George Washington

Other books in The American Statesmen series:

Thomas Jefferson by John T. Morse Jr.

Mount Vernon

George Washington

HENRY CABOT LODGE

The AMERICAN STATESMEN Series

Foreword by George Grant

CUMBERLAND HOUSE
NASHVILLE, TENNESSEE

Published by
CUMBERLAND HOUSE PUBLISHING, INC.
431 Harding Industrial Drive
Nashville, TN 37211

Foreword copyright © 2004 by George Grant

Cover design: Gore Studio, Inc.
Text design: Lisa Taylor

Library of Congress Cataloging-in-Publication Data

Lodge, Henry Cabot, 1850-1924.
  George Washington / Henry Cabot Lodge ; foreword by George Grant.
     p. cm. — (The American statesmen series)
  Reprint. Originally published: Boston : Houghton Mifflin, c1898.
  Includes index.
  ISBN 1-58182-415-7 (pbk.)
  1. Washington, George, 1732-1799. 2. Presidents—United States—Biography. I. Title. II. American statesmen series (Nashville, Tenn)
  E312.L834 2004
  973.4'1'092—dc22

                                                                    2004020899

Printed in the United States of America
1 2 3 4 5 6 7 8 — 09 08 07 06 05 04

★ CONTENTS ★

★ ILLUSTRATIONS ★

From the original painting by Emanuel Leutze in the New York Metropolitan Museum. The United States flag shown in the picture is an anachronism. The stars and stripes were first adopted by Congress in June, 1777; and any flag carried by Washington's army in December, 1776, would have consisted of the stripes with the crosses of St. George and St. Andrew in the blue field where the stars now appear.

From the original painting by Trumbull in the Art Gallery of Yale University.

From a contemporary French folio engraving in the Emmet collection, New York Public Library, Lenox Building.

From the original portrait by Gilbert Stuart in the Museum of Fine Arts, Boston. Autograph from Winsor's "America."

From the original painting by C. W. Peale, by kind permission of Mrs. Wm. Brenton Greene Jr., Princeton, N. J. Autograph from Winsor's "America."

Foreword

ACCORDING TO THE majority of eighteenth- and nineteenth-century historians, the most remarkable event during America's Founding Era did not take place on a battlefield. It did not occur during the course of the constitutional debates. It was not recorded during the great diplomatic negotiations with France, Spain, or Holland. It did not take place at sea, or in the assemblies of the states, or in the counsels of war. It was instead when the field commander of the continental armies surrendered his commission to the congressional authorities at Annapolis. It was instead a humble demonstration of servanthood. It was when General George Washington resigned his officer's commission.

At the time, he was the idol of the country and his soldiers. The army was unpaid, and the veteran troops, well armed and fresh from their victory at Yorktown, were eager to have him take control of the disordered country. Some wanted to crown him king. Others thought to make him a dictator—rather like Cromwell had been a century earlier in England.

With the loyal support of the army and the enthusiasm of the populous, it would have been easy enough for Washington to make himself the ruler of the new nation. But instead, he resigned. He appeared before President Thomas Mifflin and his cabinet and submitted himself to their governance on December 23, 1783.

Writing of the remarkable scene that then ensued, Henry Wadsworth Longfellow exclaimed, "Which was the most splendid spectacle ever witnessed—the opening feast of Prince George in London, or the resignation of Washington? Which is the noble character for after-ages to admire—yon fribble dancing in lace and spangles, or yon hero who sheaths his sword after a life of spotless honor, a purity unreproached, a courage indomitable, and a consummate victory?"

The answer to most Americans was obvious: Washington was "first in war, first in peace, and first in the hearts of his countrymen."

Though he had often wrangled in disagreement with his superiors over matters of military strategy, pay schedules, supply shipments, troop deployment, and the overlap of civil and martial responsibilities, there was never any question of his ultimate loyalty or allegiance. In the end, he always submitted himself to the authority God had placed over him. And that was no mean feat.

"His true greatness was evidenced," said Henry Adams, "in the fact that he never sought greatness, but rather service." The dean of American historians, Francis Parkman, concurred that it was this "remarkable spirit of the servant" that ultimately "elevated him even higher in his countrymen's estimations than he already was." And biographer Paul Butterfield wrote, "He never countenanced the sin of omission when it came to duty to God or country. His was a life of constant service in the face of mankind's gravest need." Thus, historian John Richard Green commented, "no nobler figure ever stood in the forefront of a country's life. Never did he shrink from meeting the need of the hour. He was our national guardian."

George Washington lived a life of service. Writing at the threshold of the twentieth century, Henry Cabot Lodge (1850–1924) believed that a recovery of such statesmanship was the only hope for the American nation—then mired in political corruption, bureaucratic wrangling, and legislative gridlock. Thus, it was a story he was particularly eager to tell.

Lodge was a wealthy Boston Brahmin—the scion of two of the most distinguished families in New England. After short stints teaching at Harvard, practicing law, and holding local political office, he served in the United States Senate for more than thirty years. He was an expert in foreign affairs and served as the chairman of the Senate's powerful International Relations Committee, where he gained fame following the First World War as a fierce opponent of any and all entangling alliances that might compromise the sovereignty of the United States. Indeed, Lodge almost single-handedly caused the demise of Woodrow Wilson's pet project, the League of Nations. In addition though, he was an accomplished scholar and wrote or edited a number of important works, including a rich twelve-volume anthology of the world's greatest literary classics and definitive works on the pioneering thought of the great American Federalists Alexander Hamilton and Fisher Ames.

While at Harvard he had become enthralled with the idea of recovering the old servant leadership ideals of Washington and the other Founding Fathers. That passion had been largely instilled in him through the lectures of Henry Brooks Adams (1838–1918). Adams had long been an influential voice at Harvard, serving as an adjunct lecturer in history off and on since 1858. But it was when he was appointed Professor of Mediaeval History in 1870 that he gained an especially ardent following among students, alumni, and faculty alike—among them men such as John Morse and Theodore Roosevelt. Over the course of the next few years, Adams and his enthusiastic followers bucked the trend of the scholastic and scientific modernists, emphasizing instead a much more classical approach to Moral Philosophy. In the process he revolutionized both Harvard and the discipline of history.

Morse enlisted the help of Lodge, Roosevelt, and several of the other Harvard intellectuals who had been influenced by Adams and his classical view of Moral Philosophy to put together a whole series of new biographies of the American Founders and the succeeding generations of like-minded American Patriots—of which this present volume was one. The series was immediately lauded by the critics and embraced by the reading public. Several of the volumes became blockbuster bestsellers and have in the intervening years been repeatedly reprinted. But perhaps more importantly, the books helped to usher in a new era of political and social reform, which enabled the still gangly young American nation to become an undisputed world power and a beacon light of freedom to oppressed peoples everywhere.

The re-publication of this volume—and this series—just over a century later is a welcome opportunity to remind yet another new generation of leaders of the great story of liberty. In an age when politicians abound but statesmen are all too rare, Lodge's portrayal of Washington is timelier than ever before.

George Washington

INTRODUCTION

FEBRUARY 9TH IN the year 1800 was a gala day in Paris. Napoleon had decreed a triumphal procession, and on that day a splendid military ceremony was performed in the Champ de Mars, and the trophies of the Egyptian expedition were exultingly displayed. There were, however, two features in all this pomp and show which seemed strangely out of keeping with the glittering pageant and the sounds of victorious rejoicing. The standards and flags of the army were hung with crape, and after the grand parade the dignitaries of the land proceeded solemnly to the Temple of Mars, and heard the eloquent M. de Fontanes deliver an "Eloge Funèbre."*

About the same time, if tradition may be trusted, the flags upon the conquering Channel fleet of England were lowered to half-mast in token

---

*A report recently discovered shows that more even was intended than was actually done.

The following is a translation of the paper, the original of which is Nos. 172 and 173 of volume 51 of the manuscript series known as *Etats-Unis*, 1799, 1800 (years 7 and 8 of the French republic): —

"*Report of Talleyrand, Minister of Foreign Affairs, on the occasion of the death of George Washington.*

"A nation which some day will be a great nation, and which to-day is the wisest and happiest on the face of the earth, weeps at the bier of a man whose courage and genius contributed the most to free it from bondage, and elevate it to the rank of an independent and sovereign power. The regrets caused by the death of this great man, the memories aroused by these regrets, and a proper veneration for all that is held dear and sacred by mankind, impel us to give expression to our sentiments by taking part in an event which deprives the world of one of its brightest ornaments, and removes to the realm of history one of the noblest lives that ever honored the human race.

"The name of Washington is inseparably linked with a memorable epoch. He adorned this epoch by his talents and the nobility of his character, and with virtues that even envy dared not assail. History offers few examples of such renown. Great from the outset of his career, patriotic before his country had become a nation, brilliant and universal despite the passions and

3

of grief for the same event which had caused the armies of France to wear the customary badges of mourning.

If some "traveller from an antique land" had observed these manifestations, he would have wondered much whose memory it was that had called them forth from these two great nations, then struggling fiercely with each other for supremacy on land and sea. His wonder would not have abated had he been told that the man for whom they mourned had wrested an empire from one, and at the time of his death was arming his countrymen against the other.

These signal honors were paid by England and France to a simple Virginian gentleman who had never left his own country, and who when he died held no other office than the titular command of a provisional army. Yet although these marks of respect from foreign nations were notable and striking, they were slight and formal in comparison with the silence and grief which fell upon the people of the United States when they heard that Washington was dead. He had died in the fullness of time, quietly, quickly, and in his own house, and yet his death called out a display of grief which has rarely been equalled in history. The trappings

---

political resentments that would gladly have checked his career, his fame is to-day imperishable,—fortune having consecrated his claim to greatness, while the prosperity of a people destined for grand achievements is the best evidence of a fame ever to increase.

"His own country now honors his memory with funeral ceremonies, having lost a citizen whose public actions and unassuming grandeur in private life were a living example of courage, wisdom, and unselfishness; and France, which from the dawn of the American Revolution hailed with hope a nation, hitherto unknown, that was discarding the vices of Europe, which foresaw all the glory that this nation would bestow on humanity, and the enlightenment of governments that would ensue from the novel character of the social institutions and the new type of heroism of which Washington and America were models for the world at large,—France, I repeat, should depart from established usages and do honor to one whose fame is beyond comparison with that of others.

"The man who, amid the decadence of modern ages, first dared believe that he could inspire degenerate nations with courage to rise to the level of republican virtues, lived for all nations and for all centuries; and this nation, which first saw in the life and success of that illustrious man a foreboding of his destiny, and therein recognized a future to be realized and duties to be performed, has every right to class him as a fellow-citizen. I therefore submit to the First Consul the following decree: —

"Bonaparte, First Consul of the republic, decrees as follows: —

"Article 1. A statue is to be erected to General Washington.

"Article 2. This statue is to be placed in one of the squares of Paris, to be chosen by the minister of the interior, and it shall be his duty to execute the present decree."

and suits of woe were there of course, but what made this mourning memorable was that the land seemed hushed with sadness, and that the sorrow dwelt among the people and was neither forced nor fleeting. Men carried it home with them to their firesides and to their churches, to their offices and their workshops. Every preacher took the life which had closed as the noblest of texts, and every orator made it the theme of his loftiest eloquence. For more than a year the newspapers teemed with eulogy and elegy, and both prose and poetry were severely taxed to pay tribute to the memory of the great one who had gone. The prose was often stilted and the verse was generally bad, but yet through it all, from the polished sentences of the funeral oration to the humble effusions of the obscurest poet's corner, there ran a strong and genuine feeling, which the highest art could not refine nor the clumsiest fine-writing degrade.

From that time to this, the stream of praise has flowed on, ever deepening and strengthening, both at home and abroad. Washington alone in history seems to have risen so high in the estimation of men that criticism has shrunk away abashed, and has only been heard whispering in corners or growling hoarsely in the now famous house in Cheyne Row.

There is a world of meaning in all this, could we but rightly interpret it. It cannot be brushed aside as mere popular superstition, formed of fancies and prejudices, to which intelligent opposition would be useless. Nothing is in fact more false than the way in which popular opinions are often belittled and made light of. The opinion of the world, however reached, becomes in the course of years or centuries the nearest approach we can make to final judgment on things human. Don Quixote may be dumb to one man, and the sonnets of Shakespeare may leave another cold and weary. But the fault is in the reader. There is no doubt of the greatness of Cervantes or Shakespeare, for they have stood the test of time, and the voices of generations of men, from which there is no appeal, have declared them to be great. The lyrics that all the world loves and repeats, the poetry which is often called hackneyed, is on the whole the best poetry. The pictures and statues that have drawn crowds of admiring gazers for centuries are the best. The things that are "caviare to the general" often undoubtedly have much merit, but they lack quite as often the warm, generous, and immortal vitality which appeals alike to rich and poor, to the ignorant and to the learned.

So it is with men. When years after his death the world agrees to call a man great, the verdict must be accepted. The historian may whiten or blacken, the critic may weigh and dissect, the form of the judgment may be altered, but the central fact remains, and with the man, whom the world in its vague way has pronounced great, history must reckon one way or the other, whether for good or ill.

When we come to such a man as Washington, the case is still stronger. Men seem to have agreed that here was greatness which no one could question, and character which no one could fail to respect. Around other leaders of men, even around the greatest of them, sharp controversies have arisen, and they have their partisans dead as they had them living. Washington had enemies who assailed him, and friends whom he loved, but in death as in life he seems to stand alone, above conflict and superior to malice. In his own country there is no dispute as to his greatness or his worth. Englishmen, the most unsparing censors of everything American, have paid homage to Washington, from the days of Fox and Byron to those of Tennyson and Gladstone. In France his name has always been revered, and in distant lands those who have scarcely heard of the existence of the United States know the country of Washington. To the mighty cairn which the nation and the states have raised to his memory, stones have come from Greece, sending a fragment of the Parthenon; from Brazil and Switzerland, Turkey and Japan, Siam and India beyond the Ganges. On that sent by China we read: "In devising plans, Washington was more decided than Ching Shing or Woo Kwang; in winning a country he was braver than Tsau Tsau or Ling Pi. Wielding his four-footed falchion, he extended the frontiers and refused to accept the Royal Dignity. The sentiments of the Three Dynasties have reappeared in him. Can any man of ancient or modern times fail to pronounce Washington peerless?" These comparisons so strange to our ears tell of a fame which has reached farther than we can readily conceive.

Washington stands as a type, and has stamped himself deep upon the imagination of mankind. Whether the image be true or false is of no consequence: the fact endures. He rises up from the dust of history as a Greek statue comes pure and serene from the earth in which it has lain for centuries. We know his deeds; but what was it in the man which has given him such a place in the affection, the respect, and the imagination of his fellow-men throughout the world?

Perhaps this question has been fully answered already. Possibly every one who has thought upon the subject has solved the problem, so that even to state it is superfluous. Yet a brilliant writer, the latest historian of the American people, has said: "General Washington is known to us, and President Washington. But George Washington is an unknown man." These are pregnant words, and that they should be true seems to make any attempt to fill the great gap an act of sheer and hopeless audacity. Yet there can be certainly no reason for adding another to the almost countless lives of Washington unless it be done with the object in view which Mr. McMaster indicates. Any such attempt may fail in execution, but if the purpose be right it has at least an excuse for its existence.

To try to add to the existing knowledge of the facts in Washington's career would have but little result beyond the multiplication of printed pages. The antiquarian, the historian, and the critic have exhausted every source, and the most minute details have been and still are the subject of endless writing and constant discussion. Every house he ever lived in has been drawn and painted; every portrait, and statue, and medal has been catalogued and engraved. His private affairs, his servants, his horses, his arms, even his clothes, have all passed beneath the merciless microscope of history. His biography has been written and rewritten. His letters have been drawn out from every lurking place, and have been given to the world in masses and in detachments. His battles have been fought over and over again, and his state papers have undergone an almost verbal examination. Yet, despite his vast fame and all the labors of the antiquarian and biographer, Washington is still not understood,—as a man he is unfamiliar to the posterity that reverences his memory. He has been misrepresented more or less covertly by hostile critics and by candid friends, and has been disguised and hidden away by the mistaken eulogy and erroneous theories of devout admirers. All that any one now can do, therefore, is to endeavor from this mass of material to depict the very man himself in the various conjunctures of his life, and strive to see what he really was and what he meant then, and what he is and what he means to us and to the world to-day.

In the progress of time Washington has become in the popular imagination largely mythical; for mythical ideas grow up in this nineteenth century, notwithstanding its boasted intelligence, much as they did in the infancy of the race. The old sentiment of humanity, more ancient and more lasting than any records or monuments, which led men in the dawn of history to worship their ancestors and the founders of states, still endures. As the centuries have gone by, this sentiment has lost its religious flavor, and has become more and more restricted in its application, but it has never been wholly extinguished. Let some man arise great above the ordinary bounds of greatness, and the feeling which caused our progenitors to bow down at the shrines of their forefathers and chiefs leads us to invest our modern hero with a mythical character, and picture him in our imagination as a being to whom, a few thousand years ago, altars would have been builded and libations poured out.

Thus we have to-day in our minds a Washington grand, solemn, and impressive. In this guise he appears as a man of lofty intellect, vast moral force, supremely successful and fortunate, and wholly apart from and above all his fellow-men. This lonely figure rises up to our imagination with all the imperial splendor of the Livian Augustus, and with about as much warmth and life as that unrivalled statue. In this vague but quite serious idea there is a great deal of truth, but not the whole truth. It is the myth of genuine love and veneration springing from the inborn gratitude of man to the founders and chiefs of his race, but it is not by any means the only one of its family. There is another, equally diffused, of wholly different parentage. In its inception this second myth is due to the itinerant parson, bookmaker, and bookseller, Mason Weems. He wrote a brief biography of Washington, of trifling historical value, yet with sufficient literary skill to make it widely popular. It neither appealed to nor was read by the cultivated and instructed few, but it reached the homes of the masses of the people. It found its way to the bench of the mechanic, to the house of the farmer, to the log cabins of the frontiersman and pioneer. It was carried across the continent on the first waves of advancing settlement. Its anecdotes and its simplicity of thought commended it to children both at home and at school, and, passing through edition after edition, its statements were widely spread, and it colored insensibly the ideas of hundreds of persons who never had heard even the name of the author. To Weems we owe the anecdote of the cherry-tree, and other tales of a similar nature. He wrote with Dr. Beattie's life of his son before him as a model, and the result is that Washington comes out in his pages a faultless prig. Whether Weems intended it or not, that is the result which he produced, and that is the Washington who was developed from the wide sale of his book. When this idea took definite and permanent shape it caused a reaction. There was a revolt against it, for the hero thus engendered had qualities which the national sense of humor could not endure in silence. The consequence is, that the Washington of Weems has afforded an endless theme for joke and burlesque. Every professional American humorist almost has tried his hand at it; and with each recurring 22d of February the hard-worked jesters of the daily newspapers take it up and make a little fun out of it, sufficient for the day that is passing over them. The opportunity is tempting, because of the ease with which fun can be made when that fundamental source of humor, a violent contrast, can be employed. But there is no irreverence in it all, for the jest is not aimed at the real Washington, but at the Washington portrayed in the Weems biography. The worthy "rector of Mount Vernon," as he called himself, meant no harm, and there is a good deal of truth, no doubt, in his book. But the blameless and priggish boy, and the equally faultless and uninteresting man, whom he originated, have become in the process of development a myth. So in its further development is the Washington of the humorist a myth. Both alike are utterly and crudely false. They resemble their great original as much as Greenough's classically nude statue, exposed to the incongruities of the North American climate, resembles in dress and appearance the general of our armies and the first President of the United States.

Such are the myth-makers. They are widely different from the critics who have assailed Washington in a sidelong way, and who can be better dealt with in a later chapter. These last bring charges which can be met: the myth-maker presents a vague conception, extremely difficult to handle because it is so elusive.

One of our well-known historical scholars and most learned antiquarians, not long ago, in an essay vindicating the "traditional Washington," treated with scorn the idea of a "new Washington," being discovered. In one sense this is quite right, in another totally wrong. There can be no new Washington discovered, because there never was but one. But the real man has been so overlaid with myths and traditions, and so distorted by misleading criticisms, that, as has already been suggested, he has been wellnigh lost. We have the religious or statuesque myth, we have the Weems myth, and the ludicrous myth of the writer of paragraphs. We have the stately hero of Sparks, and Everett, and Marshall, and Irving, with all his great deeds as general and president duly recorded and set down in polished and eloquent sentences; and we know him to be very great and wise and pure, and, be it said with bated breath, very dry and cold. We are also familiar with the commonplace man who so wonderfully illustrated the power of character as set forth by various persons, either from love of novelty or because the great chief seemed to get in the way of their own heroes.

If this is all, then the career of Washington and his towering fame present a problem of which the world has never seen the like. But this cannot be all: there must be more behind. Every one knows the famous Stuart portrait of Washington. The last effort of the artist's cunning is there employed to paint his great subject for posterity. How serene and beautiful it is! It is a noble picture for future ages to look upon. Still it is not all. There is in the dining-room of Memorial Hall at Cambridge another portrait, painted by Savage. It is cold and dry, hard enough to serve for the signboard of an inn, and able, one would think, to withstand all weathers. Yet this picture has something which Stuart left out. There is a rugged strength in the face which gives us pause, there is a massiveness in the jaw, telling of an iron grip and a relentless will, which has infinite meaning.

Here's John the Smith's rough-hammered head. Great eye.
Gross jaw, and griped lips do what granite can
To give you the crown-grasper. What a man!

In death as in life, there is something about Washington, call it greatness, dignity, majesty, what you will, which seems to hold men aloof and
keep them from knowing him. In truth he was a most difficult man to
know. Carlyle, crying out through hundreds of pages and myriads of
words for the "silent man," passed by with a sneer the most absolutely
silent great man that history can show. Washington's letters and speeches
and messages fill many volumes, but they are all on business. They are
profoundly silent as to the writer himself. From this Carlyle concluded
apparently that there was nothing to tell,—a very shallow conclusion if it
was the one he really reached. Such an idea was certainly far, very far,
from the truth.

Behind the popular myths, behind the statuesque figure of the orator and the preacher, behind the general and the president of the historian, there was a strong, vigorous man, in whose veins ran warm, red
blood, in whose heart were stormy passions and deep sympathy for
humanity, in whose brain were far-reaching thoughts, and who was
informed throughout his being with a resistless will. The veil of his
silence is not often lifted, and never intentionally, but now and then
there is a glimpse behind it; and in stray sentences and in little incidents
strenuously gathered together; above all, in the right interpretation of the
words, and the deeds, and the true history known to all men, we can
surely find George Washington "the noblest figure that ever stood in the
forefront of a nation's life."

The Home of the Washington Family

CHAPTER I

THE OLD DOMINION

TO KNOW GEORGE Washington, we must first of all know the society in which he was born and brought up. As certain lilies draw their colors from the subtle qualities of the soil hidden beneath the water upon which they float, so are men profoundly affected by the obscure and insensible influences which surround their childhood and youth. The art of the chemist may discover perhaps the secret agent which tints the white flower with blue or pink, but very often the elements, which analysis detects, nature alone can combine. The analogy is not strained or fanciful when we apply it to a past society. We can separate, and classify, and label the various elements, but to combine them in such a way as to form a vivid picture is a work of surpassing difficulty. This is especially true of such a land as Virginia in the middle of the last century. Virginian society, as it existed at that period, is utterly extinct, John Randolph said it had departed before the year 1800. Since then another century, with all its manifold changes, has wellnigh come and gone. Most important of all, the last surviving institution of colonial Virginia has been swept away in the crash of civil war, which has opened a gulf between past and present wider and deeper than any that time alone could make.

Life and society as they existed in the Virginia of the eighteenth century seem, moreover, to have been sharply broken and ended. We cannot trace our steps backward, as is possible in most cases, over the road by which the world has travelled since those days. We are compelled to take a long leap mentally in order to land ourselves securely in the Virginia which honored the second George, and looked up to Walpole and Pitt as the arbiters of its fate.

We live in a period of great cities, rapid communication, vast and varied business interests, enormous diversity of occupation, great industries, diffused intelligence, farming by steam, and with everything and everybody pervaded by an unresting, high-strung activity. We transport ourselves to the Virginia of Washington's boyhood, and find a people without cities or towns, with no means of communication except what was afforded by rivers and wood roads; having no trades, no industries, no means of spreading knowledge, only one occupation, clumsily performed; and living a quiet, monotonous existence, which can now hardly be realized. It is "a far cry to Loch-Awe," as the Scotch proverb has it; and this old Virginian society, although we should find it sorry work living in it, is both pleasant and picturesque in the pages of history.

The population of Virginia, advancing toward half a million, and divided pretty equally between the free whites and the enslaved blacks, was densest, to use a most inappropriate word, at the water's edge and near the mouths of the rivers. Thence it crept backwards, following always the lines of the watercourses, and growing ever thinner and more scattered until it reached the Blue Ridge. Behind the mountains was the wilderness, haunted, as old John Lederer said a century earlier, by monsters, and inhabited, as the eighteenth-century Virginians very well knew, by savages and wild beasts, much more real and dangerous than the hobgoblins of their ancestors.

The population, in proportion to its numbers, was very widely distributed. It was not collected in groups, after the fashion with which we are now familiar, for then there were no cities or towns in Virginia. The only place which could pretend to either name was Norfolk, the solitary seaport, which, with its six or seven thousand inhabitants, formed the most glaring exception that any rule solicitous of proof could possibly desire. Williamsburg, the capital, was a straggling village, somewhat overweighted with the public buildings and those of the college. It would light up into life and vivacity during the season of politics and society, and then relapse again into the country stillness. Outside of Williamsburg and Norfolk there were various points which passed in the catalogue and on the map for towns, but which in reality were merely the shadows of a name. The most populous consisted of a few houses inhabited by store-keepers and traders, some tobacco warehouses, and a tavern, clustered about the church or court-house. Many others had only the church, or, if a county seat, the church and court-house, keeping solitary state in the woods. There once a week the sound of prayer and gossip, or at longer intervals the voices of lawyers and politicians, and the shouts of the wrestlers on the green, broke through the stillness which with the going down of the sun resumed its sway in the forests.

There was little chance here for that friction of mind with mind, or for that quick interchange of thought and sentiment and knowledge which are familiar to the dwellers in cities, and which have driven forward more rapidly than all else what we call civilization. Rare meetings for special objects with persons as solitary in their lives and as ill-informed as himself, constituted to the average Virginian the world of society, and there was nothing from outside to supply the deficiencies at home. Once a fortnight a mail crawled down from the North, and once a month another crept on to the South. George Washington was four years old when the first newspaper was published in the colony, and he was twenty when the first actors appeared at Williamsburg. What was not brought was not sought. The Virginians did not go down to the sea in ships. They were not a seafaring race, and as they had neither trade nor commerce they were totally destitute of the inquiring, enterprising spirit, and of the knowledge brought by those pursuits which involve travel and adventure. The English tobacco ships worked their way up the rivers, taking the great staple, and leaving their varied goods, and their tardy news from Europe, wherever they stopped. This was the sum of the information and intercourse which Virginia got from across the sea, for travellers were practically unknown. Few came on business, fewer still from curiosity. Stray peddlers from the North, or trappers from beyond the mountains with their packs of furs, chiefly constituted what would now be called the travelling public. There were in truth no means of travelling except on foot, on horseback, or by boat on the rivers, which formed the best and most expeditious highways. Stage-coaches, or other public conveyances, were unknown. Over some of the roads the rich man, with his six horses and black outriders, might make his way in a lumbering carriage, but most of the roads were little better than woodland paths; and the rivers, innocent of bridges, offered in the uncertain fords abundance of inconvenience, not unmixed with peril. The taverns were execrable, and only the ever-ready hospitality of the people made it possible to get from place to place. The result was that the Virginians stayed at home, and sought and welcomed the rare stranger at their gates as if they were well aware that they were entertaining angels.

It is not difficult to sift this home-keeping people, and find out that portion which was Virginia, for the mass was but an appendage of the small fraction which ruled, led, and did the thinking for the whole community. Half the people were slaves, and in that single wretched word their history is told. They were, on the whole, well and kindly treated, but they have no meaning in history except as an institution, and as an influence in the lives, feelings, and character of the men who made the state.

Above the slaves, little better than they, but separated from them by the wide gulf of race and color, were the indented white servants, some convicts, some redemptioners. They, too, have their story told when we have catalogued them. We cross another gulf and come to the farmers, to the men who grew wheat as well as tobacco on their own land, sometimes working alone, sometimes the owners of a few slaves. Some of these men were of the class well known since as the "poor whites" of the South, the weaker brothers who could not resist the poison of slavery, but sank under it into ignorance and poverty. They were contented because their skins were white, and because they were thereby part of an aristocracy to whom labor was a badge of serfdom. The larger portion of this middle class, however, were thrifty and industrious enough. Including as they did in their ranks the hunters and pioneers, the traders and merchants, all the freemen in fact who toiled and worked, they formed the mass of the white population, and furnished the bone and sinew and some of the intellectual power of Virginia. The only professional men were the clergy, for the lawyers were few, and growing to importance only as the Revolution began; while the physicians were still fewer, and as a class of no importance at all. The clergy were a picturesque element in the social landscape, but they were as a body very poor representatives of learning, religion, and morality. They ranged from hedge parsons and Fleet chaplains, who had slunk away from England to find a desirable obscurity in the new world, to divines of real learning and genuine piety, who were the supporters of the college, and who would have been a credit to any society. These last, however, were lamentably few in number. The mass of the clergy were men who worked their own lands, sold tobacco, were the boon companions of the planters, hunted, shot, drank hard, and lived well, performing their sacred duties in a perfunctory and not always in a decent manner.

The clergy, however, formed the stepping-stone socially between the farmers, traders, and small planters, and the highest and most important class in Virginian society. The great planters were the men who owned, ruled, and guided Virginia. Their vast estates were scattered along the rivers from the seacoast to the mountains. Each plantation was in itself a small village, with the owner's house in the centre, surrounded by outbuildings and negro cabins, and the pastures, meadows, and fields of tobacco stretching away on all sides. The rare traveller, pursuing his devious way on horseback or in a boat, would catch sight of these noble estates opening up from the road or the river, and then the forest would close in around him for several miles, until through the thinning trees he would see again the white cabins and the cleared fields of the next plantation.

In such places dwelt the Virginian planters, surrounded by their families and slaves, and in a solitude broken only by the infrequent and eagerly welcomed stranger, by their duties as vestrymen and magistrates, or by the annual pilgrimage to Williamsburg in search of society, or to sit in the House of Burgesses. They were occupied by the care of their plantations, which involved a good deal of riding in the open air, but which was at best an easy and indolent pursuit made light by slave labor and trained overseers. As a result the planters had an abundance of spare time, which they devoted to cock-fighting, horse-racing, fishing, shooting, and fox-hunting,—all, save the first, wholesome and manly sports, but which did not demand any undue mental strain. There is, indeed, no indication that the Virginians had any great love for intellectual exertion. When the amiable attorney-general of Charles II. said to the Virginian commissioners, pleading the cause of learning and religion, "Damn your souls! grow tobacco!" he uttered a precept which the mass of the planters seem to pave laid to heart. For fifty years there were no schools, and down to the Revolution even the apologies bearing that honored name were few, and the college was small and struggling. In some of the great families, the eldest sons would be sent to England and to the great universities: they would make the grand tour, play a part in the fashionable society of London, and come back to their plantations fine gentlemen and scholars. Such was Colonel Byrd, in the early part of the eighteenth century, a friend of the Earl of Orrery, and the author of certain amusing memoirs. Such at a later day was Arthur Lee, doctor and diplomat, student and politician. But most of these young gentlemen thus sent abroad to improve their minds and manners led a life not materially different from that of our charming friend, Harry Warrington, after his arrival in England.

The sons who stayed at home sometimes gathered a little learning from the clergyman of the parish, or received a fair education at the College of William and Mary, but very many did not have even so much as this. There was not in truth much use for learning in managing a plantation or raising horses, and men get along surprisingly well without that which they do not need, especially if the acquisition demands labor. The Virginian planter thought little and read less, and there were no learned professions to hold out golden prizes and stimulate the love of knowledge. The women fared even worse, for they could not go to Europe or to William and Mary's, so that after exhausting the teaching capacity of the parson they settled down to a round of household duties and to the cares of a multitude of slaves, working much harder and more steadily than their lords and masters ever thought of doing.

The only general form of intellectual exertion was that of governing. The planters managed local affairs through the vestries, and ruled Virginia in the House of Burgesses. To this work they paid strict attention, and, after the fashion of their race, did it very well and very efficiently. They were an extremely competent body whenever they made up their minds to do anything; but they liked the life and habits of Squire Western, and saw no reason for adopting any others until it was necessary.

There were, of course, vast differences in the condition of the planters. Some counted their acres by thousands and their slaves by hundreds, while others scrambled along as best they might with one plantation and a few score of negroes. Some dwelt in very handsome houses, picturesque and beautiful, like Gunston Hall or Stratford, or in vast, tasteless, and extravagant piles like Rosewell. Others were contented with very modest houses, consisting of one story with a gabled roof, and flanked by two massive chimneys. In some houses there was a brave show of handsome plate and china, fine furniture, and London-made carriages, rich silks and satins, and brocaded dresses. In others there were earthenware and pewter, homespun and woollen, and little use for horses except in the plough or under the saddle.

But there were certain qualities common to all the Virginia planters. The luxury was imperfect. The splendor was sometimes barbaric. There were holes in the brocades, and the fresh air of heaven would often blow through a broken window upon the glittering silver and the costly china. It was an easy-going aristocracy, unfinished, and frequently slovenly in its appointments, after the fashion of the warmer climates and the regions of slavery.

Everything was plentiful except ready money. In this rich and poor were alike. They were all ahead of their income, and it seems as if, from one cause or another, from extravagance or improvidence, from horses or the gaming-table, every Virginian family went through bankruptcy about once in a generation.

When Harry Warrington arrived in England, all his relations at Castlewood regarded the handsome young fellow as a prince, with his acres and his slaves. It was a natural and pleasing delusion, born of the possession of land and serfs, to which the Virginians themselves gave ready credence. They forgot that the land was so plentiful that it was of little value; that slaves were the most wasteful form of labor; and that a failure of the tobacco crop, pledged before it was gathered, meant ruin, although they had been reminded more than once of this last impressive fact. They knew that they had plenty to eat and drink, and a herd of people to wait upon them and cultivate their land, as well as obliging London merchants always ready to furnish every luxury in return for the mortgage of a crop or an estate. So they gave themselves little anxiety as to the future and lived in the present, very much to their own satisfaction.

To the communities of trade and commerce, to the mercantile and industrial spirit of to-day, such an existence and such modes of life appear distressingly lax and unprogressive. The sages of the bank parlors and the counting-rooms would shake their heads at such spendthrifts as these, refuse to discount their paper, and confidently predict that by no possibility could they come to good. They had their defects, no doubt, these planters and farmers of Virginia. The life they led was strongly developed on the animal side, and was perhaps neither stimulating nor elevating. The living was the reverse of plain, and the thinking was neither extremely high nor notably laborious. Yet in this very particular there is something rather restful and pleasant to the eye wearied by the sight of incessant movement, and to the ear deafened by the continual shout that nothing is good that does not change, and that all change must be good. We should probably find great discomforts and many unpleasant limitations in the life and habits of a hundred years ago on any part of the globe, and yet at a time when it seems as if rapidity and movement were the last words and the ultimate ideals of civilization, it is rather agreeable to turn to such a community as the eighteenth-century planters of Virginia. They lived contentedly on the acres of their fathers, and except at rare and stated intervals they had no other interests than those furnished by their ancestral domain. At the courthouse or the vestry, or at Williamsburg, they met their neighbors and talked very keenly about the politics of Europe, or the affairs of the colony. They were little troubled about religion, but they worshipped after the fashion of their fathers, and had a serious fidelity to church and king. They wrangled with their governors over appropriations, but they lived on good terms with those eminent persons, and attended state balls at what they called the palace, and danced and made merry with much stateliness and grace. Their everyday life ran on in the quiet of their plantations as calmly as one of their own rivers. The English trader would come and go; the infrequent stranger would be received and welcomed; Christmas would be kept in hearty English fashion; young men from a neighboring estate would ride over through the darkening woods to court, or dance, or play the fiddle, like Patrick Henry or Thomas Jefferson; and these simple events were all that made a ripple on the placid stream. Much time was given to sports, rough, hearty, manly sports, with a spice of danger, and these, with an occasional adventurous dash into the wilderness, kept them sound and strong and brave, both in body and mind. There was nothing languid or effeminate about the Virginian planter. He was a robust man, quite ready to fight or work when the time came, and well fitted to deal with affairs when he was needed. He was a free-handed, hospitable, generous being, not much given to study or thought, but thoroughly public-spirited and keenly alive to the interests of Virginia. Above all things he was an aristocrat, set apart by the dark line of race, color, and hereditary servitude, as proud as the proudest Austrian with his endless quarterings, as sturdy and vigorous as an English yeoman, and as jealous of his rights and privileges as any baron who stood by John at Runnymede. To this aristocracy, careless and indolent, given to rough pleasures and indifferent to the finer and higher sides of life, the call came, as it comes to all men sooner or later, and in response they gave their country soldiers, statesmen, and jurists of the highest order, and fit for the great work they were asked to do. We must go back to Athens to find another instance of a society so small in numbers, and yet capable of such an outburst of ability and force. They were of sound English stock, with a slight admixture of the Huguenot, the best blood of France; and although for a century and a half they had seemed to stagnate in the New World, they were strong and fruitful and effective beyond the measure of ordinary races when the hour of peril and trial was at hand.

CHAPTER II

THE WASHINGTONS

SUCH WAS THE world and such the community which counted as a small fraction the Washington family. Our immediate concern is with that family, for before we approach the man we must know his ancestors. The greatest leader of scientific thought in this century has come to the aid of the genealogist, and given to the results of the latter's somewhat discredited labors a vitality and meaning which it seemed impossible that dry and dusty pedigrees and barren tables of descent should ever possess. We have always selected our race-horses according to the doctrines of evolution, and we now study the character of a great man by examining first the history of his forefathers.

Washington made so great an impression upon the world in his lifetime that genealogists at once undertook for him the construction of a suitable pedigree. The excellent Sir Isaac Heard, garter king-at-arms, worked out a genealogy which seemed reasonable enough, and then wrote to the president in relation to it. Washington in reply thanked him for his politeness, sent him the Virginian genealogy of his own branch, and after expressing a courteous interest said, in his simple and direct fashion, that he had been a busy man and had paid but little attention to the subject. His knowledge about his English forefathers was in fact extremely slight. He had heard merely that the first of the name in Virginia had come from one of the northern counties of England, but whether from Lancashire or Yorkshire, or one still more northerly, he could not tell. Sir

23

Isaac was not thoroughly satisfied with the correctness of his own work, but presently Baker took it up in his history of Northamptonshire, and perfected it to his own satisfaction and that of the world in general. This genealogy derived Washington's descent from the owners of the manor of Sulgrave, in Northamptonshire, and thence carried it back to the Norman knight, Sir William de Hertburn. According to this pedigree the Virginian settlers, John and Lawrence, were the sons of Lawrence Washington of Sulgrave Manor, and this genealogy was adopted by Sparks and Irving, as well as by the public at large. Twenty years ago, however, Colonel Chester, by his researches, broke beyond repair the most essential link in the chain forged by Heard and Baker, proving clearly that the Virginian settlers could not have been the sons of Lawrence of Sulgrave, as identified by the garter king-at-arms. Still more recently the mythical spirit has taken violent possession of the Washington ancestry, and an ingenious gentleman has traced the pedigree of our first president back to Thorfinn and thence to Odin, which is sufficiently remote, dignified, and lofty to satisfy the most exacting Welshman that ever lived. Still the breach made by Colonel Chester has not been repaired, although many writers, including some who should know better, cling with undiminished faith to the Heard pedigree. It is known that Colonel Chester himself believed that he had found the true line, coming, it is supposed, through a younger branch of the Sulgrave race, but he died before he had discovered the one bit of evidence necessary to prove an essential step, and he was too conscientiously accurate to leave anything to conjecture.

Thus we are left with no certain knowledge of Washington's forefathers beyond the Virginian settlers, John and Lawrence. There can be, however, little doubt that the two emigrants came of the Sulgrave stock, although the exact connection has not been established. The identity of arms and of Christian names seems to prove them scions of that race, and the failure to connect them with any other family of the name in England corroborates this theory.* In that interesting land where everything,

---

*Colonel Chester (*N. E. Historical Register*, vol. xxi., 1867, p. 25) lays stress on the president's statement that his ancestor was said to come from Lancashire or Yorkshire, or some more

according to our narrow ideas, is upside down, it is customary, when an individual arrives at distinction, to confer nobility upon his ancestors instead of his children. The Washingtons offer an interesting example of the application of this Chinese system in the Western world, for, if they have not been actually ennobled in recognition of the deeds of their great descendant, they have at least become the subjects of intense and general interest. Every one of the name who could be discovered anywhere has been dragged forth into the light, and has had all that was known about him duly recorded and set down. By scanning family trees and pedigrees, and picking up stray bits of information here and there, we can learn in a rude and general fashion what manner of men those were who claimed descent from William of Hertburn, and who bore the name of Washington in the mother-country. As Mr. Galton passes a hundred faces before the same highly sensitized plate, and gets a photograph which is a likeness of no one of his subjects, and yet resembles them all, so we may turn the camera of history upon these Washingtons, as they flash up for a moment from the dim past, and hope to get what Professor Huxley calls a "generic" picture of the race, even if the outlines be somewhat blurred and indistinct.

In the North of England, in the region conquered first by Saxons and then by Danes, lies the little village of Washington. It came into the possession of Sir William de Hertburn, and belonged to him at the time of

---

northerly county, and seems to imply that this, excluding as it does Northamptonshire, makes against the identity of Sir Isaac Heard's John Washington with the Virginian emigrant. I have found a little evidence on this subject which seems to have been hitherto unnoticed, and which tends to show that the Virginia emigrants were not from the northerly counties. The well-known account of the Baconian troubles, written by Mrs. Ann Cotton in 1676 (Force's *Hist. Tracts*, i.), is addressed "to Mr. C. H., at Yardly, in Northamptonshire," probably Yardly-Hastings, about eight miles from Northampton, and consequently very near Sulgrave Manor. At the beginning (p. 1) the writer refers to the commander of the Virginians in the first campaign against the Indians as "one Colonel Washington (him whom you have sometimes seen at your house)." This suggests very strongly that John Washington, the first Virginian of the name, was of Northamptonshire, and that he came from, or lived in the neighborhood of, Sulgrave Manor, and therefore belonged to that family. Had he lived all his life in Yorkshire it is not probable that Mr. C. H. would have seen him much at his house in Yardly. [Since the publication of these volumes, the researches of Mr. Waters have proved Washington's descent from the Sulgrave family and therefore the correctness of the theory advanced in the text.]

the Boldon Book in 1183. Soon after, he or his descendants took the name of De Wessyngton, and there they remained for two centuries, knights of the palatinate, holding their lands by a military tenure, fighting in all the wars, and taking part in tournaments with becoming splendor. By the beginning of the fifteenth century the line of feudal knights of the palatinate was extinct, and the manor passed from the family by the marriage of Dionisia de Wessyngton. But the main stock had in the mean time thrown out many offshoots, which had taken firm root in other parts of England. We hear of several who came in various ways to eminence. There was the learned and vigorous prior of Durham, John De Wessyngton, probably one of the original family, and the name appears in various places after his time in records and on monuments, indicating a flourishing and increasing race. Lawrence Washington, in the sixteenth century, was the mayor of Northampton, and received from King Henry VIII. the manor of Sulgrave in 1538. In the next century we find traces of Robert Washington of the Adwick family, a rich merchant of Leeds, and of his son Joseph Washington, a learned lawyer and author, of Gray's Inn. About the same time we hear of Richard Washington and Philip Washington holding high places at University College, Oxford. The Sulgrave branch, however, was the most numerous and prosperous. From the mayor of Northampton were descended Sir William Washington, who married the half-sister of George Villiers, Duke of Buckingham; Sir Henry Washington, who made a desperate defence of Worcester against the forces of the Parliament in 1646; Lieutenant-Colonel James Washington, who fell at the siege of Pontefract, fighting for King Charles; another James, of a later time, who was implicated in Monmouth's rebellion, fled to Holland and became the progenitor of a flourishing and successful family, which has spread to Germany and there been ennobled; Sir Lawrence Washington, of Garsdon, whose granddaughter married Robert Shirley, Baron Ferrers; and others of less note, but all men of property and standing. They seem to have been a successful, thrifty race, owning lands and estates, wise magistrates and good soldiers, marrying well, and increasing their wealth and strength from generation to generation. They were of Norman stock, knights and gentlemen in the full

sense of the word before the French Revolution, and we can detect in
them here and there a marked strain of the old Norse blood, carrying
with it across the centuries the wild Berserker spirit which made the
adventurous Northmen for centuries the terror of Europe. They were a
strong race evidently, these Washingtons, whom we see now only by
glimpses through the mists of time, not brilliant apparently, never winning the very highest fortune, having their failures and reverses no
doubt, but on the whole prudent, bold men, always important in their
several stations, ready to fight and ready to work, and as a rule successful
in that which they set themselves to do.

In 1658 the two brothers, John and Lawrence, appeared in Virginia.
They seem to have been men of substance, for they purchased lands and
established themselves at Bridges Creek, in Westmoreland County. With
this brief statement, Lawrence disappears, leaving us nothing further
than the knowledge that he had numerous descendants. John, with
whom we are more concerned, figures at once in the colonial records of
Maryland. He made complaint to the Maryland authorities, soon after his
arrival, against Edward Prescott, merchant, and captain of the ship in
which he had come over, for hanging a woman during the voyage for
witchcraft. We have a letter of his, explaining that he could not appear at
the first trial because he was about to baptize his son, and had bidden the
neighbors and gossips to the feast. A little incident this, dug out of the
musty records, but it shows us an active, generous man, intolerant of
oppression, public-spirited and hospitable, social, and friendly in his new
relations. He soon after was called to mourn the death of his English wife
and of two children, but he speedily consoled himself by taking a second
wife, Anne Pope, by whom he had three children, Lawrence, John, and
Anne. According to the Virginian tradition, John Washington the elder
was a surveyor, and made a location of lands which was set aside because
they had been assigned to the Indians. It is quite apparent that he was a
forehanded person who acquired property and impressed himself upon
his neighbors. In 1667, when he had been but ten years in the colony, he
was chosen to the House of Burgesses; and eight years later he was made
a colonel and sent with a thousand men to join the Marylanders in

destroying the "Susquehannocks," at the "Piscataway" fort, on account of some murdering begun by another tribe. As a feat of arms, the expedition was not a very brilliant affair. The Virginians and Marylanders killed half a dozen Indian chiefs during a parley, and then invested the fort. After repulsing several sorties, they stupidly allowed the Indians to escape in the night and carry murder and pillage through the outlying settlements, lighting up first the flames of savage war and then the fiercer fire of domestic insurrection. In the next year we hear again of John Washington in the House of Burgesses, when Sir William Berkeley assailed his troops for the murder of the Indians during the parley. Popular feeling, however, was clearly with the colonel, for nothing was done and the matter dropped. At that point, too, in 1676, John Washington disappears from sight, and we know only that as his will was proved in 1677, he must have died soon after the scene with Berkeley. He was buried in the family vault at Bridges Creek, and left a good estate to be divided among his children. The colonel was evidently both a prudent and popular man, and quite disposed to bustle about in the world in which he found himself. He acquired lands, came to the front at once as a leader although a new-comer in the country, was evidently a fighting man as is shown by his selection to command the Virginian forces, and was honored by his neighbors, who gave his name to the parish in which he dwelt. Then he died and his son Lawrence reigned in his stead, and became by his wife, Mildred Warner, the father of John, Augustine and Mildred Washington.

This second son, Augustine, farmer and planter like his forefathers, married first Jane Butler, by whom he had three sons and a daughter, and second, Mary Ball, by whom he had four sons and two daughters. The eldest child of these second nuptials was named George, and was born on February 11 (O. S.), 1732, at Bridges Creek. The house in which this event occurred was a plain, wooden farmhouse of the primitive Virginian pattern, with four rooms on the ground floor, an attic story with a long, sloping roof, and a massive brick chimney. Three years after George Washington's birth it is said to have been burned, and the family for this or some other reason removed to another estate in what is now Stafford

County. The second house was like the first, and stood on rising ground looking across a meadow to the Rappahannock, and beyond the river to the village of Fredericksburg, which was nearly opposite. Here, in 1743, Augustine Washington died somewhat suddenly, at the age of forty-nine, from an attack of gout brought on by exposure in the rain, and was buried with his fathers in the old vault at Bridges Creek. Here, too, the boyhood of Washington was passed, and therefore it becomes necessary to look about us and see what we can learn of this important period of his life.

We know nothing about his father, except that he was kindly and affectionate, attached to his wife and children, and apparently absorbed in the care of his estates. On his death the children came wholly under the maternal influence and direction. Much has been written about the "mother of Washington," but as a matter of fact, although she lived to an advanced age, we know scarcely more about her than we do about her husband. She was of gentle birth, and possessed a vigorous character and a good deal of business capacity. The advantages of education were given in but slight measure to the Virginian ladies of her time, and Mrs. Washington offered no exception to the general rule. Her reading was confined to a small number of volumes, chiefly of a devotional character, her favorite apparently being Hale's "Moral and Divine Contemplations." She evidently knew no language but her own, and her spelling was extremely bad even in that age of uncertain orthography. Certain qualities, however, are clear to us even now through all the dimness. We can see that Mary Washington was gifted with strong sense, and had the power of conducting business matters providently and exactly. She was an imperious woman, of strong will, ruling her kingdom alone. Above all she was very dignified, very silent, and very sober-minded. That she was affectionate and loving cannot be doubted, for she retained to the last a profound hold upon the reverential devotion of her son, and yet as he rose steadily to the pinnacle of human greatness, she could only say that "George had been a good boy, and she was sure he would do his duty." Not a brilliant woman evidently, not one suited to shine in courts, conduct intrigues, or adorn literature, yet able to transmit moral qualities to her oldest son, which, mingled with those of the Washingtons, were of infinite value in the foundation of a great Republic. She found herself a widow at an early age, with a family of young children to educate and support. Her means were narrow, for although Augustine Washington was able to leave what was called a landed estate to each son, it was little more than idle capital, and the income in ready money was by no means so evident as the acres.

Many are the myths, and deplorably few the facts, that have come down to us in regard to Washington's boyhood. For the former we are indebted to the illustrious Weems, and to that personage a few more words must be devoted. Weems has been held up to the present age in various ways, usually, it must be confessed, of an unflattering nature, and "mendacious" is the adjective most commonly applied to him. There has been in reality a good deal of needless confusion about Weems and his book, for he was not a complex character, and neither he nor his writings are difficult to value or understand. By profession a clergyman or preacher, by nature an adventurer, Weems loved notoriety, money, and a wandering life. So he wrote books which he correctly believed would be popular, and sold them not only through the regular channels, but by peddling them himself as he travelled about the country. In this way he gratified all his propensities, and no doubt derived from life a good deal of simple pleasure. Chance brought him near Washington in the closing days, and his commercial instinct told him that here was the subject of all others for his pen and his market. He accordingly produced the biography which had so much success. Judged solely as literature, the book is beneath contempt. The style is turgid, overloaded, and at times silly. The statements are loose, the mode of narration confused and incoherent, and the moralizing is flat and commonplace to the last degree. Yet there was a certain sincerity of feeling underneath all the bombast and platitudes, and this saved the book. The biography did not go, and was not intended to go, into the hands of the polite society of the great eastern towns. It was meant for the farmers, the pioneers, and the backwoodsmen of the country. It went into their homes, and passed with them beyond the Alleghanies and out to the plains and valleys of the great West. The very defects of the book helped it to success among the simple, hard-working, hard-fighting race engaged in the conquest of the American continent. To them its heavy and tawdry style, its staring morals, and its real patriotism all seemed eminently befitting the national hero, and thus Weems created the Washington of the popular fancy. The idea grew up with the country, and became so ingrained in the popular thought that finally everybody was affected by it, and even the most stately and solemn of the Washington biographers adopted the unsupported tales of the itinerant parson and book-peddler.

In regard to the public life of Washington, Weems took the facts known to every one, and drawn for the most part from the gazettes. He then dressed them up in his own peculiar fashion and gave them to the world. All this, forming of course nine tenths of his book, has passed, despite its success, into oblivion. The remaining tenth described Washington's boyhood until his fourteenth or fifteenth year, and this, which is the work of the author's imagination, has lived. Weems, having set himself up as absolutely the only authority as to this period, has been implicitly followed, and has thus come to demand serious consideration. Until Weems is weighed and disposed of, we cannot even begin an attempt to get at the real Washington.

Weems was not a cold-blooded liar, a mere forger of anecdotes. He was simply a man destitute of historical sense, training, or morals, ready to take the slenderest fact and work it up for the purposes of the market until it became almost as impossible to reduce it to its original dimensions as it was for the fisherman to get the Afrit back into his jar. In a word, Weems was an approved mythmaker. No better example can be given than the way in which he described himself. It is believed that he preached once, and possibly oftener, to a congregation which numbered Washington among its members. Thereupon he published himself in his book as the rector of Mount Vernon parish. There was, to begin with, no such parish. There was Truro parish, in which was a church called indifferently Pohick or Mount Vernon church. Of this church Washington was a vestryman until 1785, when he joined the church at Alexandria. The Rev. Lee Massey was the clergyman of the Mount Vernon church, and the church at Alexandria had nothing to do with Mount Vernon. There never was, moreover, such a person as the rector of Mount Vernon parish, but it was the Weems way of treating his appearance before the great man, and of deceiving the world with the notion of an intimacy which the title implied.

Weems, of course, had no difficulty with the public life, but in describing the boyhood he was thrown on his own resources, and out of them he evolved the cherry-tree, the refusal to fight or permit fighting among the boys at school, and the initials in the garden. This last story is to the effect that Augustine Washington planted seeds in such a manner that when they sprouted they formed on the earth the initials of his son's name, and the boy being much delighted thereby, the father explained to him that it was the work of the Creator, and thus inculcated a profound belief in God. This tale is taken bodily from Dr. Beattie's biographical sketch of his son, published in England in 1799, and may be dismissed at once. As to the other two more familiar anecdotes there is not a scintilla of evidence that they had any foundation, and with them may be included the colt story, told by Mr. Custis, a simple variation of the cherry-tree theme, which is Washington's early love of truth. Weems says that his stories were told him by a lady, and "a good old gentleman," who remembered the incidents, while Mr. Custis gives no authority for his minute account of a trivial event over a century old when he wrote. To a writer who invented the rector of Mount Vernon, the further invention of a couple of Boswells would be a trifle. I say Boswells advisedly, for these stories are told with the utmost minuteness, and the conversations between Washington and his father are given as if from a stenographic report. How Mr. Custis, usually so accurate, came to be so far infected with the Weems myth as to tell the colt story after the Weems manner, cannot now be determined. There can be no doubt that Washington, like most healthy boys, got into a good deal of mischief, and it is not at all impossible that he injured fruit-trees and confessed that he had done so. It may be accepted as certain that he rode and mastered many unbroken thorough-bred colts, and it is possible that one of them burst a blood-vessel in the process and died, and that the boy promptly told his mother of the accident.

But this is the utmost credit which these two anecdotes can claim. Even so much as this cannot be said of certain other improving tales of like nature. That Washington lectured his playmates on the wickedness of fighting, and in the year 1754 allowed himself to be knocked down in the presence of his soldiers, and thereupon begged his assailant's pardon for having spoken roughly to him, are stories so silly and so foolishly impossible that they do not deserve an instant's consideration.

There is nothing intrinsically impossible in either the cherry-tree or the colt incident, nor would there be in a hundred others which might be readily invented. The real point is that these stories, as told by Weems and Mr. Custis, are on their face hopelessly and ridiculously false. They are so, not merely because they have no vestige of evidence to support them, but because they are in every word and line the offspring of a period more than fifty years later. No English-speaking people, certainly no Virginians, ever thought or behaved or talked in 1740 like the personages in Weems's stories, whatever they may have done in 1790, or at the beginning of the next century. These precious anecdotes belong to the age of Miss Edgeworth and Hannah More and Jane Taylor. They are engaging specimens of the "Harry and Lucy" and "Purple Jar" morality, and accurately reflect the pale didacticism which became fashionable in England at the close of the last century. They are as untrue to nature and to fact at the period to which they are assigned as would be efforts to depict Augustine Washington and his wife in the dress of the French revolution discussing the propriety of worshipping the Goddess of Reason.

To enter into any serious historical criticism of these stories would be to break a butterfly. So much as this even has been said only because these wretched fables have gone throughout the world, and it is time that they were swept away into the dust-heaps of history. They represent Mr. and Mrs. Washington as affected and priggish people, given to cheap moralizing, and, what is far worse, they have served to place Washington himself in a ridiculous light to an age which has outgrown the educational foibles of seventy-five years ago. Augustine Washington and his wife were a gentleman and lady of the eighteenth century, living in Virginia. So far as we know without guessing or conjecture, they were simple,

honest, and straightforward, devoted to the care of their family and
estate, and doing their duty sensibly and after the fashion of their time.
Their son, to whom the greatest wrong has been done, not only never
did anything common or mean, but from the beginning to the end of his
life he was never for an instant ridiculous or affected, and he was as
utterly removed from canting or priggishness as any human being could
well be. Let us therefore consign the Weems stories and their offspring
to the limbo of historical rubbish, and try to learn what the plain facts tell
us of the boy Washington.

Unfortunately these same facts are at first very few, so few that they
tell us hardly anything. We know when and where Washington was born;
and how, when he was little more than three years old,* he was taken
from Bridges Creek to the banks of the Rappahannock. There he was
placed under the charge of one Hobby, the sexton of the parish, to learn
his alphabet and his pothooks; and when that worthy man's store of learning was exhausted he was sent back to Bridges Creek, soon after his
father's death, to live with his half-brother Augustine, and obtain the
benefits of a school kept by a Mr. Williams. There he received what
would now be called a fair common-school education, wholly destitute of
any instruction in languages, ancient or modern, but apparently with
some mathematical training.

That he studied faithfully cannot be doubted, and we know, too, that
he matured early, and was a tall, active, and muscular boy. He could out-
walk and outrun and outride any of his companions. As he could no doubt
have thrashed any of them too, he was, in virtue of these qualities, which
are respected everywhere by all wholesome minds, and especially by
boys, a leader among his school-fellows. We know further that he was
honest and true, and a lad of unusual promise, not because of the goody-
goody anecdotes of the myth-makers, but because he was liked and
trusted by such men as his brother Lawrence and Lord Fairfax.

There he was, at all events, in his fourteenth year, a big, strong, hearty

---

*There is a conflict about the period of this removal (see above, p. 28). Tradition places it in
1735, but the Rev. Mr. McGuire (*Religious Opinions of Washington*) puts it in 1739.

boy, offering a serious problem to his mother, who was struggling along with many acres, little money, and five children. Mrs. Washington's chief desire naturally was to put George in the way of getting a living, which no doubt seemed far more important than getting an education, and, as he was a sober-minded boy, the same idea was probably profoundly impressed on his own mind also. This condition of domestic affairs led to the first attempt to give Washington a start in life, which has been given to us until very lately in a somewhat decorated form. The fact is, that in casting about for something to do, it occurred to some one, very likely to the boy himself, that it would be a fine idea to go to sea. His masculine friends and relatives urged the scheme upon Mrs. Washington, who consented very reluctantly, if at all, not liking the notion of parting with her oldest son, even in her anxiety to have him earn his bread. When it came to the point, however, she finally decided against his going, determined probably by a very sensible letter from her brother, Joseph Ball, an English lawyer. In all the ornamented versions we are informed that the boy was to enter the royal navy, and that a midshipman's warrant was procured for him. There does not appear to be any valid authority for the royal navy, the warrant, or the midshipman. The contemporary Virginian letters speak simply of "going to sea," while Mr. Ball says distinctly that the plan was to enter the boy on a tobacco ship, with an excellent chance of being pressed on a man-of-war, and a very faint prospect of either getting into the navy, or even rising to be the captain of one of the petty trading-vessels familiar to Virginian planters. Some recent writers have put Mr. Ball aside as not knowing what was intended in regard to his nephew, but in view of the difficulty at that time of obtaining commissions in the navy without great political influence, it seems probable that Mrs. Washington's brother knew very well what he was talking about, and he certainly wrote a very sensible letter. A bold, adventurous boy, eager to earn his living and make his way in the world, would, like many others before him, look longingly to the sea as the highway to fortune and success. To Washington the romance of the sea was represented by the tobacco ship creeping up the river and bringing all the luxuries and many of the necessaries of life from vaguely distant countries. No doubt he wished to go on one of these vessels and try his luck, and very possibly the royal navy was hoped for as the ultimate result. The effort was certainly made to send him to sea, but it failed, and he went back to school to study more mathematics.

Apart from the fact that the exact sciences in moderate degree were about all that Mr. Williams could teach, this branch of learning had an immediate practical value, inasmuch as surveying was almost the only immediately gainful pursuit open to a young Virginia gentleman, who sorely needed a little ready money that he might buy slaves and work a plantation. So Washington studied on for two years more, and fitted himself to be a surveyor. There are still extant some early papers belonging to this period, chiefly fragments of school exercises, which show that he already wrote the bold, handsome hand with which the world was to become familiar, and that he made geometrical figures and notes of surveys with the neatness and accuracy which clung to him in all the work of his life, whether great or small. Among those papers too were found many copies of legal forms, and a set of rules, over a hundred in number, as to etiquette and behavior, carefully written out. It has always been supposed that these rules were copied, but it was reserved apparently for the storms of a mighty civil war to lay bare what may have been, if not the source of the rules themselves, the origin and suggestion of their compilation. At that time a little volume was found in Virginia bearing the name of George Washington in a boyish hand on the fly-leaf, and the date 1742. The book was entitled, "The Young Man's Companion." It was an English work, and had passed through thirteen editions, which was little enough in view of its varied and extensive information. It was written by W. Mather, in a plain and easy style, and treated of arithmetic, surveying, forms for legal documents, the measuring of land and lumber, gardening, and many other useful topics, and it contained general precepts which, with the aid of Hale's "Contemplations," may readily have furnished the hints for the rules found in manuscript among Washington's papers.* These rules were in the main wise and sensible, and it is evident they had occupied deeply the

---

*An account of this volume was given in the *New York Tribune* in 1866, and also in the *Historical Magazine* (x. 47).

boy's mind.* They are for the most part concerned with the commonplaces of etiquette and good manners, but there is something not only apt but quite prophetic in the last one; "Labor to keep alive in your breast that little spark of celestial fire called conscience." To suppose that Washington's character was formed by these sententious bits of not very profound wisdom would be absurd; but that a series of rules which most lads would have regarded as simply dull should have been written out and pondered by this boy indicates a soberness and thoughtfulness of mind which certainly are not usual at that age. The chief thought that runs through all the sayings is to practice self-control, and no man ever displayed that most difficult of virtues to such a degree as George Washington. It was no ordinary boy who took such a lesson as this to heart before he was fifteen, and carried it into his daily life, never to be forgotten. It may also be said that very few boys ever needed it more; but those persons who know what they chiefly need, and pursue it, are by no means common.

---

*The most important are given in Sparks' *Writings of Washington*, ii. 412, and they may be found complete in the little pamphlet concerning them, excellently edited by Dr. J. M. Toner, of Washington.

CHAPTER III

ON THE FRONTIER

WHILE WASHINGTON WAS working his way through the learning purveyed by Mr. Williams, he was also receiving another education, of a much broader and better sort, from the men and women among whom he found himself, and with whom he made friends. Chief among them was his eldest brother, Lawrence, fourteen years his senior, who had been educated in England, had fought with Vernon at Carthagena, and had then returned to Virginia, to be to him a generous father and a loving friend. As the head of the family, Lawrence Washington had received the lion's share of the property, including the estate at Hunting Creek, on the Potomac, which he christened Mount Vernon, after his admiral, and where he settled down and built him a goodly house. To this pleasant spot George Washington journeyed often in vacation time, and there he came to live and further pursue his studies, after leaving school in the autumn of 1747.

Lawrence Washington had married the daughter of William Fairfax, the proprietor of Belvoir, a neighboring plantation, and the agent for the vast estates held by his family in Virginia. George Fairfax, Mrs. Washington's brother, had married a Miss Cary, and thus two large and agreeable family connections were thrown open to the young surveyor when he emerged from school. The chief figure, however, in that pleasant winter of 1747–48, so far as an influence upon the character of Washington is concerned, was the head of the family into which Lawrence Washington had married. Thomas, Lord Fairfax, then sixty

39

years of age, had come to Virginia to live upon and look after the kingdom which he had inherited in the wilderness. He came of a noble and distinguished race. Graduating at Oxford with credit, he served in the army, dabbled in literature, had his fling in the London world, and was jilted by a beauty who preferred a duke, and gave her faithful but less titled lover an apparently incurable wound. His life having been thus early twisted and set awry, Lord Fairfax, when well past his prime, had determined finally to come to Virginia, bury himself in the forests, and look after the almost limitless possessions beyond the Blue Ridge, which he had inherited from his maternal grandfather, Lord Culpeper, of unsavory Restoration memory. It was a piece of great good-fortune which threw in Washington's path this accomplished gentleman, familiar with courts and camps, disappointed, but not morose, disillusioned, but still kindly and generous. From him the boy could gain that knowledge of men and manners which no school can give, and which is as important in its way as any that a teacher can impart.

Lord Fairfax and Washington became fast friends. They hunted the fox together, and hunted him hard. They engaged in all the rough sports and perilous excitements that Virginia winter life could afford, and the boy's bold and skilful riding, his love of sports and his fine temper, commended him to the warm and affectionate interest of the old nobleman. Other qualities, too, the experienced man of the world saw in his young companion: a high and persistent courage, robust and calm sense, and, above all, unusual force of will and character. Washington impressed profoundly everybody with whom he was brought into personal contact, a fact which is one of the most marked features of his character and career, and one which deserves study more than almost any other. Lord Fairfax was no exception to the rule. He saw in Washington not simply a promising, brave, open-hearted boy, diligent in practising his profession, and whom he was anxious to help, but something more; something which so impressed him that he confided to this lad a task which, according to its performance, would affect both his fortune and his peace. In a word, he trusted Washington, and told him, as the spring of 1748 was opening, to go forth and survey the vast Fairfax estates beyond the Ridge, define their boundaries, and save them from future litigation. With this commission from Lord Fairfax, Washington entered on the first period of his career. He passed it on the frontier, fighting nature, the Indians, and the French. He went in a schoolboy; he came out the first soldier in the colonies, and one of the leading men of Virginia. Let us pause a moment and look at him as he stands on the threshold of this momentous period, rightly called momentous because it was the formative period in the life of such a man.

He had just passed his sixteenth birthday. He was tall and muscular, approaching the stature of more than six feet which he afterwards attained. He was not yet filled out to manly proportions, but was rather spare, after the fashion of youth. He had a well-shaped, active figure, symmetrical except for the unusual length of the arms, indicating uncommon strength. His light brown hair was drawn back from a broad forehead, and grayish-blue eyes looked happily, and perhaps a trifle soberly, on the pleasant Virginia world about him. The face was open and manly, with a square, massive jaw, and a general expression of calmness and strength. "Fair and florid," big and strong, he was, take him for all in all, as fine a specimen of his race as could be found in the English colonies.

Let us look a little closer through the keen eyes of one who studied many faces to good purpose. The great painter of portraits, Gilbert Stuart, tells us of Washington that he never saw in any man such large eye-sockets, or such a breadth of nose and forehead between the eyes, and that he read there the evidences of the strongest passions possible to human nature. John Bernard the actor, a good observer, too, saw in Washington's face, in 1797, the signs of an habitual conflict and mastery of passions, witnessed by the compressed mouth and deeply indented brow. The problem had been solved then; but in 1748, passion and will alike slumbered, and no man could tell which would prevail, or whether they would work together to great purpose or go jarring on to nothingness. He rises up to us out of the past in that early springtime a fine, handsome, athletic boy, beloved by those about him, who found him a charming companion and did not guess that he might be a terribly dangerous foe. He rises up instinct with life and strength, a being capable, as we know, of great things whether for good or evil, with hot blood pulsing in his veins and beating in his heart, with violent passions and relentless will still undeveloped, and no one in all that jolly, generous Virginian society even dimly dreamed what that development would be, or what it would mean to the world.

It was in March, 1748, that George Fairfax and Washington set forth on their adventures, and passing through Ashby's Gap in the Blue Ridge, entered the valley of Virginia. Thence they worked their way up the valley of the Shenandoah, surveying as they went, returned and swam the swollen Potomac, surveyed the lands about its south branch and in the mountainous region of Frederick County, and finally reached Mount Vernon again on April 12th. It was a rough experience for a beginner, but a wholesome one, and furnished the usual vicissitudes of frontier life. They were wet and cold and hungry, or warm and dry and well fed, by turns. They slept in a tent, or the huts of the scattered settlers, and oftener still beneath the stars. They met a war party of Indians, and having plied them with liquor, watched one of their mad dances round the camp-fire. In another place they came on a straggling settlement of Germans, dull, patient, and illiterate, strangely unfit for the life of the wilderness. All these things, as well as the progress of their work and their various resting-places, Washington noted down briefly but methodically in a diary, showing in these rough notes the first evidences of that keen observation of nature and men and daily incidents which he developed to such good purpose in after-life. There are no rhapsodies and no reflections in these hasty jottings, but the employments and the discomforts are all set down in a simple and matter-of-fact way, which omitted no essential thing and excluded all that was worthless. His work, too, was well done, and Lord Fairfax was so much pleased by the report that he moved across the Blue Ridge, built a hunting lodge preparatory to something more splendid which never came to pass, and laid out a noble manor, to which he gave the name of Greenway Court. He also procured for Washington an appointment as a public surveyor, which conferred authority on his surveys and provided him with regular work. Thus started, Washington toiled at his profession for three years, living and working as he did on his first expedition. It was a rough life, but a manly and robust one, and the men who live it, although often rude and coarse, are never weak or effeminate. To Washington it was an admirable school. It strengthened his muscles and hardened him to exposure and fatigue. It accustomed him to risks and perils of various kinds, and made him fertile in expedients and confident of himself, while the nature of his work rendered him careful and industrious. That his work was well done is shown by the fact that his surveys were considered of the first authority, and stand unquestioned to this day, like certain other work which he was subsequently called to do. It was part of his character, when he did anything, to do it in a lasting fashion, and it is worth while to remember that the surveys he made as a boy were the best that could be made.

He wrote to a friend at this time: "Since you received my letter of October last, I have not slept above three or four nights in a bed, but, after walking a good deal all the day, I have lain down before the fire upon a little hay, straw, fodder, or a bearskin, whichever was to be had, with man, wife, and children, like dogs and cats; and happy is he who gets the berth nearest the fire. Nothing would make it pass off tolerably but a good reward. A doubloon is my constant gain every day that the weather will permit of my going out, and sometimes six pistoles." He was evidently a thrifty lad, and honestly pleased with honest earnings. He was no mere adventurous wanderer, but a man working for results in money, reputation, or some solid value, and while he worked and earned he kept an observant eye upon the wilderness, and bought up when he could the best land for himself and his family, laying the foundations of the great landed estate of which he died possessed.

There was also a lighter and pleasanter side to this hard-working existence, which was quite as useful, and more attractive, than toiling in the woods and mountains. The young surveyor passed much of his time at Greenway Court, hunting the fox and rejoicing in all field sports which held high place in that kingdom, while at the same time he profited much in graver fashion by his friendship with such a man as Lord Fairfax. There, too, he had a chance at a library, and his diaries show that he read carefully the history of England and the essays of the "Spectator."

Neither in early days nor at any other time was he a student, for he had few opportunities, and his life from the beginning was out of doors and among men. But the idea sometimes put forward that Washington cared nothing for reading or for books is an idle one. He read at Greenway Court and everywhere else when he had a chance, and he read well and to some purpose, studying men and events in books as he did in the world, and though he never talked of his reading, preserving silence on that as on other things concerning himself, no one ever was able to record an instance in which he showed himself ignorant of history or of literature. He was never a learned man, but so far as his own language could carry him he was an educated one. Thus while he developed the sterner qualities by hard work and a rough life, he did not bring back the coarse habits of the backwoods and the camp-fire, but was able to refine his manners and improve his mind in the excellent society and under the hospitable roof of Lord Fairfax.

Three years slipped by, and then a domestic change came which much affected Washington's whole life. The Carthagena campaign had undermined the strength of Lawrence Washington and sown the seeds of consumption, which showed itself in 1749, and became steadily more alarming. A voyage to England and a summer at the warm springs were tried without success, and finally, as a last resort, the invalid sailed for the West Indies, in September, 1751. Thither his brother George accompanied him, and we have the fragments of a diary kept during this first and last wandering outside his native country. He copied the log, noted the weather, and evidently strove to get some idea of nautical matters while he was at sea and leading a life strangely unfamiliar to a woodsman and pioneer. When they arrived they were immediately asked to breakfast and dine with Major Clarke, the military magnate of the place, and our young Virginian remarked, with characteristic prudence and a certain touch of grim humor, "We went,—myself with some reluctance, as the smallpox was in the family." He fell a victim to his good manners, for two weeks later he was "strongly attacked with the smallpox," and was then housed for a month, getting safely and successfully through this dangerous and then almost universal ordeal. Before the disease declared itself, however, he went about everywhere, innocently scattering infection, and greatly enjoying the pleasures of the island. It is to be regretted that any part of this diary should have been lost, for it is pleasant reading, and exhibits the writer in an agreeable and characteristic fashion. He commented on the country and the scenery, inveighed against the extravagance of the charges for board and lodging, told of his dinner-parties and his friends, and noted the marvelous abundance and variety of the tropical fruits, which contrasted strangely with the British dishes of beefsteak and tripe. He also mentioned being treated to a ticket to see the play of "George Barnwell," on which he offered this cautious criticism: "The character of Barnwell and several others were said to be well performed. There was music adapted and regularly conducted."

Soon after his recovery Washington returned to Virginia, arriving there in February, 1752. The diary concluded with a brief but perfectly effective description of Barbadoes, touching on its resources and scenery, its government and condition, and the manners and customs of its inhabitants. All through these notes we find the keenly observant spirit, and the evidence of a mind constantly alert to learn. We see also a pleasant, happy temperament, enjoying with hearty zest all the pleasures that youth and life could furnish. He who wrote these lines was evidently a vigorous, good-humored young fellow, with a quick eye for the world opening before him, and for the delights as well as the instruction which it offered.

From the sunshine and ease of this tropical winter Washington passed to a long season of trial and responsibility at home and abroad. In July, 1752, his much-loved brother Lawrence died, leaving George guardian of his daughter, and heir to his estates in the event of that daughter's death. Thus the current of his home life changed, and responsibility came into it, while outside the mighty stream of public events changed too, and swept him along in the swelling torrent of a world-wide war.

In all the vast wilderness beyond the mountains there was not room for both French and English. The rival nations had been for years slowly approaching each other, until in 1749 each people proceeded at last to take possession of the Ohio country after its own fashion. The French sent a military expedition which sank and nailed up leaden plates; the English formed a great land company to speculate and make money, and both set diligently to work to form Indian alliances. A man of far less perception than Lawrence Washington, who had become the chief manager of the Ohio Company, would have seen that the conditions on the frontier rendered war inevitable, and he accordingly made ready for the future by preparing his brother for the career of a soldier, so far as it could be done. He brought to Mount Vernon two old companions-in-arms of the Carthagena time, Adjutant Muse, a Virginian, and Jacob Van Braam, a Dutch soldier of fortune. The former instructed Washington in the art of war, tactics, and the manual of arms, the latter in fencing and the sword exercise. At the same time Lawrence Washington procured for his brother, then only nineteen years of age, an appointment as one of the adjutants-general of Virginia, with the rank of major. To all this the young surveyor took kindly enough so far as we can tell, but his military avocations were interrupted by his voyage to Barbadoes, by the illness and death of his brother, and by the cares and responsibilities thereby thrust upon him.

Meantime the French aggressions had continued, and French soldiers and traders were working their way up from the South and down from the North, bullying and cajoling the Indians by turns, taking possession of the Ohio country, and selecting places as they went for that chain of forts which was to hem in and slowly strangle the English settlements. Governor Dinwiddie had sent a commissioner to remonstrate against these encroachments, but his envoy had stopped a hundred and fifty miles short of the French posts, alarmed by the troublous condition of things, and by the defeat and slaughter which the Frenchmen had already inflicted upon the Indians. Some more vigorous person was evidently needed to go through the form of warning France not to trespass on the English wilderness and thereupon Governor Dinwiddie selected for the task George Washington, recently reappointed adjutant-general of the northern division, and major in the Virginian forces. He was a young man for such an undertaking, not yet twenty-two, but clearly of good reputation. It is plain enough that Lord Fairfax and others had said to the governor, "Here is the very man for you; young, daring, and adventurous, but yet sober-minded and responsible, who only lacks opportunity to show the stuff that is in him."

Thus, then, in October, 1753, Washington set forth with Van Braam, and various servants and horses, accompanied by the boldest of Virginian frontiersmen, Christopher Gist. He wrote a report in the form of a journal, which was sent to England and much read at the time as part of the news of the day, and which has an equal although different interest now. It is a succinct, clear, and sober narrative. The little party was formed at Will's Creek, and thence through woods and over swollen rivers made its way to Logstown. Here they spent some days among the Indians, whose leaders Washington got within his grasp after much speech-making; and here, too, he met some French deserters from the South, and drew from them all the knowledge they possessed of New Orleans and the military expeditions from that region. From Logstown he pushed on, accompanied by his Indian chiefs, to Venango, on the Ohio, the first French outpost. The French officers asked him to sup with them. The wine flowed freely, the tongues of the hosts were loosened, and the young Virginian, temperate and hard-headed, listened to all the conversation, and noted down mentally much that was interesting and valuable. The next morning the Indian chiefs, prudently kept in the background, appeared, and a struggle ensued between the talkative, clever Frenchmen and the quiet, persistent Virginian, over the possession of these important savages. Finally Washington got off, carrying his chiefs with him, and made his way seventy miles further to the fort on French Creek. Here he delivered the governor's letter, and while M. de St. Pierre wrote a vague and polite answer, he sketched the fort and informed himself in regard to the military condition of the post. Then came another struggle over the Indians, and finally Washington got off with them once more, and worked his way back to Venango. Another struggle for the savages followed, rum being always the principal factor in the negotiation, and at last the chiefs determined to stay behind. Nevertheless, the work had been well done, and the important Half-King remained true to the English cause.

Leaving his horses, Washington and Gist then took to the woods on foot. The French Indians lay in wait for them and tried to murder them, and Gist, like a true frontiersman, was for shooting the scoundrel whom they captured. But Washington stayed his hand, and they gave the savage the slip and pressed on. It was the middle of December and cold and stormy. In crossing a river, Washington fell from the raft into deep water, amid the floating ice, but fought his way out, and he and his companion passed the night on an island, with their clothes frozen upon them. So through peril and privation, and various dangers, stopping in the midst of it all to win another savage potentate, they reached the edge of the settlements and thence went on to Williamsburg, where great praise and glory were awarded to the youthful envoy, the hero of the hour in the little Virginia capital.

It is worth while to pause over this expedition a moment and to consider attentively this journal which recounts it, for there are very few incidents or documents which tell us more of Washington. He was not yet twenty-two when he faced this first grave responsibility, and he did his work absolutely well. Cool courage, of course, he showed, but also patience and wisdom in handling the Indians, a clear sense that the crafty and well-trained Frenchmen could not blind, and a strong faculty for dealing with men, always a rare and precious gift. As in the little Barbadoes diary, so also in this journal, we see, and far more strongly, the penetration and perception that nothing could escape, and which set down all things essential and let the "huddling silver, little worth," go by. The clearness, terseness, and entire sufficiency of the narrative are obvious and lie on the surface; but we find also another quality of the man which is one of the most marked features in his character, and one which we must dwell upon again and again, as we follow the story of his life. Here it is that we learn directly for the first time that Washington was a profoundly silent man. The gospel of silence has been preached in these latter days by Carlyle, with the fervor of a seer and prophet, and the world owes him a debt for the historical discredit which he has brought upon the man of words as compared with the man of deeds. Carlyle brushed Washington aside as "a bloodless Cromwell," a phrase to which we must revert later on other grounds, and, as has already been said, failed utterly to see that he was the most supremely silent of the great men of action that the world can show. Like Cromwell and Frederic, Washington wrote countless letters, made many speeches, and was agreeable in conversation. But this was all in the way of business, and a man may be profoundly silent and yet talk a great deal. Silence in the fine and true sense is neither mere holding of the tongue nor an incapacity of expression. The greatly silent man is he who is not given to words for their own sake, and who never talks about himself. Both Cromwell, greatest of Englishmen, and the great Frederic, Carlyle's especial heroes, were fond of talking of themselves. So in still larger measure was Napoleon, and many others of less importance. But Washington differs from them all. He had abundant power of words, and could use them with much force and point when he was so minded, but he never used them needlessly or to hide his meaning, and he never talked about himself. Hence the inestimable difficulty of knowing him. A brief sentence here and there, a rare gleam of light across the page of a letter, is all that we can find. The rest is silence. He did as great work as has fallen to the lot of man, he wrote volumes of correspondence, he talked with innumerable men and women, and of himself he said nothing. Here in this youthful journal we have a narrative of wild adventure, wily diplomacy, and personal peril, impossible of condensation, and yet not a word of the writer's thoughts or feelings. All that was done or said important to the business in hand was set down, and nothing was overlooked, but that is all. The work was done, and we know how it was done, but the man is silent as to all else. Here, indeed, is the man of action and of real silence, a character to be much admired and wondered at in these or any other days.

Washington's report looked like war, and its author was shortly afterwards appointed lieutenant-colonel of a Virginian regiment, Colonel Fry commanding. Now began that long experience of human stupidity and inefficiency with which Washington was destined to struggle through all the years of his military career, suffering from them, and triumphing in spite of them to a degree unequalled by any other great commander. Dinwiddie, the Scotch governor, was eager enough to fight, and full of energy and good intentions, but he was hasty and not overwise, and was filled with an excessive idea of his prerogatives. The assembly, on its side, was sufficiently patriotic, but its members came from a community which for more than half a century had had no fighting, and they knew nothing of war or its necessities. Unaccustomed to the large affairs into which they were suddenly plunged, they displayed a narrow and provincial spirit. Keenly alive to their own rights and privileges, they were more occupied in quarrelling with Dinwiddie than in prosecuting the war. In the weak proprietary governments of Maryland and Pennsylvania there was the same condition of affairs, with every evil exaggerated tenfold. The fighting spirit was dominant in Virginia, but in Quaker-ridden Pennsylvania it seems to have been almost extinct. These three were not very promising communities to look to for support in a difficult and costly war.

With all this inertia and stupidity Washington was called to cope, and he rebelled against it in vigorous fashion. Leaving Colonel Fry to follow with the main body of troops, Washington set out on April 2, 1754, with two companies from Alexandria, where he had been recruiting amidst most irritating difficulties. He reached Will's Creek three weeks later; and then his real troubles began. Captain Trent, the timid and halting envoy, who had failed to reach the French, had been sent out by the wise authorities to build a fort at the junction of the Alleghany and Monongahela, on the admirable site selected by the keen eye of Washington. There Trent left his men and returned to Will's Creek, where Washington found him, but without the pack-horses that he had promised to provide. Presently news came that the French in overwhelming numbers had swept down upon Trent's little party, captured their fort, and sent them packing back to Virginia. Washington took this to be war, and determined at once to march against the enemy. Having impressed from the inhabitants, who were not bubbling over with patriotism, some horses and wagons, he set out on his toilsome march across the mountains.

It was a wild and desolate region, and progress was extremely slow. By May 9th he was at the Little Meadows, twenty miles from his starting-place; by the 18th at the Youghiogany River, which he explored and found unnavigable. He was therefore forced to take up his weary march again for the Monongahela, and by the 27th he was at the Great Meadows, a few miles further on. The extreme danger of his position does not seem to have occurred to him, but he was harassed and angered by the conduct of the assembly. He wrote to Governor Dinwiddie that he had no idea of giving up his commission. "But," he continued, "let me serve voluntarily; then I will, with the greatest pleasure in life, devote my services to the expedition, without any other reward than the satisfaction of serving my country; but to be slaving dangerously for the shadow of pay, through woods, rocks, mountains,—I would rather prefer the great toil of a daily laborer, and dig for a maintenance, provided I were reduced to the necessity, than serve upon such ignoble terms; for I really do not see why the lives of his Majesty's subjects in Virginia should be of less value than those in other parts of his American dominions, especially when it is well known that we must undergo double their hardship." Here we have a high-spirited, high-tempered young gentleman, with a contempt for shams that it is pleasant to see, and evidently endowed also with a fine taste for fighting and not too much patience.

Indignant letters written in vigorous language were, however, of little avail, and Washington prepared to shift for himself as best he might. His Indian allies brought him news that the French were on the march and had thrown out scouting parties. Picking out a place in the Great Meadows for a fort, "a charming field for an encounter," he in his turn sent out a scouting party, and then on fresh intelligence from the Indians set forth himself with forty men to find the enemy. After a toilsome march they discovered their foes in camp. The French, surprised and surrounded, sprang to arms, the Virginians fired, there was a sharp exchange of shots, and all was over. Ten of the French were killed and twenty-one were taken prisoners, only one of the party escaping to carry back the news.

This little skirmish made a prodigious noise in its day, and was much heralded in France. The French declared that Jumonville, the leader, who fell at the first fire, was foully assassinated, and that he and his party were ambassadors and sacred characters. Paris rang with this fresh instance

of British perfidy, and a M. Thomas celebrated the luckless Jumonville in
a solemn epic poem in four books. French historians, relying on the
account of the Canadian who escaped, adopted the same tone, and at a
later day mourned over this black spot on Washington's character. The
French view was simple nonsense. Jumonville and his party, as the
papers found on Jumonville showed, were out on a spying and scouting
expedition. They were seeking to surprise the English when the English
surprised them, with the usual backwoods result. The affair has a dramatic interest because it was the first blood shed in a great struggle, and
was the beginning of a series of world-wide wars and social and political
convulsions, which terminated more than half a century later on the
plains of Waterloo. It gave immortality to an obscure French officer by
linking his name with that of his opponent, and brought Washington for
the moment before the eyes of the world, which little dreamed that this
Virginian colonel was destined to be one of the principal figures in the
great revolutionary drama to which the war then beginning was but the
prologue.

Washington, well satisfied with his exploit, retraced his steps, and
having sent his prisoners back to Virginia, proceeded to consider his situation. It was not a very cheerful prospect. Contrecœur, with the main
body of the French and Indians, was moving down from the
Monongahela a thousand strong. This of course was to have been anticipated, and it does not seem to have in the least damped Washington's
spirits. His blood was up, his fighting temper thoroughly roused, and he
prepared to push on. Colonel Fry had died meanwhile, leaving
Washington in command; but his troops came forward, and also not long
after a useless "independent" company from South Carolina. Thus reinforced Washington advanced painfully some thirteen miles, and then
receiving sure intelligence of the approach of the French in great force
fell back with difficulty to the Great Meadows, where he was obliged by
the exhausted condition of his men to stop. He at once resumed work on
Fort Necessity, and made ready for a desperate defence, for the French
were on his heels, and on July 3d appeared at the Meadows. Washington
offered battle outside the fort, and this being declined withdrew to his

trenches, and skirmishing went on all day. When night fell it was apparent that the end had come. The men were starved and worn-out. Their muskets in many cases were rendered useless by the rain, and their ammunition was spent. The Indians had deserted, and the foe outnumbered them four to one. When the French therefore offered a parley, Washington was forced reluctantly to accept. The French had no stomach for the fight, apparently, and allowed the English to go with their arms, exacting nothing but a pledge that for a year they would not come to the Ohio.

So ended Washington's first campaign. His friend the Half-King, the celebrated Seneca chief, Thanacarishon, who prudently departed on the arrival of the French, has left us a candid opinion of Washington and his opponents. "The colonel," he said, "was a good-natured man, but had no experience; he took upon him to command the Indians as his slaves, and would have them every day upon the scout and to attack the enemy by themselves, but would by no means take advice from the Indians. He lay in one place from one full moon to the other, without making any fortifications, except that little thing on the meadow; whereas, had he taken advice, and built such fortifications as I advised him, he might easily have beat off the French. But the French in the engagement acted like cowards, and the English like fools."[*]

There is a deal of truth in this opinion. The whole expedition was rash in the extreme. When Washington left Will's Creek he was aware that he was going to meet a force of a thousand men with only a hundred and fifty raw recruits at his back. In the same spirit he pushed on; and after the Jumonville affair, although he knew that the wilderness about him was swarming with enemies, he still struggled forward. When forced to retreat he made a stand at the Meadows and offered battle in the open to his more numerous and more prudent foes, for he was one of those men who by nature regard courage as a substitute for everything, and who have a contempt for hostile odds. He was ready to meet any number

---

[*]*Enquiry into the Causes of the Alienation of the Delaware and Shawanese Indians*, etc. London, 1759. By Charles Thomson, afterwards Secretary of Congress.

of French and Indians with cheerful confidence and with real pleasure. He wrote, in a letter which soon became famous, that he loved to hear bullets whistle, a sage observation which he set down in later years as a folly of youth. Yet this boyish outburst, foolish as it was, has a meaning to us, for it was essentially true. Washington had the fierce fighting temper of the Northmen. He loved battle and danger, and he never ceased to love them and to give way to their excitement, although he did not again set down such sentiments in boastful phrase that made the world laugh. Men of such temper, moreover, are naturally imperious and have a fine disregard of consequences, with the result that their allies, Indian or otherwise, often become impatient and finally useless. The campaign was perfectly wild from the outset, and if it had not been for the utter indifference to danger displayed by Washington, and the consequent timidity of the French, that particular body of Virginians would have been permanently lost to the British Empire.

But we learn from all this many things. It appears that Washington was not merely a brave man, but one who loved fighting for its own sake. The whole expedition shows an arbitrary temper and the most reckless courage, valuable qualities, but here unrestrained, and mixed with very little prudence. Some important lessons were learned by Washington from the rough teachings of inexorable and unconquerable facts. He received in this campaign the first taste of that severe experience which by its training developed the self-control and mastery of temper for which he became so remarkable. He did not spring into life a perfect and impossible man, as is so often represented. On the contrary, he was educated by circumstances; but the metal came out of the furnace of experience finely tempered, because it was by nature of the best and with but little dross to be purged away. In addition to all this he acquired for the moment what would now be called a European reputation. He was known in Paris as an assassin, and in England, thanks to the bullet letter, as a "fanfaron" and brave braggart. With these results he wended his way home much depressed in spirits, but not in the least discouraged, and fonder of fighting than ever.

Virginia, however, took a kinder view of the campaign than did her defeated soldier. She appreciated the gallantry of the offer to fight in the open and the general conduct of the troops, and her House of Burgesses passed a vote of thanks to Washington and his officers, and gave money to his men. In August he rejoined his regiment, and renewed the vain struggle against incompetence and extravagance, and as if this were not enough, his sense of honor was wounded and his temper much irritated by the governor's playing false to the prisoners taken in the Jumonville fight. While thus engaged, news came that the French were off their guard at Fort Duquesne, and Dinwiddie was for having the regiment of undisciplined troops march again into the wilderness. Washington, however, had learned something, if not a great deal, and he demonstrated the folly of such an attempt in a manner too clear to be confuted.

Meantime the Burgesses came together, and more money being voted, Dinwiddie hit on a notable plan for quieting dissensions between regulars and provincials by dividing all the troops into independent companies, with no officer higher than a captain. Washington, the only officer who had seen fighting and led the regiment, resented this senseless policy, and resigning his commission withdrew to Mount Vernon to manage the estate and attend to his own affairs. He was driven to this course still more strongly by the original cause of Dinwiddie's arrangement. The English government had issued an order that officers holding the king's commission should rank provincial officers, and that provincial generals and field officers should have no rank when a general or field officer holding a royal commission was present. The degradation of being ranked by every whipper-snapper who might hold a royal commission by virtue, perhaps, of being the bastard son of some nobleman's cast-off mistress was more than the temper of George Washington could bear, and when Governor Sharpe, general by the king's commission, and eager to secure the services of the best fighter in Virginia, offered him a company and urged his acceptance, he replied in language that must have somewhat astonished his excellency. "You make mention in your letter," he wrote to Colonel Fitzhugh, Governor Sharpe's second in command, "of my continuing in the service, and retaining my colonel's commission. This idea has filled me with surprise; for, if you think me capable of holding a commission that has neither rank nor emolument annexed to it, you must entertain a very contemptible opinion of my weakness, and believe me to be more empty than the commission itself. . . . In short every captain, bearing the king's commission, every half-pay officer, or others appearing with such a commission, would rank before me. . . . Yet my inclinations are strongly bent to arms."

It was a bitter disappointment to withdraw from military life, but Washington had an intense sense of personal dignity; not the small vanity of a petty mind, but the quality of a proud man conscious of his own strength and purpose. It was of immense value to the American people at a later day, and there is something very instructive in this early revolt against the stupid arrogance which England has always thought it wise to display toward this country. She has paid dearly for indulging it, but it has seldom cost her more than when it drove Washington from her service, and left in his mind a sense of indignity and injustice.

Meantime this Virginian campaigning had started a great movement. England was aroused, and it was determined to assail France in Nova Scotia, from New York and on the Ohio. In accordance with this plan General Braddock arrived in Virginia February 20, 1755, with two picked regiments, and encamped at Alexandria. Thither Washington used to ride and look longingly at the pomp and glitter, and wish that he were engaged in the service. Presently this became known, and Braddock, hearing of the young Virginian's past experience, offered him a place on his staff with the rank of colonel where he would be subject only to the orders of the general, and could serve as a volunteer. He therefore accepted at once, and threw himself into his new duties with hearty good-will. Every step was full of instruction. At Annapolis he met the governors of the other colonies, and was interested and attracted by this association with distinguished public men. In the army to which he was attached he studied with the deepest attention the best discipline of Europe, observing everything and forgetting nothing, thus preparing himself unconsciously to use against his teachers the knowledge he acquired.

He also made warm friends with the English officers, and was treated with consideration by his commander. The universal practice of all

Englishmen was to behave contemptuously to the colonists, but there was something about Washington which made this impossible. They all treated him with the utmost courtesy, vaguely conscious that beneath the pleasant, quiet manner there was a strength of character and ability such as is rarely found, and that this was a man whom it was unsafe to affront. There is no stronger instance of Washington's power of impressing himself upon others than that he commanded now the respect and affection of his general, who was the last man to be easily or favorably affected by a young provincial officer.

Edward Braddock was a veteran soldier, a skilled disciplinarian, and a rigid martinet. He was narrow-minded, brutal, and brave. He had led a fast life in society, indulging in coarse and violent dissipations, and was proud with the intense pride of a limited intelligence and a nature incapable of physical fear. It would be difficult to conceive of a man more unfit to be entrusted with the task of marching through the wilderness and sweeping the French from the Ohio. All the conditions which confronted him were unfamiliar and beyond his experience. He cordially despised the provincials who were essential to his success, and lost no opportunity of showing his contempt for them. The colonists on their side, especially in Pennsylvania, gave him, unfortunately, only too much ground for irritation and disgust. They were delighted to see this brilliant force come from England to fight their battles, but they kept on wrangling and holding back, refusing money and supplies, and doing nothing. Braddock chafed and delayed, swore angrily, and lingered still. Washington strove to help him, but defended his country fearlessly against wholesale and furious attacks.

Finally the army began to move, but so slowly and after so much delay that they did not reach Will's Creek until the middle of May. Here came another exasperating pause, relieved only by Franklin, who by giving his own time, ability, and money, supplied the necessary wagons. Then they pushed on again, but with the utmost slowness. With supreme difficulty they made an elaborate road over the mountains as they marched, and did not reach the Little Meadows until June 16th. Then at last Braddock turned to his young aide for the counsel which had already been proffered and rejected many times. Washington advised the division of the army, so that the main body could hurry forward in light marching order while a detachment remained behind and brought up the heavy baggage. This plan was adopted, and the army started forward, still too heavily burdened, as Washington thought, but in somewhat better trim for the wilderness than before. Their progress, quickened as it was, still seemed slow to Washington, but he was taken ill with a fever, and finally was compelled by Braddock to stop for rest at the ford of Youghiogany. He made Braddock promise that he should be brought up before the army reached Fort Duquesne, and wrote to his friend Orme that he would not miss the impending battle for five hundred pounds.

As soon as his fever abated a little he left Colonel Dunbar, and, being unable to sit on a horse, was conveyed to the front in a wagon, coming up with the army on July 8th. He was just in time, for the next day the troops forded the Monongahela and marched to attack the fort. The splendid appearance of the soldiers as they crossed the river roused Washington's enthusiasm; but he was not without misgivings. Franklin had already warned Braddock against the danger of surprise, and had been told with a sneer that while these savages might be a formidable enemy to raw American militia, they could make no impression on disciplined troops. Now at the last moment Washington warned the general again and was angrily rebuked.

The troops marched on in ordered ranks, glittering and beautiful. Suddenly firing was heard in the front, and presently the van was flung back on the main body. Yells and war-whoops resounded on every side, and an unseen enemy poured in a deadly fire. Washington begged Braddock to throw his men into the woods, but all in vain. Fight in platoons they must, or not at all. The result was that they did not fight at all. They became panic-stricken, and huddled together, overcome with fear, until at last when Braddock was mortally wounded they broke in wild rout and fled. Of the regular troops, seven hundred, and of the officers, who showed the utmost bravery, sixty-two out of eighty-six, were killed or wounded. Two hundred Frenchmen and six hundred Indians achieved this signal victory. The only thing that could be called fighting on the

English side was done by the Virginians, "the raw American militia," who, spread out as skirmishers, met their foes on their own ground, and were cut off almost to a man.

Washington at the outset flung himself headlong into the fight. He rode up and down the field, carrying orders and striving to rally "the dastards," as he afterwards called the regular troops. He endeavored to bring up the artillery, but the men would not serve the guns, although he aimed and discharged one himself. All through that dreadful carnage he rode fiercely about, raging with the excitement of battle, and utterly exposed from beginning to end. Even now it makes the heart beat quicker to think of him amid the smoke and slaughter as he dashed hither and thither, his face glowing and his eyes shining with the fierce light of battle, leading on his own Virginians, and trying to stay the tide of disaster. He had two horses shot under him and four bullets through his coat. The Indians thought he bore a charmed life, while his death was reported in the colonies, together with his dying speech, which, he dryly wrote to his brother, he had not yet composed.

When the troops broke it was Washington who gathered the fugitives and brought off the dying general. It was he who rode on to meet Dunbar, and rallying the fugitives enabled the wretched remnants to take up their march for the settlements. He it was who laid Braddock in the grave four days after the defeat, and read over the dead the solemn words of the English service. Wise, sensible, and active in the advance, splendidly reckless on the day of battle, cool and collected on the retreat, Washington alone emerged from that history of disaster with added glory. Again he comes before us as, above all things, the fighting man, hot-blooded and fierce in action, and utterly indifferent to the danger which excited and delighted him. But the earlier lesson had not been useless. He showed a prudence and wisdom in counsel which were not apparent in the first of his campaigns, and he no longer thought that courage was all-sufficient, or that any enemy could be despised. He was plainly one of those who could learn. His first experience had borne good fruit, and now he had been taught a series of fresh and valuable lessons. Before his eyes had been displayed the most brilliant European discipline, both in camp and on the march. He had studied and absorbed it all, talking with veterans and hearing from them many things that he could have acquired nowhere else. Once more had he been taught, in a way not to be forgotten, that it is never well to underrate one's opponent. He had looked deeper, too, and had seen what the whole continent soon understood, that English troops were not invincible, that they could be beaten by Indians, and that they were after all much like other men. This was the knowledge, fatal to British supremacy, which Braddock's defeat brought to Washington and to the colonists, and which was never forgotten. Could he have looked into the future, he would have seen also in this ill-fated expedition an epitome of much future history. The expedition began with stupid contempt toward America and all things American, and ended in ruin and defeat. It was a bitter experience, much heeded by the colonists, but disregarded by England, whose indifference was paid for at a heavy cost.

After the hasty retreat, Colonel Dunbar, stricken with panic, fled onward to Philadelphia, abandoning everything, and Virginia was left naturally in a state of great alarm. The assembly came together, and at last, thoroughly frightened, voted abundant money, and ordered a regiment of a thousand men to be raised. Washington, who had returned to Mount Vernon ill and worn-out, was urged to solicit the command, but it was not his way to solicit, and he declined to do so now. August 14th, he wrote to his mother: "If it is in my power to avoid going to the Ohio again, I shall; but if the command is pressed upon me by the general voice of the country, and offered upon such terms as cannot be objected against, it would reflect dishonor on me to refuse it." The same day he was offered the command of all the Virginian forces on his own terms, and accepted. Virginia believed in Washington, and he was ready to obey her call.

He at once assumed command and betook himself to Winchester, a general without an army, but still able to check by his presence the existing panic, and ready to enter upon the trying, dreary, and fruitless work that lay before him. In April, 1757, he wrote: "I have been posted then, for more than twenty months past, upon our cold and barren frontiers, to perform, I think I may say, impossibilities; that is, to protect from the cruel incursions of a crafty, savage enemy a line of inhabitants, of more than three hundred and fifty miles in extent, with a force inadequate to the task." This terse statement covers all that can be said of the next three years. It was a long struggle against a savage foe in front, and narrowness, jealousy, and stupidity behind; apparently without any chance of effecting anything, or gaining any glory or reward. Troops were voted, but were raised with difficulty, and when raised were neglected and ill-treated by the wrangling governor and assembly, which caused much ill-suppressed wrath in the breast of the commander-in-chief who labored day and night to bring about better discipline in camp, and who wrote long letters to Williamsburg recounting existing evils and praying for a new militia law.

The troops, in fact, were got out with vast difficulty even under the most stinging necessity, and were almost worthless when they came. Of one "noble captain" who refused to come, Washington wrote: "With coolness and moderation this great captain answered that his wife, family, and corn were all at stake; so were those of his soldiers; therefore it was impossible for him to come. Such is the example of the officers; such the behavior of the men; and upon such circumstances depends the safety of our country!" But while the soldiers were neglected, and the assembly faltered, and the militia disobeyed, the French and Indians kept at work on the long, exposed frontier. There panic reigned, farm-houses and villages went up in smoke, and the fields were reddened with slaughter at each fresh incursion. Gentlemen in Williamsburg bore these misfortunes with reasonable fortitude, but Washington raged against the abuses and the inaction, and vowed that nothing but the imminent danger prevented his resignation. "The supplicating tears of the women," he wrote, "and moving petitions of the men melt me into such deadly sorrow that I solemnly declare, if I know my own mind, I could offer myself a willing sacrifice to the butchering enemy, provided that would contribute to the people's ease." This is one of the rare flashes of personal feeling which disclose the real man, warm of heart and temper, full of human sympathy, and giving vent to hot indignation in words which still ring clear and strong across the century that has come and gone.

Serious troubles, moreover, were complicated by petty annoyances. A Maryland captain, at the head of thirty men, undertook to claim rank over the Virginian commander-in-chief because he had held a king's commission; and Washington was obliged to travel to Boston in order to have the miserable thing set right by Governor Shirley. This affair settled, he returned to take up again the old disheartening struggle, and his outspoken condemnation of Dinwiddie's foolish schemes and of the shortcomings of the government began to raise up backbiters and malcontents at Williamsburg. "My orders," he said, "are dark, doubtful, and uncertain; to-day approved, to-morrow condemned. Left to act and proceed at hazard, accountable for the consequences, and blamed without the benefit of defence." He determined nevertheless to bear with his trials until the arrival of Lord Loudon, the new commander-in-chief, from whom he expected vigor and improvement. Unfortunately he was destined to have only fresh disappointment from the new general, for Lord Loudon was merely one more incompetent man added to the existing confusion. He paid no heed to the South, matters continued to go badly in the North, and Virginia was left helpless. So Washington toiled on with much discouragement, and the disagreeable attacks upon him increased. That it should have been so is not surprising, for he wrote to the governor, who now held him in much disfavor, to the speaker, and indeed to every one, with a most galling plainness. He was only twenty-five, be it remembered, and his high temper was by no means under perfect control. He was anything but diplomatic at that period of his life, and was far from patient, using language with much sincerity and force, and indulging in a blunt irony of rather a ferocious kind. When he was accused finally of getting up reports of imaginary dangers, his temper gave way entirely. He wrote wrathfully to the governor for justice, and added in a letter to his friend, Captain Peachey: "As to Colonel C.'s gross and infamous reflections on my conduct last spring, it will be needless, I dare say, to observe further at this time than that the liberty which he has been pleased to allow himself in sporting with my character is little else than a comic entertainment, discovering at one view his passionate fondness for your friend, his inviolable love of truth, his unfathomable knowledge, and the masterly strokes of his wisdom in displaying it. You are heartily welcome to make use of any letter or letters which I may at any time have written to you; for although I keep no copies of epistles to my friends, nor can remember the contents of all of them, yet I am sensible that the narrations are just, and that truth and honesty will appear in my writings; of which, therefore, I shall not be ashamed, though criticism may censure my style."

Perhaps a little more patience would have produced better results, but it is pleasant to find one man, in that period of stupidity and incompetency, who was ready to free his mind in this refreshing way. The only wonder is that he was not driven from his command. That they insisted on keeping him there shows beyond everything that he had already impressed himself so strongly on Virginia that the authorities, although they smarted under his attacks, did not dare to meddle with him. Dinwiddie and the rest could foil him in obtaining a commission in the king's army, but they could not shake his hold upon the people.

In the winter of 1758 his health broke down completely. He was so ill that he thought that his constitution was seriously injured; and therefore withdrew to Mount Vernon, where he slowly recovered. Meantime a great man came at last to the head of affairs in England, and, inspired by William Pitt, fleets and armies went forth to conquer. Reviving at the prospect, Washington offered his services to General Forbes, who had come to undertake the task which Braddock had failed to accomplish. Once more English troops appeared, and a large army was gathered. Then the old story began again, and Washington, whose proffered aid had been gladly received, chafed and worried all summer at the fresh spectacle of delay and stupidity which was presented to him. His advice was disregarded, and all the weary business of building new roads through the wilderness was once more undertaken. A detachment, sent forward contrary to his views, met with the fate of Braddock, and as the summer passed, and autumn changed to winter, it looked as if nothing would be gained in return for so much toil and preparation. But Pitt had conquered the Ohio in Canada, news arrived of the withdrawal of the French, the army pressed on, and, with Washington in the van, marched into the smoking ruins of Fort Duquesne, henceforth to be known to the world as Fort Pitt.

So closed the first period in Washington's public career. We have seen him pass through it in all its phases. It shows him as an adventurous pioneer, as a reckless frontier fighter, and as a soldier of great promise. He learned many things in this time, and was taught much in the hard school of adversity. In the effort to conquer Frenchmen and Indians he studied the art of war, and at the same time he learned to bear with and to overcome the dulness and inefficiency of the government he served. Thus he was forced to practise self-control in order to attain his ends, and to acquire skill in the management of men. There could have been no better training for the work he was to do in the after years, and the future showed how deeply he profited by it. Let us turn now, for a moment, to the softer and pleasanter side of life, and having seen what Washington was, and what he did as a fighting man, let us try to know him in the equally important and far more attractive domain of private and domestic life.

CHAPTER IV

LOVE AND MARRIAGE

LEWIS WILLIS, OF Fredericksburg, who was at school with Washington, used to speak of him as an unusually studious and industrious boy, but recalled one occasion when he distinguished himself and surprised his schoolmates by "romping with one of the largest girls."[*] Half a century later, when the days of romping were long over and gone, a gentleman writing of a Mrs. Hartley, whom Washington much admired, said that the general always liked a fine woman.[†] It is certain that from romping he passed rapidly to more serious forms of expressing regard, for by the time he was fourteen he had fallen deeply in love with Mary Bland of Westmoreland, whom he calls his "Lowland Beauty," and to whom he wrote various copies of verses, preserved amid the notes of surveys, in his diary for 1747–48. The old tradition identified the "Lowland Beauty" with Miss Lucy Grymes, perhaps correctly, and there are drafts of letters addressed to "Dear Sally," which suggest that the mistake in identification might have arisen from the fact that there were several ladies who answered to that description. In the following sentence from the draft of a letter to a masculine sympathizer, also preserved in the tell-tale diary of 1748, there is certainly an indication that the constancy of the lover was not perfect. "Dear Friend Robin," he wrote: "My place of residence at present is at his

[*]Quoted from the Willis MS. by Mr. Conway, in *Magazine of American History*, March, 1887, p. 196.
[†]*Magazine of American History*, i. 324.

Lordship's, where I might, were my heart disengaged, pass my time very pleasantly, as there is a very agreeable young lady in the same house, Colonel George Fairfax's wife's sister. But that only adds fuel to the fire, as being often and unavoidably in company with her revives my former passion for your Lowland Beauty; whereas were I to live more retired from young women, I might in some measure alleviate my sorrow by burying that chaste and troublesome passion in oblivion; I am very well assured that this will be the only antidote or remedy." Our gloomy young gentleman, however, did not take to solitude to cure the pangs of despised love, but proceeded to calm his spirits by the society of this same sister-in-law of George Fairfax, Miss Mary Cary. One "Lowland Beauty," Lucy Grymes, married Henry Lee, and became the mother of "Legion Harry," a favorite

MARY CARY

officer and friend of Washington, and the grandmother of Robert E. Lee, the great soldier of the Southern Confederacy. The affair with Miss Cary went on apparently for some years, fitfully pursued in the intervals of war and Indian fighting, and interrupted also by matters of a more tender nature. The first diversion occurred about 1752, when we find Washington writing to William Fauntleroy, at Richmond, that he proposed to come to his house to see his sister, Miss Betsy, and that he hoped for a revocation of her former cruel sentence.* Miss Betsy, however, seems to have been obdurate, and we hear no more of love affairs until much later, and then in connection with matters of a graver sort.

---

* *Historical Magazine*, 3d series, 1873. Letter communicated by Fitzhugh Lee.

When Captain Dagworthy, commanding thirty men in the Maryland service, undertook in virtue of a king's commission to outrank the commander-in-chief of the Virginian forces, Washington made up his mind that he would have this question at least finally and properly settled. So, as has been said, he went to Boston, saw Governor Shirley, and had the dispute determined in his own favor. He made the journey on horseback, and had with him two of his aides and two servants. An old letter, luckily preserved, tells us how he looked, for it contains orders to his London agents for various articles, sent for perhaps in anticipation of this very expedition. In Braddock's campaign the young surveyor and frontier soldier had been thrown among a party of dashing, handsomely equipped officers fresh from London, and their appearance had engaged his careful attention. Washington was a thoroughly simple man in all ways, but he was also a man of taste and a lover of military discipline. He had a keen sense of appropriateness, a valuable faculty which stood him in good stead in grave as well as trivial matters all through his career, and which in his youth came out most strongly in the matter of manners and personal appearance. He was a handsome man, and liked to be well dressed and to have everything about himself or his servants of the best. Yet he was not a mere imitator of fashions or devoted to fine clothes. The American leggings and fringed hunting-shirt had a strong hold on his affections, and he introduced them into Forbes's army, and again into the army of the Revolution, as the best uniform for the backwoods fighters. But he learned with Braddock that the dress of parade has as real military value as that of service, and when he travelled northward to settle about Captain Dagworthy, he felt justly that he now was going on parade for the first time as the representative of his troops and his colony. Therefore with excellent sense he dressed as befitted the occasion, and at the same time gratified his own taste.

Thanks to these precautions, the little cavalcade that left Virginia on February 4, 1756, must have looked brilliant enough as they rode away through the dark woods. First came the colonel, mounted of course on the finest of animals, for he loved and understood horses from the time when he rode bareback in the pasture to those later days when he acted as judge at a horse-race and saw his own pet colt "Magnolia" beaten. In this expedition he wore, of course, his uniform of buff and blue, with a white and scarlet cloak over his shoulders, and a sword-knot of red and gold. His "horse furniture" was of the best London make, trimmed with "livery lace," and the Washington arms were engraved upon the housings. Close by his side rode his two aides, likewise in buff and blue, and behind came his servants, dressed in the Washington colors of white and scarlet and wearing hats laced with silver. Thus accoutred, they all rode on together to the North.

The colonel's fame had gone before him, for the hero of Braddock's stricken field and the commander of the Virginian forces was known by reputation throughout the colonies. Every door flew open to him as he passed, and every one was delighted to welcome the young soldier. He was dined and wined and fêted in Philadelphia, and again in New York, where he fell in love at apparently short notice with the heiress Mary Philipse, the sister-in-law of his friend Beverly Robinson. Tearing himself away from these attractions he pushed on to Boston, then the most important city on the continent, and the headquarters of Shirley, the commander-in-chief. The little New England capital had at that time a society which, rich for those days, was relieved from its Puritan sombreness by the gayety and life brought in by the royal officers. Here Washington lingered ten days, talking war and politics with the governor, visiting in state the "great and general court," dancing every night at some ball, dining with and being fêted by the magnates of the town. His business done, he returned to New York, tarried there awhile for the sake of the fair dame, but came to no conclusions, and then, like the soldier in the song, he gave his bridle-rein a shake and rode away again to the South, and to the harassed and ravaged frontier of Virginia.

How much this little interlude, pushed into a corner as it has been by the dignity of history,—how much it tells of the real man! How the statuesque myth and the priggish myth and the dull and solemn myth melt away before it! Wise and strong, a bearer of heavy responsibility beyond his years, daring in fight and sober in judgment, we have here the other and the more human side of Washington. One loves to picture that gallant, generous, youthful figure, brilliant in color and manly in form, riding gayly on from one little colonial town to another, feasting, dancing, courting, and making merry. For him the myrtle and ivy were entwined with the laurel, and fame was sweetened by youth. He was righteously ready to draw from life all the good things which fate and fortune then smiling upon him could offer, and he took his pleasure frankly, with an honest heart.

We know that he succeeded in his mission and put the captain of thirty men in his proper place, but no one now can tell how deeply he was affected by the charms of Miss Philipse. The only certain fact is that he was able not long after to console himself very effectually. Riding away from Mount Vernon once more, in the spring of 1758, this time to Williamsburg with despatches, he stopped at William's Ferry to dine with his friend Major Chamberlayne, and there he met Martha Dandridge, the widow of Daniel Parke Custis. She was young, pretty, intelligent, and an heiress, and her society seemed to attract the young soldier. The afternoon wore away, the horses came to the door at the appointed time, and after being walked back and forth for some hours were returned to the stable. The sun went down, and still the colonel lingered. The next morning he rode away with his despatches, but on his return he paused at the White House, the home of Mrs. Custis, and then and there plighted his troth with the charming widow. The wooing was brief and decisive, and the successful lover departed for the camp, to feel more keenly than ever the delays of the British officers and the shortcomings of the colonial government. As soon as Fort Duquesne had fallen he hurried home, resigned his commission in the last week of December, and was married on January 6, 1759. It was a brilliant wedding party which assembled on that winter day in the little church near the White House. There were gathered Francis Fauquier, the gay, free-thinking, high-living governor, gorgeous in scarlet and gold; British officers, red-coated and gold-laced, and all the neighboring gentry in the handsomest clothes that London credit could furnish. The bride was attired in silk and satin, laces and brocade, with pearls on her neck and in her ears; while the bridegroom appeared in blue and silver trimmed with scarlet, and with gold buckles at his knees and on his shoes. After the ceremony the bride was taken home in a coach and six, her husband riding beside her, mounted on a splendid horse and followed by all the gentlemen of the party.

The sunshine and glitter of the wedding-day must have appeared to Washington deeply appropriate, for he certainly seemed to have all that heart of man could desire. Just twenty-seven, in the first flush of young manhood, keen of sense and yet wise in experience, life must have looked very fair and smiling. He had left the army with a well-earned fame, and had come home to take the wife of his choice and enjoy the good-will and respect of all men. While away on his last campaign he had been elected a member of the House of Burgesses, and when he took his seat on removing to Williamsburg, three months after his marriage, Mr. Robinson, the speaker, thanked him publicly in eloquent words for his services to the country. Washington rose to reply, but he was so utterly unable to talk about himself that he stood before the House stammering and blushing, until the speaker said, "Sit down, Mr. Washington; your modesty equals your valor, and that surpasses the power of any language I possess." It is an old story, and as graceful as it is old, but it was all very grateful to Washington, especially as the words of the speaker bodied forth the feelings of Virginia. Such an atmosphere, filled with deserved respect and praise, was pleasant to begin with, and then he had everything else too.

He not only continued to sit in the House year after year and help to rule Virginia, but he served on the church vestry, and so held in his hands the reins of local government. He had married a charming woman, simple, straightforward, and sympathetic, free from gossip or pretence, and as capable in practical matters as he was himself. By right of birth a member of the Virginian aristocracy, he had widened and strengthened his connections through his wife. A man of handsome property by the death of Lawrence Washington's daughter, he had become by his marriage one of the richest men of the country. Acknowledged to be the first soldier on the continent, respected and trusted in public, successful and happy in private life, he had attained before he was thirty to all that Virginia could give of wealth, prosperity, and honor, a fact of which he was well aware, for there never breathed a man more wisely contented than George Washington at this period.

He made his home at Mount Vernon, adding many acres to the estate, and giving to it his best attention. It is needless to say that he was successful, for that was the case with everything he undertook. He loved country life, and he was the best and most prosperous planter in Virginia, which was really a more difficult achievement than the mere statement implies. Genuinely profitable farming in Virginia was not common, for the general system was a bad one. A single great staple, easily produced by the reckless exhaustion of land, and varying widely in the annual

value of crops, bred improvidence and speculation. Everything was bought upon long credits, given by the London merchants, and this, too, contributed largely to carelessness and waste. The chronic state of a planter in a business way was one of debt, and the lack of capital made his conduct of affairs extravagant and loose. With all his care and method Washington himself was often pinched for ready money, and it was only by his thoroughness and foresight that he prospered and made money while so many of his neighbors struggled with debt and lived on in easy luxury, not knowing what the morrow might bring forth.

A far more serious trouble than bad business methods was one which was little heeded at the moment, but which really lay at the foundation of the whole system of society and business. This was the character of the labor by which the plantations were worked. Slave labor is well known now to be the most expensive and the worst form of labor that can be employed. In the middle of the eighteenth century, however, its evils were not appreciated, either from an economical or a moral point of view. This is not the place to discuss the subject of African slavery in America. But it is important to know Washington's opinions in regard to an institution which was destined to have such a powerful influence upon the country, and it seems most appropriate to consider those opinions at the moment when slaves became a practical factor in his life as a Virginian planter.

Washington accepted the system as he found it, as most men accept the social arrangements to which they are born. He grew up in a world where slavery had always existed, and where its rightfulness had never been questioned. Being on the frontier, occupied with surveying and with war, he never had occasion to really consider the matter at all until he found himself at the head of large estates, with his own prosperity dependent on the labor of slaves. The first practical question, therefore, was how to employ this labor to the best advantage. A man of his clear perceptions soon discovered the defects of the system, and he gave great attention to feeding and clothing his slaves, and to their general management. Parkinson* says in a general way that Washington treated his slaves

---

* *Tour in America*, 1798–1800.

harshly, spoke to them sharply, and maintained a military discipline, to which he attributed the General's rare success as a planter. There can be no doubt of the success, and the military discipline is probably true, but the statement as to harshness is unsupported by any other authority. Indeed, Parkinson even contradicts it himself, for he says elsewhere that Washington never bought or sold a slave, a proof of the highest and most intelligent humanity; and he adds in his final sketch of the General's character, that he "was incapable of wrong-doing, but did to all men as he would they should do to him. Therefore it is not to be supposed that he would injure the negro." This agrees with what we learn from all other sources. Humane by nature, he conceived a great interest and pity for these helpless beings, and treated them with kindness and forethought. In a word, he was a wise and good master, as well as a successful one, and the condition of his slaves was as happy, and their labor as profitable, as was possible to such a system.

So the years rolled by; the war came and then the making of the government, and Washington's thoughts were turned more and more, as was the case with all the men of his time in that era of change and of new ideas, to the consideration of human slavery in its moral, political, and social aspects. To trace the course of his opinions in detail is needless. It is sufficient to summarize them, for the results of his reflection and observation are more important than the processes by which they were reached. Washington became convinced that the whole system was thoroughly bad, as well as utterly repugnant to the ideas on which the Revolution was fought and the government of the United States founded. With a prescience wonderful for those days and on that subject, he saw that slavery meant the up-growth in the United States of two systems so radically hostile, both socially and economically, that they could lead only to a struggle for political supremacy, which in its course he feared would imperil the Union. For this reason he deprecated the introduction of the slavery question into the debates of the first Congress, because he realized its character, and he did not believe that the Union or the government at that early day could bear the strain which in this way would be produced. At the same time he felt that a right solution must be found or inconceivable evils would ensue. The inherent and everlasting wrong of the system made its continuance, to his mind, impossible. While it existed, he believed that the laws which surrounded it should be maintained, because he thought that to violate these only added one wrong to another. He also doubted, as will be seen in a later chapter, where his conversation with John Bernard is quoted, whether the negroes could be immediately emancipated with safety either to themselves or to the whites, in their actual condition of ignorance, illiteracy, and helplessness. The plan which he favored, and which, it would seem, was his hope and reliance, was first the checking of importation, followed by a gradual emancipation, with proper compensation to the owners and suitable preparation and education for the slaves. He told the clergymen Asbury and Coke, when they visited him for that purpose, that he was in favor of emancipation, and was ready to write a letter to the assembly to that effect.[*] He wished fervently that such a spirit might take possession of the people of the country, but he wrote to Lafayette that he despaired of seeing it. When he died he did all that lay within his power to impress his views upon his countrymen by directing that all his slaves should be set free on the death of his wife. His precepts and his example in this grave matter went unheeded for many years by the generations that came after him. But now that slavery is dead, to the joy of all men, it is well to remember that on this terrible question Washington's opinions were those of a humane man, impatient of wrong, and of a noble and far-seeing statesman, watchful of the evils that threatened his country.[†]

After this digression let us return to the Virginian farmer, whose mind was not disturbed as yet by thoughts of the destiny of the United States, or considerations of the rights of man, but who was much exercised by the task of making an honest income out of his estates. To do this he grappled with details as firmly as he did with the general system under which all plantations in that day were carried on. He understood every branch of farming; he was on the alert for every improvement; he rose

---

[*]*Magazine of American History*, 1880, p. 158.
[†]For some expressions of Washington's opinions on slavery, see Sparks, viii. 414, ix. 159–163, and x. 224.

early, worked steadily, gave to everything his personal supervision, kept his own accounts with wonderful exactness, and naturally enough his brands of flour went unquestioned everywhere, his credit was high, and he made money—so far as it was possible under existing conditions. Like Shakespeare, as Bishop Blougram has it, he

Saved money, spent it, owned the worth of things.

He had no fine and senseless disregard for money or the good things of this world, but on the contrary saw in them not the value attached to them by vulgar minds, but their true worth. He was a solid, square, evenly-balanced man in those days, believing that whatever he did was worth doing well. So he farmed, as he fought and governed, better than anybody else.

While thus looking after his own estates at home, he went further afield in search of investments, keeping a shrewd eye on the western lands, and buying wisely and judiciously whenever he had the opportunity. He also constituted himself now, as in a later time, the champion of the soldiers, for whom he had the truest sympathy and affection, and a large part of the correspondence of this period is devoted to their claims for the lands granted them by the assembly. He distinguished carefully among them, however, those who were undeserving, and to the major of the regiment, who had been excluded from the public thanks on account of cowardice at the Great Meadows, he wrote as follows: "Your impertinent letter was delivered to me yesterday. As I am not accustomed to receive such from any man, nor would have taken the same language from you personally without letting you feel some marks of my resentment, I would advise you to be cautious in writing me a second of the same tenor. But for your stupidity and sottishness you might have known, by attending to the public gazette, that you had your full quantity of ten thousand acres of land allowed you. But suppose you had really fallen short, do you think your superlative merit entitles you to greater indulgence than others? . . . All my concern is that I ever engaged in behalf of so ungrateful a fellow as you are." The writer of this letter, be it said in passing, was the man whom Mr. Weems and others tell us was knocked down before his soldiers, and then apologized to his assailant. It may be suspected that it was well for the recipient of this letter that he did not have a personal interview with its author, and it may be doubted if he ever sought one subsequently. Just, generous, and magnanimous to an extraordinary degree, Washington had a dangerous temper, held well under control, but blazing out now and again against injustice, impertinence, or oppression. He was a peaceful man, leading a peaceful life, but the fighting spirit only slumbered, and it would break out at wrong of any sort, in a way which was extremely unpleasant and threatening to those who aroused it.

Apart from lands and money and the management of affairs, public and private, there were many other interests of varied nature which all had their share of Washington's time and thought. He was a devoted husband, and gave to his step-children the most affectionate care. He watched over and protected them, and when the daughter died, after a long and wasting illness, in 1773, he mourned for her as if she had been his own, with all the tenderness of a deep and reserved affection. The boy, John Custis, he made his friend and companion from the beginning, and his letters to the lad and about him are wise and judicious in the highest degree. He spent much time and thought on the question of education, and after securing the best instructors took the boy to New York and entered him at Columbia College in 1773. Young Custis however did not remain there long, for he had fallen in love, and the following year was married to Eleanor Calvert, not without some misgivings on the part of Washington, who had observed his ward's somewhat flighty disposition, and who gave a great deal of anxious thought to his future. At home as abroad he was an undemonstrative man, but he had abundance of that real affection which labors for those to whom it goes out more unselfishly and far more effectually than that which bubbles and boils upon the surface like a shallow, noisy brook.

From the suggestions that he made in regard to young Custis, it is evident that Washington valued and respected education, and that he had that regard for learning for its own sake which always exists in large measure in every thoughtful man. He read well, even if his active life prevented his reading much, as we can see by his vigorous English, and by his occasional allusions to history. From his London orders we see, too, that everything about his house must have denoted that its possessor had refinement and taste. His intense sense of propriety and unfailing instinct for what was appropriate are everywhere apparent. His dress, his furniture, his harnesses, the things for the children, all show the same fondness for simplicity, and yet a constant insistence that everything should be the best of its kind. We can learn a good deal about any man by the ornaments of his house, and by the portraits which hang on his walls; for these dumb things tell us whom among the great men of earth the owner admires, and indicate the tastes he best loves to gratify. When Washington first settled with his wife at Mount Vernon, he ordered from Europe the busts of Alexander the Great, Charles XII. of Sweden, Julius Caesar, Frederick of Prussia, Marlborough, and Prince Eugene, and in addition he asked for statuettes of "two wild beasts." The combination of soldier and statesman is the predominant admiration, then comes the reckless and splendid military adventurer, and lastly wild life and the chase. There is no mistaking the ideas and fancies of the man who penned this order which has drifted down to us from the past.

But as Washington's active life was largely out of doors, so too were his pleasures. He loved the fresh open-air existence of the woods and fields, and there he found his one great amusement. He shot and fished, but did not care much for these pursuits, for his hobby was hunting, which gratified at once his passion for horses and dogs and his love for the strong excitement of the chase, when dashed with just enough danger to make it really fascinating. He showed in his sport the same thoroughness and love of perfection that he displayed in everything else. His stables were filled with the best animals that Virginia could furnish. There were the "blooded coach-horses" for Mrs. Washington's carriage, "Magnolia," a full-blooded Arabian, used by his owner for the road, the ponies for the children, and finally, the high-bred hunters Chinkling and Valiant, Ajax and Blueskin, and the rest, all duly set down in the register in the hand-writing of the master himself. His first visit in the morning was to the stables. The next to the kennels to inspect and criticise the hounds, also methodically registered and described, so that we can read the names of Vulcan and Ringwood, Singer and Truelove, Music and Sweetlips, to which the Virginian woods once echoed nearly a century and a half ago. His hounds were the subject of much thought, and were so constantly and critically drafted as to speed, keenness, and bottom, that when in full cry they ran so closely bunched that tradition says, in classic phrase, they could have been covered with a blanket. The hounds met three times a week in the season, usually at Mount Vernon, sometimes at Belvoir. They would get off at daybreak, Washington in the midst of his hounds, splendidly mounted, generally on his favorite Blueskin, a powerful iron-gray horse of great speed and endurance. He wore a blue coat, scarlet waistcoat, buckskin breeches, and a velvet cap. Closely followed by his huntsman and the neighboring gentlemen, with the ladies, headed, very likely, by Mrs. Washington in a scarlet habit, he would ride to the appointed covert and throw in. There was no difficulty in finding, and then away they would go, usually after a gray fox, sometimes after a big black fox, rarely to be caught. Most of the country was wild and unfenced, rough in footing, and offering hard and dangerous going for the horses, but Washington always made it a rule to stay with his hounds. Cautious or timid riders, if they were so minded, could gallop along the wood roads with the ladies, and content themselves with glimpses of the hunt, but the master rode at the front. The fields, it is to be feared, were sometimes small, but Washington hunted even if he had only his stepson or was quite alone.

His diaries abound with allusions to the sport. "Went a-hunting with Jacky Custis, and catched a fox after three hours chase; found it in the creek." "Mr. Bryan Fairfax, Mr. Grayson, and Phil. Alexander came home by sunrise. Hunted and catched a fox with these, Lord Fairfax, his brother, and Colonel Fairfax, all of whom, with Mr. Fairfax and Mr. Wilson of England, dined here." Again, November 26th and 29th, "Hunted again with the same party." "1768, Jan. 8th. Hunting again with same company. Started a fox and run him 4 hours. Took the hounds off at night." "Jan. 15. Shooting." "16. At home all day with cards; it snow-ing." "23. Rid to Muddy Hole and directed paths to be cut for fox-hunting." "Feb. 12. Catched 2 foxes." "Feb. 13. Catched 2 more foxes." "Mar. 2. Catched fox with bob'd tail and cut ears after 7 hours chase, in which most of the dogs were worsted." "Dec. 5. Fox-hunting with Lord Fairfax and his brother and Colonel Fairfax. Started a fox and lost it. Dined at Belvoir and returned in the evening."*

So the entries run on, for he hunted almost every day in the season, usually with success, but always with persistence. Like all true sportsmen Washington had a horror of illicit sport of any kind, and although he shot comparatively little, he was much annoyed by a vagabond who lurked in the creeks and inlets on his estate, and slaughtered his canvasback ducks. Hearing the report of a gun one morning, he rode through the bushes and saw his poaching friend just shoving off in a canoe. The rascal raised his gun and covered his pursuer, whereupon Washington, the cold-blooded and patient person so familiar in the myths, dashed his horse headlong into the water, seized the gun, grasped the canoe, and dragging it ashore pulled the man out of the boat and beat him soundly. If the man had yielded at once he would probably have got off easily enough, but when he put Washington's life in imminent perils the wild fighting spirit flared up as usual.

The hunting season was of course that of the most lavish hospitality. There was always a great deal of dining about, but Mount Vernon was the chief resort, and its doors, ever open, were flung far back when people came for a meet, or gathered to talk over the events of a good run. Company was the rule and solitude the exception. When only the family were at dinner, the fact was written down in the diary with great care as an unusual event, for Washington was the soul of hospitality, and although he kept early hours, he loved society and a houseful of people. Profoundly reserved and silent as to himself, a lover of solitude so far as his own thoughts and feelings were concerned, he was far from being a solitary man in the ordinary acceptation of the word. He liked life and gayety and conversation, he liked music and dancing or a game of cards

---

*MS. Diaries in State Department.

when the weather was bad, and he enjoyed heartily the presence of young people and of his own friends. So Mount Vernon was always full of guests, and the master noted in his diary that although he owned more than a hundred cows he was obliged, nevertheless, to buy butter, which suggests an experience not unknown to gentlemen farmers of any period, and also that company was never lacking in that generous, open house overlooking the Potomac.

Beyond the bounds of his own estate he had also many occupations and pleasures. He was a member of the House of Burgesses, diligent in his attention to the work of governing the colony. He was diligent also in church affairs, and very active in the vestry, which was the seat of local government in Virginia. We hear of him also as the manager of lotteries, which were a common form of raising money for local purposes, in preference to direct taxation. In a word, he was thoroughly public-spirited, and performed all the small duties which his position demanded in the same spirit that he afterwards brought to the command of armies and to the government of the nation. He had pleasure too, as well as business, away from Mount Vernon. He liked to go to his neighbors' houses and enjoy their hospitality as they enjoyed his. We hear of him, at the court-house on court days, where all the countryside gathered to talk and listen to the lawyers and hear the news, and when he went to Williamsburg his diary tells us of a round of dinners, beginning with the governor, of visits to the club, and of a regular attendance at the theatre whenever actors came to the little capital. Whether at home or abroad, he took part in all the serious pursuits, in all the interests, and in every reasonable pleasure offered by the colony.

Take it for all in all, it was a manly, wholesome, many-sided life. It kept Washington young and strong, both mentally and physically. When he was forty he flung the iron bar, at some village sports, to a point which no competitor could approach. There, was no man in all Virginia who could ride a horse with such a powerful and assured seat. There was no one who could journey farther on foot, and no man at Williamsburg who showed at the governor's receptions such a commanding presence, or who walked with such a strong and elastic step.

As with the body so with the mind. He never rusted. A practical carpenter and smith, he brought the same quiet intelligence and firm will to the forging of iron or the felling and sawing of trees that he had displayed in fighting France. The life of a country gentleman did not dull or stupefy him, or lead him to gross indulgences. He remained well-made and athletic, strong and enduring, keen in perception and in sense, and warm in his feelings and affections. Many men would have become heavy and useless in these years of quiet country life, but Washington simply ripened, and, like all slowly maturing men, grew stronger, abler, and wiser in the happy years of rest and waiting which intervened between youth and middle age.

Meantime, while the current of daily life flowed on thus gently at Mount Vernon, the great stream of public events poured by outside. It ran very calmly at first, after the war, and then with a quickening murmur, which increased to an ominous roar when the passage of the Stamp Act became known in America. Washington was always a constant attendant at the assembly, in which by sheer force of character, and despite his lack of the talking and debating faculty, he carried more weight than any other member. He was present on May 29, 1765, when Patrick Henry introduced his famous resolutions and menaced the king's government in words which rang through the continent. The resolutions were adopted, and Washington went home, with many anxious thoughts, to discuss the political outlook with his friend and neighbor George Mason, one of the keenest and ablest men in Virginia. The utter folly of the policy embodied in the Stamp Act struck Washington very forcibly. With that foresight for which he was so remarkable, he perceived what scarcely any one else even dreamt of, that persistence in this course must surely lead to a violent separation from the mother country, and it is interesting to note in this, the first instance when he was called upon to consider a political question of great magnitude, his clearness of vision and grasp of mind. In what he wrote there is no trace of the ambitious schemer, no threatening nor blustering, no undue despondency nor excited hopes. But there is a calm understanding of all the conditions, an entire freedom from self-deception, and the power of seeing facts exactly as they were, which were all characteristic of his intellectual strength, and to which we shall need to recur again and again.

The repeal of the Stamp Act was received by Washington with sober but sincere pleasure. He had anticipated "direful" results and "unhappy consequences" from its enforcement, and he freely said that those who were instrumental in its repeal had his cordial thanks. He was no agitator, and had not come forward in this affair, so he now retired again to Mount Vernon, to his farming and hunting, where he remained, watching very closely the progress of events. He had marked the dangerous reservation of the principle in the very act of repeal; he observed at Boston the gathering strength of what the wise ministers of George III. called sedition; he noted the arrival of British troops in the rebellious Puritan town; and he saw plainly enough, looming in the background, the final appeal to arms. He wrote to Mason (April 5, 1769), that "at a time when our lordly masters in Great Britain will be satisfied with nothing less than the deprivation of American freedom, something should be done to avert the stroke and maintain the liberty which we have derived from our ancestors. But the manner of doing it, to answer the purpose effectually, is the point in question. That no man should scruple or hesitate a moment to use arms in defence of so valuable a blessing is clearly my opinion. Yet arms, I would beg leave to add, should be the last resource, the *dernier resort*." He then urged the adoption of the only middle course, non-importation, but he had not much hope in this expedient, although an honest desire is evident that it may prove effectual.

When the assembly met in May, they received the new governor, Lord Botetourt, with much cordiality, and then fell to passing spirited and sharp-spoken resolutions declaring their own rights and defending Massachusetts. The result was a dissolution. Thereupon the burgesses repaired to the Raleigh tavern, where they adopted a set of non-importation resolutions and formed an association. The resolutions were offered by Washington, and were the result of his quiet country talks with Mason. When the moment for action arrived, Washington came naturally to the front, and then returned quietly to Mount Vernon, once more to go about his business and watch the threatening political horizon. Virginia did not

live up to this first non-importation agreement, and formed another a
year later. But Washington was not in the habit of presenting resolutions
merely for effect, and there was nothing of the actor in his composition.
His resolutions meant business, and he lived up to them rigidly himself.
Neither tea nor any of the proscribed articles were allowed in his house.
Most of the leaders did not realize the seriousness of the situation, but
Washington, looking forward with clear and sober gaze, was in grim
earnest, and was fully conscious that when he offered his resolutions the
colony was trying the last peaceful remedy, and that the next step would
be war.

Still he went calmly about his many affairs as usual, and gratified the
old passion for the frontier by a journey to Pittsburgh for the sake of lands
and soldiers' claims, and thence down the Ohio and into the wilderness
with his old friends the trappers and pioneers. He visited the Indian villages as in the days of the French mission, and noted in the savages an
ominous restlessness, which seemed, like the flight of birds, to express
the dumb instinct of an approaching storm. The clouds broke away
somewhat under the kindly management of Lord Botetourt, and then
gathered again more thickly on the accession of his successor, Lord
Dunmore. With both these gentlemen Washington was on the most
friendly terms. He visited them often, and was consulted by them, as it
behooved them to consult the strongest man within the limits of their
government. Still he waited and watched, and scanned carefully the
news from the North. Before long he heard that tea-chests were floating
in Boston harbor, and then from across the water came intelligence of the
passage of the Port Bill and other measures destined to crush to earth the
little rebel town.

When the Virginia assembly met again, they proceeded to congratulate the governor on the arrival of Lady Dunmore, and then suddenly, as
all was flowing smoothly along, there came a letter through the corresponding committee which Washington had helped to establish, telling
of the measures against Boston. Everything else was thrown aside at
once, a vigorous protest was entered on the journal of the House, and June
1st, when the Port Bill was to go into operation, was appointed a day of

fasting, humiliation, and prayer. The first result was prompt dissolution of the assembly. The next was another meeting in the long room of the Raleigh tavern, where the Boston bill was denounced, non-importation renewed, and the committee of correspondence instructed to take steps for calling a general congress. Events were beginning to move at last with perilous rapidity. Washington dined with Lord Dunmore on the evening of that day, rode with him, and appeared at her ladyship's ball the next night. It was not his way to bite his thumb at men from whom he differed politically, nor to call the motives of his opponents in question. But when the 1st of June arrived, he noted in his diary that he fasted all day and attended the appointed services. He always meant what he said, being of a simple nature, and when he fasted and prayed there was something ominously earnest about it, something that his excellency the governor, who liked the society of this agreeable man and wise counsellor, would have done well to consider and draw conclusions from, and which he probably did not heed at all. He might well have reflected, as he undoubtedly failed to do, that when men of the George Washington type fast and pray on account of political misdoings, it is well for their opponents to look to it carefully.

Meantime Boston had sent forth appeals to form a league among the colonies, and thereupon another meeting was held in the Raleigh tavern, and a letter was dispatched advising the burgesses to consider this matter of a general league and take the sense of their respective counties. Virginia and Massachusetts had joined hands now, and they were sweeping the rest of the continent irresistibly forward with them. As for Washington, he returned to Mount Vernon and at once set about taking the sense of his county, as he had agreed. Before doing so he had some correspondence with his old friend Bryan Fairfax. The Fairfaxes naturally sided with the mother-country, and Bryan was much distressed by the course of Virginia, and remonstrated strongly, and at length by letter, against violent measures. Washington replied to him: "Does it not appear as clear as the sun in its meridian brightness that there is a regular, systematic plan formed to fix the right and practice of taxation on us? Does not the uniform conduct of Parliament for some years past confirm this?

Do not all the debates, especially those just brought to us in the House of Commons, on the side of government expressly declare that America must be taxed in aid of the British funds, and that she has no longer resources within herself? Is there anything to be expected from petitioning after this? Is not the attack upon the liberty and property of the people of Boston, before restitution of the loss to the India Company was demanded, a plain and self-evident proof of what they are aiming at? Do not the subsequent bills (now I dare say acts) for depriving the Massachusetts Bay of its charter, and for transporting offenders into other colonies, or to Great Britain for trial, where it is impossible from the nature of the thing that justice can be obtained, convince us that the administration is determined to stick at nothing to carry its point? Ought we not, then, to put our virtue and fortitude to the severest test?" He was prepared, he continued, for anything except confiscating British debts, which struck him as dishonorable. These were plain but pregnant questions, but what we mark in them, and in all his letters of this time, is the absence of constitutional discussion, of which America was then full. They are confined to a direct presentation of the broad political question, which underlay everything. Washington always went straight to the mark, and he now saw, through all the dust of legal and constitutional strife, that the only real issue was whether America was to be allowed to govern herself in her own way or not. In the acts of the ministry he perceived a policy which aimed at substantial power, and he believed that such a policy, if insisted on, could have but one result.

The meeting of Fairfax County was held in due course, and Washington presided. The usual resolutions for self-government and against the vindictive Massachusetts measures were adopted. Union and non-importation were urged; and then the congress, which they advocated, was recommended to address a petition and remonstrance to the king, and ask him to reflect that "from our sovereign there can be but one appeal." Everything was to be tried, everything was to be done, but the ultimate appeal was never lost sight of where Washington appeared, and the final sentence of these Fairfax County resolves is very characteristic of the leader in the meeting. Two days later he wrote to the worthy and still remonstrating Bryan Fairfax, repeating and enlarging his former questions, and adding: "Has not General Gage's conduct since his arrival, in stopping the address of his council, and publishing a proclamation more becoming a Turkish bashaw than an English governor, declaring it treason to associate in any manner by which the commerce of Great Britain is to be affected,—has not this exhibited an unexampled testimony of the most despotic system of tyranny that ever was practised in a free government? . . . Shall we after this whine and cry for relief, when we have already tried it in vain? Or shall we supinely sit and see one province after another fall a sacrifice to despotism?" The fighting spirit of the man was rising. There was no rash rushing forward, no ignorant shouting for war, no blinking of the real issue, but a foresight that nothing could dim, and a perception of facts which nothing could confuse.

On August 1st Washington was at Williamsburg, to represent his county in the meeting of representatives from all Virginia. The convention passed resolutions like the Fairfax resolves, and chose delegates to a general congress. The silent man was now warming into action. He "made the most eloquent speech that ever was made," and said, "I will raise a thousand men, subsist them at my own expense, and march them to the relief of Boston." He was capable, it would seem, of talking to the purpose with some fire and force, for all he was so quiet and so retiring. When there was anything to say, he could say it so that it stirred all who listened, because they felt that there was a mastering strength behind the words. He faced the terrible issue solemnly and firmly, but his blood was up, the fighting spirit in him was aroused, and the convention chose him as one of Virginia's six delegates to the Continental Congress. He lingered long enough to make a few preparations at Mount Vernon. He wrote another letter to Fairfax, interesting to us as showing the keenness with which he read in the meagre news reports the character of Gage and of the opposing people of Massachusetts. Then he started for the North to take the first step on the long and difficult path that lay before him.

CHAPTER V

TAKING COMMAND

IN THE WARM days of closing August, a party of three gentlemen rode away from Mount Vernon one morning, and set out upon their long journey to Philadelphia. One cannot help wondering whether a tender and somewhat sad remembrance did not rise in Washington's mind, as he thought of the last time he had gone northward, nearly twenty years before. Then, he was a light-hearted young soldier, and he and his aides, albeit they went on business, rode gayly through the forests, lighting the road with the bright colors they wore and with the glitter of lace and arms, while they anticipated all the pleasures of youth in the new lands they were to visit. Now, he was in the prime of manhood, looking into the future with prophetic eyes, and sober as was his wont when the shadow of coming responsibility lay dark upon his path. With him went Patrick Henry, four years his junior, and Edmund Pendleton, now past three-score. They were all quiet and grave enough, no doubt; but Washington, we may believe, was gravest of all, because, being the most truthful of men to himself as to others, he saw more plainly what was coming. So they made their journey to the North, and on the memorable 5th of September they met with their brethren from the other colonies in Carpenters' Hall in Philadelphia.

The Congress sat fifty-one days, occupied with debates and discussion. Few abler, more honest, or more memorable bodies of men have ever assembled to settle the fate of nations. Much debate, great and

87

earnest in all directions, resulted in a declaration of colonial rights, in an address to the king, in another to the people of Canada, and a third to the people of Great Britain; masterly state papers, seldom surpassed, and extorting even then the admiration of England. In these debates and state papers Washington took no part that is now apparent on the face of the record. He was silent in the Congress, and if he was consulted, as he unquestionably was by the committees, there is no record of it now. The simple fact was that his time had not come. He saw men of the most acute minds, liberal in education, patriotic in heart, trained in law and in history, doing the work of the moment in the best possible way. If anything had been done wrongly, or had been left undone, Washington would have found his voice quickly enough, and uttered another of the "most eloquent speeches ever made," as he did shortly before in the Virginia convention. He could speak in public when need was, but now there was no need and nothing to arouse him. The work of Congress followed the line of policy adopted by the Virginia convention, and that had proceeded along the path marked out in the Fairfax resolves, so that Washington could not be other than content. He occupied his own time, as we see by notes in his diary, in visiting the delegates from the other colonies, and in informing himself as to their ideas and purposes, and those of the people whom they represented. He was quietly working for the future, the present being well taken care of. Yet this silent man, going hither and thither, and chatting pleasantly with this member or that, was in some way or other impressing himself deeply on all the delegates, for Patrick Henry said: "If you speak of solid information and sound judgment, Colonel Washington is unquestionably the greatest man on the floor."

We have a letter, written at just this time, which shows us how Washington felt, and we see again how his spirit rose as he saw more and more clearly that the ultimate issue was inevitable. The letter is addressed to Captain Mackenzie, a British officer at Boston, and an old friend. "Permit me," he began, "with the freedom of a friend (for you know I always esteemed you), to express my sorrow that fortune should place you in a service that must fix curses to the latest posterity upon the contrivers, and, if success (which, by the by, is impossible) accompanies it, execrations upon all those who have been instrumental in the execution." This was rather uncompromising talk and not over peaceable, it must be confessed. He continued: "Give me leave to add, and I think I can announce it as a fact, that it is not the wish or intent of that government [Massachusetts], or any other upon this continent, separately or collectively, to set up for independence; but this you may at the same time rely on, that none of them will ever submit to the loss of those valuable rights and privileges which are essential to the happiness of every free state, and without which life, liberty, and property are rendered totally insecure. . . . Again give me leave to add as my opinion that more blood will be spilled on this occasion, if the ministry are determined to push matters to extremity, than history has ever yet furnished instances of in the annals of North America, and such a vital wound will be given to the peace of this great country, as time itself cannot cure or eradicate the remembrance of." Washington was not a political agitator like Sam Adams, planning with unerring intelligence to bring about independence. On the contrary, he rightly declared that independence was not desired. But although he believed in exhausting every argument and every peaceful remedy, it is evident that he felt that there now could be but one result, and that violent separation from the mother country was inevitable. Here is where he differed from his associates and from the great mass of the people, and it is to this entire veracity of mind that his wisdom and foresight were so largely due, as well as his success when the time came for him to put his hand to the plough.

When Congress adjourned, Washington returned to Mount Vernon, to the pursuits and pleasures that he loved, to his family and farm, and to his horses and hounds, with whom he had many a good run, the last that he was to enjoy for years to come. He returned also to wait and watch as before, and to see war rapidly gather in the east. When the Virginia convention again assembled, resolutions were introduced to arm and discipline men, and Henry declared in their support that an "appeal to arms and to the God of Hosts" was all that was left. Washington said nothing, but he served on the committee to draft a plan of defence, and then fell to reviewing the independent companies which were springing up every-where. At the same time he wrote to his brother John, who had raised a troop, that he would accept the command of it if desired, as it was his "full intention to devote his life and fortune in the cause we are engaged in, if needful." At Mount Vernon his old comrades of the French war began to appear, in search of courage and sympathy. Thither, too, came Charles Lee, a typical military adventurer of that period, a man of English birth and of varied service, brilliant, whimsical, and unbalanced. There also came Horatio Gates, likewise British, and disappointed with his prospects at home; less adventurous than Lee, but also less brilliant, and not much more valuable.

Thus the winter wore away; spring opened, and toward the end of April Washington started again for the North, much occupied with cer-tain tidings from Lexington and Concord which just then spread over the land. He saw all that it meant plainly enough, and after noting the fact that the colonists fought and fought well, he wrote to George Fairfax in England: "Unhappy it is to reflect that a brother's sword has been sheathed in a brother's breast, and that the once happy and peace-ful plains of America are either to be drenched in blood or inhabited by slaves. Sad alternative. But can a virtuous man hesitate in his choice?" Congress, it would seem, thought there was a good deal of room for hes-itation, both for virtuous men and others, and after the fashion of their race determined to do a little more debating and arguing, before taking any decisive step. After much resistance and discussion, a second "humble and dutiful petition" to the king was adopted, and with strange contradiction a confederation was formed at the same time, and Congress proceeded to exercise the sovereign powers thus vested in them. The most pressing and troublesome question before them was what to do with the army surrounding Boston, and with the actual hos-tilities there existing.

Washington, for his part, went quietly about as before, saying noth-ing and observing much, working hard as chairman of the military com-mittees, planning for defence, and arranging for raising an army. One act of his alone stands out for us with significance at this critical time. In this second Congress he appeared habitually on the floor in his blue and buff uniform of a Virginia colonel. It was his way of saying that the hour for action had come, and that he at least was ready for the fight whenever called upon.

Presently he was summoned. Weary of waiting, John Adams at last declared that Congress must adopt the army and make Washington, who at this mention of his name stepped out of the room, commander-in-chief. On June 15th, formal motions were made to this effect and unanimously adopted, and the next day Washington appeared before Congress and accepted the trust. His words were few and simple. He expressed his sense of his own insufficiency for the task before him, and said that as no pecuniary consideration could have induced him to undertake the work, he must decline all pay or emoluments, only looking to Congress to defray his expenses. In the same spirit he wrote to his soldiers in Virginia, to his brother, and finally, in terms at once simple and pathetic, to his wife. There was no pretence about this, but the sternest reality of self-distrust, for Washington saw and measured as did no one else the magnitude of the work before him. He knew that he was about to face the best troops of Europe, and he had learned by experience that after the first excitement was over he would be obliged to rely upon a people who were brave and patriotic, but also undisciplined, untrained, and unprepared for war, without money, without arms, without allies or credit, and torn by selfish local interests. Nobody else perceived all this as he was able to with his mastery of facts, but he faced the duty unflinchingly. He did not put it aside because he distrusted himself, for in his truthfulness he could not but confess that no other American could show one tithe of his capacity, experience, or military service. He knew what was coming, knew it, no doubt, when he first put on his uniform, and he accepted instantly.

John Adams in his autobiography speaks of the necessity of choosing a Southern general, and also says there were objectors to the selection of Washington even among the Virginia delegates. That there were political reasons for taking a Virginian cannot be doubted. But the dissent, even if it existed, never appeared on the surface, excepting in the case of John Hancock, who, with curious vanity, thought that he ought to have this great place. When Washington's name was proposed there was no murmur of opposition, for there was no man who could for one moment be compared with him in fitness. The choice was inevitable, and he himself felt it to be so. He saw it coming; he would fain have avoided the great task, but no thought of shrinking crossed his mind. He saw with his entire freedom from constitutional subtleties that an absolute parliament sought to extend its power to the colonies. To this he would not submit, and he knew that this was a question which could be settled only by one side giving way, or by the dread appeal to arms. It was a question of fact, hard, unrelenting fact, now to be determined by battle, and on him had fallen the burden of sustaining the cause of his country. In this spirit he accepted his commission, and rode forth to review the troops. He was greeted with loud acclaim wherever he appeared. Mankind is impressed by externals, and those who gazed upon Washington in the streets of Philadelphia felt their courage rise and their hearts grow strong at the sight of his virile, muscular figure as he passed before them on horseback, stately, dignified, and self-contained. The people looked upon him, and were confident that this was a man worthy and able to dare and do all things.

On June 21st he set forth accompanied by Lee and Schuyler, and with a brilliant escort. He had ridden but twenty miles when he was met by the news of Bunker Hill. "Did the militia fight?" was the immediate and characteristic question; and being told that they did fight, he exclaimed, "Then the liberties of the country are safe." Given the fighting spirit, Washington felt he could do anything. Full of this important intelligence he pressed forward to Newark, where he was received by a committee of the provincial congress, sent to conduct the commander-in-chief to New York. There he tarried long enough to appoint Schuyler to the charge of the military affairs in that colony, having mastered on the journey its complicated social and political conditions. Pushing on through Connecticut he reached Watertown, where he was received by the provincial congress of Massachusetts, on July 2d, with every expression of attachment and confidence. Lingering less than an hour for this ceremony, he rode on to the headquarters at Cambridge, and when he came within the lines the shouts of the soldiers and the booming of cannon announced his arrival to the English in Boston.

The next day he rode forth in the presence of a great multitude, and the troops having been drawn up before him, he drew his sword beneath the historical elm-tree, and took command of the first American army. "His excellency," wrote Dr. Thatcher in his journal, "was on horseback in company with several military gentlemen. It was not difficult to distinguish him from all others. He is tall and well proportioned, and his personal appearance truly noble and majestic." "He is tall and of easy and agreeable address," the loyalist Curwen had remarked a few weeks before; while Mrs. John Adams, warm-hearted and clever, wrote to her husband after the general's arrival: "Dignity, ease, and complacency, the gentleman and the soldier, look agreeably blended in him. Modesty marks every line and feature of his face. Those lines of Dryden instantly occurred to me,—

> 'Mark his majestic fabric! He's a temple
> Sacred by birth, and built by hands divine;
> His soul's the deity that lodges there;
> Nor is the pile unworthy of the God.'"

Lady, lawyer, and surgeon, patriot and tory, all speak alike, and as they wrote so New England felt. A slave-owner, an aristocrat, and a churchman, Washington came to Cambridge to pass over the heads of native generals to the command of a New England army, among a democratic people, hard working and simple in their lives, and dissenters to the backbone, who regarded episcopacy as something little short of papistry and quite equivalent to toryism. Yet the shout that went up from soldiers and people on Cambridge common on that pleasant July morning came from the heart and had no jarring note. A few of the political chiefs growled a little in later days at Washington, but the soldiers and the people, high and low, rich and poor, gave him an unstinted loyalty. On the fields of battle and throughout eight years of political strife the men of New England stood by the great Virginian with a devotion and truth in which was no shadow of turning. Here again we see exhibited most conspicuously the powerful personality of the man who was able thus to command immediately the allegiance of this naturally cold and reserved people. What was it that they saw that inspired them at once with so much confidence? They looked upon a tall, handsome man, dressed in plain uniform, wearing across his breast a broad blue band of silk, which some may have noticed as the badge and symbol of a certain solemn league and covenant once very momentous in the English-speaking world. They saw his calm, high bearing, and in every line of face and figure they beheld the signs of force and courage. Yet there must have been something more to call forth the confidence then so quickly given, and which no one ever long withheld. All felt dimly, but none the less surely, that here was a strong, able man, capable of rising to the emergency, whatever it might be, capable of continued growth and development, clear of head and warm of heart; and so the New England people gave to him instinctively their sympathy and their faith, and never took either back.

The shouts and cheers died away, and then Washington returned to his temporary quarters in the Wadsworth house, to master the task before him. The first great test of his courage and ability had come, and he faced it quietly as the excitement caused by his arrival passed by. He saw before him, to use his own words, "a mixed multitude of people, under very little discipline, order, or government." In the language of one of his aides:* "The entire army, if it deserved the name, was but an assemblage of brave, enthusiastic, undisciplined, country lads; the officers in general quite as ignorant of military life as the troops, excepting a few elderly men, who had seen some irregular service among the provincials under Lord Amherst." With this force, ill-posted and very insecurely fortified, Washington was to drive the British from Boston. His first step was to count his men, and it took eight days to get the necessary returns, which in an ordinary army would have been furnished in an hour. When he had them, he found that instead of twenty thousand, as had been represented, but fourteen thousand soldiers were actually present for duty. In

---

*John Trumbull, *Reminiscences*, p. 18.

a short time, however, Mr. Emerson, the chaplain, noted in his diary that it was surprising how much had been done, and that the lines had been so extended, and the works so shrewdly built, that it was morally impossible for the enemy to get out except in one place purposely left open. A little later the same observer remarked: "There is a great over-turning in the camp as to order and regularity; new lords, new laws. The Generals Washington and Lee are upon the lines every day. The strictest government is taking place, and great distinction is made between officers and soldiers." Bodies of troops scattered here and there by chance were replaced by well-distributed forces, posted wisely and effectively in strong intrenchments. It is little wonder that the worthy chaplain was impressed, and now, seeing it all from every side, we too can watch order come out of chaos and mark the growth of an army under the guidance of a master-mind and the steady pressure of an unbending will.

Then too there was no discipline, for the army was composed of raw militia, who elected their officers and carried on war as they pleased. In a passage suppressed by Mr. Sparks, Washington said: "There is no such thing as getting officers of this stamp to carry orders into execution—to curry favor with the men (by whom they were chosen, and on whose smile they may possibly think that they may again rely) seems to be one of the principal objects of their attention. I have made a pretty good slam amongst such kind of officers as the Massachusetts government abounds in, since I came into this camp, having broke one colonel and two captains for cowardly behavior in the action on Bunker Hill, two captains for drawing more pay and provisions than they had men in their company, and one for being absent from his post when the enemy appeared there and burnt a house just by it. Besides these I have at this time one colonel, one major, one captain, and two subalterns under arrest for trial. In short, I spare none, and yet fear it will not all do, as these people seem to be too attentive to everything but their own interests." This may be plain and homely in phrase, but it is not stilted, and the quick energy of the words shows how the New England farmers and fishermen were being rapidly brought to discipline. Bringing the army into order, however, was but a small part of his duties. It is necessary to run over all his difficulties, great and small, at this time, and count them up, in order to gain a just idea of the force and capacity of the man who overcame them.

Washington, moreover, was obliged to deal not only with his army, but with the general congress and the congress of the province. He had to teach them, utterly ignorant as they were of the needs and details of war, how to organize and supply their armies. There was no commissary department, there were no uniforms, no arrangements for ammunition, no small arms, no cannon, no resources to draw upon for all these necessaries of war. Little by little he taught Congress to provide after a fashion for these things, little by little he developed what he needed, and by his own ingenuity, and by seizing alertly every suggestion from others, he supplied for better or worse one deficiency after another. He had to deal with various governors and various colonies, each with its prejudices, jealousies, and shortcomings. He had to arrange for new levies from a people unused to war, and to settle with infinite anxiety and much wear and tear of mind and body, the conflict as to rank among officers to whom he could apply no test but his own insight. He had to organize and stimulate the arming of privateers, which, by preying on British commerce, were destined to exercise such a powerful influence on the fate of the war. It was neither showy nor attractive, such work as this, but it was very vital, and it was done.

By the end of July the army was in a better posture of defence, and then at the beginning of the next month, as the prospect was brightening, it was suddenly discovered that there was no gunpowder. An undrilled army, imperfectly organized, was facing a disciplined force and had only some nine rounds in the cartridge-boxes. Yet there is no quivering in the letters from headquarters. Anxiety and strain of nerve are apparent; but a resolute determination rises over all, supported by a ready fertility of resource. Couriers flew over the country asking for powder in every town and in every village. A vessel was even dispatched to the Bermudas to seize there a supply of powder, of which the general, always listening, had heard. Thus the immediate and grinding pressure was presently relieved, but the staple of war still remained pitifully and perilously meagre all through the winter.

Meantime, while thus overwhelmed with the cares immediately about him, Washington was watching the rest of the country. He had a keen eye upon Johnson and his Indians in the valley of the Mohawk; he followed sharply every movement of Tryon and the Tories in New York; he refused with stern good sense to detach troops to Connecticut and Long Island, knowing well when to give and when to say No, a difficult monosyllable for the new general of freshly revolted colonies. But if he would not detach in one place, he was ready enough to do so in another. He sent one expedition by Lake Champlain, under Montgomery, to Montreal, and gave Arnold picked troops to march through the wilds of Maine and strike Quebec. The scheme was bold and brilliant, both in conception and in execution, and came very near severing Canada forever from the British crown. A chapter of little accidents, each one of which proved as fatal as it was unavoidable, a moment's delay on the Plains of Abraham, and the whole campaign failed; but there was a grasp of conditions, a clearness of perception, and a comprehensiveness about the plan, which stamp it as the work of a great soldier, who saw besides the military importance, the enormous political value held out by the chance of such a victory.

The daring, far-reaching quality of this Canadian expedition was much more congenial to Washington's temper and character than the wearing work of the siege. All that man could do before Boston was done, and still Congress expected the impossible, and grumbled because without ships he did not secure the harbor. He himself, while he inwardly resented such criticism, chafed under the monotonous drudgery of the intrenchments. He was longing, according to his nature, to fight and was, it must be confessed, quite ready to attempt the impossible in his own way. Early in September he proposed to attack the town in boats and by the neck of land at Roxbury, but the council of officers unanimously voted against him. A little more than a month later he planned another attack, and was again voted down by his officers. Councils of war never fight, it is said, and perhaps in this case it was well that such was their habit, for the schemes look rather desperate now. To us they serve to show the temper of the man, and also his self-control, for Washington was ready enough to override councils when wholly free from doubt himself.

Thus the planning of campaigns, both distant and near, went on, and at the same time the current of details, difficult, vital, absolute in demanding prompt and vigorous solution, went on too. The existence of war made it necessary to settle our relations with our enemies, and that these relations should be rightly settled was of vast moment to our cause, struggling for recognition. The first question was the matter of prisoners, and on August 11th Washington wrote to Gage: —

> I understand that the officers engaged in the cause of liberty and their country, who by the fortune of war have fallen into your hands, have been thrown indiscriminately into a common gaol appropriated for felons; that no consideration has been had for those of the most respectable rank, when languishing with wounds and sickness; and that some have been even amputated in this unworthy situation.
>
> Let your opinion, sir, of the principle which actuates them be what it may, they suppose that they act from the noblest of all principles, a love of freedom and their country. But political principles, I conceive, are foreign to this point. The obligations arising from the rights of humanity and claims of rank are universally binding and extensive, except in case of retaliation. These, I should have hoped, would have dictated a more tender treatment of those individuals whom chance or war had put in your power. Nor can I forbear suggesting its fatal tendency to widen that unhappy breach which you, and those ministers under whom you act, have repeatedly declared your wish is to see forever closed.
>
> My duty now makes it necessary to apprise you, that for the future I shall regulate all my conduct towards those gentlemen who are or may be in our possession, exactly by the rule you shall observe towards those of ours now in your custody.
>
> If severity and hardship mark the line of your conduct, painful as it may be to me, your prisoners will feel its effects.

But if kindness and humanity are shown to ours, I shall with pleasure consider those in our hands only as unfortunate, and they shall receive from me that treatment to which the unfortunate are ever entitled.

This is a letter worthy of a little study. The affair does not look very important now, but it went then to the roots of things; for this letter would go out to the world, and America and the American cause would be judged by their leader. A little bluster or ferocity, any fine writing, or any absurdity, and the world would have sneered, condemned, or laughed. But no man could read this letter and fail to perceive that here was dignity and force, justice and sense, with just a touch of pathos and eloquence to recommend it to the heart. Men might differ with the writer, but they could neither laugh at him nor set him aside.

Gage replied after his kind. He was an inconsiderable person, dull and well meaning, intended for the command of a garrison town, and terribly twisted and torn by the great events in which he was momentarily caught. His masters were stupid and arrogant, and he imitated them with perfect success, except that arrogance with him dwindled to impertinence. He answered Washington's letter with denials and recriminations, lectured the American general on the political situation, and talked about "usurped authority," "rebels," "criminals," and persons destined to the "cord." Washington, being a man of his word, proceeded to put some English prisoners into jail, and then wrote a second note, giving Gage a little lesson in manners, with the vain hope of making him see that gentlemen did not scold and vituperate because they fought. He restated his case calmly and coolly, as before, informed Gage that he had investigated the counter-charge of cruelty and found it without any foundation, and then continued: "You advise me to give free operation to truth, and to punish misrepresentation and falsehood. If experience stamps value upon counsel, yours must have a weight which few can claim. You best can tell how far the convulsion, which has brought such ruin on both countries, and shaken the mighty empire of Britain to its foundation, may be traced to these malignant causes.

You affect, sir, to despise all rank not derived from the same source with your own. I cannot conceive one more honorable than that which flows from the uncorrupted choice of a brave and free people, the purest source and original fountain of all power. Far from making it a plea for cruelty, a mind of true magnanimity and enlarged ideas would comprehend and respect it.

Washington had grasped instinctively the general truth that Englishmen are prone to mistake civility for servility, and become offensive, whereas if they are treated with indifference, rebuke, or even rudeness, they are apt to be respectful and polite. He was obliged to go over the same ground with Sir William Howe, a little later, and still more sharply; and this matter of prisoners recurred, although at longer and longer intervals, throughout the war. But as the British generals saw their officers go to jail, and found that their impudence and assumption were met by keen reproofs, they gradually comprehended that Washington was not a man to be trifled with, and that in him was a pride and dignity outtopping theirs and far stronger, because grounded on responsibility borne and work done, and on the deep sense of a great and righteous cause.

It was probably a pleasure and a relief to give to Gage and Sir William Howe a little instruction in military behavior and general good manners, but there was nothing save infinite vexation in dealing with the difficulties arising on the American side of the line. As the days shortened and the leaves fell, Washington saw before him a New England winter, with no clothing and no money for his troops. Through long letters to Congress, and strenuous personal efforts, these wants were somehow supplied. Then the men began to get restless and homesick, and both privates and officers would disappear to their farms, which Washington, always impatient of wrongdoing, styled "base and pernicious conduct," and punished accordingly.

By and by the terms of enlistment ran out and the regiments began to melt away even before the proper date. Recruiting was carried on slowly and with difficulty, new levies were tardy in coming in, and

Congress could not be persuaded to stop limited enlistments. Still the task was done. The old army departed and a new one arose in its place, the posts were strengthened and ammunition secured.

Among these reinforcements came some Virginia riflemen, and it must have warmed Washington's heart to see once more these brave and hardy fighters in the familiar hunting shirt and leggings. They certainly made him warm in a very different sense by getting into a rough-and-tumble fight one winter's day with some Marblehead fishermen. The quarrel was at its height, when suddenly into the brawl rode the commander-in-chief. He quickly dismounted, seized two of the combatants, shook them, berated them, if tradition may be trusted, for their local jealousies, and so with strong arm quelled the disturbance. He must have longed to take more than one colonial governor or magnate by the throat and shake him soundly, as he did his soldiers from the woods of Virginia and the rocks of Marblehead, for to his temper there was nothing so satisfying as rapid and decisive action. But he could not quell governors and assemblies in this way, and yet he managed them and got what he wanted with a patience and tact which it must have been in the last degree trying to him to practise, gifted as he was with a nature at once masterful and passionate.

Another trial was brought about by his securing and sending out privateers which did good service. They brought in many valuable prizes which caused infinite trouble, and forced Washington not only to be a naval secretary, but also made him a species of admiralty judge. He implored the slowmoving Congress to relieve him from this burden, and suggested a plan which led to the formation of special committees and was the origin of the Federal judiciary of the United States. Besides the local jealousies and the personal jealousies, and the privateers and their prizes, he had to meet also the greed and selfishness as well of the money-making, stock-jobbing spirit which springs up rankly under the influence of army contracts and large expenditures among a people accustomed to trade and unused to war. Washington wrote savagely of these practices, but still, despite all hindrances and annoyances, he kept moving straight on to his object.

In the midst of his labors, harassed and tried in all ways, he was assailed as usual by complaint and criticism. Some of it came to him through his friend and aide, Joseph Reed, to whom he wrote in reply one of the noblest letters ever penned by a great man struggling with adverse circumstances and wringing victory from grudging fortune. He said that he was always ready to welcome criticism, hear advice, and learn the opinion of the world.

"For as I have but one capital object in view, I could wish to make my conduct coincide with the wishes of mankind, as far as I can consistently; I mean, without departing from that great line of duty which, though hid under a cloud for some time, from a peculiarity of circumstances, may, nevertheless, bear a scrutiny." Thus he held fast to "the great line of duty," though bitterly tried the while by the news from Canada, where brilliant beginnings were coming to dismal endings, and cheered only by the arrival of his wife, who drove up one day in her coach and four, with the horses ridden by black postilions in scarlet and white liveries, much to the amazement, no doubt, of the sober-minded New England folk.

Light, however, finally began to break on the work about him. Henry Knox, sent out for that purpose, returned safely with the guns captured at Ticonderoga, and thus heavy ordnance and gun-powder were obtained. By the middle of February the harbor was frozen over, and Washington arranged to cross the ice and carry Boston by storm. Again he was held back by his council, but this time he could not be stopped. If he could not cross the ice he would go by land. He had been slowly but surely advancing his works all winter, and now he determined on a decisive stroke. On the evening of Monday, March 4th, under cover of a heavy bombardment which distracted the enemy's attention, he marched a large body of troops to Dorchester Heights and began to throw up redoubts. The work went forward rapidly, and Washington rode about all night encouraging the men. The New England soldiers had sorely tried his temper, and there were many severe attacks and bitter criticisms upon them in his letters, which were suppressed or smoothed over for the most part by Mr. Sparks, but which have come to light since, as is sometimes the case with facts. Gradually, however, the General had come to know his soldiers better, and six months later he wrote to Lund Washington, praising his northern troops in the highest terms. Even now he understood them as never before, and as he watched them on that raw March night, working with the energy and quick intelligence of their race, he probably felt that the defects were superficial, but the virtues, the tenacity, and the courage were lasting and strong.

When day dawned, and the British caught sight of the formidable works which had sprung up in the night, there was a great excitement and running hither and thither in the town. Still the men on the heights worked on, and still Washington rode back and forth among them. He was stirred and greatly rejoiced at the coming of the fight, which he now believed inevitable, and as always, when he was deeply moved, the hidden springs of sentiment and passion were opened, and he reminded his soldiers that it was the anniversary of the Boston massacre, and appealed to them by the memories of that day to prepare for battle with the enemy. As with the Huguenots at Ivry, —

"Remember St. Bartholomew!" was passed from man to man.

But the fighting never came. The British troops were made ready, then a gale arose and they could not cross the bay. The next day it rained in torrents, and the next day it was too late. The American intrenchments frowned threateningly above the town, and began to send in certain ominous messengers in the shape of shot and shell. The place was now so clearly untenable that Howe determined to evacuate it. An informal request to allow the troops to depart unmolested was not answered, but Washington suspended his fire and the British made ready to withdraw. Still they hesitated and delayed, until Washington again advanced his works, and on this hint they started in earnest, on March 17th, amid confusion, pillage, and disorder, leaving cannon and much else behind them, and seeking refuge in their ships.

All was over, and the town was in the hands of the Americans. In Washington's own words, "To maintain a post within musket-shot of the enemy for six months together, without powder, and at the same time to disband one army and recruit another within that distance of twenty-odd British regiments, is more, probably, than ever was attempted." It was, in truth, a gallant feat of arms, carried through by the resolute will and strong brain of one man. The troops on both sides were brave, but the British had advantages far more than compensating for a disparity of numbers, always slight and often more imaginary than real. They had twelve thousand men, experienced, disciplined, equipped, and thoroughly supplied. They had the best arms and cannon and gunpowder. They commanded the sea with a strong fleet, and they were concentrated on the inside line, able to strike with suddenness and overwhelming force at any point of widely extended posts. Washington caught them with an iron grip and tightened it steadily until, in disorderly haste, they took to their boats without even striking a blow. Washington's great abilities, and the incapacity of the generals opposed to him, were the causes of this result. If Robert Clive, for instance, had chanced to have been there the end might possibly have been the same, but there would have been some bloody fighting before that end was reached. The explanation of the feeble abandonment of Boston lies in the stupidity of the English government, which had sown the wind and then proceeded to handle the customary crop with equal fatuity.

There were plenty of great men in England, but they were not conducting her government or her armies. Lord Sandwich had declared in the House of Lords that all "Yankees were cowards," a simple and satisfactory statement, readily accepted by the governing classes, and flung in the teeth of the British soldiers as they fell back twice from the bloody slopes of Bunker Hill. Acting on this pleasant idea, England sent out as commanders of her American army a parcel of ministerial and court favorites, thoroughly second-rate men, to whom was confided the task of beating one of the best soldiers and hardest fighters of the century. Despite the enormous material odds in favor of Great Britain, the natural result of matching the Howes and Gages and Clintons against George Washington ensued, and the first lesson was taught by the evacuation of Boston.

Washington did not linger over his victory. Even while the British fleet still hung about the harbor he began to send troops to New York to make ready for the next attack. He entered Boston in order to see that every precaution was taken against the spread of the smallpox, and then prepared to depart himself. Two ideas, during his first winter of conflict, had taken possession of his mind, and undoubtedly influenced profoundly his future course. One was the conviction that the struggle must be fought out to the bitter end, and must bring either subjugation or complete independence. He wrote in February: "With respect to myself, I have never entertained an idea of an accommodation, since I heard of the measures which were adopted in consequence of the Bunker's Hill fight;" and at an earlier date he said: "I hope my countrymen (of Virginia) will rise superior to any losses the whole navy of Great Britain can bring on them, and that the destruction of Norfolk and threatened devastation of other places will have no other effect than to unite the whole country in one indissoluble band against a nation which seems to be lost to every sense of virtue and those feelings which distinguish a civilized people from the most barbarous savages." With such thoughts he sought to make Congress appreciate the probable long duration of the struggle, and he bent every energy to giving permanency to his army, and decisiveness to each campaign. The other idea which had grown in his mind during the weary siege was that the Tories were thoroughly dangerous and deserved scant mercy. In his second letter to Gage he refers to them, with the frankness which characterized him when he felt strongly, as "execrable parricides," and he made ready to treat them with the utmost severity at New York and elsewhere. When Washington was aroused there was a stern and relentless side to his character, in keeping with the force and strength which were his chief qualities. His attitude on this point seems harsh now when the old Tories no longer look very dreadful. But they were dangerous then, and Washington, with his honest hatred of all that seemed to him to partake of meanness or treason, proposed to put them down and render them harmless, being well convinced, after his clear-sighted fashion, that war was not peace, and that mildness to domestic foes was sadly misplaced.

His errand to New England was now done and well done. His victory was won, everything was settled at Boston; and so, having sent his army forward, he started for New York, to meet the harder trials that still awaited him.

CHAPTER VI

SAVING THE REVOLUTION

AFTER LEAVING BOSTON, Washington proceeded through Rhode Island and Connecticut, pushing troops forward as he advanced, and reached New York on April 13th. There he found himself plunged at once into the same sea of difficulties with which he had been struggling at Boston, the only difference being that these were fresh and entirely untouched. The army was inadequate, and the town, which was the central point of the colonies, as well as the great river at its side, was wholly unprotected. The troops were in large measure raw and undrilled, the committee of safety was hesitating, the Tories were virulent and active, corresponding constantly with Tryon who was lurking in a British man-of-war, while from the north came tidings of retreat and disaster. All these harassing difficulties crowded upon the commander-in-chief as soon as he arrived. To appreciate him it is necessary to understand these conditions and realize their weight and consequence, albeit the details seem petty. When we comprehend the difficulties, then we can see plainly the greatness of the man who quietly and silently took them up and disposed of them. Some he scotched and some he killed, but he dealt with them all after a fashion sufficient to enable him to move steadily forward. In his presence the provincial committee suddenly stiffened and grew strong. All correspondence with Tryon was cut off, the Tories were repressed, and on Long Island steps were taken to root out "these abominable pests of society," as the commander-in-chief called them in his plain-spoken way.

107

Then forts were built, soldiers energetically recruited and drilled, arrangements made for prisoners, and despite all the present cares anxious thought was given to the Canada campaign, and ideas and expeditions, orders, suggestions and encouragement were freely furnished to the dispirited generals and broken forces of the north.

One matter, however, overshadowed all others. Nearly a year before, Washington had seen that there was no prospect or possibility of accommodation with Great Britain. It was plain to his mind that the struggle was final in its character and would be decisive. Separation from the mother country, therefore, ought to come at once, so that public opinion might be concentrated, and above all, permanency ought to be given to the army. These ideas he had been striving to impress upon Congress, for the most part less clear-sighted than he was as to facts, and as the months slipped by his letters had grown constantly more earnest and more vehement. Still Congress hesitated, and at last Washington went himself to Philadelphia and held conferences with the principal men. What he said is lost, but the tone of Congress certainly rose after his visit. The aggressive leaders found their hands so much strengthened that little more than a month later they carried through a declaration of independence, which was solemnly and gratefully proclaimed to the army by the general, much relieved to have got through the necessary boat-burning, and to have brought affairs, military and political, on to the hard ground of actual fact.

Soon after his return from Philadelphia, he received convincing proof that his views in regard to the Tories were extremely sound. A conspiracy devised by Tryon, which aimed apparently at the assassination of the commander-in-chief, and which had corrupted his life-guards for that purpose, was discovered and scattered before it had fairly hardened into definite form. The mayor of the city and various other persons were seized and thrown into prison, and one of the life-guards, Thomas Hickey by name, who was the principal tool in the plot, was hanged in the presence of a large concourse of people. Washington wrote a brief and business-like account of the affair to Congress, from which one would hardly suppose that his own life had been aimed at. It is a curious instance of his cool indifference to personal danger. The conspiracy had failed, that was sufficient for him, and he had other things besides himself to consider. "We expect a bloody summer in New York and Canada," he wrote to his brother, and even while the Canadian expedition was coming to a disastrous close, and was bringing hostile invasion instead of the hoped-for conquest, British men-of-war were arriving daily in the harbor, and a large army was collecting on Staten Island. The rejoicings over the Declaration of Independence had hardly died away, when the vessels of the enemy made their way up the Hudson without check from the embryo forts, or the obstacles placed in the stream.

July 12th Lord Howe arrived with more troops, and also with ample powers to pardon and negotiate. Almost immediately he tried to open a correspondence with Washington, but Colonel Reed, in behalf of the General, refused to receive the letter addressed to "Mr. Washington." Then Lord Howe sent an officer to the American camp with a second letter, addressed to "George Washington, Esq., etc., etc." The bearer was courteously received, but the letter was declined. "The etc., etc. implies everything," said the Englishman. It may also mean "anything," Washington replied, and added that touching the pardoning power of Lord Howe there could be no pardon where there was no guilt, and where no forgiveness was asked. As a result of these interviews, Lord Howe wrote to England that it would be well to give Mr. Washington his proper title. A small question, apparently, this of the form of address, especially to a lover of facts, and yet it was in reality of genuine importance. To the world Washington represented the young republic, and he was determined to extort from England the first acknowledgment of independence by compelling her to recognize the Americans as belligerents and not rebels. Washington cared as little for vain shows as any man who ever lived, but he had the highest sense of personal dignity, and of the dignity of his cause and country. Neither should be allowed to suffer in his hands. He appreciated the effect on mankind of forms and titles, and with unerring judgment he insisted on what he knew to be of real value. It is one of the earliest examples of the dignity and good taste which were of such inestimable value to his country.

He had abundant occasion also for the employment of these same qualities, coupled with unwearied patience and tact, in dealing with his own men. The present army was drawn from a wider range than that which had taken Boston, and sectional jealousies and disputes, growing every day more hateful to the commander-in-chief, sprang up rankly. The men of Maryland thought those of Connecticut ploughboys; the latter held the former to be fops and dandies. These and a hundred other disputes buzzed and whirled about Washington, stirring his strong temper, and exercising his sternest self-control in the untiring effort to suppress them and put them to death. "It requires," John Adams truly said, "more serenity of temper, a deeper understanding, and more courage than fell to the lot of Marlborough, to ride in this whirlwind." Fortunately these qualities were all there, and with them an honesty of purpose and an unbending directness of character to which Anne's great general was a stranger.

Meantime, while the internal difficulties were slowly diminished, the forces of the enemy rapidly increased. First it became evident that attacks were not feasible. Then the question changed to a mere choice of defences. Even as to this there was great and harassing doubt, for the enemy, having command of the water, could concentrate and attack at any point they pleased. Moreover, the British had thirty thousand of the best disciplined and best equipped troops that Europe could furnish, while Washington had some twenty thousand men, one fourth of whom were unfit for duty, and with the remaining three fourths, raw recruits for the most part, he was obliged to defend an extended line of posts, without cavalry, and with no means for rapid concentration. Had he been governed solely by military considerations he would have removed the inhabitants, burned New York, and drawing his forces together would have taken up a secure post of observation. To have destroyed the town, however, not only would have frightened the timid and the doubters, and driven them over to the Tories, but would have dispirited the patriots not yet alive to the exigencies of war, and deeply injured the American cause. That Washington well understood the need of such action is clear, both from the current rumors that the town was to be burned, and from his expressed desire to remove the women and children from New York. But political considerations overruled the military necessity, and he spared the town. It was bad enough to be thus hampered, but he was even more fettered in other ways, for he could not even concentrate his forces and withdraw to the Highlands without a battle, as he was obliged to fight in order to sustain public feeling, and thus he was driven on to almost sure defeat.

Everything, too, as the day of battle drew near, seemed to make against him. On August 22d the enemy began to land on Long Island, where Greene had drawn a strong line of redoubts behind the village of Brooklyn, to defend the heights which commanded New York, and had made every arrangement to protect the three roads through the wooded hills, about a mile from the intrenchments. Most unfortunately, and just at the critical moment, Greene was taken down with a raging fever, so that when Washington came over on the 24th he found much confusion in the camps, which he repressed as best he could, and then prepared for the attack. Greene's illness, however, had caused some oversights which were unknown to the commander-in-chief, and which, as it turned out, proved fatal.

After indecisive skirmishing for two or three days, the British started early on the morning of the 26th. They had nine thousand men and were well informed as to the country. Advancing through woodpaths and lanes, they came round to the left flank of the Americans. One of the roads through the hills was unguarded, the others feebly protected. The result is soon told. The Americans, out-generalled and out-flanked, were taken by surprise and surrounded, Sullivan and his division were cut off, and then Lord Stirling. There was some desperate fighting, and the Americans showed plenty of courage, but only a few forced their way out. Most of them were killed or taken prisoners, the total loss out of some five thousand men reaching as high as two thousand.

From the redoubts, whither he had come at the sound of the firing, Washington watched the slaughter and disaster in grim silence. He saw the British troops, flushed with victory, press on to the very edge of his works and then withdraw in obedience to command. The British generals had their prey so surely, as they believed, that they mercifully decided not to waste life unnecessarily by storming the works in the first glow of success. So they waited during that night and the two following days, while Washington strengthened his intrenchments, brought over reinforcements, and prepared for the worst. On the 29th it became apparent that there was a movement in the fleet, and that arrangements were being made to take the Americans in the rear and wholly cut them off. It was a pretty plan, but the British overlooked the fact that while they were lingering, summing up their victory, and counting the future as assured, there was a silent watchful man on the other side of the redoubts who for forty-eight hours never left the lines, and who with a great capacity for stubborn fighting could move, when the stress came, with the celerity and stealth of a panther.

Washington swiftly determined to retreat. It was a desperate undertaking, and a lesser man would have hesitated and been lost. He had to transport nine thousand men across a strait of strong tides and currents, and three quarters of a mile in width. It was necessary to collect the boats from a distance, and do it all within sight and hearing of the enemy. The boats were obtained, a thick mist settled down on sea and land, the water was calm, and as the night wore away, the entire army with all its arms and baggage was carried over, Washington leaving in the last boat. At daybreak the British awoke, but it was too late. They had fought a successful battle, they had had the American army in their grasp, and now all was over. The victory had melted away, and, as a grand result, they had a few hundred prisoners, a stray boat with three camp-followers, and the deserted works in which they stood. To make such a retreat as this was a feat of arms as great as most victories, and in it we see, perhaps as plainly as anywhere, the nerve and quickness of the man who conducted it. It is true it was the only chance of salvation, but the great man is he who is entirely master of his opportunity, even if he have but one.

The outlook, nevertheless, was, as Washington wrote, "truly distressing." The troops were dispirited, and the militia began to disappear, as they always did after a defeat. Congress would not permit the destruction of the city, different interests pulled in different directions, conflicting opinions distracted the councils of war, and, with utter inability to predict the enemy's movements, everything led to halfway measures and to intense anxiety, while Lord Howe tried to negotiate with Congress, and the Americans waited for events. Washington, looking beyond the confusion of the moment, saw that he had gained much by delay, and had his own plan well defined. He wrote: "We have not only delayed the operations of the campaign till it is too late to effect any capital incursion into the country, but have drawn the enemy's forces to one point. . . . It would be presumption to draw out our young troops into open ground against their superiors both in number and discipline, and I have never spared the spade and pickaxe." Every one else, however, saw only past defeat and present peril.

The British ships gradually made their way up the river, until it became apparent that they intended to surround and cut off the American army. Washington made preparations to withdraw, but uncertainty of information came near rendering his precautions futile. September 15th the men-of-war opened fire, and troops were landed near Kip's Bay. The militia in the breastworks at that point had been at Brooklyn and gave way at once, communicating their panic to two Connecticut regiments. Washington, galloping down to the scene of battle, came upon the disordered and flying troops. He dashed in among them, conjuring them to stop, but even while he was trying to rally them they broke again on the appearance of some sixty or seventy of the enemy, and ran in all directions. In a tempest of anger Washington drew his pistols, struck the fugitives with his sword, and was only forced from the field by one of his officers seizing the bridle of his horse and dragging him away from the British, now within a hundred yards of the spot.

Through all his trials and anxieties Washington always showed the broadest and most generous sympathy. When the militia had begun to leave him a few days before, although he despised their action and protested bitterly to Congress against their employment, yet in his letters he displayed a keen appreciation of their feelings, and saw plainly every palliation and excuse. But there was one thing which he could never appreciate nor realize. It was from first to last impossible for him to understand how any man could refuse to fight, or could think of running away. When he beheld rout and cowardly panic before his very eyes, his temper broke loose and ran uncontrolled. His one thought then was to fight to the last, and he would have thrown himself single-handed on the enemy, with all his wisdom and prudence flung to the winds. The day when the commander held his place by virtue of personal prowess lay far back in the centuries, and no one knew it better than Washington. But the old fighting spirit awoke within him when the clash of arms sounded in his ears, and though we may know the general in the tent and in the council, we can only know the man when he breaks out from all rules and customs, and shows the rage of battle, and the indomitable eagerness for the fray, which lie at the bottom of the tenacity and courage that carried the war for independence to a triumphant close.

The rout and panic over, Washington quickly turned to deal with the pressing danger. With coolness and quickness he issued his orders, and succeeded in getting his army off, Putnam's division escaping most narrowly. He then took post at King's Bridge, and began to strengthen and fortify his lines. While thus engaged, the enemy advanced, and on the 16th a sharp skirmish was fought, in which the British were repulsed, and great bravery was shown by the Connecticut and Virginia troops, the two commanding officers being killed. This affair, which was the first gleam of success, encouraged the troops, and was turned to the best account by the general. Still a successful skirmish did not touch the essential difficulties of the situation, which then as always came from within, rather than without. To face and check twenty-five thousand well equipped and highly disciplined soldiers Washington had now some twelve thousand men, lacking in everything which goes to make an army, except mere individual courage and a high average of intelligence. Even this meagre force was an inconstant and diminishing quantity, shifting, uncertain, and always threatening dissolution.

The task of facing and fighting the enemy was enough for the ablest of men; but Washington was obliged also to combat and overcome the inertness and dulness born of ignorance, and to teach Congress how to govern a nation at war. In the hours "allotted to sleep," he sat in his headquarters, writing a letter, with "blots and scratches," which told Congress with the utmost precision and vigor just what was needed. It was but one of a long series of similar letters, written with unconquerable patience and with unwearied iteration, lighted here and there by flashes of deep and angry feeling, which would finally strike home under the pressure of defeat, and bring the patriots of the legislature to sudden action, always incomplete, but still action of some sort. It must have been inexpressibly dreary work, but quite as much was due to those letters as to the battles. Thinking for other people, and teaching them what to do, is at best an ungrateful duty, but when it is done while an enemy is at your throat, it shows a grim tenacity of purpose which is well worth consideration.

In this instance the letter of September 24th, read in the light of the battles of Long Island and Kip's Bay, had a considerable effect. The first steps were taken to make the army national and permanent, to raise the pay of officers, and to lengthen enlistments. Like most of the war measures of Congress, they were too late for the immediate necessity, but they helped the future. Congress, moreover, then felt that all had been done that could be demanded, and relapsed once more into confidence. "The British force," said John Adams, chairman of the board of war, "is so divided, they will do no great matter this fall." But Washington, facing hard facts, wrote to Congress with his unsparing truth on October 4th: "Give me leave to say, sir, (I say it with due deference and respect, and my knowledge of the facts, added to the importance of the cause and the stake I hold in it, must justify the freedom,) that your affairs are in a more unpromising way than you seem to apprehend. Your army, as I mentioned in my last, is on the eve of its political dissolution. True it is, you have voted a larger one in lieu of it; but the season is late; and there is a material difference between voting battalions and raising men."

The campaign as seen from the board of war and from the Plains of Harlem differed widely. It is needless to say now which was correct; every one knows that the General was right and Congress wrong, but being in the right did not help Washington, nor did he take petty pleasure in being able to say, "I told you how it would be." The hard facts remained unchanged. There was the wholly patriotic but slumberous, and for fighting purposes quite inefficient Congress still to be waked up and kept awake, and to be instructed. With painful and plain-spoken repetition this work was grappled with and done methodically, and like all else as effectively as was possible.

Meanwhile the days slipped along, and Washington waited on the Harlem Plains, planning descents on Long Island, and determining to make a desperate stand where he was, unless the situation decidedly changed. Then the situation did change, as neither he nor any one else apparently had anticipated. The British warships came up the Hudson past the forts, brushing aside our boasted obstructions, destroying our little fleet, and getting command of the river. Then General Howe landed at Frog's Point, where he was checked for the moment by the good disposition of Heath, under Washington's direction. These two events made it evident that the situation of the American army was full of peril, and that retreat was again necessary. Such certainly was the conclusion of the council of war, on the 16th, acting this time in agreement with their chief. Six days Howe lingered on Frog's Point, bringing up stores or artillery or something; it matters little now why he tarried. Suffice it that he waited, and gave six days to his opponent. They were of little value to Howe, but they were of inestimable worth to Washington, who employed them in getting everything in readiness, in holding his council of war, and then on the 17th in moving deliberately off to very strong ground at White Plains. On his way he fought two or three slight, sharp, and successful skirmishes with the British. Sir William followed closely, but with much caution, having now a dull glimmer in his mind that at the head of the raw troops in front of him was a man with whom it was not safe to be entirely careless.

On the 28th, Howe came up to Washington's position, and found the Americans quite equal in numbers, strongly intrenched, and awaiting his attack with confidence. He hesitated, doubted, and finally feeling that he must do something, sent four thousand men to storm Chatterton Hill, an outlying post, where some fourteen hundred Americans were stationed. There was a short, sharp action, and then the Americans retreated in good order to the main army, having lost less than half as many men as their opponents. With caution now much enlarged, Howe sent for reinforcements, and waited two days. The third day it rained, and on the fourth Howe found that Washington had withdrawn to a higher and quite impregnable line of hills, where he held all the passes in the rear and awaited a second attack. Howe contemplated the situation for two or three days longer, and then broke camp and withdrew to Dobbs Ferry. Such were the great results of the victory of Long Island, two wasted months, and the American army still untouched.

Howe was resolved, however, that his campaign should not be utterly fruitless, and therefore directed his attention to the defences of the Hudson, Fort Lee, and Fort Washington, and here he met with better success. Congress, in its military wisdom, had insisted that these forts must and could be held. So thought the generals, and so most especially, and most unluckily, did Greene. Washington, with his usual accurate and keen perception, saw, from the time the men-of-war came up the Hudson, and, now that the British army was free, more clearly than ever that both forts ought to be abandoned. Sure of his ground, he overruled Congress, but was so far influenced by Greene that he gave to that officer discretionary orders as to withdrawal. This was an act of weakness, as he afterwards admitted, for which he bitterly reproached himself, never confusing or glossing over his own errors, but loyal there, as elsewhere, to facts. An attempt was made to hold both forts, and both were lost, as he had foreseen. From Fort Lee the garrison withdrew in safety. Fort Washington was carried by storm, after a severe struggle. Twenty-six hundred men and all the munitions of war fell into the hands of the enemy. It was a serious and most depressing loss, and was felt throughout the continent.

Meantime Washington had crossed into the Jerseys, and, after the loss of Fort Lee, began to retreat before the British, who, flushed with victory, now advanced rapidly under Lord Cornwallis. The crisis of his fate and of the Revolution was upon him. His army was melting away. The militia had almost all disappeared, and regiments whose term of enlistment had expired were departing daily. Lee, who had a division under his command, was ordered to come up, but paid no attention, although the orders were repeated almost every day for a month. He lingered, and loitered, and excused himself, and at last was taken prisoner. This disposed of him for a time very satisfactorily, but meanwhile he had succeeded in keeping his troops from Washington, which was a most serious misfortune.

On December 2d Washington was at Princeton with three thousand ragged men, and the British close upon his heels. They had him now surely in their grip. There could be no mistake this time, and there was therefore no need of a forced march. But they had not yet learned that to Washington even hours meant much, and when, after duly resting, they reached the Delaware, they found the Americans on the other side, and all the boats destroyed for a distance of seventy miles.

It was winter now, the short gray days had come, and with them piercing cold and storms of sleet and ice. It seemed as if the elements alone would finally disperse the feeble body of men still gathered about the commander-in-chief. Congress had sent him blank commissions and orders to recruit, which were well meant, but were not practically of much value. As Glendower could call spirits from the vasty deep, so they, with like success, sought to call soldiers from the earth in the midst of defeat, and in the teeth of a North American winter. Washington, baffling pursuit and flying from town to town, left nothing undone. North and south went letters and appeals for men, money, and supplies. Vain, very vain, it all was, for the most part, but still it was done in a tenacious spirit. Lee would not come, the Jersey militia would not turn out, thousands began to accept Howe's amnesty, and signs of wavering were apparent in some of the Middle States. Philadelphia was threatened, Newport was in the hands of the enemy, and for ninety miles Washington had retreated, evading ruin again and again only by the width of a river. Congress voted not to leave Philadelphia,—a fact which their General declined to publish,—and then fled.

No one remained to face the grim realities of the time but Washington, and he met them unmoved. Not a moment passed that he did not seek in some way to effect something. Not an hour went by that he did not turn calmly from fresh and ever renewed disappointment to work and action.

By the middle of December Howe felt satisfied that the American army would soon dissolve, and leaving strong detachments in various posts he withdrew to New York. His premises were sound, and his conclusions logical, but he made his usual mistake of overlooking and underestimating the American general. No sooner was it known that he was on his way to New York than Washington, at the head of his dissolving army, resolved to take the offensive and strike an outlying post. In a letter of December 14th, the day after Howe began to move, we catch the first glimpse of Trenton. It was a bold spirit that, in the dead of winter, with a broken army, no prospect of reinforcements, and in the midst of a terror-stricken people, could thus resolve with some four thousand men to attack an army thoroughly appointed, and numbering in all its divisions twenty-five thousand soldiers.

It is well to pause a moment and look at that situation, and at the overwhelming difficulties which hemmed it in, and then try to realize what manner of man he was who rose superior to it, and conquered it. Be it remembered, too, that he never deceived himself, and never for one instant disguised the truth. Two years later he wrote that at this supreme moment, in what were called "the dark days of America," he was never despondent; and this was true enough, for despair was not in his nature. But no delusions lent him courage. On the 18th he wrote to his brother "that if every nerve was not strained to recruit this new army the game was pretty nearly up;" and added, "You can form no idea of the perplexity of my situation. No man, I believe, ever had a greater choice of difficulties, and less means to extricate himself from them. However, under a full persuasion of the justice of our cause, I cannot entertain an idea that it will finally sink, though it may remain for some time under a cloud." There is no complaint, no boasting, no despair in this letter. We can detect a bitterness in the references to Congress and to Lee, but the tone of the letter is as calm as a May morning, and it concludes with sending love and good wishes to the writer's sister and her family.

Thus in the dreary winter Washington was planning and devising and sending hither and thither for men, and never ceased through it all to write urgent and ever sharper letters and keep a wary eye upon the future. He not only wrote strongly, but he pledged his own estate and exceeded his powers in desperate efforts to raise money and men. On the

20th he wrote to Congress: "It may be thought that I am going a good deal out of the line of my duty to adopt these measures, or to advise thus freely. A character to lose, an estate to forfeit, the inestimable blessings of liberty at stake, and a life devoted, must be my excuse." Even now across the century these words come with a grave solemnity to our ears, and we can feel as he felt when he alone saw that he stood on the brink of a great crisis. It is an awful thing to know that the life of a nation is at stake, and this thought throbs in his words, measured and quiet as usual, but deeply fraught with much meaning to him and to the world.

By Christmas all was ready, and when the Christian world was rejoicing and feasting, and the British officers in New York and in the New Jersey towns were revelling and laughing, Washington prepared to strike. His whole force, broken into various detachments, was less than six thousand men. To each division was assigned, with provident forethought, its exact part. Nothing was overlooked, nothing omitted; and then every division commander failed, for good reason or bad, to do his duty. Gates was to march from Bristol with two thousand men, Ewing was to cross at Trenton, Putnam was to come up from Philadelphia, Griffin was to make a diversion against Donop. When the moment came, Gates, disapproving the scheme, was on his way to Congress, and Wilkinson, with his message, found his way to headquarters by following the bloody tracks of the barefooted soldiers. Griffin abandoned New Jersey and fled before Donop. Putnam would not even attempt to leave Philadelphia, and Ewing made no effort to cross at Trenton. Cadwalader, indeed, came down from Bristol, but after looking at the river and the floating ice, gave it up as desperate.

But there was one man who did not hesitate nor give up, nor halt on account of floating ice. With twenty-four hundred hardy veterans, Washington crossed the Delaware. The night was bitter cold and the passage difficult. When they landed, and began their march of nine miles to Trenton, a fierce storm of sleet drove in their faces. Sullivan, marching by the river, sent word that the arms of his men were wet. "Then tell your general," said Washington, "to use the bayonet, for the town must be taken." In broad daylight they came to the town. Washington, at the front

WASHINGTON CROSSING THE DELAWARE.

and on the right of the line, swept down the Pennington road, and as he drove in the pickets he heard the shouts of Sullivan's men, as, with Stark leading the van, they charged in from the river. A company of yägers and the light dragoons slipped away, there was a little confused fighting in the streets, Colonel Rahl fell, mortally wounded, his Hessians threw down their arms, and all was over. The battle had been fought and won, and the Revolution was saved.

Taking his thousand prisoners with him, Washington recrossed the Delaware to his old position. Had all done their duty, as he had planned, the British hold on New Jersey would have been shattered. As it was, it was only loosened. Congress, aroused at last, had invested Washington with almost dictatorial powers; but the time for action was short. The army was again melting away, and only by urgent appeals were some veterans retained, and enough new men gathered to make a force of five thousand men. With this army Washington prepared to finish what he had begun.

Trenton struck alarm and dismay into the British, and Cornwallis, with seven thousand of the best troops, started from New York to redeem what had been lost. Leaving three regiments at Princeton, he pushed hotly after Washington, who fell back behind the Assunpink River, skirmishing heavily and successfully. When Cornwallis reached the river he found the American army drawn up on the other side awaiting him. An attack on the bridge was repulsed, and the prospect looked uninviting. Some officers urged an immediate assault; but night was falling, and Cornwallis, sure of the game, decided to wait till the morrow. He, too, forgot that he was facing an enemy who never overlooked a mistake, and never waited an hour. With quick decision Washington left his camp-fires burning on the river bank, and taking roundabout roads, which he had already reconnoitred, marched on Princeton. By sunrise he was in the outskirts of the town. Mercer, detached with some three hundred men, fell in with Mawhood's regiment, and a sharp action ensued. Mercer was mortally wounded, and his men gave way just as the main army came upon the field. The British charged, and as the raw Pennsylvanian troops in the van wavered, Washington rode to the front, and reining his horse within thirty yards of the British, ordered his men to advance. The volleys of musketry left him unscathed, the men stood firm, the other divisions came rapidly into action, and the enemy gave way in all directions. The two other British regiments were driven through the town and routed. Had there been cavalry they would have been entirely cut off. As it was, they were completely broken, and in this short but bloody action they lost five hundred men in killed, wounded, and prisoners. It was too late to strike the magazines at Brunswick, as Washington had intended, and so he withdrew once more with his army to the high lands to rest and recruit.

His work was done, however. The country, which had been supine, and even hostile, rose now, and the British were attacked, surprised, and cut off in all directions, until at last they were shut up in the immediate vicinity of New York. The tide had been turned, and Washington had won the precious breathing-time which was all he required.

Frederic the Great is reported to have said that this was the most brilliant campaign of the century. It certainly showed all the characteristics of the highest strategy and most consummate generalship. With a force numerically insignificant as compared with that opposed to him, Washington won two decisive victories, striking the enemy suddenly with superior numbers at each point of attack. The Trenton campaign has all the quality of some of the last battles fought by Napoleon in France before his retirement to Elba. Moreover, these battles show not only generalship of the first order, but great statesmanship. They display that prescient knowledge which recognizes the supreme moment when all must be risked to save the state. By Trenton and Princeton Washington inflicted deadly blows upon the enemy, but he did far more by reviving the patriotic spirit of the country fainting under the bitter experience of defeat, and by sending fresh life and hope and courage throughout the whole people.

It was the decisive moment of the war. Sooner or later the American colonies were sure to part from the mother-country, either peaceably or violently. But there was nothing inevitable in the Revolution of 1776, nor was its end at all certain. It was in the last extremities when the British overran New Jersey, and if it had not been for Washington that particular revolution would have most surely failed. Its fate lay in the hands of the general and his army; and to the strong brain growing ever keener and quicker as the pressure became more intense, to the iron will gathering a more relentless force as defeat thickened, to the high, unbending character, and to the passionate and fighting temper of Washington, we owe the brilliant campaign which in the darkest hour turned the tide and saved the cause of the Revolution.

CHAPTER VII

"MALICE DOMESTIC, AND FOREIGN LEVY"

AFTER THE "TWO lucky strokes at Trenton and Princeton," as he himself called them, Washington took up a strong position at Morristown and waited. His plan was to hold the enemy in check, and to delay all operations until spring. It is easy enough now to state his purpose, and it looks very simple, but it was a grim task to carry it out through the bleak winter days of 1777. The Jersey farmers, spurred by the sufferings inflicted upon them by the British troops, had turned out at last in deference to Washington's appeals, after the victories of Trenton and Princeton, had harassed and cut off outlying parties, and had thus straitened the movements of the enemy. But the main army of the colonies, on which all depended, was in a pitiable state. It shifted its character almost from day to day. The curse of short enlistments, so denounced by Washington, made itself felt now with frightful effect. With the new year most of the continental troops departed, while others to replace them came in very slowly, and recruiting dragged most wearisomely. Washington was thus obliged, with temporary reinforcements of raw militia, to keep up appearances; and no commander ever struggled with a more trying task. At times it looked as if the whole army would actually disappear, and more than once Washington expected that the week's or the month's end would find him with not more than five hundred men. At the beginning of March he had about four thousand men, a few weeks later only three thousand raw troops, ill-fed, ill-clad, ill-shod, ill-armed, and almost unpaid. Over against him was Howe, with eleven thousand men in the field, and still more in the city of New York, well disciplined and equipped, well-armed, well-fed, and furnished with every needful supply. The contrast is absolutely grotesque, and yet the force of one man's genius and will was such that this excellent British army was hemmed in and kept in harmless quiet by their ragged opponents.

Washington's plan, from the first, was to keep the field at all hazards, and literally at all hazards did he do so. Right and left his letters went, day after day, calling with pathetic but dignified earnestness for men and supplies. In one of these epistles, to Governor Cooke of Rhode Island, written in January, to remonstrate against raising troops for the State only, he set forth his intentions in a few words. "You must be sensible," he said, "that the season is fast approaching when a new campaign will open; nay, the former is not yet closed; nor do I intend it shall be, unless the enemy quits the Jerseys." To keep fighting all the time, and never let the fire of active resistance flicker or die out, was Washington's theory of the way to maintain his own side and beat the enemy. If he could not fight big battles, he would fight small ones; if he could not fight little battles, he would raid and skirmish and surprise; but fighting of some sort he would have, while the enemy attempted to spread over a State and hold possession of it. We can see the obstacles now, but we can only wonder how they were sufficiently overcome to allow anything to be done.

Moreover, besides the purely physical difficulties in the lack of men, money, and supplies, there were others of a political and personal kind, which were even more wearing and trying, but which, nevertheless, had to be dealt with also, in some fashion. In order to sustain the courage of the people Washington was obliged to give out, and to allow it to be supposed, that he had more men than was really the case, and so Congress and various wise and well-meaning persons grumbled because he did not do more and fight more battles. He never deceived Congress, but they either could not or would not understand the actual situation. In March he wrote to Robert Morris: "Nor is it in my power to make Congress fully sensible of the real situation of our affairs, and that it is with difficulty, if I may use the expression, that I can by every means in my power keep the life and soul of this army together. In a word, when they are at a distance, they think it is but to say, *Presto, begone*, and everything is done. They seem not to have any conception of the difficulty and perplexity attending those who are to execute." It was so easy to see what they would like to have done, and so simple to pass a resolve to that effect, that Congress never could appreciate the reality of the difficulty and the danger until the hand of the enemy was almost at their throats. They were not even content with delay and neglect, but interfered actively at times, as in the matter of the exchange of prisoners, where they made unending trouble for Washington, and showed themselves unable to learn or to keep their hands off after any amount of instruction.

In January Washington issued a proclamation requiring those inhabitants who had subscribed to Howe's declaration to come in within thirty days and take the oath of allegiance to the United States. If they failed to do so they were to be treated as enemies. The measure was an eminently proper one, and the proclamation was couched in the most moderate language. It was impossible to permit a large class of persons to exist on the theory that they were peaceful American citizens and also subjects of King George. The results of such conduct were in every way perilous and intolerable, and Washington was determined that he would divide the sheep from the goats, and know whom he was defending and whom attacking. Yet for this wise and necessary action he was called in question in Congress and accused of violating civil rights and the resolves of Congress. Nothing was actually done about it, but such an incident shows from a single point the infinite tact and resolution required in waging war under a government whose members were unable to comprehend what was meant, and who could not see that until they had beaten England it was hardly worth while to worry about civil rights, which in case of defeat would speedily cease to exist altogether.

Another fertile source of trouble arose from questions of rank. Members of Congress, in making promotions and appointments, were more apt to consider local claims than military merit, and they also allowed their own personal prejudices to affect their action in this respect far too much. Thence arose endless heart-burnings and jealousies, followed by resignations and the loss of valuable officers. Congress, having made the appointments, would go cheerfully about its business, while the swarm of grievances thus let loose would come buzzing about the devoted head of the commander-in-chief. He could not get away, but was compelled to quiet rivalries, allay irritated feelings, and ride the storm as best he might. It was all done, however, in one way or another: by personal appeals, and by letters full of dignity, patriotism, and patience, which are very impressive and full of meaning for students of character, even in this day and generation.

Then again, not content with snarling up our native appointments, Congress complicated matters still more dangerously by its treatment of foreigners. The members of Congress were colonists, and the fact that they had shaken off the yoke of the mother country did not in the least alter their colonial and perfectly natural habit of regarding with enormous respect Englishmen and Frenchmen, and indeed anybody who had had the good fortune to be born in Europe. The result was that they distributed commissions and gave inordinate rank to the many volunteers who came over the ocean, actuated by various motives, but all filled with a profound sense of their own merits. It is only fair to Congress to say that the American agents abroad were even more to blame in this respect. Silas Deane especially scattered promises of commissions with a lavish hand, and Congress refused to fulfil many of the promises thus made in its name. Nevertheless, Congress was far too lax, and followed too closely the example of its agents. Some of these foreigners were disinterested men and excellent soldiers, who proved of great value to the American cause. Many others were mere military adventurers, capable of being turned to good account, perhaps, but by no means entitled to what they claimed and in most instances received.

The ill-considered action of Congress and of our agents abroad in this respect was a source of constantly recurring troubles of a very serious nature. Native officers, who had borne the burden and heat of the day, justly resented being superseded by some stranger, unable to speak the language, who had landed in the states but a few days before. As a result, resignations were threatened which, if carried out, would affect the character of the army very deeply. Then again, the foreigners themselves, inflated by the eagerness of our agents and by their reception at the hands of Congress, would find on joining the army that they could get no commands, chiefly because there were none to give. They would then become dissatisfied with their rank and employment, and bitter complaints and recriminations would ensue. All these difficulties, of course, fell most heavily upon the commander-in-chief, who was heartily disgusted with the whole business. Washington believed from the beginning, and said over and over again in various and ever stronger terms, that this was an American war and must be fought by Americans. In no other way, and by no other persons, did he consider that it could be carried to any success worth having. He saw of course the importance of a French alliance, and deeply desired it, for it was a leading element in the solution of the political and military situation; but alliance with a foreign power was one thing, and sporadic military volunteers were another. Washington had no narrow prejudices against foreigners, for he was a man of broad and liberal mind, and no one was more universally beloved and respected by the foreign officers than he; but he was intensely American in his feelings, and he would not admit for an instant that the American war for independence could be righteously fought or honestly won by others than Americans. He was well aware that foreign volunteers had a value and use of which he largely and gratefully availed himself; but he was exasperated and alarmed by the indiscriminate and lavish way in which our agents abroad and Congress gave rank and office to them. "Hungry adventurers," he called them in one letter, when driven beyond endurance by the endless annoyances thus forced upon him; and so he pushed their pretensions aside, and managed, on the whole, to keep them in their proper place. The operation was delicate, difficult, and unpleasant, for it seemed to savor of ingratitude. But Washington was never shaken for an instant in his policy, and while he checked the danger, he showed in many instances, like Lafayette and Steuben, that he could appreciate and use all that was really valuable in the foreign contingent.

The service rendered by Washington in this matter has never been justly understood or appreciated. If he had not taken this position, and held it with an absolute firmness which bordered on harshness, we should have found ourselves in a short time with an army of American soldiers officered by foreigners, many of them mere mercenaries, "hungry adventurers," from France, Poland or Hungary, from Germany, Ireland or England. The result of such a combination would have been disorganization and defeat. That members of Congress and some of our representatives in Europe did not see the danger, and that they were impressed by the foreign officers who came among them, was perfectly natural. Men are the creatures of the time in which they live, and take their color from the conditions which surround them, as the chameleon does from the grass or leaves in which it hides. The rulers and lawmakers of 1776 could not cast off their provincial awe of the natives of England and Europe as they cast off their political allegiance to the British king. The only wonder is that there should have been even one man so great in mind and character that he could rise at a single bound from the level of a provincial planter to the heights of a great national leader. He proved himself such in all ways, but in none more surely than in his ability to consider all men simply as men, and, with a judgment that nothing could confuse, to ward off from his cause and country the dangers inherent in colonial habits of thought and action, so menacing to a people struggling for independence. We can see this strong, high spirit of nationality running through Washington's whole career, but it never did better service than when it stood between the American army and lavish favor to foreign volunteers.

Among other disagreeable and necessary truths, Washington had told Congress that Philadelphia was in danger, that Howe probably meant to occupy it, and that it would be nearly impossible to prevent his doing so. This warning being given and unheeded, he continued to watch his antagonist, doing so with increased vigilance, as signs of activity began to appear in New York. Toward the end of May he broke up his cantonments, having now about seven thousand men, and took a strong position within ten miles of Brunswick. Here he waited, keeping an anxious eye on the Hudson in case he should be mistaken in his expectations, and should find that the enemy really intended to go north to meet Burgoyne instead of south to capture Philadelphia.

Washington's doubts were soon to be resolved and his expectations fulfilled. May 31st, a fleet of a hundred sail left New York, and couriers were at once sent southward to warn the States of the possibility of a speedy invasion. About the same time transports arrived with more German mercenaries, and Howe, thus reinforced, entered the Jerseys. Washington determined to decline battle, and if the enemy pushed on and crossed the Delaware, to hang heavily on their rear, while the militia from the south were drawn up to Philadelphia. He adopted this course because he felt confident that Howe would never cross the Delaware and leave the main army of the Americans behind him. His theory proved correct. The British advanced and retreated, burned houses and villages and made feints, but all in vain. Washington baffled them at every point, and finally Sir William evacuated the Jerseys entirely and withdrew to New York and Staten Island, where active preparations for some expedition were at once begun. Again came anxious watching, with the old fear that Howe meant to go northward and join the now advancing Burgoyne. The fear was groundless. On July 23d the British fleet set sail from New York, carrying between fifteen and eighteen thousand men. Not deceived by the efforts to make him think that they aimed at Boston, but still fearing that the sailing might be only a ruse and the Hudson the real object after all, Washington moved cautiously to the Delaware, holding himself ready to strike in either direction. On the 31st he heard that the enemy were at the Capes. This seemed decisive; so he sent in all directions for reinforcements, moved the main army rapidly to Germantown, and prepared to defend Philadelphia. The next news was that the fleet had put to sea again, and again messengers went north to warn Putnam to prepare for the defence of the Hudson. Washington himself was about to re-cross the Delaware, when tidings arrived that the fleet had once more appeared at the Capes, and after a few more days of doubt the ships came up the Chesapeake and anchored.

Washington thought the "route a strange one," but he knew now that he was right in his belief that Howe aimed at Philadelphia. He therefore gathered his forces and marched south to meet the enemy, passing through the city in order to impress the disaffected and the timid with the show of force. It was a motley array that followed him. There was nothing uniform about the troops except their burnished arms and the sprigs of evergreen in their hats. Nevertheless Lafayette, who had just come among them, thought that they looked like good soldiers, and the Tories woke up sharply to the fact that there was a large body of men known as the American army, and that they had a certain obvious fighting capacity visible in their appearance. Neither friends nor enemies knew, however, as they stood on the Philadelphia sidewalks and watched the troops go past, that the mere fact of that army's existence was the greatest victory of skill and endurance which the war could show, and that the question of success lay in its continuance.

Leaving Philadelphia, Washington pushed on to the junction of the Brandywine and Christiana Creek, and posted his men along the heights. August 25th, Howe landed at the Head of Elk, and Washington threw out light parties to drive in cattle, carry off supplies, and annoy the enemy. This was done, on the whole, satisfactorily, and after some successful skirmishing on the part of the Americans, the two armies on the 5th of September found themselves within eight or ten miles of each other. Washington now determined to risk a battle in the field, despite his inferiority in every way. He accordingly issued a stirring proclamation to the soldiers, and then fell back behind the Brandywine, to a strong position, and prepared to contest the passage of the river.

Early on September 11th, the British advanced to Chad's Ford, where Washington was posted with the main body, and after some skirmishing began to cannonade at long range. Meantime Cornwallis, with the main body, made a long détour of seventeen miles, and came upon the right flank and rear of the Americans. Sullivan, who was on the right, had failed to guard the fords above, and through lack of information was practically surprised. Washington, on rumors that the enemy were marching toward his right, with the instinct of a great soldier was about to cross the river in his front and crush the enemy there, but he also was misled and kept back by false reports. When the truth was known, it was too late. The right wing had been beaten and flung back, the enemy were nearly in the rear, and were now advancing in earnest in front. All that man could do was done. Troops were pushed forward and a gallant stand was made at various points; but the critical moment had come and gone, and there was nothing for it but a hasty retreat, which came near degenerating into a rout.

The causes of this complete defeat, for such it was, are easily seen. Washington had planned his battle and chosen his position well. If he had not been deceived by the first reports, he even then would have fallen upon and overwhelmed the British centre before they could have reached his right wing. But the Americans, to begin with, were outnumbered. They had only eleven thousand effective men, while the British brought fifteen of their eighteen thousand into action. Then the Americans suffered, as they constantly did, from misinformation, and from an absence of system in learning the enemy's movements. Washington's attack was fatally checked in this way, and Sullivan was surprised from the same causes, as well as from his own culpable ignorance of the country beyond him, which was the reason of his failure to guard the upper fords. The Americans lost, also, by the unsteadiness of new troops when the unexpected happens, and when the panic-bearing notion that they are surprised and likely to be surrounded comes upon them with a sudden shock.

This defeat was complete and severe, and it was followed in a few days by that of Wayne, who narrowly escaped utter ruin. Yet through all this disaster we can see the advance which had been made since the equally unfortunate and very similar battle on Long Island. Then, the troops seemed to lose heart and courage, the army was held together with difficulty, and could do nothing but retreat. Now, in the few days which Howe, as usual, gave up with such fatal effect to himself, Washington rallied his army, and finding them in excellent spirits marched down the Lancaster road to fight again. On the eve of battle a heavy storm came on, which so injured the arms and munitions that with bitter disappointment he was obliged to withdraw, but nevertheless it is plain how much this forward movement meant. At the moment, however, it looked badly enough, especially after the defeat of Wayne, for Howe pressed forward, took possession of Philadelphia, and encamped the main body of his army at Germantown.

Meantime Washington, who had not in the least given up his idea of fighting again, recruited his army, and having a little more than eight thousand men, determined to try another stroke at the British, while they were weakened by detachments. On the night of October 3d he started, and reached Germantown at daybreak on the 4th. At first the Americans swept everything before them, and flung the British back in rout and confusion. Then matters began to go wrong, as is always likely to happen when, as in this case, widely separated and yet accurately concerted action is essential to success. Some of the British threw themselves into a stone house, and instead of leaving them there under guard, the whole army stopped to besiege, and a precious half hour was lost. Then Greene and Stephen were late in coming up, having made a circuit, and although when they arrived all seemed to go well, the Americans were seized with an inexplicable panic, and fell back, as Wayne truly said, in the very moment of victory. One of those unlucky accidents, utterly unavoidable, but always dangerous to extensive combinations, had a principal effect on the result. The morning was very misty, and the fog, soon thickened by the smoke, caused confusion, random firing, and, worst of all, that uncertainty of feeling and action which something or nothing converted into a panic. Nevertheless, the Americans rallied quickly this time, and a good retreat was made, under the lead of Greene, until safety was reached. The action, while it lasted, had been very sharp, and the losses on both sides were severe, the Americans suffering most.

Washington, as usual when matters went ill, exposed himself recklessly, to the great alarm of his generals, but all in vain. He was deeply disappointed, and expressed himself so at first, for he saw that the men had unaccountably given way when they were on the edge of victory. The underlying cause was of course, as at Long Island and Brandywine, the unsteadiness of raw troops, and Washington felt rightly, after the first sting had passed, that he had really achieved a great deal. Congress applauded the attempt, and when the smoke of the battle had cleared away, men generally perceived that its having been fought at all was in reality the important fact. It made also a profound impression upon the French cabinet. Eagerly watching the course of events, they saw the significance of the fact that an army raised within a year could fight a battle in the open field, endure a severe defeat, and then take the offensive and make a bold and well-planned attack, which narrowly missed being overwhelmingly successful. To the observant and trained eyes of Europe, the defeat at Germantown made it evident that there was fighting material among these untrained colonists, capable of becoming formidable; and that there was besides a powerful will and directing mind, capable on its part of bringing this same material into the required shape and condition. To dispassionate onlookers, England's grasp on her colonies appeared to be slipping away very rapidly. Washington himself saw the meaning of it all plainly enough, for it was but the development of his theory of carrying on the war.

There is no indication, however, that England detected, in all that had gone on since her army landed at the Head of Elk, anything more than a couple of natural defeats for the rebels. General Howe was sufficiently impressed to draw in his troops, and keep very closely shut up in Philadelphia, but his country was not moved at all. The fact that it had taken forty-seven days to get their army from the Elk River to Philadelphia, and that in that time they had fought two successful battles and yet had left the American army still active and menacing, had no effect upon the British mind. The English were thoroughly satisfied that the colonists were cowards and were sure to be defeated, no matter what the actual facts might be. They regarded Washington as an upstart militia colonel, and they utterly failed to comprehend that they had to do with a great soldier, who was able to organize and lead an army, overcome incredible difficulties, beat and outgeneral them, bear defeat, and then fight again. They were unable to realize that the mere fact that such a man could be produced and such an army maintained meant the inevitable loss of colonies three thousand miles away. Men there were in England, undoubtedly, like Burke and Fox, who felt and understood the significance of these things, but the mass of the people, as well as the aristocracy, the king, and the cabinet, would have none of them. Rude contempt for other people is a warming and satisfying feeling, no doubt, and the English have had unquestionably great satisfaction from its free indulgence. No one should grudge it to them, least of all Americans. It is a comfort for which they have paid, so far as this country is concerned, by the loss of their North American colonies, and by a few other settlements with the United States at other and later times.

But although Washington and his army failed to impress England, events had happened in the north, during this same summer, which were so sharp-pointed that they not only impressed the English people keenly and unpleasantly, but they actually penetrated the dull comprehension of George III. and his cabinet. "Why," asked an English lady of an American naval officer, in the year of grace 1887—"why is your ship named the Saratoga?" "Because," was the reply, "at Saratoga an English general and an English army of more than five thousand men surrendered to an American army and laid down their arms." Although apparently neglected now in the general scheme of British education, Saratoga was a memorable event in the summer of 1777, and the part taken by Washington in bringing about the great result has never, it would seem, been properly set forth. There is no need to trace here the history of that campaign, but it is necessary to show how much was done by the commander-in-chief, five hundred miles away, to win the final victory.

In the winter of 1776–77 reports came that a general and an army were to be sent to Canada to invade the colonies from the north by way of Lake Champlain. The news does not seem to have made a very deep impression generally, nor to have been regarded as anything beyond the ordinary course of military events. But there was one man, fortunately, who in an instant perceived the full significance of this movement. Washington saw that the English had at last found an idea, or, at least, a general possessed of one. So long as the British confined themselves to fighting one or two battles, and then, taking possession of a single town, were content to sit down and pass their winter in good quarters, leaving the colonists in undisturbed control of all the rest of the country, there was nothing to be feared. The result of such campaigning as this could not be doubtful for a moment to any clear-sighted man. But when a plan was on foot, which, if successful, meant the control of the lakes and the Hudson, and of a line of communication from the north to the great colonial seaport, the case was very different. Such a campaign as this would cause the complete severance of New England, the chief source for men and supplies, from the rest of the colonies. It promised the mastery, not of a town, but of half a dozen States, and this to the American cause probably would be ruin.

So strongly and clearly did Washington feel all this that his counter-plan was at once ready, and before people had fairly grasped the idea that there was to be a northern invasion, he was sending, early in March, urgent letters to New England to rouse up the militia and have them in readiness to march at a moment's notice. To Schuyler, in command of the northern department, he began now to write constantly, and to unfold the methods which must be pursued in order to compass the defeat of the invaders. His object was to delay the army of Burgoyne by every possible device, while steadily avoiding a pitched battle. Then the militia and hardy farmers of New England and New York were to be rallied, and were to fall upon the flank and rear of the British, harass them constantly, cut off their outlying parties, and finally hem them in and destroy them. If the army and people of the North could only be left undisturbed, it is evident from his letters that Washington felt no doubt as to the result in that quarter.

But the North included only half the conditions essential to success. The grave danger feared by Washington was that Howe would understand the situation, and seeing his opportunity, would throw everything else aside, and marching northward with twenty thousand men, would make himself master of the Hudson, effect a junction with Burgoyne at Albany, and so cut the colonies in twain. From all he could learn, and from his knowledge of his opponent's character, Washington felt satisfied that Howe intended to capture Philadelphia, advancing, probably, through the Jerseys. Yet, despite his well-reasoned judgment on this point, it seemed so incredible that any soldier could fail to see that decisive victory lay in the north, and in a junction with Burgoyne, that

Washington could not really and fully believe in such fatuity until he knew that Howe was actually landing at the Head of Elk. This is the reason for the anxiety displayed in the correspondence of that summer, for the changing and shifting movements, and for the obvious hesitation of opinion, so unusual with Washington at any time. Be it remembered, moreover, that it was an awful doubt which went to bed and got up and walked with him through all those long nights and days. If Howe, the dull and lethargic, should awake from his dream of conquering America by taking now and again an isolated town, and should break for the north with twenty thousand men, the fortunes of the young republic would come to their severest test.

In that event, Washington knew well enough what he meant to do. He would march his main army to the Hudson, unite with the strong body of troops which he kept there constantly, contest every inch of the country and the river with Howe, and keep him at all hazards from getting to Albany. But he also knew well that if this were done the odds would be fearfully against him, for Howe would then not only outnumber him very greatly, but there would be ample time for the British to act, and but a short distance to be covered. We can imagine, therefore, his profound sense of relief when he found that Howe and his army were really south of Philadelphia, after a waste of many precious weeks. He could now devote himself singlehearted to the defence of the city, for distance and time were at last on his side, and all that remained was to fight Howe so hard and steadily that neither in victory nor defeat would he remember Burgoyne. Pitt said that he would conquer Canada on the plains of Germany, and Burgoyne was compelled to surrender in large measure by the campaign of Washington in New Jersey and Pennsylvania.

If we study carefully Washington's correspondence during that eventful summer, grouping together that relating to the northern campaign, and comparing it with that which dealt with the affairs of his own army, all that has just been said comes out with entire clearness, and it is astonishing to see how exactly events justified his foresight. If he could only hold Howe in the south, he was quite willing to trust Burgoyne to the rising of the people and to the northern wilderness. Every effort he made was in this direction, beginning, as has been said, by his appeals to the New England governors in March. Schuyler, on his part, was thoroughly imbued with Washington's other leading idea, that the one way to victory was by retarding the enemy. At the outset everything went utterly and disastrously wrong. Washington counted on an obstinate struggle, and a long delay at Ticonderoga, for he had not been on the ground, and could not imagine that our officers would fortify everything but the one commanding point.

The loss of the forts appalled the country and disappointed Washington, but did not shake his nerve for an instant. He wrote to Schuyler: "This stroke is severe indeed, and has distressed us much. But notwithstanding things at present have a dark and gloomy aspect, I hope a spirited opposition will check the progress of General Burgoyne's army, and that the confidence derived from his success will hurry him into measures that will, in their consequences, be favorable to us. We should never despair; our situation has before been unpromising, and has changed for the better; so I trust it will again. If new difficulties arise we must only put forth new exertions, and proportion our efforts to the exigency of the times." Even after this seemingly crushing defeat he still felt sure of Burgoyne, so long as he was unsupported. Suiting the action to the word, he again bent every nerve to rouse New England and get out her militia. When he was satisfied that Howe was landing below Philadelphia, the first thing he did was to send forth the same cry in the same quarter, to bring out more men against Burgoyne. He showed, too, the utmost generosity toward the northern army, sending thither all the troops he could possibly spare, and even parting with his favorite corps of Morgan's riflemen. Despite his liberality, the commanders in the north were unreasonable in their demands, and when they asked too much, Washington flatly declined to send more men, for he would not weaken himself unduly, and he knew what they did not see, that the fate of the northern invasion turned largely on his own ability to cope with Howe.

The blame for the loss of the forts fell of course upon Schuyler, who was none too popular in Congress, and who with St. Clair was accordingly made a scape-goat. Congress voted that Washington should appoint a new commander, and the New England delegates visited him to urge the selection of Gates. This task Washington refused to perform, alleging as a reason that the northern department had always been considered a separate command, and that he had never done more than advise. These reasons do not look very weighty or very strong, and it is not quite clear what the underlying motive was. Washington never shrank from responsibility, and he knew very well that he could pick out the best man more unerringly than Congress. But he also saw that Congress favored Gates, whom he would not have chosen, and he therefore probably felt that it was more important to have some one whom New England believed in and approved than a better soldier who would have been unwelcome to her representatives. It is certain that he would not have acted thus, had he thought that generalship was an important element in the problem; but he relied on a popular uprising, and not on the commander, to defeat Burgoyne. He may have thought, too, that it was a mistake to relieve Schuyler, who was working in the directions which he had pointed out, and who, if not a great soldier, was a brave, high-minded, and sensible man, devoted to his chief and to the country. It was Schuyler indeed who, by his persistent labor in breaking down bridges, tearing up roads, and felling trees, while he gathered men industriously in all directions, did more than any one else at that moment to prepare the way for an ultimate victory.

Whatever his feelings may have been in regard to the command of the northern department, Washington made no change in his own course after Gates had been appointed. He knew that Gates was at least harmless, and not likely to block the natural course of events. He therefore felt free to press his own policy without cessation, and without apprehension. He took care that Lincoln and Arnold should be there to look after the New England militia, and he wrote to Governor Clinton, in whose energy and courage he had great confidence, to rouse up the men of New York. He suggested the points of attack, and at every moment advised and counselled and watched, holding all the while a firm grip on Howe. Slowly and surely the net, thus painfully set, tightened round Burgoyne.

The New Englanders whipped one division at Bennington, and the New Yorkers shattered another at Oriskany and Fort Schuyler. The country people turned out in defence of their invaded homes and poured into the American camp. Burgoyne struggled and advanced, fought and retreated. Gates, stupid, lethargic, and good-natured, did nothing, but there was no need of generalship; and Arnold was there, turbulent and quarrelsome, but full of daring; and Morgan, too, equally ready; and they and others did all the necessary fighting.

Poor Burgoyne, a brave gentleman, if not a great general, had the misfortune to be a clever man in the service of a stupid administration, and he met the fate usually meted out under such circumstances to men of ideas. Howe went off to the conquest of Philadelphia, Clinton made a brief burning and plundering raid up the river, and the northern invasion, which really had meaning, was left to its fate. It was a hard fate, but there was no escape. Outnumbered, beaten, and caught, Burgoyne surrendered. If there had been a fighting-man at the head of the American army, the British would have surrendered as prisoners of war, and not on conditions. Schuyler, we may be sure, whatever his failings, would never have let them off so easily. But it was sufficient as it was. The wilderness, and the militia of New York and New England swarming to the defence of their homes, had done the work. It all fell out just as Washington had foreseen and planned, and England, despising her enemy and their commander, saw one of her armies surrender, and might have known, if she had had the wit, that the colonies were now lost forever. The Revolution had been saved at Trenton; it was established at Saratoga. In the one case it was the direct, in the other the indirect, work of Washington.

Poor Gates, with his dull brain turning under the impression that this crowning mercy had been his own doing, lost his head, forgot that there was a commander-in-chief, and sending his news to Congress, left Washington to find out from chance rumors, and a tardy letter from Putnam, that Burgoyne had actually surrendered. This gross slight, however, had deeper roots than the mere exultation of victory acting on a heavy and common mind. It represented a hostile feeling which had been slowly increasing for some time, which had been carefully nurtured by those interested in its growth, and which blossomed rapidly in the heated air of military triumph. From the outset it had been Washington's business to fight the enemy, manage the army, deal with Congress, and consider in all its bearings the political situation at home and abroad; but he was now called upon to meet a trouble outside the line of duty, and to face attacks from within, which, ideally speaking, ought never to have existed, but which, in view of our very fallible humanity, were certain to come sooner or later. Much domestic malice Washington was destined to encounter in the later years of political strife, but this was the only instance in his military career where enmity came to overt action and open speech. The first and the last of its kind, this assault upon him has much interest, for a strong light is thrown upon his character by studying him, thus beset, and by seeing just how he passed through this most trying and disagreeable of ordeals.

The germ of the difficulties was to be found where we should expect it, in the differences between the men of speech and the man of action, between the lawmakers and the soldier. Washington had been obliged to tell Congress a great many plain and unpleasant truths. It was part of his duty, and he did it accordingly. He was always dignified, calm, and courteous, but he had an alarmingly direct way with him, especially when he was annoyed. He was simple almost to bluntness, but now and then would use a grave irony which must have made listening ears tingle. Congress was patriotic and well-intentioned, and on the whole stood bravely by its general, but it was unversed in war, very impatient, and at times wildly impracticable. Here is a letter which depicts the situation, and the relation between the general and his rulers, with great clearness. March 14, 1777, Washington wrote to the President: "Could I accomplish the important objects so eagerly wished by Congress,—'confining the enemy within their present quarters, preventing their getting supplies from the country, and totally subduing them before they are reinforced,' —I should be happy indeed. But what prospect or hope can there be of my effecting so desirable a work at this time?"

We can imagine how exasperating such requests and suggestions must have been. It was very much as if Congress had said: "Good General, bring in the Atlantic tides and drown the enemy; or pluck the moon from the sky and give it to us, as a mark of your loyalty." Such requests are not soothing to any man struggling his best with great anxieties, and with a host of petty cares. Washington, nevertheless, kept his temper, and replied only by setting down a few hard facts which answered the demands of Congress in a final manner, and with all the sting of truth. Thus a little irritation had been generated in Congress against the general, and there were some members who developed a good deal of pronounced hostility. Sam Adams, a born agitator and a trained politician, unequalled almost in our history as an organizer and manager of men, able, narrow, coldly fierce, the man of the town meeting and the caucus, had no possibility of intellectual sympathy with the silent, patient, hardgripping soldier, hemmed with difficulties, but ever moving straight forward to his object, with occasional wild gusts of reckless fighting passion. John Adams, too, brilliant of speech and pen, ardent, patriotic, and highminded, was, in his way, out of touch with Washington. Although he moved Washington's appointment, he began almost immediately to find fault with him, an exercise to which he was extremely prone. Inasmuch as he could see how things ought to be done, he could not understand why they were not done in that way at once, for he had a fine forgetfulness of other people's difficulties, as is the case with most of us. The New England representatives generally took their cue from these two, especially James Lovell, who carried his ideas into action, and obtained a little niche in the temple of fame by making himself disagreeably conspicuous in the intrigue against the commander-in-chief, when it finally developed.

There were others, too, outside New England who were discontented, and among them Richard Henry Lee, from the General's own State. He was evidently critical and somewhat unfriendly at this time, although the reasons for his being so are not now very distinct. Then there was Mr. Clark of New Jersey, an excellent man, who thought the General was invading popular rights; and to him others might be added who vaguely felt that things ought to be better than they were. This party, adverse to Washington, obtained the appointment of Gates to the northern department, under whom the army won a great victory, and they were correspondingly happy. John Adams wrote his wife that one cause of thanksgiving was that the tide had not been turned by the commander-in-chief and southern troops, for the adulation would have been intolerable; and that a man may be wise and virtuous and not a deity.

Here, so far as the leading and influential men were concerned, the matter would have dropped, probably; but there were lesser men like Lovell who were much encouraged by the surrender of Burgoyne, and who thought that they now might supplant Washington with Gates. Before long, too, they found in the army itself some active and not over-scrupulous allies. The most conspicuous figure among the military malcontents was Gates himself, who, although sluggish in all things, still had a keen eye for his own advancement. He showed plainly how much his head had been turned by the victory at Saratoga when he failed to inform Washington of the fact, and when he afterward delayed sending back troops until he was driven to it by the determined energy of Hamilton, who was sent to bring him to reason. Next in importance to Gates was Thomas Mifflin, an ardent patriot, but a rather light-headed person, who espoused the opposition to Washington for causes now somewhat misty, but among which personal vanity played no inconsiderable part. About these two leaders gathered a certain number of inferior officers of no great moment then or since.

The active and moving spirit in the party, however, was one Conway, an Irish adventurer, who made himself so prominent that the whole affair passed into history bearing his name, and the "Conway cabal" has obtained an enduring notoriety which its hero never acquired by any public services. Conway was one of the foreign officers who had gained the favor of Congress and held the rank of brigadier-general, but this by no means filled the measure of his pretensions, and when De Kalb was made a major-general Conway immediately started forward with claims to the same rank. He received strong support from the factious opposition, and there was so much stir that Washington sharply interfered, for to his general objection to these lavish gifts of excessive rank was added an especial distrust in this particular case. In his calm way he had evidently observed Conway, and with his unerring judgment of men had found him wanting. "I may add," he wrote to Lee, "and I think with truth, that it will give a fatal blow to the existence of the army. Upon so interesting a subject I must speak plainly. General Conway's merit then as an officer, and his importance in this army, exist more in his own imagination than in reality." This plain talk soon reached Conway, drove him at once into furious opposition, and caused him to impart to the faction a cohesion and vigor which they had before lacked. Circumstances favored them. The victory at Saratoga gave them something tangible to go upon, and the first move was made when Gates failed to inform Washington of the surrender, and then held back the troops sent for so urgently by the commander-in-chief, who had sacrificed so much from his own army to secure that of the north.

At this very moment, indeed, when Washington was calling for troops, he was struggling with the utmost tenacity to hold control of the Delaware. He made every arrangement possible to maintain the forts, and the first assaults upon them were repulsed with great slaughter, the British in the attack on Fort Mercer losing Count Donop, the leader, and four hundred men. Then came a breathing space, and then the attacks were renewed, supported by vessels, and both forts were abandoned after the works had been levelled to the ground by the enemy's fire. Meanwhile Hamilton, sent to the north, had done his work; Gates had been stirred, and Putnam, well-meaning but stubborn, had been sharply brought to his bearings. Reinforcements had come, and Washington meditated an attack on Philadelphia. There was a good deal of clamor for something brilliant and decisive, for both the army and the public were a little dizzy from the effects of Saratoga, and with sublime blindness to different conditions, could not see why the same performance should not be repeated to order everywhere else. To oppose this wish was trying, doubly trying to a man eager to fight, and with his full share of the very human desire to be as successful as his neighbor. It required great nerve to say No; but Washington did not lack that quality, and as general and statesman he reconnoitred the enemy's works, weighed the chances, said No decisively, and took up an almost impregnable position at White Marsh.

Thereupon Howe announced that he would drive Washington beyond the mountains, and on December 4th he approached the American lines with this highly proper purpose. There was some skirmishing along the foot of the hills of an unimportant character, and on the third day Washington, in high spirits, thought an attack would be made, and rode among the soldiers directing and encouraging them. Nothing came of it, however, but more skirmishing, and the next day Howe marched back to Philadelphia. He had offered battle in all ways, he had invited action; but again, with the same pressure both from his own spirit and from public opinion, Washington had said No. On his own ground he was more than ready to fight Howe, but despite the terrible temptation he would fight on no other. Not the least brilliant exploit of Wellington was the retreat to the shrewdly prepared lines of Torres Vedras, and one of the most difficult successes of Washington was his double refusal to fight as the year 1777 drew to a close.

Like most right and wise things, Washington's action looks now, a century later, so plainly sensible that it is hard to imagine how any one could have questioned it; and one cannot, without a great effort, realize the awful strain upon will and temper involved in thus refusing battle. If the proposed attack on Philadelphia had failed, or if our army had come down from the hills and been beaten in the fields below, no American army would have remained. The army of the north, of which men were talking so proudly, had done its work and dispersed. The fate of the Revolution rested where it had been from the beginning, with Washington and his soldiers. Drive them beyond the mountains and there was no other army to fall back upon. On their existence everything hinged, and when Howe got back to Philadelphia, there they were still existent, still coherent, hovering on his flank, cooping him up in his lines, and leaving him master of little more than the ground his men encamped upon, and the streets his sentinels patrolled. When Franklin was told in Paris that Howe had taken Philadelphia, his reply was, "Philadelphia has taken Howe."

But, with the exception of Franklin, contemporary opinion in the month of December, 1777, was very different from that of to-day, and the cabal had been at work ever since the commander-in-chief had stepped between Conway and the exorbitant rank he coveted. Washington, indeed, was perfectly aware of what was going on. He was quiet and dignified, impassive and silent, but he knew when men, whether great or small, were plotting against him, and he watched them with the same keenness as he did Howe and the British.

In the midst of his struggle to hold the Delaware forts, and of his efforts to get back his troops from the north, a story came to him that arrested his attention. Wilkinson, of Gates's staff, had come to Congress with the news of the surrender. He had been fifteen days on the road and three days getting his papers in order, and when it was proposed to give him a sword, Dr. Witherspoon, canny Scot as he was, suggested that they had better "gie the lad a pair of spurs." This thrust and some delay seem to have nettled Wilkinson, who was swelling with importance, and although he was finally made a brigadier-general, he rode off to the north much ruffled. In later years Wilkinson was secretive enough; but in his hot youth he could not hold his tongue, and on his way back to Gates he talked. What he said was marked and carried to headquarters, and on November 9th Washington wrote to Conway:

> A letter which I received last night contained the following paragraph,—"In a letter from General Conway to General Gates he says, '*Heaven has determined to save your country, or a weak general and bad counsellors would have ruined it.*' I am, sir, your humble servant," etc.

This curt note fell upon Conway with stunning effect. It is said that he tried to apologize, and he certainly resigned. As for Gates, he fell to writing letters filled with expressions of wonder as to who had betrayed him, and writhed most pitiably under the exposure. Washington's replies are models of cold dignity, and the calm indifference with which he treated the whole matter, while holding Gates to the point with relentless grasp, is very interesting. The cabal was seriously shaken by this sudden blow. It must have dawned upon them dimly that they might have mistaken their man, and that the silent soldier was perhaps not so easy to dispose of by an intrigue as they had fancied. Nevertheless, they rallied, and taking advantage of the feeling in Congress created by Burgoyne's surrender, they set to work to get control of military matters. The board of war was enlarged to five, with Gates at its head and Mifflin a member, and, thus constituted, it proceeded to make Conway inspector-general, with the rank of major-general. This, after Conway's conduct, was a direct insult to Washington, and marks the highest point attained by his opponents.

In Congress, too, they became more active, and John Jay said that there was in that body a party bitterly hostile to Washington. We know little of the members of that faction now, for they never took the trouble to refer to the matter in after years, and did everything that silence could do to have it all forgotten. But the party existed none the less, and significant letters have come down to us, one of them written by Lovell, and two anonymous, addressed respectively to Patrick Henry and to Laurens, then president, which show a bitter and vindictive spirit, and breathe but one purpose. The same thought is constantly reiterated, that with a good general the northern army had won a great victory, and that the main army, if commanded in the same way, would do likewise. The plan was simple and coherent. The cabal wished to drive Washington out of power and replace him with Gates. With this purpose they wrote to Henry and Laurens; with this purpose they made Conway inspector-general.

When they turned from intrigue to action, however, they began to fail. One of their pet schemes was the conquest of Canada, and with this object Lafayette was sent to the lakes, only to find that no preparations had been made, because the originators of the idea were ignorant and inefficient. The expedition promptly collapsed and was abandoned, with much instruction in consequence to Congress and people. Under their control the commissariat also went hopelessly to pieces, and a committee of Congress proceeded to Valley Forge and found that in this direction, too, the new managers had grievously failed. Then the original Conway letter, uncovered so unceremoniously by Washington, kept returning to plague its author. Gates's correspondence went on all through the winter, and with every letter Gates floundered more and more, and Washington's replies grew more and more freezing and severe. Gates undertook to throw the blame on Wilkinson, who became loftily indignant and challenged him. The two made up their quarrel very soon in a ludicrous manner, but Wilkinson in the interval had an interview with Washington, which revealed an amount of duplicity and perfidy on the part of the cabal, so shocking to the former's sensitive nature, that he resigned his secretaryship of the board of war on account, as he frankly said, of the treachery and falsehood of Gates. Such a quarrel of course hurt the cabal, but it was still more weakened by Gates himself, whose only idea seemed to be to supersede Washington by slighting him, refusing troops, and declining to propose his health at dinner,—methods as unusual as they were feeble.

The cabal, in fact, was so weak in ability and character that the moment any responsibility fell upon its members it was certain to break down, but the absolutely fatal obstacle to its schemes was the man it aimed to overthrow. The idea evidently was that Washington could be driven to resign. They knew that they could not get either Congress or public opinion to support them in removing him, but they believed that a few well placed slights and insults would make him remove himself. It was just here that they made their mistake. Washington, as they were aware, was sensitive and high-spirited to the last degree, and he had no love for office, but he was not one of those weaklings who leave power and place in a pet because they are criticised and assailed. He was not ambitious in the ordinary personal sense, but he had a passion for success. Whether it was breaking a horse, or reclaiming land, or fighting Indians, or saving a state, whatever he set his hand to, that he carried through to the end. With him there never was any shadow of turning back. When, without any self-seeking, he was placed at the head of the Revolution, he made up his mind that he would carry it through everything to victory, if victory were possible. Death or a prison could stop him, but neither defeat nor neglect, and still less the forces of intrigue and cabal.

When he wrote to his brother announcing Burgoyne's surrender, he had nothing to say of the slight Gates put upon him, but merely added in a postscript, "I most devoutly congratulate my country and every well-wisher to the cause on this signal stroke of Providence." This was his tone to every one, both in private and public. His complaint of not being properly notified he made to Gates alone, and put it in the form of a rebuke. He knew of the movement against him from the beginning, but apparently the first person he confided in was Conway, when he sent him the brief note of November 9th. Even after the cabal was fully developed, he wrote about it only once or twice, when compelled to do so, and there is no evidence that he ever talked about it except, perhaps, to a few most intimate friends. In a letter to Patrick Henry he said that he was obliged to allow a false impression as to his strength to go abroad, and that he suffered in consequence; and he added, with a little touch of feeling, that while the yeomanry of New York and New England poured into the camp of Gates, outnumbering the enemy two to one, he could get no aid of that sort from Pennsylvania, and still marvels were demanded of him.

Thus he went on his way through the winter, silent except when obliged to answer some friend, and always ready to meet his enemies. When Conway complained to Congress of his reception at camp, Washington wrote the president that he was not given to dissimulation, and that he certainly had been cold in his manner. He wrote to Lafayette that slander had been busy, and that he had urged his officers to be cool and dispassionate as to Conway, adding, "I have no doubt that everything happens for the best, that we shall triumph over all our misfortunes, and in the end be happy; when, my dear Marquis, if you will give me your company in Virginia, we will laugh at our past difficulties and the folly of others." But though he wrote thus lightly to his friends, he followed Gates sternly enough, and kept that gentleman occupied as he drove him from point to point. Among other things he touched upon Conway's character with sharp irony, saying, "It is, however, greatly to be lamented that this adept in military science did not employ his abilities in the progress of the campaign, in pointing out those wise measures which were calculated to give us 'that degree of success we could reasonably expect.'"

Poor Gates did not find these letters pleasant reading, and one more curt note, on February 24th, finished the controversy. By that time the cabal was falling to pieces, and in a little while was dispersed. Wilkinson's resignation was accepted, Mifflin was put under Washington's orders, and Gates was sent to his command in the north. Conway resigned one day in a pet, and found his resignation accepted and his power gone with unpleasant suddenness. He then got into a quarrel with General Cadwalader on account of his attacks on the commander-in-chief. The quarrel ended in a duel. Conway was badly wounded, and thinking himself dying, wrote a contrite note of apology to Washington, then recovered, left the country, and disappeared from the ken of history. Thus domestic malice and the "bitter party" in Congress failed and perished. They had dashed themselves in vain against the strong man who held firmly both soldiers and people. "While the public are satisfied with my endeavors, I mean not to shrink from the cause." So Washington wrote to Gordon as the cabal was coming to an end, and in that spirit he crushed silently and thoroughly the faction that sought to thwart his purpose, and drive him from office by sneers, slights, and intrigues.

These attacks upon him came at the darkest moment of his military career. Defeated at Brandywine and Germantown, he had been forced from the forts after a desperate struggle, had seen Philadelphia and the river fall completely into the hands of the enemy, and, bitterest of all, he had been obliged to hold back from another assault on the British lines, and to content himself with baffling Howe when that gentleman came out and offered battle. Then the enemy withdrew to their comfortable quarters, and he was left to face again the harsh winter and the problem of existence. It was the same ever recurring effort to keep the American army, and thereby the American Revolution, alive. There was nothing in this task to stir the blood and rouse the heart. It was merely a question of grim tenacity of purpose and of the ability to comprehend its overwhelming importance. It was not a work that appealed to or inspired any one, and to carry it through to a successful issue rested with the commander-in-chief alone.

In the frost and snow he withdrew to Valley Forge, within easy striking distance of Philadelphia. He had literally nothing to rely upon but his own stern will and strong head. His soldiers, steadily dwindling in numbers, marked their road to Valley Forge by the blood from their naked feet.

They were destitute and in rags. When they reached their destination they had no shelter, and it was only by the energy and ingenuity of the General that they were led to build huts, and thus secure a measure of protection against the weather. There were literally no supplies, and the Board of War failed completely to remedy the evil. The army was in such straits that it was obliged to seize by force the commonest necessaries. This was a desperate expedient and shocked public opinion, which Washington, as a statesman, watched and cultivated as an essential element of success in his difficult business. He disliked to take extreme measures, but there was nothing else to be done when his men were starving, when nearly three thousand of them were unfit for duty because "barefoot and otherwise naked," and when a large part of the army were obliged to sit up all night by the fires for warmth's sake, having no blankets with which to cover themselves if they lay down. With nothing to eat, nothing to burn, nothing wherewith to clothe themselves, wasting away from exposure and disease, we can only wonder at the forbearance which stayed the hand of violent seizure so long. Yet, as Washington had foreseen, there was even then an outcry against him. Nevertheless, his action ultimately did more good than harm in the very matter of public opinion, for it opened men's eyes, and led to some tardy improvements and some increased effort.

Worse even than this criticism was the remonstrance of the legislature of Pennsylvania against the going into winter-quarters. They expected Washington to keep the open field, and even to attack the British, with his starving, ragged army, in all the severity of a northern winter. They had failed him at every point and in every promise, in men, clothing, and supplies. They were not content that he covered their State and kept the Revolution alive among the huts of Valley Forge. They wished the impossible. They asked for the moon, and then cried out because it was not given to them. It was a stupid, unkind thing to do, and Washington answered their complaints in a letter to the president of Congress. After setting forth the shortcomings of the Pennsylvanians in the very plainest of plain English, he said: "But what makes this matter still more extraordinary in my eye is that these very gentlemen should think a winter's campaign, and the covering of these States from the invasion of an enemy, so easy and practicable a business. I can assure those gentlemen, that it is a much easier and less distressing thing to draw remonstrances in a comfortable room, by a good fireside, than to occupy a cold, bleak hill, and sleep under frost and snow, without clothes or blankets. However, although they seem to have little feeling for the naked and distressed soldiers, I feel superabundantly for them, and from my soul I pity those miseries which it is neither in my power to relieve or prevent."

This was not a safe man for the gentlemen of Pennsylvania to cross too far, nor could they swerve him, with all his sense of public opinion, one jot from what he meant to do. In the stern rebuke, and in the deep pathos of these sentences, we catch a glimpse of the silent and self-controlled man breaking out for a moment as he thinks of his faithful and suffering men. Whatever happened, he would hold them together, for in this black time we detect the fear which haunted him, that the people at large might give way. He was determined on independence. He felt a keen hatred against England for her whole conduct toward America, and this hatred was sharpened by the efforts of the English to injure him personally by forged letters and other despicable contrivances. He was resolved that England should never prevail, and his language in regard to her has a fierceness of tone which is full of meaning. He was bent, also, on success, and if under the long strain the people should weaken or waver, he was determined to maintain the army at all hazards.

So, while he struggled against cold and hunger and destitution, while he contended with faction at home and lukewarmness in the administration of the war, even then, in the midst of these trials, he was devising a new system for the organization and permanence of his forces. Congress meddled with the matter of prisoners and with the promotion of officers, and he argued with and checked them, and still pressed on in his plans. He insisted that officers must have better provision, for they had begun to resign. "You must appeal to their interest as well as to their patriotism," he wrote, "and you must give them half-pay and full pay in proper measure." "You must follow the same policy with the men," he said; "you must have done with short enlistments. In a word, gentlemen, you must give me an army, a lasting, enduring, continental army, for therein lies independence."* It all comes out now, through the dust of details and annoyances, through the misery and suffering of that wretched winter, through the shrill cries of ignorance and hostility,—the great, clear, strong policy which meant to substitute an army for militia, and thereby secure victory and independence. It is the burden of all his letters to the governors of States, and to his officers everywhere. "I will hold the army together," he said, "but you on all sides must help me build it up."*

Thus with much strenuous labor and many fervent appeals he held his army together in some way, and slowly improved it. His system began to be put in force, his reiterated lessons were coming home to Congress, and his reforms and suggestions were in some measure adopted. Under the sound and trained guidance of Baron Steuben a drill and discipline were introduced, which soon showed marked results. Greene succeeded Mifflin as quartermaster-general, and brought order out of chaos. The Conway cabal went to pieces, and as spring opened Washington began to see light once more. To have held on through that winter was a great feat, but to have built up and improved the army at such a time was much more wonderful. It shows a greatness of character and a force of will rarer than military genius, and enables us to understand better, perhaps, than almost any of his victories, why it was that the success of the Revolution lay in the hands of one man.

After Howe's withdrawal from the Jerseys in the previous year, a contemporary wrote that Washington was left with the remnants of an army "to scuffle for liberty." The winter had passed, and he was prepared to scuffle again. On May 11th Sir Henry Clinton relieved Sir William Howe at Philadelphia, and the latter took his departure in a blaze of mock glory and resplendent millinery, known as the Mischianza, a fit close to a career of failure, which he was too dull to appreciate. The new commander was

---

*These two quotations are not literal, of course, but give the substance of many letters.

more active than his predecessor, but no cleverer, and no better fitted to cope with Washington. It was another characteristic choice on the part of the British ministry, who could never muster enough intellect to understand that the Americans would fight, and that they were led by a really great soldier. The coming of Clinton did not alter existing conditions.

Expecting a movement by the enemy, Washington sent Lafayette forward to watch Philadelphia. Clinton, fresh in office, determined to cut him off, and by a rapid movement nearly succeeded in so doing. Timely information, presence of mind, and quickness alone enabled the young Frenchman to escape, narrowly but completely. Meantime, a cause for delay, that curse of the British throughout the war, supervened. A peace commission, consisting of the Earl of Carlisle, William Eden, and Governor Johnstone, arrived. They were excellent men, but they came too late. Their propositions three years before would have been well enough, but as it was they were worse than nothing. Coolly received, they held a fruitless interview with a committee of Congress, tried to bribe and intrigue, found that their own army had been already ordered to evacuate Philadelphia without their knowledge, and finally gave up their task in angry despair, and returned to England to join in the chorus of fault-finding which was beginning to sound very loud in ministerial ears.

Meanwhile, Washington waited and watched, puzzled by the delay, and hoping only to harass Sir Henry with militia on the march to New York. But as the days slipped by, the Americans grew stronger, while Sir Henry weakened himself by sending five thousand men to the West Indies, and three thousand to Florida. When he finally started, he had with him less than ten thousand men, while the Americans had thirteen thousand, nearly all continental troops. Under these circumstances, Washington determined to bring on a battle. He was thwarted at the outset by his officers, as was wont to be the case. Lee had returned more whimsical than ever, and at the moment was strongly adverse to an attack, and was full of wise saws about building a bridge of gold for the flying enemy. The ascendancy which, as an English officer, he still retained enabled him to get a certain following, and the councils of war which were held compared unfavorably, as Hamilton put it, with the deliberations of midwives. Washington was harassed of course by all this, but he did not stay his purpose, and as soon as he knew that Clinton actually had marched, he broke camp at Valley Forge and started in pursuit. There were more councils of an old-womanish character, but finally Washington took the matter into his own hands, and ordered forth a strong detachment to attack the British rear-guard. They set out on the 25th, and as Lee, to whom the command belonged, did not care to go, Lafayette was put in charge. As soon as Lafayette had departed, however, Lee changed his mind, and insisted that all the detachments in front, amounting to six thousand men, formed a division so large that it was unjust not to give him the command. Washington, therefore, sent him forward next day with two additional brigades, and then Lee by seniority took command on the 27th of the entire advance.

In the evening of that day, Washington came up, reconnoitred the enemy, and saw that, although their position was a strong one, another day's unmolested march would make it still stronger. He therefore resolved to attack the next morning, and gave Lee then and there explicit orders to that effect. In the early dawn he despatched similar orders, but Lee apparently did nothing except move feebly forward, saying to Lafayette, "You don't know the British soldiers; we cannot stand against them." He made a weak attempt to cut off a covering party, marched and countermarched, ordered and countermanded, until Lafayette and Wayne, eager to fight, knew not what to do, and sent hot messages to Washington to come to them.

Thus hesitating and confused, Lee permitted Clinton to get his baggage and train to the front, and to mass all his best troops in the rear under Cornwallis, who then advanced against the American lines. Now there were no orders at all, and the troops did not know what to do, or where to go. They stood still, then began to fall back, and then to retreat. A very little more and there would have been a rout. As it was, Washington alone prevented disaster. His early reports from the front from Dickinson's outlying party, and from Lee himself, were all favorable. Then he heard the firing, and putting the main army in motion, he rode rapidly forward. First he encountered a straggler, who talked of defeat. He could not believe it, and the fellow was pushed aside and silenced. Then came another and another, all with songs of death. Finally, officers and regiments began to come. No one knew why they fled, or what had happened. As the ill tidings grew thicker, Washington spurred sharper and rode faster through the deep sand, and under the blazing mid-summer sun. At last he met Lee and the main body all in full retreat. He rode straight at Lee, savage with anger, not pleasant to look at, one may guess, and asked fiercely and with a deep oath, tradition says, what it all meant. Lee was no coward, and did not usually lack for words. He was, too, a hardened man of the world, and, in the phrase of that day, impudent to boot. But then and there he stammered and hesitated. The fierce question was repeated. Lee gathered himself and tried to excuse and palliate what had happened, but although the brief words that followed are variously reported to us across the century, we know that Washington rebuked him in such a way, and with such passion, that all was over between them. Lee had committed the one unpardonable sin in the eyes of his commander. He had failed to fight when the enemy was upon him. He had disobeyed orders and retreated. It was the end of him. He went to the rear, thence to a court-martial, thence to dismissal and to a solitary life. He was an intelligent, quick-witted, unstable man, much overrated because he was an English officer among a colonial people. He was ever treated magnanimously by Washington after the day of battle at Monmouth, but he then disappeared from the latter's life.

When Lee bowed before the storm and stepped aside, Washington was left to deal with the danger and confusion around him. Thus did he tell the story afterwards to his brother: "A retreat, however, was the fact, be the causes what they may; and the disorder arising from it would have proved fatal to the army, had not that bountiful Providence, which has never failed us in the hour of distress, enabled me to form a regiment or two (of those that were retreating) in the face of the enemy, and under their fire; by which means a stand was made long enough (the place through which the enemy were pressing being narrow) to form the troops, that were advancing, upon an advantageous piece of ground in the rear." We cannot add much to these simple and modest words, for they tell the whole story. Having put Lee aside, Washington rallied the broken troops, brought them into position, turned them back, and held the enemy in check. It was not an easy feat, but it was done, and when Lee's division again fell back in good order the main army was in position, and the action became general. The British were repulsed, and then Washington, taking the offensive, drove them back until he occupied the battlefield of the morning. Night came upon him still advancing. He halted his army, lay down under a tree, his soldiers lying on their arms about him, and planned a fresh attack, to be made at daylight. But when the dawn came it was seen that the British had crept off, and were far on their road. The heat prevented a rapid pursuit, and Clinton got into New York. Between there and Philadelphia he had lost two thousand men, Washington said, and modern authorities put it at about fifteen hundred, of whom nearly five hundred fell at Monmouth.

It is worth while to pause a moment and compare this battle with the rout of Long Island, the surprise at the Brandywine, and the fatal unsteadiness at Germantown. Here, too, a check was received at the out-set, owing to blundering which no one could have foreseen. The troops, confused and without orders, began to retreat, but without panic or disorder. The moment Washington appeared they rallied, returned to the field, showed perfect steadiness, and the victory was won. Monmouth has never been one of the famous battles of the Revolution, and yet there is no other which can compare with it as an illustration of Washington's ability as a soldier. It was not so much the way in which it was fought, although that was fine enough, but its importance lies in the evidence which it gives of the way in which Washington, after a series of defeats, during a winter of terrible suffering and privation, had yet developed his ragged volunteers into a well-disciplined and effective army. The battle was a victory, but the existence and the quality of the army that won it were a far greater triumph.

The dreary winter at Valley Forge had indeed borne fruit. With a slight numerical superiority Washington had fought the British in the open field, and fairly defeated them. "Clinton gained no advantage," said the great Frederic, "except to reach New York with the wreck of his army; America is probably lost for England." Another year had passed, and England had lost an army, and still held what she had before, the city of New York. Washington was in the field with a better army than ever, and an army flushed with a victory which had been achieved after difficulties and trials that no one now can rightly picture or describe. The American Revolution was advancing, held firm by the master-hand of its leader. Into it, during these days of struggle and of battle, a new element had come, and the next step is to see how Washington dealt with the fresh conditions upon which the great conflict had entered.

CHAPTER VIII

THE ALLIES

ON MAY 4TH, 1778, Congress ratified the treaties of commerce and alliance with France. On the 6th, Washington, waiting at Valley Forge for the British to start from Philadelphia, caused his army, drawn out on parade, to celebrate the great event with cheers and with salvos of artillery and musketry. The alliance deserved cheers and celebration, for it marked a long step onward in the Revolution. It showed that America had demonstrated to Europe that she could win independence, and it had been proved to the traditional enemy of England that the time had come when it would be profitable to help the revolted colonies. But the alliance brought troubles as well as blessings in its train. It induced a relaxation in popular energy, and carried with it new and difficult problems for the commander-in-chief. The successful management of allies, and of allied forces, had been one of the severest tests of the statesmanship of William III, and had constituted one of the principal glories of Marlborough. A similar problem now confronted the American general.

Washington was free from the diplomatic and political portion of the business, but the military and popular part fell wholly into his hands, and demanded the exercise of talents entirely different from those of either a general or an administrator. It has been not infrequently written more or less plainly, and it is constantly said, that Washington was great in character, but that in brains he was not far above the commonplace. It is even hinted sometimes that the father of his country was a dull man, a notion

161

which we shall have occasion to examine more fully further on. At this point let the criticism be remembered merely in connection with the fact that to coöperate with allies in military matters demands tact, quick perception, firmness, and patience. In a word, it is a task which calls for the finest and most highly trained intellectual powers, and of which the difficulty is enhanced a thousand-fold when the allies were, on the one side, an old, aristocratic, punctilious people, and on the other, colonists utterly devoid of tradition, etiquette, or fixed habits, and very much accustomed to go their own way and speak their own minds with careless freedom. With this problem Washington was obliged suddenly to deal, both in ill success and good success, as well as in many attempts which came to nothing. Let us see how he solved it at the very outset, when everything went most perversely wrong.

On July 14th he heard that D'Estaing's fleet was off the coast, and at once, without a trace of elation or excitement, he began to consider the possibility of intercepting the British fleet expected to arrive shortly from Cork. As soon as D'Estaing was within reach he sent two of his aides on board the flagship, and at once opened a correspondence with his ally. These letters of welcome, and those of suggestion which followed, are models, in their way, of what such letters ought always to be. They were perfectly adapted to satisfy the etiquette and the love of good manners of the French, and yet there was not a trace of anything like servility, or of an effusive gratitude which outran the favors granted. They combined stately courtesy with simple dignity, and are phrased with a sober grace which shows the thoroughly strong man, as capable to turn a sentence, if need be, as to rally retreating soldiers in the face of the enemy.

In this first meeting of the allies nothing happened fortunately. D'Estaing had had a long passage, and was too late to cut off Lord Howe at the Delaware. Then he turned to New York, and was too late there, and found further that he could not get his ships over the bar. Hence more delays, so that he was late again in getting to Newport, where he was to unite with Sullivan in driving the British from Rhode Island, as Washington had planned, in case of failure at New York, while the French were still hovering on the coast. When D'Estaing finally reached

Newport, there was still another delay of ten days, and then, just as he and Sullivan were preparing to attack, Lord Howe, with his squadron reinforced, appeared off the harbor. Promising to return, D'Estaing sailed out to give the enemy battle, and after much manœuvring both fleets were driven off by a severe storm, and D'Estaing came back only to tell Sullivan that he must go to Boston at once to refit. Then came the protest addressed to the Count and signed by all the American officers; then the departure of D'Estaing, and an indiscreet proclamation to the troops by Sullivan, reflecting on the conduct of the allies.

When D'Estaing had actually gone, and the Americans were obliged to retreat, there was much grumbling in all directions, and it looked as if the first result of the alliance was to be a very pretty quarrel. It was a bad and awkward business. Congress had the good sense to suppress the protest of the officers, and Washington, disappointed, but perhaps not wholly surprised, set himself to work to put matters right. It was no easy task to soothe the French, on the one hand, who were naturally aggrieved at the utterances of the American officers and at the popular feeling, and on the other to calm his own people, who were, not without reason, both disappointed and provoked. To Sullivan, fuming with wrath, he wrote: "Should the expedition fail through the abandonment of the French fleet, the officers concerned will be apt to complain loudly. But prudence dictates that we should put the best face upon the matter, and to the world attribute the removal to Boston to necessity. The reasons are too obvious to need explaining." And again, a few days later: "First impressions, you know, are generally longest remembered, and will serve to fix in a great degree our national character among the French. In our conduct towards them we should remember that they are a people old in war, very strict in military etiquette, and apt to take fire when others scarcely seem warmed. Permit me to recommend, in the most particular manner, the cultivation of harmony and good agreement, and your endeavor to destroy that ill-humor which may have got into officers." To Lafayette he wrote: "Everybody, sir, who reasons, will acknowledge the advantages which we have derived from the French fleet, and the zeal of the commander of it; but in a free and republican government you cannot restrain the voice of the multitude. Every man will speak as he thinks, or, more properly, without thinking, and consequently will judge of effects without attending to the causes. The censures which have been levelled at the French fleet would more than probably have fallen in a much higher degree upon a fleet of our own, if we had had one in the same situation. It is the nature of man to be displeased with everything that disappoints a favorite hope or flattering project; and it is the folly of too many of them to condemn without investigating circumstances." Finally he wrote to D'Estaing, deploring the difference which had arisen, mentioning his own efforts and wishes to restore harmony, and said: "It is in the trying circumstances to which your Excellency has been exposed that the virtues of a great mind are displayed in their brightest lustre, and that a general's character is better known than in the moment of victory. It was yours by every title that can give it; and the adverse elements that robbed you of your prize can never deprive you of the glory due you. Though your success has not been equal to your expectations, yet you have the satisfaction of reflecting that you have rendered essential services to the common cause." This is not the letter of a dull man. Indeed, there is a nicety about it that partakes of cleverness, a much commoner thing than greatness, but something which all great men by no means possess. Thus by tact and comprehension of human nature, by judicious suppression and judicious letters, Washington, through the prudent exercise of all his commanding influence, quieted his own people and soothed his allies. In this way a serious disaster was averted, and an abortive expedition was all that was left to be regretted, instead of an ugly quarrel, which might readily have neutralized the vast advantages flowing from the French alliance.

Having refitted, D'Estaing bore away for the West Indies, and so closed the first chapter in the history of the alliance with France. Nothing more was heard of the allies until the spring was well advanced, when M. Gérard, the minister, wrote, intimating that D'Estaing was about to return, and asking what we would do. Washington replied at length, professing his willingness to coöperate in any way, and offering, if the French would send ships, to abandon everything, run all risks, and make an attack on New York. Nothing further came of it, and Washington heard that the fleet had gone to the Southern States, which he learned without regret, as he was apprehensive as to the condition of affairs in that region. Again, in the autumn, it was reported that the fleet was once more upon the northern coast. Washington at once sent officers to be on the lookout at the most likely points, and he wrote elaborately to D'Estaing, setting forth with wonderful perspicuity the incidents of the past, the condition of the present, and the probabilities of the future. He was willing to do anything, or plan anything, provided his allies would join with him. The jealousy so habitual in humanity, which is afraid that some one else may get the glory of a common success, was unknown to Washington, and if he could but drive the British from America, and establish American independence, he was perfectly willing that the glory should take care of itself. But all his wisdom in dealing with the allies was, for the moment, vain. While he was planning for a great stroke, and calling out the militia of New England, D'Estaing was making ready to relieve Georgia, and a few days after Washington wrote his second letter, the French and Americans assaulted the British works at Savannah, and were repulsed with heavy losses. Then D'Estaing sailed away again, and the second effort of France to aid England's revolted colonies came to an end. Their presence had had a good moral effect, and the dread of D'Estaing's return had caused Clinton to withdraw from Newport and concentrate in New York. This was all that was actually accomplished, and there was nothing for it but to await still another trial and a more convenient season.

With all his courtesy and consideration, with all his readiness to fall in with the wishes and schemes of the French, it must not be supposed that Washington ever went an inch too far in this direction. He valued the French alliance, and proposed to use it to great purpose, but he was not in the least dazzled or blinded by it. Even in the earliest glow of excitement and hope produced by D'Estaing's arrival, Washington took occasion to draw once more the distinction between a valuable alliance and volunteer adventurers, and to remonstrate again with Congress about their reckless profusion in dealing with foreign officers. To Gouverneur

Morris he wrote on July 24, 1778: "The lavish manner in which rank has hitherto been bestowed on these gentlemen will certainly be productive of one or the other of these two evils: either to make it despicable in the eyes of Europe, or become the means of pouring them in upon us like a torrent and adding to our present burden. But it is neither the expense nor the trouble of them that I most dread. There is an evil more extensive in its nature, and fatal in its consequences, to be apprehended, and that is the driving of all our own officers out of the service, and throwing not only our army, but our military councils, entirely into the hands of foreigners. . . . Baron Steuben, I now find, is also wanting to quit his inspectorship for a command in the line. This will be productive of much discontent to the brigadiers. In a word, although I think the baron an excellent officer, I do most devoutly wish that we had not a single foreigner among us except the Marquis de Lafayette, who acts upon very different principles from those which govern the rest." A few days later he said, on the same theme, to the president of Congress: "I trust you think me so much a citizen of the world as to believe I am not easily warped or led away by attachments merely local and American; yet I confess I am not entirely without them, nor does it appear to me that they are unwarrantable, if confined within proper limits. Fewer promotions in the foreign line would have been productive of more harmony, and made our warfare more agreeable to all parties." Again, he said of Steuben: "I regret that there should be a necessity that his services should be lost to the army; at the same time I think it my duty explicitly to observe to Congress that his desire of having an actual and permanent command in the line cannot be complied with without wounding the feelings of a number of officers, whose rank and merits give them every claim to attention; and that the doing of it would be productive of much dissatisfaction and extensive ill consequences."

Washington's resistance to the colonial deference for foreigners has already been pointed out, but this second burst of opposition, coming at this especial time, deserves renewed attention. The splendid fleet and well-equipped troops of our ally were actually at our gates, and everybody was in a paroxysm of perfectly natural gratitude. To the colonial mind, steeped in colonial habits of thought, the foreigner at this particular juncture appeared more than ever to be a splendid and superior being. But he did not in the least confuse or sway the cool judgment that guided the destinies of the Revolution. Let us consider well the pregnant sentences just quoted, and the letters from which they are taken. They deserve it, for they throw a strong light on a side of Washington's mind and character too little appreciated. One hears it said not infrequently, it has been argued even in print with some solemnity, that Washington was, no doubt, a great man and rightly a national hero, but that he was not an American. It will be necessary to recur to this charge again and consider it at some length. It is sufficient at this point to see how it tallies with his conduct in a single matter, which was a very perfect test of the national and American quality of the man. We can get at the truth by contrasting him with his own contemporaries, the only fair comparison, for he was a man and an American of his own time and not of the present day, which is a point his critics overlook.

Where he differed from the men of his own time was in the fact that he rose to a breadth and height of Americanism and of national feeling which no other man of that day touched at all. Nothing is more intense than the conservatism of mental habits, and although it requires now an effort to realize it, it should not be forgotten that in every habit of thought the inhabitants of the thirteen colonies were wholly colonial. If this is properly appreciated we can understand the mental breadth and vigor which enabled Washington to shake off at once all past habits and become an independent leader of an independent people. He felt to the very core of his being the need of national self-respect and national dignity. To him, as the chief of the armies and the head of the Revolution, all men, no matter what tongue they spake or what country they came from, were to be dealt with on a footing of simple equality, and treated according to their merits. There was to him no glamour in the fact that this man was a Frenchman and that an Englishman. His own personal pride extended to his people, and he bowed to no national superiority anywhere. Hamilton was national throughout, but he was born outside the thirteen colonies, and knew his fellow-citizens only as Americans. Franklin was national by the force of his own commanding genius. John Adams grew to the same conception, so far as our relations to other nations were concerned. But beyond these three we may look far and closely before we find another among all the really great men of the time who freed himself wholly from the superstition of the colonist about the nations of Europe.

When Washington drew his sword beneath the Cambridge elm he stood forth as the first American, the best type of man that the New World could produce, with no provincial taint upon him, and no shadow of the colonial past clouding his path. It was this great quality that gave the struggle which he led a character it would never have attained without a leader so constituted. Had he been merely a colonial Englishman, had he not risen at once to the conception of an American nation, the world would have looked at us with very different eyes. It was the splendid dignity of the man, quite as much as his fighting capacity, which impressed Europe. Kings and ministers, looking on dispassionately, soon realized that here was a really considerable man, no ordinary agitator or revolutionist, but a great man on a great stage with great conceptions. England, indeed, talked about a militia colonel, but this chatter disappeared in the smoke of Trenton, and even England came to look upon him as the all-powerful spirit of the Revolution. Dull men and colonial squires do not grasp a great idea and carry it into action on the world's stage in a few months. To stand forward at the head of raw armies and of a colonial people as a national leader, calm, dignified, and far-seeing, requires not only character, but intellect of the highest and strongest kind. Now that we have come as a people, after more than a century's struggle, to the national feeling which Washington compassed in a moment, it is well to consider that single achievement and to meditate on its meaning, whether in estimating him, or in gauging what he was to the American people when they came into existence.

Let us take another instance of the same quality, shown also in the winter of 1778. Congress had from the beginning a longing to conquer Canada, which was a wholly natural and entirely laudable desire, for conquest is always more interesting than defence. Washington, on the other hand, after the first complete failure, which was so nearly a success in the then undefended and unsuspicious country, gave up pretty thoroughly all ideas of attacking Canada again, and opposed the various plans of Congress in that direction. When he had a life-and-death struggle to get together and subsist enough men to protect their own firesides, he had ample reason to know that invasions of Canada were hopeless. Indeed, not much active opposition from the commander-in-chief was needed to dispose of the Canadian schemes, for facts settled them as fast as they arose. When the cabal got up its Canadian expedition, it consisted of Lafayette, and penetrated no farther than Albany. So Washington merely kept his eye watchfully on Canada, and argued against expeditions thither, until this winter of 1778, when something quite new in that direction came up.

Lafayette's imagination had been fired by the notion of conquering Canada. His idea was to get succors from France for this especial purpose, and with them and American aid to achieve the conquest. Congress was impressed and pleased by the scheme, and sent a report upon it to Franklin, to communicate to the French court, but Washington, when he heard of the plan, took a very different view. He sent at once a long despatch to Congress, urging every possible objection to the proposed campaign, on the ground of its utter impracticability, and with this official letter, which was necessarily confined to the military side of the question, went another addressed to President Laurens personally, which contained the deeper reasons of his opposition. He said that there was an objection not touched upon in his public letter, which was absolutely insurmountable. This was the introduction of French troops into Canada to take possession of the capital, in the midst of a people of their own race and religion, and but recently severed from them.

He pointed out the enormous advantages which would accrue to France from the possession of Canada, such as independent posts, control of the Indians, and the Newfoundland trade. "France . . . possessed of New Orleans on our right, Canada on our left, and seconded by the numerous tribes of Indians in our rear, . . . would, it is much to be apprehended, have it in her power to give law to these States." He went on to show that France might easily find an excuse for such conduct, in seeking a surety for her advances of money, and that she had but little to fear from the contingency of our being driven to reunite with England. He continued: "Men are very apt to run into extremes. Hatred to England may carry some into an excess of confidence in France, especially when motives of gratitude are thrown into the scale. Men of this description would be unwilling to suppose France capable of acting so ungenerous a part. I am heartily disposed to entertain the most favorable sentiments of our new ally, and to cherish them in others to a reasonable degree. But it is a maxim, founded on the universal experience of mankind, that no nation is to be trusted farther than it is bound by its own interest; and no prudent statesman or politician will venture to depart from it. In our circumstances we ought to be particularly cautious; for we have not yet attained sufficient vigor and maturity to recover from the shock of any false steps into which we may unwarily fall."

We shall have occasion to recall these utterances at a later day, but at this time they serve to show yet again how broadly and clearly Washington judged nations and policies. Uppermost in his mind was the destiny of his own nation, just coming into being, and from that firm point he watched and reasoned. His words had no effect on Congress, but as it turned out, the plan failed through adverse influences in the quarter where Washington least expected them. He believed that this Canadian plan had been put into Lafayette's mind by the cabinet of Louis XVI, and he could not imagine that a policy of such obvious wisdom could be overlooked by French statesmen. In this he was completely mistaken, for France failed to see what seemed so simple to the American general, that the opportunity had come to revive her old American policy and reëstablish her colonies under the most favorable conditions. The ministers of Louis XVI, moreover, did not wish the colonies to conquer Canada, and the plan of Lafayette and the Congress received no aid in Paris and came to nothing. But the fruitless incident exhibits in the strongest light the attitude of Washington as a purely American statesman, and the comprehensiveness of his mind in dealing with large affairs.

The French alliance and the coming of the French fleet were of incalculable advantage to the colonies, but they had one evil effect, as has already been suggested. To a people weary with unequal conflict, it was a debilitating influence, and America needed at that moment more than ever energy and vigor, both in the council and the field. Yet the general outlook was distinctly better and more encouraging. Soon after Washington had defeated Clinton at Monmouth, and had taken a position whence he could watch and check him, he wrote to his friend General Nelson in Virginia: —

> It is not a little pleasing, nor less wonderful to contemplate, that, after two years' manœuvring and undergoing the strangest vicissitudes that perhaps ever attended any one contest since the creation, both armies are brought back to the very point they set out from, and that the offending party at the beginning is now reduced to the spade and pick-axe for defence. The hand of Providence has been so conspicuous in all this that he must be worse than an infidel that lacks faith, and more than wicked that has not gratitude enough to acknowledge his obligations. But it will be time enough for me to turn preacher when my present appointment ceases.

He had reason to congratulate himself on the result of his two years' campaigning, but as the summer wore away and winter came on he found causes for fresh and deep alarm, despite the good outlook in the field. The demoralizing effects of civil war were beginning to show themselves in various directions. The character of Congress, in point of ability, had declined alarmingly, for the able men of the first Congress, with few exceptions, had departed. Some had gone to the army, some to the diplomatic service, and many had remained at home, preferring the honors and offices of the States to those of the Confederation. Their successors, patriotic and well-meaning though they were, lacked the energy and force of those who had started the Revolution, and, as a consequence, Congress had become feeble and ineffective, easily swayed by influential schemers, and unable to cope with the difficulties which surrounded them.

Outside the government the popular tone had deteriorated sadly. The lavish issues of irredeemable paper by the Confederation and the States had brought their finances to the verge of absolute ruin. The continental currency had fallen to something like forty to one in gold, and the decline was hastened by the forged notes put out by the enemy. The fluctuations of this paper soon bred a spirit of gambling, and hence came a class of men, both inside and outside of politics, who sought, more or less corruptly, to make fortunes by army contracts, and by forestalling the markets. These developments filled Washington with anxiety, for in the financial troubles he saw ruin to the army. The unpaid troops bore the injustice done them with wonderful patience, but it was something that could not last, and Washington knew the danger. In vain did he remonstrate. It seemed to be impossible to get anything done, and at last, in the following spring, the outbreak began. Two New Jersey regiments refused to march until the assembly made provision for their pay. Washington took high ground with them, but they stood respectfully firm, and finally had their way. Not long after came another outbreak in the Connecticut line, with similar results. These object lessons had some result, and by foreign loans and the ability of Robert Morris the country was enabled to stumble along; but it was a frightful and wearing anxiety to the commander-in-chief.

Washington saw at once that the root of the evil lay in the feebleness of Congress, and although he could not deal with the finances, he was able to strive for an improvement in the governing body. Not content with letters, he left the army and went to Philadelphia, in the winter of 1779, and there appealed to Congress in person, setting forth the perils which beset them, and urging action. He wrote also to his friends everywhere, pointing out the deficiencies of Congress, and begging them to send better and stronger men. To Benjamin Harrison he wrote: "It appears to me as clear as ever the sun did in its meridian brightness, that America never stood in more eminent need of the wise, patriotic, and spirited exertions of her sons than at this period; . . . the States separately are too much engaged in their local concerns, and have too many of their ablest men withdrawn from the general council, for the good of the common weal." He took the same high tone in all his letters, and there can be seen through it all the desperate endeavor to make the States and the people understand the dangers which he realized, but which they either could not or would not appreciate.

On the other hand, while his anxiety was sharpened to the highest point by the character of Congress, his sternest wrath was kindled by the gambling and money-making which had become rampant. To Reed he wrote in December, 1778: "It gives me sincere pleasure to find that there is likely to be a coalition of the Whigs in your State, a few only excepted, and that the assembly is so well disposed to second your endeavors in bringing those murderers of our cause, the monopolizers, forestallers, and engrossers, to condign punishment. It is much to be lamented that each State, long ere this, has not hunted them down as pests to society and the greatest enemies we have to the happiness of America. I would to God that some one of the most atrocious in each State was hung in gibbets upon a gallows five times as high as the one prepared by Haman. No punishment, in my opinion, is too great for the man who can build his greatness upon his country's ruin." He would have hanged them too had he had the power, for he was always as good as his word.

It is refreshing to read these righteously angry words, still ringing as sharply as when they were written. They clear away all the myths—the priggish, the cold, the statuesque, the dull myths—as the strong gusts of the northwest wind in autumn sweep off the heavy mists of lingering August. They are the hot words of a warm-blooded man, a good hater, who loathed meanness and treachery, and who would have hanged those who battened upon the country's distress. When he went to Philadelphia, a few weeks later, and saw the state of things with nearer view, he felt the wretchedness and outrage of such doings more than ever. He wrote to Harrison: "If I were to be called upon to draw a picture of the times and of men, from what I have seen, heard, and in part know, I should in one word say, that idleness, dissipation, and extravagance seem to have laid fast hold of most of them; that speculation, peculation, and an insatiable thirst for riches seem to have got the better of every other consideration, and almost of every order of men; that party disputes and personal quarrels are the great business of the day; whilst the momentous concerns of an empire, a great and accumulating debt, ruined finances, depreciated money, and want of credit, which, in its consequences, is the want of everything, are but secondary considerations, and postponed from day to day, from week to week, as if our affairs wore the most promising aspect."

Other men talked about empire, but he alone grasped the great conception, and felt it in his soul. To see not only immediate success imperilled, but the future paltered with by small, mean, and dishonest men, cut him to the quick. He set himself doggedly to fight it, as he always fought every enemy, using both speech and pen in all quarters. Much, no doubt, he ultimately effected, but he was contending with the usual results of civil war, which are demoralizing always, and especially so among a young people in a new country. At first, therefore, all seemed vain. The selfishness, "peculation, and speculation" seemed to get worse, and the tone of Congress and the people lower, as he struggled against them. In March, 1779, he wrote to James Warren of Massachusetts: "Nothing, I am convinced, but the depreciation of our currency, aided by stock-jobbing and party dissensions, has fed the hopes of the enemy, and kept the British arms in America to this day. They do not scruple to declare this themselves, and add that we shall be our own conquerors. Can not our common country, America, possess virtue enough to disappoint them? Is the paltry consideration of a little pelf to individuals to be placed in competition with the essential rights and liberties of the present generation, and of millions yet unborn? Shall a few designing men, for their own aggrandizement, and to gratify their own avarice, overset the goodly fabric we have been rearing, at the expense of so much time, blood, and treasure? And shall we at last become the victims of our own lust of gain? Forbid it, Heaven! Forbid it, all and every State in the Union, by enacting and enforcing efficacious laws for checking the growth of these monstrous evils, and restoring matters, in some degree, to the state they were in at the commencement of the war.

"Our cause is noble. It is the cause of mankind, and the danger to it is to be apprehended from ourselves. Shall we slumber and sleep, then, while we should be punishing those miscreants who have brought these troubles upon us, and who are aiming to continue us in them; while we should be striving to fill our battalions, and devising ways and means to raise the value of the currency, on the credit of which everything depends?" Again we see the prevailing idea of the future, which haunted him continually. Evidently, he had some imagination, and also a power of terse and eloquent expression which we have heard of before, and shall note again.

Still the appeals seemed to sound in deaf ears. He wrote to George Mason: "I have seen, without despondency, even for a moment, the hours which America has styled her gloomy ones; but I have beheld no day since the commencement of hostilities that I have thought her liberties in such imminent danger as at present. . . . Indeed, we are verging so fast to destruction that I am filled with sensations to which I have been a stranger till within these three months." To Gouverneur Morris he said: "If the enemy have it in their power to press us hard this campaign, I know not what may be the consequence." He had faced the enemy, the bleak winters, raw soldiers, and all the difficulties of impecunious government, with a cheerful courage that never failed. But the spectacle of widespread popular demoralization, of selfish scrambles for plunder, and of feeble administration at the centre of government weighed upon him heavily. It was not the general's business to build up Congress and grapple with finance, but Washington addressed himself to the new task with his usual persistent courage. It was slow and painful work. He seemed to make no progress, and then it was that his spirits sank at the prospect of ruin and defeat, not coming on the field of battle, but from our own vices and our own lack of energy and wisdom. Yet his work told in the end, as it always did. His vast and steadily growing influence made itself felt even through the dense troubles of the uneasy times. Congress turned with energy to Europe for fresh loans. Lafayette worked away to get an army sent over. The two Morrises, stimulated by Washington, flung themselves into the financial difficulties, and feeble but distinct efforts toward a more concentrated and better organized administration of public affairs were made both in the States and the confederation.

But, although Washington's spirits fell, and his anxieties became wellnigh intolerable in this period of reaction which followed the French alliance, he made no public show of it, but carried on his own work with the army and in the field as usual, contending with all the difficulties, new and old, as calmly and efficiently as ever. After Clinton slipped away from Monmouth and sought refuge in New York, Washington took post at convenient points and watched the movements of the enemy. In this way the summer passed. As always, Washington's first object was to guard the Hudson, and while he held this vital point firmly, he waited, ready to strike elsewhere if necessary. It looked for a time as if the British intended to descend on Boston, seize the town, and destroy the French fleet, which had gone there to refit. Such was the opinion of Gates, then commanding in that department, and as Washington inclined to the same belief, the fear of this event gave him many anxious moments. He even moved his troops so as to be in readiness to march eastward at short notice; but he gradually became convinced that the enemy had no such plan. Much of his thought, now and always, was given to efforts to divine the intentions of the British generals. They had so few settled ideas, and were so tardy and lingering when they had plans, that it is small wonder that their opponents were sorely puzzled in trying to find out what their purposes were, when they really had none. The fact was that Washington saw their military opportunities with the eye of a great soldier, and so much better than they, that he suffered a good deal of needless anxiety in devising methods to meet attacks which they had not the wit to undertake. He had a profound contempt for their policy of holding towns, and believing that they must see the utter futility of it, after several years of trial, he constantly expected from them a well-planned and extensive campaign, which in reality they were incapable of devising.

The main army, therefore, remained quiet, and when the autumn had passed went into winter-quarters in well-posted detachments about New York. In December Clinton made an ineffectual raid, and then all was peaceful again, and Washington was able to go to Philadelphia and struggle with Congress, leaving his army more comfortable and secure than they had been in any previous winter.

In January he informed Congress as to the next campaign. He showed them the impossibility of undertaking anything on a large scale, and announced his intention of remaining on the defensive. It was a trying policy to a man of his temper, but he could do no better, and he knew, now as always, what others could not yet see, that by simply holding on and keeping his army in the field he was slowly but surely winning independence. He tried to get Congress to do something with the navy, and he planned an expedition, under the command of Sullivan, to overrun the Indian country and check the barbarous raids of the Tories and savages on the frontier; and with this he was fain to be content. In fact, he perceived very clearly the direction in which the war was tending. He kept up his struggle with Congress for a permanent army, and with the old persistency pleaded that something should be done for the officers, and at the same time he tried to keep the States in good humor when they were grumbling about the amount of protection afforded them.

But all this wear and tear of heart and brain and temper, while given chiefly to hold the army together, was not endured with any notion that he and Clinton were eventually to fight it out in the neighborhood of New York. Washington felt that that part of the conflict was over. He now hoped and believed that the moment would come, when, by uniting his army with the French, he should be able to strike the decisive blow. Until that time came, however, he knew that he could do nothing on a great scale, and he felt that meanwhile the British, abandoning practically the eastern and middle States, would make one last desperate struggle for victory, and would make it in the south. Long before any one else, he appreciated this fact, and saw a peril looming large in that region, where everybody was considering the British invasion as little more than an exaggerated raid. He foresaw, too, that we should suffer more there than we had in the extreme north, because the south was full of Tories and less well organized.

All this, however, did not change his own plans one jot. He believed that the south must work out its own salvation, as New York and New England had done with Burgoyne, and he felt sure that in the end it would be successful. But he would not go south, nor take his army there.

The instinct of a great commander for the vital point in a war or a battle, is as keen as that of the tiger is said to be for the jugular vein of its victim. The British might overrun the north or invade the south, but he would stay where he was, with his grip upon New York and the Hudson River. The tide of invasion might ebb and flow in this region or that, but the British were doomed if they could not divide the eastern colonies from the others. When the appointed hour came, he was ready to abandon everything and strike the final and fatal blow; but until then he waited and stood fast with his army, holding the great river in his grasp. He felt much more anxiety about the south than he had felt about the north, and expected Congress to consult him as to a commander, having made up his mind that Greene was the man to send. But Congress still believed in Gates, who had been making trouble for Washington all winter; and so Gates was sent, and Congress in due time got their lesson, and found once more that Washington understood men better than they did.

In the north the winter was comparatively uneventful. The spring passed, and in June Clinton came out and took possession of Stony Point and Verplanck's Point, and began to fortify them. It looked a little as if Clinton might intend to get control of the Hudson by slow approaches, fortifying, and then advancing until he reached West Point. With this in mind, Washington at once determined to check the British by striking sharply at one of their new posts. Having made up his mind, he sent for Wayne and asked him if he would storm Stony Point. Tradition says that Wayne replied, "I will storm hell, if you will plan it." A true tradition, probably, in keeping with Wayne's character, and pleasant to us to-day as showing with a vivid gleam of rough human speech the utter confidence of the army in their leader, that confidence which only a great soldier can inspire. So Washington planned, and Wayne stormed, and Stony Point fell. It was a gallant and brilliant feat of arms, one of the most brilliant of the war. Over five hundred prisoners were taken, the guns were carried off, and the works destroyed, leaving the British to begin afresh with a good deal of increased caution and respect. Not long after, Harry Lee stormed Paulus Hook with equal success, and the British were checked and arrested, if they intended any extensive movement. On the frontier, Sullivan, after some delays, did his work effectively, ravaging the Indian towns and reducing them to quiet, thus taking away another annoyance and danger.

In these various ways Clinton's circle of activity was steadily narrowed, but it may be doubted whether he had any coherent plan. The principal occupation of the British was to send out marauding expeditions and cut off outlying parties. Tryon burned and pillaged in Connecticut, Matthews in Virginia, and others on a smaller scale elsewhere in New Jersey and New York. The blundering stupidity of this system of warfare was only equalled by its utter brutality. Houses were burned, peaceful villages went up in smoke, women and children were outraged, and soldiers were bayoneted after they had surrendered. These details of the Revolution are wellnigh forgotten now, but when the ear is wearied with talk about English generosity and love of fair play, it is well to turn back and study the exploits of Tryon, and it is not amiss in the same connection to recall that English budgets contained a special appropriation for scalping-knives, a delicate attention to the Tories and Indians who were burning and butchering on the frontier.

Such methods of warfare Washington despised intellectually, and hated morally. He saw that every raid only hardened the people against England, and made her cause more hopeless. The misery caused by these raids angered him, but he would not retaliate in kind, and Wayne bayoneted no English soldiers after they laid down their arms at Stony Point. It was enough for Washington to hold fast to the great objects he had in view, to check Clinton and circumscribe his movements. Steadfastly he did this through the summer and winter of 1779, which proved one of the worst that he had yet endured. Supplies did not come, the army dwindled, and the miseries of Valley Forge were renewed. Again was repeated the old and pitiful story of appeals to Congress and the States, and again the undaunted spirit and strenuous exertions of Washington saved the army and the Revolution from the internal ruin which was his worst enemy. When the new year began, he saw that he was again condemned to a defensive campaign, but this made little difference now, for what he had foreseen in the spring of 1779 became certainty in the autumn. The active war was transferred to the south, where the chapter of disasters was beginning, and Clinton had practically given up everything except New York. The war had taken on the new phase expected by Washington. Weak as he was, he began to detach troops, and prepared to deal with the last desperate effort of England to conquer her revolted colonies from the south.

CHAPTER IX

ARNOLD'S TREASON, AND THE WAR IN THE SOUTH

THE SPRING OF 1780 was the beginning of a period of inactivity and disappointment, of diligent effort and frustrated plans. During the months which ensued before the march to the south, Washington passed through a stress of harassing anxiety, which was far worse than anything he had to undergo at any other time. Plans were formed, only to fail. Opportunities arose, only to pass by unfulfilled. The network of hostile conditions bound him hand and foot, and it seemed at times as if he could never break the bonds that held him, or prevent or hold back the moral, social, and political dissolution going on about him. With the aid of France, he meant to strike one decisive blow, and end the struggle. Every moment was of importance, and yet the days and weeks and months slipped by, and he could get nothing done. He could neither gain control of the sea, nor gather sufficient forces of his own, although delay now meant ruin. He saw the British overrun the south, and he could not leave the Hudson. He was obliged to sacrifice the southern States, and yet he could get neither ships nor men to attack New York. The army was starving and mutinous, and he sought relief in vain. The finances were ruined, Congress was helpless, the States seemed stupefied. Treason of the most desperate kind suddenly reared its head, and threatened the very citadel of the Revolution. These were the days of the war least familiar to posterity. They are unmarked in the main by action or fighting, and on this dreary monotony nothing stands out

181

except the black stain of Arnold's treason. Yet it was the time of all others when Washington had most to bear. It was the time of all others when his dogged persistence and unwavering courage alone seemed to sustain the flickering fortunes of the war.

In April Washington was pondering ruefully on the condition of affairs at the south. He saw that the only hope of saving Charleston was in the defence of the bar; and when that became indefensible, he saw that the town ought to be abandoned to the enemy, and the army withdrawn to the country. His military genius showed itself again and again in his perfectly accurate judgment on distant campaigns. He seemed to apprehend all the conditions at a glance, and although his wisdom made him refuse to issue orders when he was not on the ground, those generals who followed his suggestions, even when a thousand miles away, were successful, and those who disregarded them were not. Lincoln, commanding at Charleston, was a brave and loyal man, but he had neither the foresight nor the courage to withdraw to the country, and then, hovering on the lines of the enemy, to confine them to the town. He yielded to the entreaties of the citizens and remained, only to surrender. Washington had retreated from New York, and after five years of fighting the British still held it, and had gone no further. He had refused to risk an assault to redeem Philadelphia at the expense of much grumbling and cursing, and had then beaten the enemy when they hastily retreated thence in the following spring. His cardinal doctrine was that the Revolution depended upon the existence of the army, and not on the possession of any particular spot of ground, and his masterly adherence to this theory brought victory, slowly but surely. Lincoln's very natural inability to grasp it, and to withstand popular pressure, cost us for a time the southern States and a great deal of bloody fighting.

In the midst of this anxiety about the south, and when he foresaw the coming disasters, Washington was cheered and encouraged by the arrival of Lafayette, whom he loved, and who brought good tidings of his zealous work for the United States in Paris. An army and a fleet were on their way to America, with a promise of more to follow. This was great news indeed. It is interesting to note how Washington took it, for we see here with unusual clearness the readiness of grasp and quickness of thought which have been noted before, but which are not commonly attributed to him. It has been the fashion to treat Washington as wise and prudent, but as distinctly slow, and when he was obliged to concentrate public opinion, either military or civil, or when doubt overhung his course, he moved with great deliberation. When he required no concentration of opinion, and had made up his mind, he could strike with a terribly swift decision, as at Trenton or Monmouth. So when a new situation presented itself he seized with wonderful rapidity every phase and possibility opened by changed conditions.

The moment he learned from Lafayette that the French succors were actually on the way, he began to lay out plans in a manner which showed how he had taken in at the first glance every chance and every contingency. He wrote that the decisive moment was at hand, and that the French succors would be fatal if not used successfully now. Congress must improve their methods of administration, and for this purpose must appoint a small committee to cooperate with him. This step he demanded, and it was taken at once. Fresh from his interview with Lafayette, he sent out orders to have inquiries made as to Halifax and its defences. Possibly a sudden and telling blow might be struck there, and nothing should be overlooked. He also wrote to Lafayette to urge upon the French commander an immediate assault on New York the moment he landed. Yet despite his thought for New York, he even then began to see the opportunities which were destined to develop into Yorktown. He had longed to go to the south before, and had held back only because he felt that the main army and New York were still the key of the position, and could not be safely left. Now, while planning the capture of New York, he asked in a letter whether the enemy was not more exposed at the southward and therefore a better subject for a combined attack there. Clearness and precision of plan as to the central point, joined to a perfect readiness to change suddenly and strike hard and decisively in a totally different quarter, are sure marks of the great commander. We can find them all through the correspondence, but here in May, 1780, they come out with peculiar vividness. They are qualities arising from a wide foresight, and from a sure and quick perception. They are not the qualities of a slow or heavy mind.

On June 1st came the news of the surrender of Charleston and the loss of the army, which was followed by the return of Clinton to New York. The southern States lay open now to the enemy, and it was a severe trial to Washington to be unable to go to their rescue; but with the same dogged adherence to his ruling idea, he concentrated his attention on the Hudson with renewed vigilance on account of Clinton's return. Adversity and prosperity alike were unable to divert him from the control of the great river and the mastery of the middle States until he saw conclusive victory elsewhere fairly within his grasp. In the same unswerving way he pushed on the preparations for what he felt to be the coming of the decisive campaign and the supreme moment of the war. To all the governors went urgent letters, calling on the States to fill their lines in the continental army, and to have their militia in readiness.

In the midst of these anxieties and preparations, the French arrived at Newport, bringing a well-equipped army of some five thousand men, and a small fleet. They brought, too, something quite as important, in the way of genuine goodwill and full intention to do all in their power for their allies. After a moment's hesitation, born of unlucky memories, the people of Rhode Island gave De Rochambeau a hearty welcome, and Washington sent him the most cordial greeting. With the greeting went the polite but earnest request for immediate action, together with plans for attacking New York; and, at the same time, another urgent call went out to the States for men, money, and supplies. The long looked-for hour had arrived, a fine French army was in Newport, a French fleet rode in the harbor, and instead of action, immediate and effective, the great event marked only the beginning of a period of delays and disappointment, wearing heart and nerve almost beyond endurance.

First it appeared that the French ships could not get into New York harbor. Then there was sickness in the French army. Then the British menaced Newport, and rapid preparations had to be made to meet that danger. Then it came out that De Rochambeau was ordered to await the arrival of the second division of the army, with more ships; and after due waiting, it was discovered that the aforesaid second division, with their ships, were securely blockaded by the English fleet at Brest. On our side it was no better; indeed, it was rather worse. There was lack of arms and powder. The drafts were made with difficulty, and the new levies came in slowly. Supplies failed altogether, and on every hand there was nothing but delay, and ever fresh delay, and in the midst of it all Washington, wrestling with sloth and incoherence and inefficiency, trampled down one failure and disappointment only to encounter another, equally important, equally petty, and equally harassing.

On August 20th he wrote to Congress a long and most able letter, which set forth forcibly the evil and perilous condition of affairs. After reading that letter no man could say that there was not need of the utmost exertion, and for the expenditure of the last ounce of energy. In it Washington struck especially at the two delusions with which the people and their representatives were lulling themselves into security, and by which they were led to relax their efforts. One was the belief that England was breaking down; the other, that the arrival of the French was synonymous with the victorious close of the war. Washington demonstrated that England still commanded the sea, and that as long as she did so there was a great advantage on her side.

She was stronger, on the whole, this year than the year before, and her financial resources were still ample. There was no use in looking for victory in the weakness of the enemy, and on the other hand, to rely wholly on France was contemptible as well as foolish. After stating plainly that the army was on the verge of dissolution, he said: "To me it will appear miraculous if our affairs can maintain themselves much longer in their present train. If either the temper or the resources of the country will not admit of an alteration, we may expect soon to be reduced to the humiliating condition of seeing the cause of America, in America, upheld by foreign arms. The generosity of our allies has a claim to all our confidence and all our gratitude, but it is neither for the honor of America, nor for the interest of the common cause, to leave the work entirely to them."

It must have been bitter to Washington above all men, with his high dignity and keen sense of national honor, to write such words as these, or

make such an argument to any of his countrymen. But it was a work
which the time demanded, and he did it without flinching. Having thus
laid bare the weak places, he proceeded to rehearse once more, with a
weariness we can easily fancy, the old, old lesson as to organization, a permanent army, and a better system of administration. This letter neither
scolded, nor bewailed, nor desponded; but it told the truth with great
force and vigor. It, of course, had but slight results, comparatively speaking, still it did something, and the final success of the Revolution is due
to the series of strong truth-telling letters, of which this is an example, as
much as to any one thing done by Washington. There was need of some
one, not only to fight battles and lead armies, but to drive Congress into
some sort of harmony, spur the careless and indifferent to action, arouse
the States, and kill various fatal delusions, and in Washington the robust
teller of unwelcome truths was found.

Still, even the results actually obtained by such letters came but
slowly, and Washington felt that he must strike at all hazards. Through
Lafayette he tried to get De Rochambeau to agree to an immediate
attack on New York. His army was on the very eve of dissolution, and he
began with reason to doubt his own power of holding it together longer.
The finances of the country were going ever faster to irremediable ruin,
and it seemed impossible that anything could postpone open and avowed
bankruptcy. So, with his army crumbling, mutinous, and half starved, he
turned to his one unfailing resource of fighting, and tried to persuade De
Rochambeau to join him. Under the circumstances, Washington was right
to wish to risk a battle, and De Rochambeau, from his point of view, was
equally so in refusing to take the offensive, unless the second division
arrived or De Guichen came with his fleet, or the English force at New
York was reduced.

In these debates and delays, mingled with an appeal to De Guichen
in the West Indies, the summer was fast wearing away, and, by way of
addition, early in September came tidings of the battle of Camden, and
the utter rout of Gates's army. Despite his own needs and trials,
Washington's first idea was to stem the current of disaster at the south,
and he ordered the fresh Maryland troops to turn back at once and march

to the Carolinas, but Gates fled so fast and far that it was some time before anything was heard of him. As more news came of Camden and its beaten general, Washington wrote to Rutledge that he should ultimately come southward. Meantime, he could only struggle with his own difficulties, and rack his brains for men and means to rescue the south. It must have seemed to Washington, in those lovely September days, as if fate could not have any worse trials in store, and that if he could only breast the troubles now surging about him, he might count on sure and speedy success. Yet the bitterest trial of all was even then hanging over his head, and with a sort of savage sarcasm it came upon him in one of those rare moments when he had an hour of rest and sunshine.

The story of Arnold's treason is easily told. Its romantic side has made it familiar to all Americans, and given it a factitious importance. Had it succeeded it would have opened vast opportunities of disaster to America. It failed, and had no result whatever. It has passed into history simply as a picturesque episode, charged with possibilities which fascinate the imagination, but having, in itself, neither meaning nor consequences beyond the two conspirators. To us it is of interest, because it shows Washington in one of the sharpest and bitterest experiences of his life. Let us see how he met it and dealt with it.

From the day when the French landed, both De Rochambeau and Washington had been most anxious to meet. The French general had been particularly urgent, but it was difficult for Washington to get away. As he wrote on August 21st: "We are about ten miles from the enemy. Our popular government imposes a necessity of great circumspection. If any misfortune should happen in my absence, it would be attended with every inconvenience. I will, however, endeavor if possible, and as soon as possible, to meet you at some convenient rendezvous." In accordance with this promise, a few weeks later, he left Greene in command of the army, and, not without misgivings, started on September 18th to meet De Rochambeau. On his way he had an interview with Arnold, who came to him to show a letter from the loyalist Colonel Robinson, and thus disarm suspicion as to his doings. On the 20th, the day when André and Arnold met to arrange the terms of the sale, Washington was with De Rochambeau at Hartford. News had arrived, meantime, that De Guichen had sailed for Europe; the command of the sea was therefore lost, and the opportunity for action had gone by. There was no need for further conference, and Washington accordingly set out on his return at once, two or three days earlier than he had intended.

He was accompanied by his own staff, and by Knox and Lafayette with their officers. With him, too, went the young Count Dumas, who has left a description of their journey, and of the popular enthusiasm displayed in the towns through which they passed. In one village, which they reached after nightfall, all the people turned out, the children bearing torches, and men and women hailed Washington as father, and pressed about him to touch the hem of his garments. Turning to Dumas he said, "We may be beaten by the English; it is the chance of war; but there is the army they will never conquer." Political leaders grumbled, and military officers caballed, but the popular feeling went out to Washington with a sure and utter confidence. The people in that little village recognized the great and unselfish leader as they recognized Lincoln a century later, and from the masses of the people no one ever heard the cry that Washington was cold or unsympathetic. They loved him, and believed in him, and such a manifestation of their devotion touched him deeply. His spirits rose under the spell of appreciation and affection, always so strong upon human nature, and he rode away from Fishkill the next morning at daybreak with a light heart.

The company was pleasant and lively, the morning was fair, and as they approached Arnold's headquarters at the Robinson house, Washington turned off to the redoubts by the river, telling the young men that they were all in love with Mrs. Arnold and would do well to go straight on and breakfast with her. Hamilton and McHenry followed his advice, and while they were at breakfast a note was brought to Arnold. It was the letter of warning from André announcing his capture, which Colonel Jameson, who ought to have been cashiered for doing it, had forwarded. Arnold at once left the table, and saying that he was going to West Point, jumped into his boat and was rowed rapidly down the river to the British man-of-war. Washington on his arrival was told that Arnold had gone to the fort, and so after a hasty breakfast he went over there himself. On reaching West Point no salute broke the stillness, and no guard turned out to receive him. He was astonished to learn that his arrival was unexpected, and that Arnold had not been there for two days. Still unsuspecting he inspected the works, and then returned.

Meantime, the messenger sent to Hartford with the papers taken on André reached the Robinson house and delivered them to Hamilton, together with a letter of confession from André himself. Hamilton read them, and hurrying out met Washington just coming up from the river. He took his chief aside, said a few words to him in a low voice, and they went into the house together. When they came out, Washington looked as calm as ever, and calling to Lafayette and Knox gave them the papers, saying simply, "Whom can we trust now?" He despatched Hamilton at once to try to intercept Arnold at Verplanck's Point, but it was too late; the boat had passed, and Arnold was safe on board the Vulture. This done, Washington bade his staff sit down with him to dinner, as the general was absent, and Mrs. Arnold was ill in her room. Dinner over, he immediately set about guarding the post, which had been so near betrayal. To Colonel Wade at West Point he wrote: "Arnold has gone to the enemy; you are in command, be vigilant." To Jameson he sent word to guard André closely. To the colonels and commanders of various outlying regiments he sent orders to bring up their troops. Everything was done that should have been done, quickly, quietly, and without comment. The most sudden and appalling treachery had failed to shake his nerve, or confuse his mind.

Yet the strong and silent man was wrung to the quick, and when everything possible had been done, and he had retired to his room, the guard outside the door heard him marching back and forth through all the weary night. The one thing he least expected, because he least understood it, had come to pass. He had been a good and true friend to the villain who had fled, for Arnold's reckless bravery and dare-devil fighting had appealed to the strongest passion of his nature, and he had stood by him always. He had grieved over the refusal of Congress to promote him in due order, and had interceded with ultimate success in his behalf. He had sympathized with him in his recent troubles in Philadelphia, and had administered the reprimand awarded by the court-martial so that rebuke seemed turned to praise. He had sought to give him every opportunity that a soldier could desire, and had finally conferred upon him the command of West Point. He had admired his courage and palliated his misconduct, and now the scoundrel had turned on him and fled. Mingled with the bitterness of these memories of betrayed confidence was the torturing ignorance of how far this base treachery had extended. For all he knew there might be a brood of traitors about him in the very citadel of America. We can never know Washington's thoughts at that time, for he was ever silent, but as we listen in imagination to the sound of the even footfalls which the guard heard all through that September night, we can dimly guess the feelings of the strong and passionate nature, wounded and distressed almost beyond endurance.

There is but little more to tell. The conspiracy stopped with Arnold. He had no accomplices, and meant to deliver the fort and pocket the booty alone. The British tried to spread the idea that other officers had been corrupted, but the attempt failed, and Washington's prompt measures of defence checked any movement against the forts. Every effort was made by Clinton to save André, but in vain. He was tried by a court composed of the highest officers in the American service, among whom was Lafayette. On his own statement, but one decision was possible. He was condemned as a spy, and as a spy he was sentenced to be hanged. He made a manly appeal against the manner of his death, and begged to be shot. Washington declined to interfere, and André went to the gallows.

The British, at the time, and some of their writers afterwards, attacked Washington for insisting on this mode of execution, but there never was an instance in his career when he was more entirely right. André was a spy and briber, who sought to ruin the American cause by means of the treachery of an American general. It was a dark and dangerous game, and he knew that he staked his life on the result. He failed, and paid the penalty. Washington could not permit, he would have been grossly and feebly culpable if he had permitted, such an attempt to pass without extreme punishment. He was generous and magnanimous, but he was not a sentimentalist, and he punished this miserable treason, so far as he could reach it, as it deserved. It is true that André was a man of talent, well-bred and courageous, and of engaging manners. He deserved all the sympathy and sorrow which he excited at the time, but nothing more. He was not only technically a spy, but he had sought his ends by bribery, he had prostituted a flag of truce, and he was to be richly paid for his work. It was all hire and salary. No doubt André was patriotic and loyal. Many spies have been the same, and have engaged in their dangerous exploits from the highest motives. Nathan Hale, whom the British hanged without compunction, was as well-born and well-bred as André, and as patriotic as man could be, and moreover he was a spy and nothing more. André was a trafficker in bribes and treachery, and however we may pity his fate, his name has no proper place in the great temple at Westminster, where all English-speaking people bow with reverence, and only a most perverted sentimentality could conceive that it was fitting to erect a monument to his memory in this country.

Washington sent André to the gallows because it was his duty to do so, but he pitied him none the less, and whatever he may have thought of the means André employed to effect his end, he made no comment upon him, except to say that "he met his fate with that fortitude which was to be expected from an accomplished man and gallant officer." As to Arnold, he was almost equally silent. When obliged to refer to him he did so in the plainest and simplest way, and only in a familiar letter to Laurens do we get a glimpse of his feelings. He wrote: "I am mistaken if at this time Arnold is undergoing the torment of a mental hell. He wants feeling. From some traits of his character which have lately come to my knowledge, he seems to have been so hackneyed in villainy, and so lost to all sense of honor and shame, that, while his faculties will enable him to continue his sordid pursuits, there will be no time for remorse." With this single expression of measureless contempt, Washington let Arnold drop from his life. The first shock had touched him to the quick, although it could not shake his steady mind. Reflection revealed to him the extraordinary baseness of Arnold's real character, and he cast the thought of him out forever, content to leave the traitor to the tender mercies of history. The calmness and dignity, the firmness and deep feeling which Washington exhibited, are of far more interest than the abortive treason, and have as real a value now as they had then, when suspicion for a moment ran riot, and men wondered "whom they could trust."

The treason of Arnold swept like a black cloud across the sky, broke, and left everything as before. That such a base peril should have existed was alarming and hateful. That it should have been exploded harmlessly made all men give a deep sigh of relief. But neither the treason nor its discovery altered the current of events one jot. The summer had come and gone. The French had arrived, and no blow had been struck. There was nothing to show for the campaign but inaction, disappointment, and the loss of the Carolinas. With the commander-in-chief, through it all, were ever present two great questions, getting more portentous and more difficult of solution with each succeeding day. How he was to keep his army in existence was one, and how he was to hold the government together was the other. He had thirteen tired States, a general government almost impotent, a bankrupt treasury, and a broken credit. The American Revolution had come down to the question of whether the brain, will, and nerve of one man could keep the machine going long enough to find fit opportunity for a final and decisive stroke. Washington had confidence in the people of the country and in himself, but the difficulties in the way were huge, and the means of surmounting them slight. There is here and there a passionate undertone in the letters of this period, which shows us the moments when the waves of trouble and disaster seemed to sweep over him. But the feeling passed, or was trampled under foot, for there was no break in the steady fight against untoward circumstances, or in the grim refusal to accept defeat.

It is almost impossible now to conceive the actual condition at that time of every matter of detail which makes military and political existence possible. No general phrases can do justice to the situation of the army; and the petty miseries and privations, which made life unendurable, went on from day to day in ever varying forms. While Washington was hearing the first ill news from the south and struggling with the problem on that side, and at the same time was planning with Lafayette how to take advantage of the French succors, the means of subsisting his army were wholly giving out. The men actually had no food. For days, as Washington wrote, there was no meat at all in camp. Goaded by hunger, a Connecticut regiment mutinied. They were brought back to duty, but held out steadily for their pay, which they had not received for five months. Indeed, the whole army was more or less mutinous, and it was only by the utmost tact that Washington kept them from wholesale desertion. After the summer had passed and the chance for a decisive campaign had gone with it, the excitement of expected action ceased to sustain the men, and the unclothed, unpaid, unfed soldiers began again to get restive. We can imagine what the condition of the rank and file must have been when we find that Washington himself could not procure an express from the quarter-master-general, and was obliged to send a letter to the Minister of France by the unsafe and slow medium of the post. He was expected to carry on a war against a rich and powerful enemy, and he could not even pay a courier to carry his dispatches.

With the commander-in-chief thus straitened, the sufferings of the men grew to be intolerable, and the spirit of revolt which had been checked through the summer began again to appear. At last, in January, 1781, it burst all the bounds. The Pennsylvania line mutinied and threatened Congress. Attempts on the part of the English to seduce them failed, but they remained in a state of open rebellion. The officers were powerless, and it looked as if the disaffection would spread, and the whole army go to pieces in the very face of the enemy. Washington held firm, and intended in his unshaken way to bring them back to their duty without yielding in a dangerous fashion. But the government of Pennsylvania, at last thoroughly frightened, rushed into the field, and patched up a compromise which contained most perilous concessions. The natural consequence was a fresh mutiny in the New Jersey line, and this time Washington determined that he would not be forestalled. He sent forward at once some regiments of loyal troops, suppressed the mutiny suddenly and with a strong hand, and hanged two of the ringleaders. The difficulty was conquered, and discipline restored.

To take this course required great boldness, for these mutinies were of no ordinary character. In the first place, it was impossible to tell whether any troops would do their duty against their fellows, and failure would have been fatal. In the second place, the grievances of the soldiers were very great, and their complaints were entirely righteous. Washington felt the profoundest sympathy with his men, and it was no easy matter to maintain order with soldiers tried almost beyond endurance, against their comrades whose claims were just. Two things saved the army. One was Washington's great influence with the men and their utter belief in him. The other was the quality of the men themselves. Lafayette said they were the most patient and patriotic soldiers the world had seen, and it is easy to believe him. The wonder is, not that they mutinied when they did, but that the whole army had not mutinied and abandoned the struggle years before. The misfortunes and mistakes of the Revolution, to whomever due, were in no respect to be charged to the army, and the conduct of the troops through all the dreary months of starvation and cold and poverty is a proof of the intelligent patriotism and patient courage of the American soldier which can never be gainsaid. To fight successful battles is the test of a good general, but to hold together a suffering army through years of unexampled privations, to meet endless failure of details with unending expedients, and then to fight battles and plan campaigns, shows a leader who was far more than a good general. Such multiplied trials and difficulties are overcome only by a great soldier who with small means achieves large results, and by a great man who by force of will and character can establish with all who follow him a power which no miseries can conquer, and no suffering diminish.

The height reached by the troubles in the army and their menacing character had, however, a good as well as a bad side. They penetrated the indifference and carelessness of both Congress and the States. Gentlemen in the confederate and local administrations and legislatures woke up to a realizing sense that the dissolution of the army meant a general wreck, in which their own necks would be in very considerable danger; and they also had an uneasy feeling that starving and mutinous soldiers were very uncertain in taking revenge. The condition of the army gave a sudden and piercing reality to Washington's indignant words to Mathews on October 4th: "At a time when public harmony is so essential, when we should aid and assist each other with all our abilities, when our hearts should be open to information and our hands ready to administer relief, to find distrusts and jealousies taking possession of the mind and a party spirit prevailing affords a most melancholy reflection, and forebodes no good." The hoarse murmur of impending mutiny emphasized strongly the words written on the same day to Duane: "The history of the war is a history of false hopes and temporary expedients. Would to God they were to end here."

The events in the south, too, had a sobering effect. The congressional general Gates had not proved a success. His defeat at Camden had been terribly complete, and his flight had been too rapid to inspire confidence in his capacity for recuperation. The members of Congress were thus led to believe that as managers of military matters they left much to be desired; and when Washington, on October 11th, addressed to them one of his long and admirable letters on reorganization, it was received in a very chastened spirit. They had listened to many such letters before, and had benefited by them always a little, but danger and defeat gave this one peculiar point. They therefore accepted the situation, and adopted all the suggestions of the commander-in-chief. They also in the same reasonable frame of mind determined that Washington should select the next general for the southern army. A good deal could have been saved had this decision been reached before; but even now it was not too late. October 14th, Washington appointed Greene to this post of difficulty and danger, and Greene's assumption of the command marks the turning-point in the tide of disaster, and the beginning of the ultimate expulsion of the British from the only portion of the colonies where they had made a tolerable campaign.

The uses of adversity, moreover, did not stop here. They extended to the States, which began to grow more vigorous in action, and to show signs of appreciating the gravity of the situation and the duties which rested upon them. This change and improvement both in Congress and the States came none too soon. Indeed, as it was, the results of their

renewed efforts were too slow to be felt at once by the army, and
mutinies broke out even after the new spirit had shown itself.
Washington also sent Knox to travel from State to State, to see the various governors, and lay the situation of affairs before them; yet even
with such a text it was a difficult struggle to get the States to make
quick and strong exertions sufficient to prevent a partial mutiny from
becoming a general revolt. The lesson, however, had had its effect. For
the moment, at least, the cause was saved. The worst defects were tem-
porarily remedied, and something was done toward supplies and subsis-
tence. The army would be able to exist through another winter, and
face another summer. Then the next campaign might bring the decisive moment; but still, who could tell? Years, instead of months, might
yet elapse before the end was reached, and then no man could say what
the result would be.

Washington saw plainly enough that the relief and improvement
were only temporary, and that carelessness and indifference were likely
to return, and be more case-hardened than ever. He was too strong and
sane a man to waste time in fighting shadows or in nourishing himself
with hopes. He dealt with the present as he found it, and fought down
difficulties as they sprang up in his path. But he was also a man of
extraordinary prescience, with a foresight as penetrating as it was judicious. It was, perhaps, his most remarkable gift, and while he controlled
the present he studied the future. Outside of the operations of armies,
and the plans of campaign, he saw, as the war progressed, that the really
fatal perils were involved in the political system. At the beginning of the
Revolution there was no organization outside the local state governments. Congress voted and resolved in favor of anything that seemed
proper, and the States responded to their appeal. In the first flush of revolution, and the first excitement of freedom, this was all very well. But
as the early passion cooled, and a long and stubborn struggle, replete
with sufferings and defeat, developed itself, the want of system began
to appear.

One of the earliest tasks of Congress was the formation of articles for
a general government, but state jealousies, and the delays incident to the

movements of thirteen sovereignties, prevented their adoption until the war was nearly over. Washington, suffering from all the complicated troubles of jarring States and general incoherence, longed for and urged the adoption of the act of confederation. He saw sooner than any one else, and with more painful intensity, the need of better union and more energetic government. As the days and months of difficulties and trials went by, the suggestions on this question in his letters grew more frequent and more urgent, and they showed the insight of the statesman and practical man of affairs. How much he hoped from the final acceptance of the act of confederation it is not easy to say, but he hoped for some improvement certainly. When at last it went into force, he saw almost at once that it would not do, and in the spring of 1780 he knew it to be a miserable failure. The system which had been established was really no better than that which had preceded it. With alarm and disgust Washington found himself flung back on what he called "the pernicious state system," and with worse prospects than ever.

Up to the time of the Revolution he had never given attention to the philosophy or science of government, but when it fell to his lot to fight the war for independence he perceived almost immediately the need of a strong central government, and his suggestions, scattered broadcast among his correspondents, manifested a knowledge of the conditions of the political problem possessed by no one else at that period. When he was satisfied of the failure of the confederation, his efforts to improve the existing administration multiplied, and he soon had the assistance of his aide-de-camp, Alexander Hamilton, who then wrote, although little more than a boy, his remarkable letters on government and finance, which were the first full expositions of the political necessities from which sprang the Constitution of the United States. Washington was vigorous in action and methodical in business, while the system of thirteen sovereignties was discordant, disorderly, and feeble in execution. He knew that the vices inherent in the confederation were ineradicable and fatal, and he also knew that it was useless to expect any comprehensive reforms until the war was over. The problem before him was whether the existing machine could be made to work until the British were finally driven from the country. The winter of 1780–81 was marked, therefore, on his part, by an urgent striving for union, and by unceasing efforts to mend and improve the rickety system of the confederation. It was with this view that he secured the despatch of Laurens, whom he carefully instructed to get money in Paris; for he was satisfied that it was only possible to tide over the financial difficulties by foreign loans from those interested in our success. In the same spirit he worked to bring about the establishment of executive departments, which was finally accomplished, after delays that sorely tried his patience. These two cases were but the most important among many of similar character, for he was always at work on these perplexing questions.

It is an astonishing proof of the strength and power of his mind that he was able to solve the daily questions of army existence, to deal with the allies, to plan attacks on New York, to watch and scheme for the southern department, to cope with Arnold's treason, with mutiny, and with administrative imbecility, and at the very same time consider the gravest governmental problems, and send forth wise suggestions, which met the exigencies of the moment, and laid the foundation of much that afterwards appeared in the Constitution of the United States. He was not a speculator on government, and after his fashion he was engaged in dealing with the questions of the day and hour. Yet the ideas that he put forth in this time of confusion and conflict and expedients were so vitally sound and wise that they deserve the most careful study in relation to after events. The political trials and difficulties of this period were the stern teachers from whom Washington acquired the knowledge and experience which made him the principal agent in bringing about the formation and adoption of the Constitution of the United States. We shall have occasion to examine these opinions and views more closely when they were afterwards brought into actual play. At this point it is only necessary to trace the history of the methods by which he solved the problem of the Revolution before the political system of the confederation became absolutely useless.

CHAPTER X

YORKTOWN

THE FAILURE TO accomplish anything in the north caused Washington, as the year drew to a close, to turn his thoughts once more toward a combined movement at the south. In pursuance of this idea, he devised a scheme of uniting with the Spaniards in the seizure of Florida, and of advancing thence through Georgia to assail the English in the rear. De Rochambeau did not approve the plan and it was abandoned; but the idea of a southern movement was still kept steadily in sight. The governing thought now was, not to protect this place or that, but to cast aside everything else in order to strike one great blow which would finish the war. Where he could do this, time alone would show, but if one follows the correspondence closely, it is apparent that Washington's military instinct turned more and more toward the south.

In that department affairs changed their aspect rapidly. January 17th, Morgan won his brilliant victory at the Cowpens, withdrew in good order with his prisoners, and united his army with that of Greene. Cornwallis was terribly disappointed by this unexpected reverse, but he determined to push an, defeat the combined American army, and then join the British forces on the Chesapeake. Greene was too weak to risk a battle, and made a masterly retreat of two hundred miles before Cornwallis, escaping across the Dan only twelve hours ahead of the enemy. The moment the British moved away, Greene recrossed the river and hung upon their rear. For a month he kept in their neighborhood, checking the rising of the Tories, and declining battle. At last he received reinforcements, felt strong enough to stand his ground, and on March 15th the battle of Guilford Court House was fought. It was a sharp and bloody fight; the British had the advantage, and Greene abandoned the field, bringing off his army in good order. Cornwallis, on his part, had suffered so heavily, however, that his victory turned to ashes. On the 18th he was in full retreat, with Greene in hot chase, and it was not until the 28th that he succeeded in getting over the Deep River and escaping to Wilmington. Thence he determined to push on and transfer the seat of war to the Chesapeake. Greene, with the boldness and quickness which showed him to be a soldier of a high order, now dropped the pursuit and turned back to fight the British in detachments and free the southern States. There is no need to follow him in the brilliant operations which ensued, and by which he achieved this result. It is sufficient to say here that he had altered the whole aspect of the war, forced Cornwallis into Virginia within reach of Washington, and begun the work of redeeming the Carolinas.

The troops which Cornwallis intended to join had been sent in detachments to Virginia during the winter and spring. The first body had arrived early in January under the command of Arnold, and a general marauding and ravaging took place. A little later General Phillips arrived with reinforcements and took command. On May 13th, General Phillips died, and a week later Cornwallis appeared at Petersburg, assumed control, and sent Arnold back to New York.

Meantime Washington, though relieved by Morgan's and Greene's admirable work, had a most trying and unhappy winter and spring. He sent every man he could spare, and more than he ought to have spared, to Greene, and he stripped himself still further when the invasion of Virginia began. But for the most part he was obliged, from lack of any naval strength, to stand helplessly by and see more and more British troops sent to the south, and witness the ravaging of his native State, without any ability to prevent it. To these grave trials was added a small one, which stung him to the quick. The British came up the Potomac, and Lund Washington, in order to preserve Mount Vernon, gave them refreshments, and treated them in a conciliatory manner. He meant well but acted ill, and Washington wrote:

> It would have been a less painful circumstance to me to have heard that, in consequence of your noncompliance with their request, they had burnt my house and laid the plantation in ruins. You ought to have considered yourself as my representative, and should have reflected on the bad example of communicating with the enemy, and making a voluntary offer of refreshments to them, with a view to prevent a conflagration.

What a clear glimpse this little episode gives of the earnestness of the man who wrote these lines. He could not bear the thought that any favor should be shown him on any pretence. He was ready to take his share of the marauding and pillaging with the rest, but he was deeply indignant at the idea that any one representing him should even appear to ask a favor of the British.

Altogether, the spring of 1781 was very trying, for there was nothing so galling to Washington as to be unable to fight. He wanted to get to the south, but he was bound hand and foot by lack of force. Yet the obstacles did not daunt or depress him. He wrote in June that he felt sure of bringing the war to a happy conclusion, and in the division of the British forces he saw his opportunity taking shape. Greene had the southern forces well in hand. Cornwallis was equally removed from Clinton on the north and Rawdon on the south, and had come within reach; so that if he could but have naval strength he could fall upon Cornwallis with superior force and crush him. In naval matters fortune thus far had dealt hardly with him, yet he could not but feel that a French fleet of sufficient force must soon come. He grasped the situation with a master-hand, and began to prepare the way. Still he kept his counsel strictly to himself, and set to work to threaten, and if possible to attack, New York, not with much hope of succeeding in any such attempt, but with a view of frightening Clinton and of inducing him either to withdraw troops from Virginia, or at least to withhold reinforcements. As he began his Virginian campaign in this distant and remote fashion at the mouth of the Hudson, he was cheered by news that De Grasse, the French admiral, had sent recruits to Newport, and intended to come himself to the American coast. He at once wrote De Grasse not to determine absolutely to come to New York, hinting that it might prove more advisable to operate to the southward. It required great tact to keep the French fleet where he needed it, and yet not reveal his intentions, and nothing showed Washington's foresight more plainly than the manner in which he made the moves in this campaign, when miles of space and weeks of time separated him from the final object of his plans. To trace this mastery of details, and the skill with which every point was remembered and covered, would require a long and minute narrative. They can only be indicated here sufficiently to show how exactly each movement fitted in its place, and how all together brought the great result.

Fortified by the good news from De Grasse, Washington had an interview with De Rochambeau, and effected a junction with the French army. Thus strengthened, he opened his campaign against Cornwallis by beginning a movement against Clinton. The troops were massed above the city, and an effort was made to surprise the upper posts and destroy Delancey's partisan corps. The attempt, although well planned, failed of its immediate purpose, giving Washington opportunity only for an effective reconnoissance of the enemy's positions. But the move was perfectly successful in its real and indirect object. Clinton was alarmed. He began to write to Cornwallis that troops should be returned to New York, and he gave up absolutely the idea of sending more men to Virginia. Having thus convinced Clinton that New York was menaced, Washington then set to work to familiarize skilfully the minds of his allies and of Congress with the idea of a southern campaign. With this end in view, he wrote on August 2d that, if more troops arrived from Virginia, New York would be impracticable, and that the next point was the south. The only contingency, as he set forth, was the all-important one of obtaining naval superiority. August 15th this essential condition gave promise of fulfilment, for on that day definite news arrived that De Grasse with his fleet was on his way to the Chesapeake. Without a moment's hesitation, Washington began to move, and at the same time he sent an urgent letter to the New England governors, demanding troops with an earnestness which he had never surpassed.

In Virginia, meanwhile, during these long mid-summer days, while Washington was waiting and planning, Cornwallis had been going up and down, harrying, burning, and plundering. His cavalry had scattered the legislature, and driven Governor Jefferson in headlong flight over the hills, while property to the value of more than three millions had been destroyed. Lafayette, sent by Washington to maintain the American cause, had been too weak to act decisively, but he had been true to his general's teaching, and, refusing battle, had hung upon the flanks of the British and harassed and checked them. Joined by Wayne, he had fought an unsuccessful engagement at Green Springs, but brought off his army, and with steady pertinacity followed the enemy to the coast, gathering strength as he moved. Now, when all was at last ready, Washington began to draw his net about Cornwallis, whom he had been keenly watching during the victorious marauding of the summer. On the news of the coming of the French fleet, he wrote to Lafayette to be prepared to join him when he reached Virginia, to retain Wayne, who intended to join Greene, and to stop Cornwallis at all hazards, if he attempted to go southward.

Cornwallis, however, had no intention of moving. He had seen the peril of his position, and had wished to withdraw to Charleston; but the ministry, highly pleased with his performances, wished him to remain on the Chesapeake, and decisive orders came to him to take a permanent post in that region. Clinton, moreover, was jealous of Cornwallis, and, impressed and deceived by Washington's movements, he not only sent no reinforcements, but detained three thousand Hessians, who had lately arrived. Cornwallis, therefore, had no choice, and with much writing for aid, and some protesting, he obeyed his orders, planted himself at Yorktown and Gloucester, and proceeded to fortify, while Lafayette kept close watch upon him. Cornwallis was a good soldier and a clever man, suffering, as Burgoyne did, from a stupid ministry and a dull and jealous commander-in-chief. Thus hampered and burdened, he was ready to fall a victim to the operations of a really great general, whom his official superiors in England undervalued and despised.

August 17th, as soon as he had set his own machinery in motion, Washington wrote to De Grasse to meet him in the Chesapeake. He was working now more anxiously and earnestly than at any time in the Revolution, not merely because he felt that success depended on the blow, but because he descried a new and alarming danger. He had perceived it in June, and the idea pursued him until all was over, and kept recurring in his letters during this strained and eager summer. To Washington's eyes, watching campaigns and government at home and the politics of Europe abroad, the signs of exhaustion, of mediation, and of coming peace across the Atlantic were plainly visible. If peace should come as things then were, America would get independence, and be shorn of many of her most valuable possessions. The sprawling British campaign of maraud and plunder, so bad in a military point of view, and about to prove fatal to Cornwallis, would, in case of sudden cessation of hostilities, be capable of the worst construction. Time, therefore, had become of the last importance. The decisive blow must be given at once, and before the slow political movements could come to a head. On July 14th, Washington had his plan mapped out. He wrote in his diary:

> Matters having now come to a crisis, and a decided plan to be determined on, I was obliged—from the shortness of Count De Grasse's promised stay on this coast, the apparent disinclination of their naval officers to force the harbor of New York, and the feeble compliance of the States with my requisitions for men hitherto, and the little prospect of greater exertions in future—to give up all ideas of attacking New York, and instead thereof to remove the French troops and a detachment from the American army to the Head of Elk, to be transported to Virginia for the purpose of coöperating with the force from the West Indies against the troops in that State.

Like most of Washington's plans, this one was clear-cut and direct, and looks now simple enough, but at the moment it was hedged with almost inconceivable difficulties at every step. The ever-present and ever-growing obstacles at home were there as usual. Appeals to Morris for money were met by the most discouraging responses, and the States seemed more lethargic than ever. Neither men nor supplies could be obtained; neither transportation nor provision for the march could be promised. Then, too, in addition to all this, came a wholly new set of stumbling-blocks arising among the allies. Everything hinged on the naval force. Washington needed it for a short time only; but for that crucial moment he must have not only superiority but supremacy at sea. Every French ship that could be reached must be in the Chesapeake, and Washington had had too many French fleets slip away from him at the last moment and bring everything to naught to take any chances in this direction. To bring about his naval supremacy required the utmost tact and good management, and that he succeeded is one of the chief triumphs of the campaign. In fact, at the very outset he was threatened in this quarter with a serious defection. De Barras, with the American squadron, was at Boston, and it was essential that he should be united with De Grasse at Yorktown. But De Barras was nettled by the favoritism which had made De Grasse, his junior in service, his superior in command. He determined therefore to take advantage of his orders and sail away to the north to Nova Scotia and Newfoundland, and leave De Grasse to fight it out alone. It is a hard thing to beat an opposing army, but it is equally hard to bring human jealousies and ambitions into the narrow path of self-sacrifice and subordination. Alarmed beyond measure at the suggested departure of the Boston squadron, Washington wrote a letter, which De Rochambeau signed with him, urging De Barras to turn his fleet toward the Chesapeake. It was a skilfully drawn missive, an adroit mingling of appeals to honor and sympathy and of vigorous demands to perform an obvious duty. The letter did its work, the diplomacy of Washington was successful, and De Barras suppressed his feelings of disappointment, and agreed to go to the Chesapeake and serve under De Grasse.

This point made, Washington pushed on his preparations, or rather pushed on despite his lack of preparations, and on August 17th, as has been said, wrote to De Grasse to meet him in the Chesapeake. He left the larger part of his own troops with Heath, to whom in carefully drawn instructions he entrusted the grave duty of guarding the Hudson and watching the British in New York. This done, he gathered his forces together, and on August 21st the army started on its march to the south. On the 23d and 24th it crossed the Hudson, without annoyance from the British of any kind. Washington had threatened New York so effectively, and manœuvred so successfully, that Clinton could not be shaken in his belief that the real object of the Americans was his own army; and it was not until September 2d that he realized that his enemy was going to the south, and that Cornwallis was in danger. He even then hesitated and delayed, but finally dispatched Admiral Graves with the fleet to the Chesapeake. The Admiral came upon the French early on September 5th, the very day that Washington was rejoicing in the news that De Grasse had arrived in the Chesapeake and had landed St. Simon and three thousand men to support Lafayette. As soon as the English fleet appeared, the French, although many of their men were on shore, sailed out and gave battle. An indecisive action ensued, in which the British suffered so much that five days later they burned one of their frigates and withdrew to New York. De Grasse returned to his anchorage, to find that De Barras had come in from Newport with eight ships and ten transports carrying ordnance.

While everything was thus moving well toward the consummation of the campaign, Washington, in the midst of his delicate and important work of breaking camp and beginning his rapid march to the south, was harassed by the ever-recurring difficulties of the feeble and bankrupt government of the confederation. He wrote again and again to Morris for money, and finally got some. His demands for men and supplies remained almost unheeded, but somehow he got provisions enough to start. He foresaw the most pressing need, and sent messages in all directions for shipping to transport his army down the Chesapeake. No one responded, but still he gathered the transports; at first a few, then more, and finally, after many delays, enough to move his army to Yorktown. The spectacle of such a struggle, so heroically made, one would think, might have inspired every soul on the continent with enthusiasm; but at this very moment, while Washington was breaking camp and marching southward, Congress was considering the reduction of the army!—which was as appropriate as it would have been for the English Parliament to have reduced the navy on the eve of Trafalgar, or for Lincoln to have advised the restoration of the army to a peace footing while Grant was fighting in the Wilderness. The fact was that the Continental Congress was weakened in ability and very tired in point of nerve and will-power. They saw that peace was coming, and naturally thought that the sooner they could get it the better. They entirely failed to see, as Washington saw, that in a too sudden peace lurked the danger of the *uti possidetis*, and that the mere fact of peace by no means implied necessarily complete success. They did not, of course, effect their reductions, but they remained inert, and so for the most part did the state governments, becoming drags upon the wheels of war instead of helpers to the man who was driving the Revolution forward to its goal. Both state and confederate governments still meant well, but they were worn out and relaxed. Yet over and through all these heavy masses of misapprehension and feebleness, Washington made his way. Here again all that can be said is that somehow or other the thing was done. We can take account of the resisting forces, but we cannot tell just how they were dealt with. We only know that one strong man trampled them down and got what he wanted done.

Pushing on after the joyful news of the arrival of De Grasse had been received, Washington left the army to go by water from the Head of Elk, and hurried to Mount Vernon, accompanied by De Rochambeau. It was six years since he had seen his home. He had left it a Virginian colonel, full of forebodings for his country, with a vast and unknown problem awaiting solution at his hands. He returned to it the first soldier of his day, after six years of battle and trial, of victory and defeat, on the eve of the last and crowning triumph. As he paused on the well-beloved spot, and gazed across the broad and beautiful river at his feet, thoughts and

remembrances must have come thronging to his mind which it is given
to few men to know. He lingered there two days, and then pressing on
again, was in Williamsburg on the 14th, and on the 17th went on board
the Ville de Paris to congratulate De Grasse on his victory, and to concert
measures for the siege.

The meeting was most agreeable. All had gone well, all promised
well, and everything was smiling and harmonious. Yet they were on the
eve of the greatest peril which occurred in the campaign. Washington had
managed to scrape together enough transports; but his almost unassisted
labors had taken time, and delay had followed. Then the transports were
slow, and winds and tides were uncertain, and there was further delay.
The interval permitted De Grasse to hear that the British fleet had
received reinforcements, and to become nervous in consequence. He
wanted to get out to sea; the season was advancing, and he was anxious
to return to the West Indies; and above all he did not wish to fight in the
bay. He therefore proposed firmly and vigorously to leave two ships in
the river, and stand out to sea with his fleet. The Yorktown campaign
began to look as if it had reached its conclusion. Once again Washington
wrote one of his masterly letters of expostulation and remonstrance, and
once more he prevailed, aided by the reasoning and appeals of Lafayette,
who carried the message. De Grasse consented to stay, and Washington,
grateful beyond measure, wrote him that "a great mind knows how to
make personal sacrifice to secure an important general good." Under the
circumstances, and in view of the general truth of this complimentary
sentiment, one cannot help rejoicing that De Grasse had "a great mind."

At all events he stayed, and thereafter everything went well. The
northern army landed at Williamsburg and marched for Yorktown on the
28th. They reconnoitred the outlying works the next day, and prepared
for an immediate assault; but in the night Cornwallis abandoned all his
outside works and withdrew into the town. Washington thereupon
advanced at once, and prepared for the siege. On the night of the 5th, the
trenches were opened only six hundred yards from the enemy's line, and
in three days the first parallel was completed. On the 11th the second
parallel was begun, and on the 14th the American batteries played on the

two advanced redoubts with such effect that the breaches were pronounced practicable. Washington at once ordered an assault. The smaller
redoubt was stormed by the Americans under Hamilton and taken in ten
minutes. The other, larger and more strongly garrisoned, was carried by
the French with equal gallantry, after half an hour's fighting. During the
assault Washington stood in an embrasure of the grand battery, watching
the advance of the men. He was always given to exposing himself recklessly when there was fighting to be done, but not when he was only an
observer. This night, however, he was much exposed to the enemy's fire.
One of his aides, anxious and disturbed for his safety, told him that the
place was perilous. "If you think so," was the quiet answer, "you are at
liberty to step back." The moment was too exciting, too fraught with
meaning, to think of peril. The old fighting spirit of Braddock's field was
unchained for the last time. He would have liked to head the American
assault, sword in hand, and as he could not do that he stood as near his
troops as he could, utterly regardless of the bullets whistling in the air
about him. Who can wonder at his intense excitement at that moment?
Others saw a brilliant storming of two outworks, but to Washington the
whole Revolution, and all the labor and thought and conflict of six years
were culminating in the smoke and din on those redoubts, while out of
the dust and heat of the sharp quick fight success was coming. He had
waited long, and worked hard, and his whole soul went out as he watched
the troops cross the abattis and scale the works. He could have no
thought of danger then, and when all was over he turned to Knox and
said, "The work is done, and well done. Bring me my horse."

Washington was not mistaken. The work was indeed done. Tarleton
early in the siege had dashed out against Lauzun on the other side of the
river and been repulsed. Cornwallis had been forced back steadily into
the town, and his redoubts, as soon as taken, were included in the second
parallel. A sortie to retake the redoubts failed, and a wild attempt to
transport the army across the river was stopped by a gale of wind. On the
17th Cornwallis was compelled to face much bloody and useless slaughter, or to surrender. He chose the latter course, and after opening negotiations and trying in vain to obtain delay, finally signed the capitulation

and gave up the town. The next day the troops marched out and laid down their arms. Over 7000 British and Hessian troops surrendered. It was a crushing defeat. The victorious army consisted in round numbers of 5500 continentals, 3500 militia, and 7000 French, and they were backed by the French fleet with entire control of the sea.

When Washington had once reached Yorktown with his fleet and army, the campaign was really at an end, for he held Cornwallis in an iron grip from which there was no escape. The masterly part of the Yorktown campaign lay in the manner in which it was brought about, in the management of so many elements, and in the rapidity of movement which carried an army without any proper supplies or means of transportation from New York to the mouth of Chesapeake Bay. The control of the sea had been the great advantage of the British from the beginning, and had enabled them to achieve all that they ever gained. With these odds against him, with no possibility of obtaining a fleet of his own, Washington saw that his only chance of bringing the war to a quick and successful issue was by means of the French. It is difficult to manage allied troops. It is still more difficult to manage allied troops and an allied fleet. Washington did both with infinite address, and won. The chief factor of his success in this direction lay in his profound personal influence on all men with whom he came in contact. His courtesy and tact were perfect, but he made no concessions, and never stooped. The proudest French noble who came here shrank from disagreement with the American general, and yet not one of them had anything but admiration and respect to express when they wrote of Washington in their memoirs, diaries, and letters. He impressed them one and all with a sense of power and greatness which could not be disregarded. Many times he failed to get the French fleet in coöperation, but finally it came. Then he put forth all his influence and all his address, and thus he got De Barras to the Chesapeake, and kept De Grasse at Yorktown.

This was one side of the problem, the most essential because everything hinged on the fleet, but by no means the most harassing. The doubt about the control of the sea made it impossible to work steadily for a sufficient time toward any one end. It was necessary to have a plan for every contingency, and be ready to adopt any one of several plans at short notice. With a foresight and judgment that never failed, Washington planned an attack on New York, another on Yorktown, and a third on Charleston. The division of the British forces gave him his opportunity of striking at one point with an overwhelming force, but there was always the possibility of their suddenly reuniting. In the extreme south he felt reasonably sure that Greene would hold Rawdon, but he was obliged to deceive and amuse Clinton, and at the same time, with a ridiculously inferior force, to keep Cornwallis from marching to South Carolina. Partly by good fortune, partly by skill, Cornwallis was kept in Virginia, while by admirably managed feints and threats Clinton was held in New York in inactivity. When the decisive moment came, and it was evident that the control of the sea was to be determined in the Chesapeake, Washington, overriding all sorts of obstacles, moved forward, despite a bankrupt and inert government, with a rapidity and daring which have been rarely equalled. It was a bold stroke to leave Clinton behind at the mouth of the Hudson, and only the quickness with which it was done, and the careful deception which had been practised, made it possible. Once at Yorktown, there was little more to do. The combination was so perfect, and the judgment had been so sure, that Cornwallis was crushed as helplessly as if he had been thrown before the car of Juggernaut. There was really but little fighting, for there was no opportunity to fight. Washington held the British in a vice, and the utter helplessness of Cornwallis, the entire inability of such a good and gallant soldier even to struggle, are the most convincing proofs of the military genius of his antagonist.

CHAPTER XI

PEACE

FORTITUDE IN MISFORTUNE is more common than composure in the hour of victory. The bitter medicine of defeat, however unpalatable, is usually extremely sobering, but the strong new wine of success generally sets the heads of poor humanity spinning, and leads often to worse results than folly. The capture of Cornwallis was enough to have turned the strongest head, for the moment at least, but it had no apparent effect upon the man who had brought it to pass, and who, more than any one else, knew what it meant. Unshaken and undismayed in the New Jersey winter, and among the complicated miseries of Valley Forge, Washington turned from the spectacle of a powerful British army laying down their arms as coolly as if he had merely fought a successful skirmish, or repelled a dangerous raid. He had that rare gift, the attribute of the strongest minds, of leaving the past to take care of itself. He never fretted over what could not be undone, nor dallied among pleasant memories while aught still remained to do. He wrote to Congress in words of quiet congratulation, through which pierced the devout and solemn sense of the great deed accomplished, and then, while the salvos of artillery were still booming in his ears, and the shouts of victory were still rising about him, he set himself, after his fashion, to care for the future and provide for the immediate completion of his work.

He wrote to De Grasse, urging him to join in an immediate movement against Charleston, such as he had already suggested, and he presented in the strongest terms the opportunities now offered for the sudden and complete ending of the struggle. But the French admiral was by no means imbued with the tireless and determined spirit of Washington. He had had his fill even of victory, and was so eager to get back to the West Indies, where he was to fall a victim to Rodney, that he would not even transport troops to Wilmington. Thus deprived of the force which alone made comprehensive and extended movements possible, Washington returned, as he had done so often before, to making the best of cramped circumstances and straitened means. He sent all the troops be could spare to Greene, to help him in wresting the southern States from the enemy, the work to which he had in vain summoned De Grasse. This done, he prepared to go north. On his way he was stopped at Eltham by the illness and death of his wife's son, John Custis, a blow which he felt severely, and which saddened the great victory he had just achieved. Still the business of the state could not wait on private grief. He left the house of mourning, and, pausing for an instant only at Mount Vernon, hastened on to Philadelphia. At the very moment of victory, and while honorable members were shaking each other's hands and congratulating each other that the war was now really over, the commander-in-chief had fallen again to writing them letters in the old strain, and was once more urging them to keep up the army, while he himself gave his personal attention to securing a naval force for the ensuing year, through the medium of Lafayette. Nothing was ever finished with Washington until it was really complete throughout, and he had as little time for rejoicing as he had for despondency or despair, while a British force still remained in the country. He probably felt that this was as untoward a time as he had ever met in a pretty large experience of unsuitable occasions, for offering sound advice, but he was not deterred thereby from doing it. This time, however, he was destined to an agreeable disappointment, for on his arrival at Philadelphia he found an excellent spirit prevailing in Congress. That body was acting cheerfully on his advice, it had filled the departments of the government, and set on foot such measures as it could to keep up the army. So Washington remained for some time at Philadelphia, helping and counselling Congress in its work, and writing to the States vigorous letters, demanding pay and clothing for the soldiers, ever uppermost in his thoughts.

But although Congress was compliant, Washington could not convince the country of the justice of his views, and of the continued need of energetic exertion. The steady relaxation of tone, which the strain of a long and trying war had produced, was accelerated by the brilliant victory of Yorktown. Washington for his own part had but little trust in the sense or the knowledge of his enemy. He felt that Yorktown was decisive, but he also thought that Great Britain would still struggle on, and that her talk of peace was very probably a mere blind, to enable her to gain time, and, by taking advantage of our relaxed and feeble condition, to strike again in hope of winning back all that had been lost. He therefore continued his appeals in behalf of the army, and reiterated everywhere the necessity for fresh and ample preparations.

As late as May 4th he wrote sharply to the States for men and money, saying that the change of ministry was likely to be adverse to peace, and that we were being lulled into a false and fatal sense of security. A few days later, on receiving information from Sir Guy Carleton of the address of the Commons to the king for peace, Washington wrote to Congress: "For my own part, I view our situation as such that, instead of relaxing, we ought to improve the present moment as the most favorable to our wishes. The British nation appear to me to be staggered, and almost ready to sink beneath the accumulating weight of debt and misfortune. If we follow the blow with vigor and energy, I think the game is our own."

Again he wrote in July. "Sir Guy Carleton is using every art to soothe and lull our people into a state of security. Admiral Digby is capturing all our vessels, and suffocating as fast as possible in prisonships all our seamen who will not enlist into the service of his Britannic Majesty; and Haldimand, with his savage allies, is scalping and burning on the frontiers." Facts always were the object of Washington's first regard, and while gentlemen on all sides were talking of peace, war was going on, and he could not understand the supineness which would permit our seamen to be suffocated, and our borderers scalped, because some people thought the war ought to be and practically was over. While the other side was fighting, he wished to be fighting too. A month later he wrote to Greene: "From the former infatuation, duplicity, and perverse system of British policy, I confess I am induced to doubt everything, to suspect everything." He could say heartily with the Trojan priest, "*Quicquid id est timeo Danaos et dona ferentes.*" Yet again, a month later still, when the negotiations were really going forward in Paris, he wrote to McHenry: "If we are wise, let us prepare for the worst. There is nothing which will so soon produce a speedy and honorable peace as a state of preparation for war; and we must either do this, or lay our account to patch up an inglorious peace, after all the toil, blood, and treasure we have spent."

No man had done and given so much as Washington, and at the same time no other man had his love of thoroughness, and his indomitable fighting temper. He found few sympathizers, his words fell upon deaf ears, and he was left to struggle on and maintain his ground as best he might, without any substantial backing. As it turned out, England was more severely wounded than he dared to hope, and her desire for peace was real. But Washington's distrust and the active policy which he urged were, in the conditions of the moment, perfectly sound, both in a military and a political point of view. It made no real difference, however, whether he was right or wrong in his opinion. He could not get what he wanted, and he was obliged to drag through another year, fettered in his military movements, and oppressed with anxiety for the future. He longed to drive the British from New York, and was forced to content himself, as so often before, with keeping his army in existence. It was a trying time, and fruitful in nothing but anxious forebodings. All the fighting was confined to skirmishes of outposts, and his days were consumed in vain efforts to obtain help from the States, while he watched with painful eagerness the current of events in Europe, down which the fortunes of his country were feebly drifting.

Among the petty incidents of the year there was one which, in its effects, gained an international importance, which has left a deep stain upon the English arms, and which touched Washington deeply. Captain Huddy, an American officer, was captured in a skirmish and carried to

New York, where he was placed in confinement. Thence he was taken on April 12th by a party of Tories in the British service, commanded by Captain Lippencott, and hanged in the broad light of day on the heights near Middletown. Testimony and affidavits to the fact, which was never questioned, were duly gathered and laid before Washington. The deed was one of wanton barbarity, for which it would be difficult to find a parallel in the annals of modern warfare. The authors of this brutal murder, to our shame be it said, were of American birth, but they were fighting for the crown and wore the British uniform. England, which for generations has deafened the world with paeans of praise for her own love of fair play and for her generous humanity, stepped in here and threw the mantle of her protection over these cowardly hangmen. It has not been uncommon for wild North American savages to deliver up criminals to the vengeance of the law, but English ministers and officers condoned the murder of Huddy, and sheltered his murderers.

When the case was laid before Washington it stirred him to the deepest wrath. He submitted the facts to twenty-five of his general officers, who unanimously advised what he was himself determined upon, instant retaliation. He wrote at once to Sir Guy Carleton, and informed him that unless the murderers were given up he should be compelled to retaliate. Carleton replied that a court-martial was ordered, and some attempt was made to recriminate; but Washington pressed on in the path he had marked out, and had an English officer selected by lot and held in close confinement to await the action of the enemy. These sharp measures brought the British, as nothing else could have done, to some sense of the enormity of the crime that had been committed. Sir Guy Carleton wrote in remonstrance, and Washington replied: "Ever since the commencement of this unnatural war my conduct has borne invariable testimony against those inhuman excesses, which, in too many instances, have marked its progress. With respect to a late transaction, to which I presume your excellency alludes, I have already expressed my resolution, a resolution formed on the most mature deliberation, and from which I shall not recede." The affair dragged along, purposely protracted by the British, and the court-martial on a technical point acquitted Lippencott.

Sir Guy Carleton, however, who really was deeply indignant at the outrage, wrote, expressing his abhorrence, disavowed Lippencott, and promised a further inquiry. This placed Washington in a very trying position,
more especially as his humanity was touched by the situation of the
unlucky hostage. The fatal lot had fallen upon a mere boy, Captain Asgill,
who was both amiable and popular, and Washington was beset with
appeals in his behalf, for Lady Asgill moved heaven and earth to save her
son. She interested the French court, and Vergennes made a special
request that Asgill should be released. Even Washington's own officers,
notably Hamilton, sought to influence him, and begged him to recede. In
these difficult circumstances, which were enhanced by the fact that contrary to his orders to select an unconditional prisoner, the lot had fallen
on a Yorktown prisoner protected by the terms of the capitulation,* he
hesitated, and asked instructions from Congress. He wrote to Duane in
September: "While retaliation was apparently necessary, however disagreeable in itself, I had no repugnance to the measure. But when the
end proposed by it is answered by a disavowal of the act, by a dissolution
of the board of refugees, and by a promise (whether with or without
meaning to comply with it, I shall not determine) that further inquisition
should be made into the matter, I thought it incumbent upon me, before
I proceeded any farther in the matter, to have the sense of Congress, who
had most explicitly approved and impliedly indeed ordered retaliation to
take place. To this hour I am held in darkness."

He did not long remain in doubt. The fact was that the public, as is
commonly the case, had forgotten the original crime and saw only the
misery of the man who was to pay the just penalty, and who was, in this
instance, an innocent and vicarious sufferer. It was difficult to refuse
Vergennes, and Congress, glad of the excuse and anxious to oblige their
allies, ordered the release of Asgill. That Washington, touched by the
unhappy condition of his prisoner, did not feel relieved by the result, it
would be absurd to suppose. But he was by no means satisfied, for the
murderous wrong that had been done rankled in his breast. He wrote to

---

*MS. letter to Lincoln.

Vergennes: "Captain Asgill has been released, and is at perfect liberty to return to the arms of an affectionate parent, whose pathetic address to your Excellency could not fail of interesting every feeling heart in her behalf. I have no right to assume any particular merit from the lenient manner in which this disagreeable affair has terminated."

There is a perfect honesty about this which is very wholesome. He had been freely charged with cruelty, and had regarded the accusation with indifference. Now, when it was easy for him to have taken the glory of mercy by simply keeping silent, he took pains to avow that the leniency was not due to him. He was not satisfied, and no one should believe that he was, even if the admission seemed to justify the charge of cruelty. If he erred at all it was in not executing some British officer at the very start, unless Lippencott had been given up within a limited time. As it was, after delay was once permitted, it is hard to see how he could have acted otherwise than he did, but Washington was not in the habit of receding from a fixed purpose, and being obliged to do so in this case troubled him, for he knew that he did well to be angry. But the frankness of the avowal to Vergennes is a good example of his entire honesty and absolute moral fearlessness.

The matter, however, which most filled his heart and mind during these weary days of waiting and doubt was the condition and the future of his soldiers. To those persons who have suspected or suggested that Washington was cold-blooded and unmindful of others, the letters he wrote in regard to the soldiers may be commended. The man whose heart was wrung by the sufferings of the poor people on the Virginian frontier, in the days of the old French war, never in fact changed his nature. Fierce in fight, passionate and hot when his anger was stirred, his love and sympathy were keen and strong toward his army. His heart went out to the brave men who had followed him, loved him, and never swerved in their loyalty to him and to their country. Washington's affection for his men, and their devotion to him, had saved the cause of American independence more often than strategy or daring. Now, when the war was practically over, his influence with both officers and soldiers was destined to be put to its severest tests.

The people of the American colonies were self-governing in the extremest sense, that is, they were accustomed to very little government interference of any sort. They were also poor and entirely unused to war. Suddenly they found themselves plunged into a bitter and protracted conflict with the most powerful of civilized nations. In the first flush of excitement, patriotic enthusiasm supplied many defects; but as time wore on, and year after year passed, and the whole social and political fabric was shaken, the moral tone of the people relaxed. In such a struggle, coming upon an unprepared people of the habits and in the circumstances of the colonists, this relaxation was inevitable. It was likewise inevitable that, as the war continued, there should be in both national and state governments, and in all directions, many shortcomings and many lamentable errors. But for the treatment accorded the army, no such excuse can be made, and no sufficient explanation can be offered. There was throughout the colonies an inborn and a carefully cultivated dread of standing armies and military power. But this very natural feeling was turned most unreasonably against our own army, and carried in that direction to the verge of insanity. This jealousy of military power indeed pursued Washington from the beginning to the end of the Revolution. It cropped out as soon as he was appointed, and came up in one form or another whenever he was obliged to take strong measures. Even at the very end, after he had borne the cause through to triumph, Congress was driven almost to frenzy because Vergennes proposed to commit the disposition of a French subsidy to the commander-in-chief.

If this feeling could show itself toward Washington, it is easy to imagine that it was not restrained toward his officers and men, and the treatment of the soldiers by Congress and by the States was not only ungrateful to the last degree, but was utterly unpardonable. Again and again the menace of immediate ruin and the stern demands of Washington alone extorted the most grudging concessions, and saved the army from dissolution. The soldiers had every reason to think that nothing but personal fear could obtain the barest consideration from the civil power. In this frame of mind, they saw the war which they had fought and won drawing to a close with no prospect of either provision or reward for them, and every indication that they would be disbanded when they were no longer needed, and left in many cases to beggary and want. In the inaction consequent upon the victory at Yorktown, they had ample time to reflect upon these facts, and their reflections were of such a nature that the situation soon became dangerous. Washington, who had struggled in season and out of season for justice to the soldiers, labored more zealously than ever during all this period, aided vigorously by Hamilton, who was now in Congress. Still nothing was done, and in October, 1782, he wrote to the Secretary of War in words warm with indignant feeling: "While I premise that no one I have seen or heard of appears opposed to the principle of reducing the army as circumstances may require, yet I cannot help fearing the result of the measure in con- templation, under present circumstances, when I see such a number of men, goaded by a thousand stings of reflection on the past and of antici- pation on the future, about to be turned into the world, soured by penury and what they call the ingratitude of the public, involved in debts, with- out one farthing of money, to carry them home after having spent the flower of their days, and many of them their patrimonies, in establishing the freedom and independence of their country, and suffered everything that human nature is capable of enduring on this side of death. . . . You may rely upon it, the patriotism and long-suffering of this army are almost exhausted, and that there never was so great a spirit of discontent as at this instant. While in the field I think it may be kept from breaking into acts of outrage; but when we retire into winter-quarters, unless the storm is previously dissipated, I cannot be at ease respecting the consequences. It is high time for a peace."

These were grave words, coming from such a man as Washington, but they passed unheeded. Congress and the States went blandly along as if everything was all right, and as if the army had no grievances. But the sol- diers thought differently. "Dissatisfactions rose to a great and alarming height, and combinations among officers to resign at given periods in a body were beginning to take place." The outlook was so threatening that Washington, who had intended to go to Mount Vernon, remained in camp, and by management and tact thwarted these combinations and converted these dangerous movements into an address to Congress from the officers, asking for half-pay, arrearages, and some other equally proper concessions. Still Congress did not stir. Some indefinite resolutions were passed, but nothing was done as to the commutation of half-pay into a fixed sum, and after such a display of indifference the dissatisfaction increased rapidly, and the army became more and more restless. In March a call was issued for a meeting of officers, and an anonymous address, written with much skill,—the work, as afterwards appeared, of Major John Armstrong,—was published at the same time. The address was well calculated to inflame the passions of the troops; it advised a resort to force, and was scattered broadcast through the camp. The army was now in a ferment, and the situation was full of peril. A weak man would have held his peace; a rash one would have tried to suppress the meeting. Washington did neither, but quietly took control of the whole movement himself. In general orders he censured the call and the address as irregular, and then appointed a time and place for the meeting. Another anonymous address thereupon appeared, quieter in tone, but congratulating the army on the recognition accorded by the commander-in-chief.

When the officers assembled, Washington arose with a manuscript in his hand, and as he took out his glasses said, simply, "You see, gentlemen, I have grown both blind and gray in your service." His address was brief, calm, and strong. The clear, vigorous sentences were charged with meaning and with deep feeling. He exhorted them one and all, both officers and men, to remain loyal and obedient, true to their glorious past and to their country. He appealed to their patriotism, and promised them that which they had always had, his own earnest support in obtaining justice from Congress. When he had finished he quietly withdrew. The officers were deeply moved by his words, and his influence prevailed. Resolutions were passed, reiterating the demands of the army, but professing entire faith in the government. This time Congress listened, and the measures granting half-pay in commutation and certain other requests were passed. Thus this very serious danger was averted, not by the reluctant action of Congress, but by the wisdom and strength of the general, who was loved by his soldiers after a fashion that few conquerors could boast.

Underlying all these general discontents, there was, besides, a well-defined movement, which saw a solution of all difficulties and a redress of all wrongs in a radical change of the form of government, and in the elevation of Washington to supreme power. This party was satisfied that the existing system was a failure, and that it was not and could not be made either strong, honest, or respectable. The obvious relief was in some kind of monarchy, with a large infusion of the one-man power; and it followed, as a matter of course, that the one man could be no other than the commander-in-chief. In May, 1782, when the feeling in the army had risen very high, this party of reform brought their ideas before Washington through an old and respected friend of his, Colonel Nicola. The colonel set forth very clearly the failure and shortcomings of the existing government, argued in favor of the substitution of something much stronger, and wound up by hinting very plainly that his correspondent was the man for the crisis and the proper savior of society. The letter was forcible and well written, and Colonel Nicola was a man of character and standing. It could not be passed over lightly or in silence, and Washington replied as follows: —

> With a mixture of surprise and astonishment, I have read with attention the sentiments you have submitted to my perusal. Be assured, sir, no occurrence in the course of the war has given me more painful sensations than your information of there being such ideas existing in the army as you have expressed, and [which] I must view with abhorrence and reprehend with severity. For the present, the communication of them will rest in my own bosom, unless some further agitation of the matter shall make a disclosure necessary. I am much at a loss to conceive what part of my conduct could have given encouragement to an address which seems to me big with the greatest mischiefs that can befall my country. If I am not deceived in the knowledge of myself, you could not have found a person to whom your schemes are more disagreeable. At the same time, in justice

chaos on the instant. But this is a woful misunderstanding of the man. To put aside a crown for love of country is noble, but to look down upon such an opportunity indicates a much greater loftiness and strength of mind. Washington was wholly free from the vulgar ambition of the usurper, and the desire of mere personal aggrandizement found no place in his nature. His ruling passion was the passion for success, and for thorough and complete success. What he could not bear was the least shadow of failure. To have fought such a war to a victorious finish, and then turned it to his own advantage, would have been to him failure of the meanest kind. He fought to free the colonies from England, and make them independent, not to play the part of a Cæsar or a Cromwell in the wreck and confusion of civil war. He flung aside the suggestion of supreme power, not simply as dishonorable and unpatriotic, but because such a result would have defeated the one great and noble object at which he aimed. Nor did he act in this way through any indolent shrinking from the great task of making what he had won worth winning, by crushing the forces of anarchy and separation, and bringing order and unity out of confusion. From the surrender of Yorktown to the day of his retirement from the Presidency, he worked unceasingly to establish union and strong government in the country he had made independent. He accomplished this great labor more successfully by honest and lawful methods than if he had taken the path of the stronghanded savior of society, and his work in this field did more for the welfare of his country than all his battles. To have restored order at the head of the army was much easier than to effect it in the slow and law-abiding fashion which he adopted. To have refused supreme rule, and then to have effected in the spirit and under the forms of free government all and more than the most brilliant of military chiefs could have achieved by absolute power, is a glory which belongs to Washington alone.

Nevertheless, at that particular juncture it was, as he himself had said, "high time for a peace." The danger at Newburgh had been averted by his commanding influence and the patriotic conduct of the army. But it had been averted only, not removed. The snake was scotched, not killed. The finishing stroke was still needed in the form of an end to hostilities, and it was therefore fortunate for the United States that a fortnight later, on March 23d, news came that a general treaty of peace had been signed. This final consummation of his work, in addition to the passage by Congress of the half-pay commutation and the settlement of the army accounts, filled Washington with deep rejoicing. He felt that in a short time, a few weeks at most, he would be free to withdraw to the quiet life at Mount Vernon for which he longed. But public bodies move slowly, and one delay after another occurred to keep him still in the harness. He chafed under the postponement, but it was not possible to him to remain idle even when he awaited in almost daily expectation the hour of dismissal. He saw with the instinctive glance of statesmanship that the dangerous point in the treaty of peace was in the provisions as to the western posts on the one side, and those relating to British debts on the other. A month therefore had not passed before he brought to the attention of Congress the importance of getting immediate possession of those posts, and a little later he succeeded in having Steuben sent out as a special envoy to obtain their surrender. The mission was vain, as he had feared. He was not destined to extract this thorn for many years, and then only after many trials and troubles. Soon afterward he made a journey with Governor Clinton to Ticonderoga, and along the valley of the Mohawk, "to wear away the time," as he wrote to Congress. He wore away time to more purpose than most people, for where he travelled he observed closely, and his observations were lessons which he never forgot. On this trip he had the western posts and the Indians always in mind, and familiarized himself with the conditions of a part of the country where these matters were of great importance.

On his return he went to Princeton, where Congress had been sitting since their flight from the mutiny which he had recently suppressed, and where a house had been provided for his use. He remained there two months, aiding Congress in their work. During the spring he had been engaged on the matter of a peace establishment, and he now gave Congress elaborate and well-matured advice on that question, and on those of public lands, western settlement, and the best Indian policy. In all these directions his views were clear, far-sighted, and wise. He saw that in these questions was involved much of the future development

and well-being of the country, and he treated them with a precision and
an easy mastery which showed the thought he had given to the new problems which now were coming to the front. Unluckily, he was so far ahead,
both in knowledge and perception, of the body with which he dealt, that
he could get little or nothing done, and in September he wrote in plain
but guarded terms of the incapacity of the lawmakers. The people were
not yet ripe for his measures, and he was forced to bide his time, and see
the injuries caused by indifference and short-sightedness work themselves out. Gradually, however, the absolutely necessary business was
brought to an end. Then Washington issued a circular letter to the governors of the States, which was one of the ablest he ever wrote, and full of
the profoundest statesmanship, and he also sent out a touching address
of farewell to the army, eloquent with wisdom and with patriotism.

From Princeton he went to West Point, where the army that still
remained in service was stationed. Thence he moved to Harlem, and on
November 25th the British army departed, and Washington, with his
troops, accompanied by Governor Clinton and some regiments of local
militia, marched in and took possession. This was the outward sign that
the war was over, and that American independence had been won.
Carleton feared that the entry of the American army might be the signal
for confusion and violence, in which the Tory inhabitants would suffer;
but everything passed off with perfect tranquillity and good order, and in
the evening Clinton gave a public dinner to the commander-in-chief and
the officers of the army.

All was now over, and Washington prepared to go to Annapolis and
lay down his commission. On December 4th his officers assembled in
Fraunces' Tavern to bid him farewell. As he looked about on his faithful
friends, his usual self-command deserted him, and he could not control
his voice. Taking a glass of wine, he lifted it up, and said simply, "With a
heart full of love and gratitude I now take my leave of you, most devoutly
wishing that your latter days may be as prosperous and happy as your former ones have been glorious and honorable." The toast was drunk in
silence, and then Washington added, "I cannot come to each of you and
take my leave, but shall be obliged if you will come and take me by the

hand." One by one they approached, and Washington grasped the hand of each man and embraced him. His eyes were full of tears, and he could not trust himself to speak. In silence he bade each and all farewell, and then, accompanied by his officers, walked to Whitehall Ferry. Entering his barge, the word was given, and as the oars struck the water he stood up and lifted his hat. In solemn silence his officers returned the salute, and watched the noble and gracious figure of their beloved chief until the boat disappeared from sight behind the point of the Battery.

At Philadelphia he stopped a few days and adjusted his accounts, which he had in characteristic fashion kept himself in the neatest and most methodical way. He had drawn no pay, and had expended considerable sums from his private fortune, which he had omitted to charge to the government. The gross amount of his expenses was about 15,000 pounds sterling, including secret service and other incidental outlays. In these days of wild money-hunting, there is something worth pondering in this simple business settlement between a great general and his government, at the close of eight years of war. This done, he started again on his journey. From Philadelphia he proceeded to Annapolis, greeted with addresses and hailed with shouts at every town and village on his route, and having reached his destination, he addressed a letter to Congress on December 20th, asking when it would be agreeable to them to receive him. The 23d was appointed, and on that day, at noon, he appeared before Congress.

The following year a French orator and "maître avocat," in an oration delivered at Toulouse upon the American Revolution, described this scene in these words: "On the day when Washington resigned his commission in the hall of Congress, a crown decked with jewels was placed upon the Book of the Constitutions. Suddenly Washington seizes it, breaks it, and flings the pieces to the assembled people. How small ambitious Cæsar seems beside the hero of America." It is worth while to recall this contemporary French description, because its theatrical and dramatic untruth gives such point by contrast to the plain and dignified reality. The scene was the hall of Congress. The members representing the sovereign power were seated and covered, while all the space about was filled by the governor and state officers of Maryland, by military officers, and by the ladies and gentlemen of the neighborhood, who stood in respectful silence with uncovered heads. Washington was introduced by the Secretary of Congress, and took a chair which had been assigned to him. There was a brief pause, and then the president said that "the United States in Congress assembled were prepared to receive his communication." Washington rose, and replied as follows:

"MR. PRESIDENT: The great events, on which my resignation depended, having at length taken place, I have now the honor of offering my sincere congratulations to Congress, and of presenting myself before them, to surrender into their hands the trust committed to me, and to claim the indulgence of retiring from the service of my country.

"Happy in the confirmation of our independence and sovereignty, and pleased with the opportunity afforded the United States of becoming a respectable nation, I resign with satisfaction the appointment I accepted with diffidence; a diffidence in my abilities to accomplish so arduous a task, which; however, was superseded by a confidence in the rectitude of our cause, the support of the supreme power of the Union, and the patronage of Heaven. The successful termination of the war has verified the most sanguine expectations; and my gratitude for the interposition of Providence, and the assistance I have received from my countrymen, increases with every review of the momentous contest." Then, after a word of gratitude to the army and to his staff, he concluded as follows: "I consider it an indispensable duty to close this last solemn act of my official life by commending the interests of our dearest country to the protection of Almighty God, and those who have the superintendence of them to his holy keeping.

"Having now finished the work assigned me, I retire from the great theatre of action; and bidding an affectionate farewell to this august body, under whose orders I have so long acted, I here offer my commission, and take my leave of all the employments of public life."

In singularly graceful and eloquent words his old opponent, Thomas Mifflin, the president, replied, the simple ceremony ended, and Washington left the room a private citizen.

The great master of English fiction, touching this scene with skilful hand, has said: "Which was the most splendid spectacle ever witnessed, the opening feast of Prince George in London, or the resignation of Washington? Which is the noble character for after ages to admire,—yon fribble dancing in lace and spangles, or yonder hero who sheathes his sword after a life of spotless honor, a purity unreproached, a courage indomitable, and a consummate victory?"

There is no need to say more. Comment or criticism on such a farewell, from such a man, at the close of a long civil war, would be not only superfluous but impertinent. The contemporary newspaper, in its meagre account, said that the occasion was deeply solemn and affecting, and that many persons shed tears. Well indeed might those then present have been thus affected, for they had witnessed a scene memorable forever in the annals of all that is best and noblest in human nature. They had listened to a speech which was not equalled in meaning and spirit in American history until, eighty years later, Abraham Lincoln stood upon the slopes of Gettysburg and uttered his immortal words upon those who died that the country might live.

CHAPTER XII

WORKING FOR UNION

HAVING RESIGNED HIS commission, Washington stood not upon the order of his going, but went at once to Virginia, and reached Mount Vernon the next day, in season to enjoy the Christmas-tide at home. It was with a deep sigh of relief that he sat himself down again by his own fireside, for all through the war the one longing that never left his mind was for the banks of the Potomac. He loved home after the fashion of his race, but with more than common intensity, and the country life was dear to him in all its phases. He liked its quiet occupations and wholesome sports, and, like most strong and simple natures, he loved above all an open-air existence. He felt that he had earned his rest, with all the temperate pleasures and employments which came with it, and he fondly believed that he was about to renew the habits which he had abandoned for eight weary years. Four days after his return he wrote to Governor Clinton: "The scene is at last closed. I feel myself eased of a load of public care. I hope to spend the remainder of my days in cultivating the affections of good men and in the practice of the domestic virtues." That the hope was sincere we may well suppose, but that it was more than a hope may be doubted. It was a wish, not a belief, for Washington must have felt that there was still work which he would surely be called to do. Still for the present the old life was there, and he threw himself into it with eager zest, though age and care put some of the former habits aside. He resumed his hunting, and Lafayette sent him a pack of splendid French

233

wolf-hounds. But they proved somewhat fierce and unmanageable, and were given up, and after that the following of the hounds was never resumed. In other respects there was little change. The work of the plantation and the affairs of the estate, much disordered by his absence, once more took shape and moved on successfully under the owner's eye. There were, as of old, the long days in the saddle, the open house and generous hospitality, the quiet evenings, and the thousand and one simple labors and enjoyments of rural life. But with all this were the newer and deeper cares, born of the change which had been wrought in the destiny of the country. The past broke in and could not be pushed aside, the future knocked at the door and demanded an answer to its questionings.

He had left home a distinguished Virginian; he returned one of the most famous men in the world, and such celebrity brought its usual penalties. Every foreigner of any position who came to the country made a pilgrimage to Mount Vernon, and many Americans did the same. Their coming was not allowed to alter the mode of life, but they were all hospitably received, and they consumed many hours of their host's precious time. Then there were the artists and sculptors, who came to paint his portrait or model his bust. "*In for a penny, in for a pound* is an old adage," he wrote to Hopkinson in 1785. "I am so hackneyed to the touches of painters' pencils that I am now altogether at their beck, and sit 'like patience on a monument,' whilst they are delineating the lines of my face. It is a proof, among many others, of what habit and custom can accomplish." Then there were the people who desired to write his memoirs, and the historians who wished to have his reminiscences, in their accounts of the Revolution. Some of these inquiring and admiring souls came in person, while others assailed him by letter and added to the vast flood of correspondence which poured in upon him by every post. His correspondence, in fact, in the needless part of it, was the most formidable waste of his time. He seems to have formed no correct idea of his own fame and what it meant, for he did not have a secretary until he found not only that he could not arrange his immense mass of papers, but that he could not even keep up with his daily letters. His correspondence came from all parts of his own country, and of Europe as well. The

French officers who had been his companions in arms wrote him with affectionate interest, and he was urged by them, one and all, and even by the king and queen, to visit France. These were letters which he was only too happy to answer, and he would fain have crossed the water in response to their kindly invitation; but he professed himself too old, which was a mere excuse, and objected his ignorance of the language, which to a man of his temperament was a real obstacle. Besides these letters of friendship, there were the schemers everywhere who sought his counsel and assistance. The notorious Lady Huntington, for example, pursued him with her project of Christianizing the Indians by means of a missionary colony in our western region, and her persistent ladyship cost him a good deal of time and thought, and some long and careful letters. Then there was the inventor Rumsey, with his steam-boat, to which he gave careful attention, as he did to everything that seemed to have merit. Another class of correspondents were his officers, who wanted his aid with Congress and in a thousand other ways, and to these old comrades he never turned a deaf ear. In this connection also came the affairs of the Society of the Cincinnati. He took an active part in the formation of the society, became its head, steered it through its early difficulties, and finally saved it from the wreck with which it was threatened by unreasoning popular prejudice. All these things were successfully managed, but at much expense of time and thought.

Then again, apart from this mass of labor thrust upon him by outsiders, there were his own concerns. His personal affairs required looking after, and he regulated accounts, an elaborate business always with him, put his farms in order, corresponded with his merchants in England, and introduced agricultural improvements, which always interested him deeply. He had large investments in land, of which from boyhood he had been a bold and sagacious purchaser. These investments had been neglected and needed his personal inspection; so in September, 1784, he mounted his horse, and with a companion and a servant rode away to the western country to look after his property. He camped out, as in the early days, and heartily enjoyed it, although reports that the Indians were moving in a restless and menacing manner shortened his trip, and prevented his penetrating beyond his settled lands to the wild tracts which he owned to the westward. Still he managed to ride some six hundred and eighty miles and get a good taste of that wild life which he never ceased to love, besides gathering a stock of information on many points of deeper and wider interest than his own property.

In the midst of all these employments, too, he attended closely to his domestic duties. At frequent intervals he journeyed to Fredericksburg to visit his mother, who still lived, and to whom he was always a dutiful and affectionate son. He watched over Mrs. Washington's grandchildren, and two or three nephews of his own, whose education he had undertaken, with all the solicitude of a father, and at the expense again of much thought and many wise letters of instruction and advice.

Even from this brief list it is possible to gain some idea of the occupations which filled Washington's time, and the only wonder is that he dealt with them so easily and effectively. Yet the greatest and most important work, that which most deeply absorbed his mind, and which affected the whole country, still remains to be described. With all his

WASHINGTON RESIGNING HIS COMMISSION.

longing for repose and privacy, Washington could not separate himself from the great problems which he had solved, or from the solution of the still greater problems which he had done more than any man to bring into existence. In reality, despite his reiterated wish for the quiet of home, he never ceased to labor at the new questions which confronted the country, and the old issues which were the legacy of the Revolution.

In the latter class was the peace establishment, on which he advised Congress, much in vain; for their idea of a peace establishment was to get rid of the army as rapidly as possible, and retain only a corporal's guard in the service of the confederation. Another question was that concerning the western posts. As has been already pointed out, Washington's keen eye had at once detected that this was the perilous point in the treaty, and he made a prompt but unavailing effort to secure these posts in the first flush of good feeling when peace had just been made. After he had retired he observed with regret the feebleness of Congress in this matter, and he continued to write about it. He wrote especially to Knox, who was in charge of the war department, and advised him to establish posts on our side, since we could not obtain the withdrawal of the British. This deep anxiety as to the western posts was due not merely to his profound distrust of the intention of England, but to his extreme solicitude as to the unsettled regions of the West. He repeatedly referred to the United States, even before the close of the war, as an infant empire, and he saw before any one else the destined growth of the country.

No man of that time, with the exception of Hamilton, ever grasped and realized as he did the imperial future which stretched before the United States. It was a difficult thing for men who had been born colonists to rise to a sense of national opportunities, but Washington passed at a single step from being a Virginian to being an American, and in so doing he stood alone. He was really and thoroughly national from the beginning of the war, at a time when, except for a few oratorical phrases, no one had ever thought of such a thing as a practical and living question. In the same way he had passed rapidly to an accurate conception of the probable growth and greatness of the country, and again he stood alone. Hamilton, born outside the colonies, unhampered by local prejudices and attachments, and living in Washington's family, as soon as he turned his mind to the subject, became, like his chief, entirely national and imperial in his views; but the other American statesmen of that day, with the exception of Franklin, only followed gradually and sometimes reluctantly in adopting their opinions. Some of them never adopted them at all, but remained imbedded in local ideas, and very few got beyond the region of words and actually grasped the facts with the absolutely clear perception which Washington had from the outset. Thus it was that when the war closed, one of the two ruling ideas in Washington's mind was to assure the future which he saw opening before the country. He perceived at a glance that the key and the guarantee of that future were in the wild regions of the West. Hence his constant anxiety as to the western posts, as to our Indian policy, and as to the maintenance of a sufficient armed force upon our borders to check the aggressions of Englishmen or of savages, and to secure free scope for settlement. In advancing these ideas on a national scale, however, he was rendered helpless by the utter weakness of Congress, which even his influence was powerless to overcome. He therefore began, immediately after his retreat to private life, to formulate and bring into existence such practical measures as were possible for the development of the West, believing that if Congress could not act, the people would, if any opportunity were given to their natural enterprise.

The scheme which he proposed was to open the western country by means of inland navigation. The thought had long been in his mind. It had come to him before the Revolution, and can be traced back to the early days when he was making surveys, buying wild lands, and meditating very deeply, but very practically, on the possible commercial development of the colonies. Now the idea assumed much larger proportions and a much graver aspect. He perceived in it the first step toward the empire which he foresaw, and when he had laid down his sword and awoke in the peaceful morning at Mount Vernon, "with a strange sense of freedom from official cares," he directed his attention at once to this plan, in which he really could do something, despite an inert Congress and a dissolving confederation. His first letter on the subject was written in March, 1784, and addressed to Jefferson, who was then in Congress, and who sympathized with Washington's views without seeing how far they reached. He told Jefferson how he despaired of government aid, and how he therefore intended to revive the scheme of a company, which he had started in 1775, and which had been abandoned on account of the war. He showed the varying interests which it was necessary to concili-ate, asked Jefferson to see the governor of Maryland, so that that State might be brought into the undertaking, and referred to the danger of being anticipated and beaten by New York, a chord of local pride which he continued to touch most adroitly as the business proceeded. Very characteristically, too, he took pains to call attention to the fact that by his ownership of land he had a personal interest in the enterprise. He looked far beyond his own lands, but he was glad to have his property devel-oped, and with his usual freedom from anything like pretense, he drew attention to the fact of his personal interests.

On his return from his tour in the autumn, he proceeded to bring the matter to public attention and to the consideration of the legislature. With this end in view he addressed a long letter to Governor Harrison, in which he laid out his whole scheme. Detroit was to be the objective point, and he indicated the different routes by which inland navigation could thence be obtained, thus opening the Indian trade, and affording an outlet at the same time for the settlers who were sure to pour in when once the fear of British aggression was removed. He dwelt strongly upon the danger of Virginia losing these advantages by the action of other States, and yet at the same time he suggested the methods by which Maryland and Pennsylvania could be brought into the plan. Then he advanced a series of arguments which were purely national in their scope. He insisted on the necessity of binding to the old colonies by strong ties the Western States, which might easily be decoyed away if Spain or England had the sense to do it. This point he argued with great force, for it was now no longer a Virginian argument, but an argument for all the States.

The practical result was that the legislature took the question up, more in deference to the writer's wishes and in gratitude for his services, than from any comprehension of what the scheme meant. The companies were duly organized, and the promoter was given a hundred and fifty shares, on the ground that the legislature wished to take every opportunity of testifying their sense of "the unexampled merits of George Washington towards his country." Washington was much touched and not a little troubled by this action. He had been willing, as he said, to give up his cherished privacy and repose in order to forward the enterprise. He had gone to Maryland even, and worked to engage that State in the scheme, but he could not bear the idea of taking money for what he regarded as part of a great public policy. "I would wish," he said, "that every individual who may hear that it was a favorite plan of mine may know also that I had no other motive for promoting it than the advantage of which I conceived it would be productive to the Union, and to this State in particular, by cementing the eastern and western territory together, at the same time that it will give vigor and increase to our commerce, and be a convenience to our citizens.

"How would this matter be viewed, then, by the eye of the world, and what would be the opinion of it, when it comes to be related that George Washington has received twenty thousand dollars and five thousand pounds sterling of the public money as an interest therein?" He thought it would make him look like a "pensioner or dependent" to accept this gratuity, and he recoiled from the idea. There is something entirely frank and human in the way in which he says "George Washington," instead of using the first pronoun singular. He always saw facts as they were; he understood the fact called "George Washington" as perfectly as any other, and although he wanted retirement and privacy, he had no mock modesty in estimating his own place in the world. At the same time, while he wished to be rid of the kindly gift, he shrank from putting on what he called the appearance of "ostentatious disinterestedness" by refusing it. Finally he took the stock and endowed two charity schools with the dividends. The scheme turned out successfully, and the work still endures, like the early surveys and various other things of a very different kind to which Washington put his hand.

In the greater forces which were presently set in motion for the preservation of the future empire, the inland navigation, started in Virginia, dropped out of sight, and became merely one of the rills which fed the mighty river. But it was the only really practical movement possible at the precise moment when it was begun, and it was characteristic of its author, who always found, even in the most discouraging conditions, something that could be done. It might be only a very little something, but still that was better than nothing to the strong man ever dealing with facts as they actually were on this confused earth, and not turning aside because things were not as they ought to be. Thus many a battle and campaign had been saved, and so inland navigation played its part now. It helped, among other things, to bring Maryland and Virginia together, and their combination was the first step toward the Constitution of the United States. There is nothing fanciful in all this. No one would pretend that the Constitution of the United States was descended from Washington's James River and Potomac River companies. But he worked at them with that end in view, and so did what was nearest to his hand and most practical toward union, empire, and the development of national sentiment.

Ah, says some critic in critic's fashion, you are carried away by your subject; you see in a simple business enterprise, intended merely to open western lands, the far-reaching ideas of a statesman. Perhaps our critic is right, for as one goes on living with this Virginian soldier, studying his letters and his thoughts, one comes to believe many things of him, and to detect much meaning in his sayings and doings. Let us, however, show our evidence at least. Here is what he wrote to his friend Humphreys a year after his scheme was afoot: "My attention is more immediately engaged in a project which I think big with great political as well as commercial consequences to the States, especially the middle ones;" and then he went on to argue the necessity of fastening the Western States to the Atlantic seaboard and thus thwarting Spain and England. This looks like more than a money-making scheme; in fact, it justifies all that has been said, especially if read in connection with certain other letters of this period. Great political results, as well as lumber and peltry, were what Washington intended to float along his rivers and canals.

In this same letter to Humphreys he touched also on another point in connection with the development of the West, which was of vast importance to the future of the country, and was even then agitating men's minds. He said: "I may be singular in my ideas, but they are these: that, to open a door to, and make easy the way for those settlers to the westward (who ought to advance regularly and compactly), before we make any stir about the navigation of the Mississippi, and before our settlements are far advanced towards that river, would be our true line of policy." Again he wrote: "However singular the opinion may be, I cannot divest myself of it, that the navigation of the Mississippi, *at this time* [1785], ought to be no object with us. On the contrary, until we have a little time allowed to open and make easy the ways between the Atlantic States and the western territory, the obstructions had better remain." He was right in describing himself as "singular" in his views on this matter, which just then was exciting much attention.

At that time indeed much feeling existed, and there were many sharp divisions about the Mississippi question. One party, for the sake of a commercial treaty with Spain, and to get a troublesome business out of the way, was ready to give up our claims to a free navigation of the great river; and this was probably the prevalent sentiment in Congress, for to most of the members the Mississippi seemed a very remote affair indeed. On the other side was a smaller and more violent party, which was for obtaining the free navigation immediately and at all hazards, and was furious at the proposition to make such a sacrifice as its opponents proposed. Finally, there was Spain herself intriguing to get possession of the West, holding out free navigation as a bait to the settlers of Kentucky, and keeping paid agents in that region to foster her schemes. Washington saw too far and too clearly to think for one moment of giving up the navigation of the Mississippi, but he also perceived what no one else seems to have thought of, that free navigation at that moment would give the western settlements "the habit of trade" with New Orleans before they had formed it with the Atlantic seaboard, and would thus detach them from the United States. He wished, therefore, to have the Mississippi question left open, and all our claims reserved, so that trade by the river should be obstructed until we had time to open our inland navigation and bind the western people to us by ties too strong to be broken. The fear that the river would be lost by waiting did not disturb him in the least, provided our claims were kept alive. He wrote to Lee in June, 1786: "Whenever the new States become so populous, and so extended to the westward, as really to need it, there will be no power which can deprive them of the use of the Mississippi." Again, a year later, while the convention was sitting in Philadelphia, he said: "My sentiments with respect to the navigation of the Mississippi have been long fixed, and are not dissimilar to those which are expressed in your letter. I have ever been of opinion that the true policy of the Atlantic States, instead of contending prematurely for the free navigation of that river (which eventually, and perhaps as soon as it will be our true interest to obtain it, must happen), would be to open and improve the natural communications with the western country." The event justified his sagacity in all respects, for the bickerings went on until the United States were able to compel Spain to give what was wanted to the western communities, which by that time had been firmly bound to those of the Atlantic coast.

Much as Washington thought about holding fast the western country, there was yet one idea that overruled it as well as all others. There was one plan which he knew would be a quick solution of the dangers and difficulties for which inland navigation and trade connections were at best but palliatives. He had learned by bitter experience, as no other man had learned, the vital need and value of union. He felt it as soon as he took command of the army, and it rode like black care behind him from Cambridge to Yorktown. He had hoped something from the confederation, but he soon saw that it was as worthless as the utter lack of system which it replaced, and amounted merely to substituting one kind of impotence and confusion for another. Others might be deceived by phrases as to nationality and a general government, but he had dwelt among hard facts, and he knew that these things did not exist. He knew that what passed for them, stood in their place and wore their semblance, were merely temporary creations born of the common danger, and doomed, when the pressure of war was gone, to fall to pieces in imbecility and inertness. To the lack of a proper union, which meant to his mind national and energetic government, he attributed the failures of the campaigns, the long-drawn miseries, and in a word the needless prolongation of the Revolution. He saw, too, that what had been so nearly ruinous in war would be absolutely so in peace, and before the treaty was actually signed he had begun to call attention to the great question on the right settlement of which the future of the country depended.

To Hamilton he wrote on March 4, 1783: "It is clearly my opinion, unless Congress have powers competent to all general purposes, that the distresses we have encountered, the expense we have incurred, and the blood we have spilt, will avail us nothing." Again he wrote to Hamilton, a few weeks later: "My wish to see the union of these States established upon liberal and permanent principles, and inclination to contribute my mite in pointing out the defects of the present constitution, are equally great. All my private letters have teemed with these sentiments, and whenever this topic has been the subject of conversation, I have endeavored to diffuse and enforce them." His circular letter to the governors of the States at the close of the war, which was as eloquent as it was forcible, was devoted to urging the necessity of a better central government. "With this conviction," he said, "of the importance of the present crisis, silence in me would be a crime. I will therefore speak to your Excellency the language of freedom and of sincerity without disguise. . . . There are four things which I humbly conceive are essential to the well-being, I may even venture to say, to the existence, of the United States, as an independent power: —

"First. An indissoluble union of the States under one federal head.

"Second. A regard to public justice.

"Third. The adoption of a proper peace establishment; and,

"Fourth. The prevalence of that pacific and friendly disposition among the people of the United States, which will induce them to forget their local prejudices and policies; to make those mutual concessions which are requisite to the general prosperity; and in some instances to sacrifice their individual advantages to the interest of the community."
The same appeal went forth again in his last address to the army, when

he said: "Although the general has so frequently given it as his opinion, in the most public and explicit manner, that unless the principles of the federal government were properly supported, and the powers of the Union increased, the honor, dignity, and justice of the nation would be lost forever; yet he cannot help repeating on this occasion so interesting a sentiment, and leaving it as his last injunction to every soldier, who may view the subject in the same serious point of light, to add his best endeavors to those of his worthy fellow-citizens towards effecting those great and valuable purposes on which our very existence as a nation so materially depends."

These two papers were the first strong public appeals for union. The letter to the governors argued the question elaborately, and was intended for the general public. The address to the army was simply a watchword and last general order; for the army needed no arguments to prove the crying need of better government. Before this, Hamilton had written his famous letters to Duane and Morris, and Madison was just beginning to turn his thoughts toward the problem of federal government; but with these exceptions Washington stood alone. In sending out these two papers he began the real work that led to the Constitution. What he said was read and heeded throughout the country, for at the close of the war his personal influence was enormous, and with the army his utterances were those of an oracle. By his appeal he made each officer and soldier a missionary in the cause of the Union, and by his arguments to the governors he gave ground and motive for a party devoted to procuring better government. Thus he started the great movement which, struggling through many obstacles, culminated in the Constitution and the union of the States. No other man could have done it, for no one but Washington had a tithe of the influence necessary to arrest public attention; and, save Hamilton, no other man then had even begun to understand the situation which Washington grasped so easily and firmly in all its completeness.

He sent out these appeals as his last words to his countrymen at the close of their conflict; but he had no intention of stopping there. He had written and spoken, as he said, to every one on every occasion upon this

topic, and he continued to do so until the work was done. He had no
sooner laid aside the military harness than he began at once to push on
the cause of union. In the bottom of his heart he must have known that
his work was but half done, and with the same pen with which he reiterated his intention to live in repose and privacy, and spend his declining
years beneath his own vine and fig-tree, he wrote urgent appeals and
wove strong arguments addressed to leaders in every State. He had not
been at home five days before he wrote to the younger Trumbull, congratulating him on his father's vigorous message in behalf of better federal government, which had not been very well received by the
Connecticut legislature. He spoke of "the jealousies and contracted temper" of the States, but avowed his belief that public sentiment was
improving. "Everything," he concluded, "my dear Trumbull, will come
right at last, as we have often prophesied. My only fear is that we shall
lose a little reputation first." A fortnight later he wrote to the governor of
Virginia: "That the prospect before us is, as you justly observe, fair, none
can deny; but what use we shall make of it is exceedingly problematical;
not but that I believe all things will come right at last, but like a young
heir come a little prematurely to a large inheritance, we shall wanton and
run riot until we have brought our reputation to the brink of ruin, and
then like him shall have to labor with the current of opinion, when compelled, perhaps, to do what prudence and common policy pointed out as
plain as any problem in Euclid in the first instance." The soundness of
the view is only equaled by the accuracy of the prediction. He might five
years later have repeated this sentence, word for word, only altering the
tenses, and he would have rehearsed exactly the course of events.

While he wrote thus he keenly watched Congress, and marked its
sure and not very gradual decline. He did what he could to bring about
useful measures, and saw them one after the other come to naught. He
urged the impost scheme, and felt that its failure was fatal to the financial welfare of the country, on which so much depended. He always was
striving to do the best with existing conditions, but the hopelessness of
every effort soon satisfied him that it was a waste of time and energy. So
he turned again in the midst of his canal schemes to renew his exhorta-

tions to leading men in the various States on the need of union as the only true solution of existing troubles.

To James McHenry, of Maryland, he wrote in August, 1785: "I confess to you candidly that I can foresee no evil greater than disunion; than those unreasonable jealousies which are continually poisoning our minds and filling them with imaginary evils for the prevention of real ones." To William Grayson of Virginia, then a member of Congress, he wrote at the same time: "I have ever been a friend to adequate congressional powers; consequently I wish to see the ninth article of the confederation amended and extended. Without these powers we cannot support a national character, and must appear contemptible in the eyes of Europe. But to you, my dear Sir, I will candidly confess that in my opinion it is of little avail to give them to Congress." He was already clearly of opinion that the existing system was hopeless, and the following spring he wrote still more sharply as to the state of public affairs to Henry Lee, in Congress. "My sentiments," he said, "with respect to the federal government are well known. Publicly and privately have they been communicated without reserve; but my opinion is that there is more wickedness than ignorance in the conduct of the States, or, in other words, in the conduct of those who have too much influence in the government of them; and until the curtain is withdrawn, and the private views and selfish principles upon which these men act are exposed to public notice, I have little hope of amendment without another convulsion."

He did not confine himself, however, to letters, important as the work done in this way was, but used all his influence toward practical measures outside of Congress, of whose action he quite despaired. The plan for a commercial agreement between Maryland and Virginia was concerted at Mount Vernon, and led to a call to all the States to meet at Annapolis for the same object. This, of course, received Washington's hearty approval and encouragement, but he evidently regarded it, although important, as merely a preliminary step to something wider and better. He wrote to Lafayette describing the proposed gathering at Annapolis, and added: "A general convention is talked of by many for the purpose of revising and correcting the defects of the federal government;

but whilst this is the wish of some, it is the dread of others, from an opinion that matters are not yet sufficiently ripe for such an event." This expressed his own feeling, for although he was entirely convinced that only a radical reform would do, he questioned whether the time had yet arrived, and whether things had become bad enough, to make such a reform either possible or lasting. He was chiefly disturbed because he felt that there was "more wickedness than ignorance mixed in our councils," and he grew more and more anxious as public affairs declined without apparently producing a reaction. The growing contempt shown by foreign nations and the arrogant conduct of Great Britain especially alarmed him, while the rapid sinking of the national reputation stung him to the quick. "I do not conceive," he wrote to Jay, in August, 1786, "we can exist long as a nation without having lodged somewhere a power which will pervade the whole Union in as energetic a manner as the authority of the state governments extends over the several States." Thus with unerring judgment he put his finger on the vital point in the whole question, which was the need of a national government that should deal with the individual citizens of the whole country and not with the States. "To be fearful," he continued, "of investing Congress, constituted as that body is, with ample authorities for national purposes, appears to me the very climax of popular absurdity and madness. . . . Requisitions are actually little better than a jest and a byword throughout the land. If you tell the legislatures they have violated the treaty of peace, and invaded the prerogatives of the confederacy, they will laugh in your face. . . . It is much to be feared, as you observe, that the better kind of people, being disgusted with the circumstances, will have their minds prepared for any revolution whatever. . . . I am told that even respectable characters speak of a monarchical government without horror. From thinking proceeds speaking; thence to acting is often but a single step. But how irrevocable and tremendous! What a triumph for our enemies to verify their predictions! . . . It is not my business to embark again upon a sea of troubles. Nor could it be expected that my sentiments and opinions would have much weight on the minds of my countrymen. They have been neglected, though given as a last legacy in the most solemn manner. I had then perhaps some claims to public attention. I consider myself as having none at present."

It is interesting to observe the ease and certainty with which, in dealing with the central question, he grasped all phases of the subject and judged of the effect of the existing weakness with regard to every relation of the country and to the politics of each State. He pointed out again and again the manner in which we were exposed to foreign hostility, and analyzed the designs of England, rightly detecting a settled policy on her part to injure and divide where she had failed to conquer. Others were blind to the meaning of the English attitude as to the western posts, commerce, and international relations. Washington brought it to the attention of our leading men, educating them on this as on other points, and showing, too, the stupidity of Great Britain in her attempt to belittle the trade of a country which, as he wrote Lafayette in prophetic vein, would one day "have weight in the scale of empires."

He followed with the same care the course of events in the several States. In them all he resisted the craze for issuing irredeemable paper money, writing to his various correspondents, and urging energetic opposition to this specious and pernicious form of public dishonesty. It was to Massachusetts, however, that his attention was most strongly attracted by the social disorders which culminated in the Shays rebellion. There the miserable condition of public affairs was bearing bitter fruit, and Washington watched the progress of the troubles with profound anxiety. He wrote to Lee: "You talk, my good sir, of employing influence to appease the present tumults in Massachusetts. I know not where that influence is to be found, or, if attainable, that it would be a proper remedy for the disorders. *Influence* is not *government*. Let us have a government by which our lives, liberties, and properties will be secured, or let us know the worst at once." Through "all this mist of intoxication and folly," however, Washington saw that the Shays insurrection would probably be the means of frightening the indifferent, and of driving those who seemed impervious to every appeal to reason into an active support of some better form of government. He rightly thought that riot and bloodshed would prove convincing arguments.

In order to understand the utter demoralization of society, politics, and public opinion at that time, the offspring of a wasting civil war and of colonial habits of thought, it is interesting to contrast the attitude of Washington with that of another distinguished American in regard to the Shays rebellion. While Washington was looking solemnly at this manifestation of weakness and disorder, and was urging strong measures with passionate vehemence, Jefferson was writing from Paris in the flippant vein of the fashionable French theorists, and uttering such ineffable nonsense as the famous sentence about "once in twenty years watering the tree of liberty with the blood of tyrants." There could be no better illustration of what Washington was than this contrast between the man of words and the man of action, between the astute leader of a party, the shrewd manager of men, and the silent leader of armies, the master builder of states and governments.

I have followed Washington through the correspondence of this time with some minuteness, because it is the only way by which his work in overcoming the obstacles in the path to good government can be seen. He held no public office; he had no means of reaching the popular ear. He was neither a professional orator nor a writer of pamphlets, and the press of that day, if he had controlled it, had no power to mould or direct public thought. Yet, despite these obstacles, he set himself to develop public opinion in favor of a better government, and he worked at this difficult and impalpable task without ceasing, from the day that he resigned from the army until he was called to the presidency of the United States. He did it by means of private letters, a feeble instrument to-day, but much more effective then. Jefferson never made speeches nor published essays, but he built up a great party, and carried himself into power as its leader by means of letters. In the same fashion Washington started the scheme for internal waterways, in order to bind the East and the West together, set on foot the policy of commercial agreements between the States, and argued on the "imperial theme" with leading men everywhere. A study of these letters reveals a strong, logical, and deliberate working towards the desired end. There was no scattering fire. Whether he was writing of canals, or the Mississippi, or the Western posts, or paper money, or the impost, or the local disorders, he always was arguing and urging union and an energetic central government. These letters went to the leaders of thought and opinion, and were quoted and passed from hand to hand. They brought immediately to the cause all the soldiers and officers of the army, and they aroused and convinced the strongest and ablest men in every State. Washington's personal influence was very great, something we of this generation, with a vast territory and seventy millions of people, cannot readily understand. To many persons his word was law; to all that was best in the community, everything he said had immense weight. This influence he used with care and without waste. Every blow he struck went home. It is impossible to estimate just how much he effected, but it is safe to say that it is to Washington, aided first by Hamilton and then by Madison, that we owe the development of public opinion and the formation of the party which devised and carried the Constitution. Events of course worked with them, but they used events, and did not suffer the golden opportunities, which without them would have been lost, to slip by.

When Washington wrote of the Shays rebellion to Lee, the movement toward a better union, which he had begun, was on the brink of success. That ill-starred insurrection became, as he foresaw, a powerful spur to the policy started at Mount Vernon, and adopted by Virginia and Maryland. From this had come the Annapolis convention, and thence the call for another convention at Philadelphia. As soon as the word went abroad that a general convention was to be held, the demand for Washington as a delegate was heard on all sides. At first he shrank from it. Despite the work which he had been doing, and which he must have known would bring him once more into public service, he still clung to the vision of home life which he had brought with him from the army. November 18, 1786, he wrote to Madison, that from a sense of obligation he should go to the convention, were it not that he had declined on account of his retirement, age, and rheumatism to be at a meeting of the Cincinnati at the same time and place. But no one heeded him, and Virginia elected him unanimously to head her delegation at Philadelphia. He wrote to Governor Randolph, acknowledging the honor, but reiterating what he had said to Madison, and urging the choice of some one else in his place. Still Virginia held the question open, and on February 3 he wrote to Knox that his private intention was not to attend. The pressure continued, and, as usual when the struggle drew near, the love of battle and the sense of duty began to reassert themselves. March 8 he again wrote to Knox that he had not meant to come, but that the question had occurred to him, "Whether my non-attendance in the convention will not be considered as dereliction of republicanism; nay, more, whether other motives may not, however injuriously, be ascribed for my not exerting myself on this occasion in support of it;" and therefore he wished to be informed as to the public expectation on the matter. On March 28 he wrote again to Randolph that ill-health might prevent his going, and therefore it would be well to appoint some one in his place. April 2 he said that if representation of the States was to be partial, or powers cramped, he did not want to be a sharer in the business. "If the delegates assemble," he wrote, "with such powers as will enable the convention to probe the defects of the constitution to the bottom and point out radical cures, it would be an honorable employment; otherwise not." This idea of inefficiency and failure in the convention had long been present to his mind, and he had already said that, if their powers were insufficient, the convention should go boldly over and beyond them and make a government with the means of coercion, and able to enforce obedience, without which it would be, in his opinion, quite worthless. Thus he pondered on the difficulties, and held back his acceptance of the post; but when the hour of action drew near, the rheumatism and the misgivings alike disappeared before the inevitable, and Washington arrived in Philadelphia, punctual as usual, on May 13, the day before the opening of the convention.

The other members were by no means equally prompt, and a week elapsed before a bare quorum was obtained and the convention enabled to organize. In this interval of waiting there appears to have been some informal discussion among the members present, between those who favored an entirely new Constitution and those who timidly desired only half-way measures. On one of these occasions Washington is reported by Gouverneur Morris, in a eulogy delivered twelve years later, to have said: "It is too probable that no plan we propose will be adopted. Perhaps another dreadful conflict is to be sustained. If, to please the people, we offer what we ourselves disapprove, how can we afterwards defend our work? Let us raise a standard to which the wise and honest can repair. The event is in the hand of God." The language is no doubt that of Morris, speaking from memory and in a highly rhetorical vein, but we may readily believe that the quotation accurately embodied Washington's opinion, and that he took this high ground at the outset, and strove from the beginning to inculcate upon his fellow-members the absolute need of bold and decisive action. The words savor of the orator who quoted them, but the noble and courageous sentiment which they express is thoroughly characteristic of the man to whom they were attributed.*

---

*It is necessary to say a few words in regard to this quotation of Washington's words made by Morris, because both Mr. Bancroft (*History of the Constitution*, ii. 8) and Mr. John Fiske (*The Critical Period of American History*, p. 232) quote them as if they were absolutely and verbally authentic. It is perfectly certain that from May 25 to September 17 Washington spoke but once; that is, he spoke but once in the convention after it became such by organization. This point is determined by Madison's statement (Notes, iii. 1600), that when Washington took the floor in behalf of Gorham's amendment, it was the only occasion on which the president entered *at all* into the discussions of the convention." (The italics are mine.) I have examined the manuscript at the State Department, and these words are written in Madison's own hand in the body of the text and inclosed in brackets. Madison was the most accurate of men. His notes are only abstracts of what was said, but he was never absent from the convention, and there can be no question that if Washington had uttered the words attributed to him by Morris, a speech so important would have been given as fully as possible, and Madison would not have said distinctly that the Gorham amendment was the only occasion when the president entered into the discussions of the convention.

It is, therefore, certain that Washington said nothing in the convention except on the occasion of the Gorham amendment, and Mr. Bancroft rightly assigns the Morris quotation to some time during the week which elapsed between the date fixed for the assembling of the convention and that on which a quorum of States was obtained. The words given by Morris, if uttered at all, must have been spoken informally in the way of conversation before there was any convention, strictly speaking, and of course before Washington was chosen president. Mr. Fiske, who devotes a page to these sentences from the eulogy, describes Washington as rising from his president's chair and addressing the convention with great solemnity. There is no authority whatever to show that he rose from the chair to address the other delegates, and, if he used the words quoted by Morris, he was certainly not president of the convention when he did so. The latter blunder, however, is Morris's own, and in making it he contradicts himself. These are his words: "He is their president. It is a question previous to their first meeting what course shall be pursued." In other words, he was their president before they had met and chosen a president. This is a fair illustration of the loose and rhetorical character of the passage in which Washington's admonition is quoted. The entire paragraph, with its mixture of tenses arising

When a quorum was finally obtained, Washington was unanimously chosen to preside over the convention; and there he sat during the sessions of four months, silent, patient, except on a single occasion,* taking no part in debate, but guiding the business, and using all his powers with steady persistence to compass the great end. The debates of that remarkable body have been preserved in outline in the full and careful notes of Madison. Its history has been elaborately written, and the arguments and opinions of its members have been minutely examined and unsparingly criticised. We are still ignorant, and shall always remain ignorant, of just how much was due to Washington for the final completion of the work. His general views and his line of action are clearly to be seen in his letters and in the words attributed to him by Morris. That he labored day and night for success we know, and that his influence with his fellow-members was vast we also know, but the rest we can only conjecture. There came a time when everything was at a standstill, and when it looked as if no agreement could be reached by the men representing so many conflicting interests. Hamilton had made his great speech, and, finding the vote of his State cast against him by his two colleagues on every question, had gone home in a frame of mind which we may easily believe was neither very contented nor very sanguine. Even Franklin, most hopeful and buoyant of men, was nearly ready to despair.

---

from the use of the historical present which Morris's classical fancies led him to employ, is, in fact, purely rhetorical, and has only the authority due to performances of that character. It seems to me impossible, therefore, to fairly suppose that the words quoted by Morris were anything more than his own presentation of a sentiment which he, no doubt, heard Washington urge frequently and forcibly. Even in this limited acceptation his account is both interesting and valuable, as indicating Washington's opinion and the tone he took with his fellow-members; but this, I think, is the utmost weight that can be attached to it. I have discussed the point thus minutely because two authorities so distinguished as Mr. Bancroft and Mr. Fiske have laid so much stress on the words given by Morris, and have seemed to me to accord to them a greater weight and a higher authenticity than the facts warrant. Morris's eulogy on Washington was delivered in New York, and may be found most readily in a little volume entitled *Washingtoniana* (p. 110), published at Lancaster in 1802.

*Just at the close of the convention, when the Constitution in its last draft was in the final stage and on the eve of adoption, Mr. Gorham of Massachusetts moved to amend by reducing the limit of population in a congressional district from forty to thirty thousand. Washington took the floor and argued briefly and modestly in favor of the change. His mere request was sufficient, and the amendment was unanimously adopted.

Washington himself wrote to Hamilton, on July 10: "When I refer you to the state of the counsels which prevailed at the period you left this city, and add that they are now, if possible, in a worse train than ever, you will find but little ground on which the hope of a good establishment can be formed. In a word, I almost despair of seeing a favorable issue to the proceedings of our convention, and do therefore repent having had any agency in the business." Matters were certainly in a bad state when Washington could write in this strain, and when his passion for success was so cooled that he repented of agency in the business. There was much virtue, however, in that little word "almost." He did not quite despair yet, and, after his fashion, he held on with grim tenacity. We know what the compromises finally were, and how they were brought about, but we can never do exact justice to the iron will which held men together when all compromises seemed impossible, and which even in the darkest hour would not wholly despair. All that can be said is, that without the influence and the labors of Washington the convention of 1787, in all probability, would have failed of success.

At all events it did not fail, and after much tribulation the work was done. On September 17, 1787, a day ever to be memorable, Washington affixed his bold and handsome signature to the Constitution of the United States. Tradition has it that as he stood by the table, pen in hand, he said: "Should the States reject this excellent Constitution, the probability is that opportunity will never be offered to cancel another in peace; the next will be drawn in blood." Whether the tradition is well or ill founded, the sentence has the ring of truth. A great work had been accomplished. If it were cast aside, Washington knew that the sword and not the pen would make the next Constitution, and he regarded that awful alternative with dread. He signed first, and was followed by all the members present, with three notable exceptions. Then the delegates dined together at the city tavern, and took a cordial leave of each other. "After which," the president of the convention wrote in his diary, "I returned to my lodgings, did some business with, and received the papers from, the secretary of the convention, and retired to meditate upon the momentous work which had been executed." It is a simple sentence, but how much it means! The world would be glad to-day to know what the thoughts were which filled Washington's mind as he sat alone in the quiet of that summer afternoon, with the new Constitution lying before him. But he was then as ever silent. He did not go alone to his room to exhibit himself on paper for the admiration of posterity. He went there to meditate for his own guidance on what had been done for the benefit of his country. The city bells had rung a joyful chime when he arrived four months before. Ought they to ring again with a new gladness, or should they toll for the death of bright hopes, now the task was done? Washington was intensely human. In that hour of silent thought his heart must have swelled with a consciousness that he had led his people through a successful Revolution, and now again from the darkness of political confusion and dissolution to the threshold of a new existence. But at the same time he never deceived himself. The new Constitution was but an experiment and an opportunity. Would the States accept it? And if they accepted it, would they abide by it? Was this instrument of government, wrought out so painfully, destined to go to pieces after a few years of trial, or was it to prove strong enough to become the charter of a nation and hold the States together indissolubly against all the shocks of politics and revolution? Washington, with his foresight and strong national instinct, plainly saw these momentous questions, somewhat dim then, although clear to all the world to-day. We can guess how solemnly he thought about them as he meditated alone in his room on that September afternoon. Whatever his reflections, his conclusions were simple. He made up his mind that the only chance for the country lay in the adoption of the new scheme, but he was sober enough in his opinions as to the Constitution itself. He said of it to Lafayette the day after the signing: "It is the result of four months' deliberation. It is now a child of fortune, to be fostered by some and buffeted by others. What will be the general opinion or the reception of it is not for me to decide; nor shall I say anything for or against it. If it be good, I suppose it will work its way; if bad, it will recoil on the framers." We catch sight here of the old theory that his public life was at an end, and now, when this exceptional duty had been performed, that he would retire once more to remote privacy.

This fancy, as well as the extremely philosophical mood about the fate of the Constitution, apparent in this letter, soon disappeared. Within a week he wrote to Henry, in whom he probably already suspected the most formidable opponent of the new plan in Virginia: "I wish the Constitution, which is offered, had been more perfect; but I sincerely believe it is the best that could be obtained at this time, and as a constitutional door is opened for amendments hereafter, the adoption of it under the present circumstances of the Union is, in my opinion, desirable." Copies of this letter were sent to Harrison and Nelson, and the correspondence thus started soon increased rapidly. He wrote to Hamilton and Madison to counsel with them as to the prospects of the Constitution, and to Knox to supply him with arguments and urge him to energetic work. By January of the new year the tone of indifference and doubt manifested in the letter to Lafayette had quite gone, and we find him writing to Governor Randolph, in reply to that gentleman's objections: "There are some things in the new form, I will readily acknowledge, which never did, and I am persuaded never will, obtain my cordial approbation, but I did then conceive and do now most firmly believe that in the aggregate it is the best Constitution that can be obtained at this epoch, and that this or a dissolution of the Union awaits our choice, and is the only alternative before us. Thus believing, I had not, nor have I now, any hesitation in deciding on which to lean."

Thus the few letters to a few friends extended to many letters to many friends, and traveled into every State. They all urged the necessity of adopting the Constitution as the best that could be obtained. What Washington's precise objections to the Constitution were is not clear. In a general way it was not energetic enough to come up to his ideal, but he never particularized in his criticisms. He may have admitted the existence of defects in order simply to disarm opposition, and doubtless he, like most of the framers, was by no means completely satisfied with his work. But he brushed all faults aside, and drove steadily forward to the great end in view. He was as far removed as possible from that highly virtuous and very ineffective class of persons who will not support anything that is not perfect, and who generally contrive to do more harm than all the avowed enemies of sound government. Washington did not stop to worry over and argue about details, but sought steadily to bring to pass the main object at which he aimed. As he had labored for the convention, so he now labored for the Constitution, and his letters to his friends not only had great weight in forming a Federal party and directing its movements, but extracts from them were quoted and published, thus exerting a direct and powerful influence on public opinion.

He made himself deeply felt in this way everywhere, but of course more in his own State than anywhere else. His confidence at first in regard to Virginia changed gradually to an intense and well-grounded anxiety, and he not only used every means, as the conflict extended, to strengthen his friends and gain votes, but he received and circulated personally copies of "The Federalist," in order to educate public opinion. The contest in the Virginia convention was for a long time doubtful, but finally the end was reached, and the decision was favorable. Without Washington's influence, it is safe to say that the Constitution would have been lost in Virginia, and without Virginia the great experiment would probably have failed. In the same spirit he worked on after the new scheme had secured enough States to insure a trial. The Constitution had been ratified; it must now be made to work, and Washington wrote earnestly to the leaders in the various States, urging them to see to it that "Federalists," stanch friends of the Constitution, were elected to Congress. There was no vagueness about his notions on this point. A party had carried the Constitution and secured its ratification, and to that party he wished the administration and establishment of the new system to be intrusted. He did not take the view that, because the fight was over, it was henceforth to be considered that there had been no fight, and that all men were politically alike. He was quite ready to do all in his power to conciliate the opponents of union and the Constitution, but he did not believe that the momentous task of converting the paper system into a living organism should be confided to any hands other than those of its tried and trusty friends.

But while he was looking so carefully after the choice of the right men to fill the legislature of the new government, the people of the country turned to him with the universal demand that he should stand at the head of it, and fill the great office of first President of the Republic. In response to the first suggestion that came, he recognized the fact that he was likely to be again called upon for another great public service, and added simply that at his age it involved a sacrifice which admitted of no compensation. He maintained this tone whenever he alluded to the subject, in response to the numerous letters urging him to accept. But although he declined to announce any decision, he had made up his mind to the inevitable. He had put his hand to the plough, and he would not turn back. His only anxiety was that the people should know that he shrank from the office, and would only leave his farm to take it from a sense of over-mastering duty. Besides his reluctance to engage in a fresh struggle, and his fear that his motives might be misunderstood, he had the same diffidence in his own abilities which weighed upon him when he took command of the armies. His passion for success, which determined him to accept the presidency, if it was deemed indispensable that he should do so, made him dread failure with an almost morbid keenness, although his courage was too high and his will too strong ever to draw back. Responsibility weighed upon his spirits, but it could not daunt him. He wrote to Trumbull in December, 1788, that he saw "nothing but clouds and darkness before him," but when the hour came he was ready. The elections were favorable to the Federalists. The electoral colleges gave Washington their unanimous vote, and on April 16, having been duly notified by Congress of his election, he left Mount Vernon for New York, to assume the conduct of the government, and stand at the head of the new Union in its first battle for life.

From the early day when he went out to seek Shirley and win redress against the assumptions of British officers, Washington's journeys to the North had been memorable in their purposes. He had traveled northward to sit in the first continental congress, to take command of the army, and to preside over the constitutional convention. Now he went, in the fullness of his fame, to enter upon a task less dangerous, perhaps, than leading armies, but more beset with difficulties, and more perilous to his reputation and peace of mind, than any he had yet undertaken. He felt all this keenly, and noted in his diary: "About ten o'clock I bade adieu to Mount Vernon, to private life, and to domestic felicity; and with a mind oppressed with more anxious and painful sensations than I have words to express, set out for New York, with the best disposition to render service to my country, in obedience to its call, but with less hope of answering its expectations."

The first stage of his journey took him only to Alexandria, a few miles from his home, where a public dinner was given to him by his friends and neighbors. He was deeply moved when he rose to reply to the words of affection addressed to him by the mayor as spokesman of the people. "All that now remains for me," he said, "is to commit myself and you to the care of that beneficent Being who, on a former occasion, happily brought us together after a long and distressing separation. Perhaps the same gracious Providence will again indulge me. But words fail me. Unutterable sensations must then be left to more expressive silence, while from an aching heart I bid all my affectionate friends and kind neighbors farewell."

So he left his home, sad at the parting, looking steadily, but not joyfully, to the future, and silent as was his wont. The simple dinner with his friends and neighbors at Alexandria was but the beginning of the chorus of praise and Godspeed which rose higher and stronger as he advanced. The road, as he traveled, was lined with people, to see him and cheer him as he passed. In every village the people from the farm and workshop crowded the streets to watch for his carriage, and the ringing of bells and firing of guns marked his coming and his going. At Baltimore a cavalcade of citizens escorted him, and cannon roared a welcome. At the Pennsylvania line Governor Mifflin, with soldiers and citizens, gathered to greet him. At Chester he mounted a horse, and in the midst of a troop of cavalry rode into Philadelphia, beneath triumphal arches, for a day of public rejoicing and festivity. At Trenton, instead of snow and darkness, and a sudden onslaught upon surprised Hessians, there was mellow sunshine, an arch of triumph, and young girls walking before him, strewing flowers in his path, and singing songs of praise and gratitude. When he reached Elizabethtown Point, the committees of

Congress met him, and he there went on board a barge manned by thirteen pilots in white uniform, and was rowed to the city of New York. A long procession of barges swept after him with music and song, while the ships in the harbor, covered with flags, fired salutes in his honor. When he reached the landing he declined to enter a carriage, but walked to his house, accompanied by Governor Clinton. He was dressed in the familiar buff and blue, and, as the people caught sight of the stately figure and the beloved colors, hats went off and the crowd bowed as he went by, bending like the ripened grain when the summer wind passes over it, and breaking forth into loud and repeated cheers.

From Mount Vernon to New York it had been one long triumphal march. There was no imperial government to lend its power and military pageantry. There were no armies, with trophies to dazzle the eyes of the beholders; nor were there wealth and luxury to give pomp and splendor to the occasion. It was the simple outpouring of popular feeling, untaught and true, but full of reverence and gratitude to a great man. It was the noble instinct of hero-worship, always keen in humanity when the real hero comes to awaken it to life. Such an experience, rightly apprehended, would have impressed any man, and it affected Washington profoundly. He was deeply moved and touched, but he was neither excited nor elated. He took it all with soberness, almost with sadness, and when he was alone wrote in his diary:—

> The display of boats which attended and joined us on this occasion, some with vocal and some with instrumental music on board; the decorations of the ships, the roar of cannon and the loud acclamations of the people, which rent the skies as I passed along the wharves, filled my mind with sensations as painful (considering the reverse of this scene, which may be the case after all my labors to do good) as they were pleasing.

In the very moment of the highest personal glory, the only thought is of the work which he has to do. There is neither elation nor cynicism, neither indifference nor self-deception, but only deep feeling and a firm, clear look into the future of work and conflict which lay silent and unknown beyond the triumphal arches and the loud acclaim of the people.

On April 30 he was inaugurated. He went in procession to the hall, was received in the senate chamber, and thence proceeded to the balcony to take the oath. He was dressed in dark brown cloth of American manufacture, with a steel-hilted sword, and with his hair powdered and drawn back in the fashion of the time. When he appeared, a shout went up from the great crowd gathered beneath the balcony. Much overcome, he bowed in silence to the people, and there was an instant hush over all. Then Chancellor Livingston administered the oath. Washington laid his hand upon the Bible, bowed, and said solemnly when the oath was concluded, "I swear, so help me God," and, bending reverently, kissed the book. Livingston stepped forward, and raising his hand cried, "Long live George Washington, President of the United States!" Then the cheers broke forth again, the cannon roared, and the bells rang out. Washington withdrew to the hall, where he read his inaugural address to Congress, and the history of the United States of America under the Constitution was begun.

CHAPTER XIII

STARTING THE GOVERNMENT

WASHINGTON WAS DEEPLY gratified by his reception at the hands of the people from Alexandria to New York. He was profoundly moved by the ceremonies of his inauguration, and when he turned from the balcony to the senate chamber he showed in his manner and voice how much he felt the meaning of all that had occurred. His speech to the assembled Congress was solemn and impressive, and with simple reverence he acknowledged the guiding hand of Providence in the fortunes of the States. He made no recommendations to Congress, but expressed his confidence in their wisdom and patriotism, adjured them to remember that the success of republican government would probably be finally settled by the success of their experiment, reminded them that amendments to the Constitution were to be considered, and informed them that he could not receive any pecuniary compensation for his services, and expected only that his expenses should be paid as in the Revolution. This was all. The first inaugural of the first President expressed only one thought, but that thought was pressed home with force. Washington wished the Congress to understand as he understood the weight and meaning of the task which had been imposed upon them, for he felt that if he could do this all would be well. How far he succeeded it would be impossible to say, but there can be no doubt as to the wisdom of his position. To have attempted to direct the first movements of Congress before he had really grasped the reins of the government would have given rise, very probably, to jealousy and opposition at the outset. When he had developed a policy, then it would be time to advise the senators and representatives how to carry it out. Meanwhile it was better to arouse their patriotism, awaken their sense of responsibility, and leave them free to begin their work under the guidance of these impressions.

As for himself, his feelings remained unchanged. He had accepted the great post with solemn anxiety, and when the prayers had all been said, and the last guns fired, when the music had ceased and the cheers had died away, and the illuminations had flickered and gone out, he wrote that in taking office he had given up all expectation of private happiness, but that he was encouraged by the popular affection, as well as by the belief that his motives were appreciated, and that, thus supported, he would do his best. In a few words, written some months later, he tersely stated what his office meant to him, and what grave difficulties surrounded his path.

"The establishment of our new government," he said, "seemed to be the last great experiment for promoting human happiness by a reasonable compact in civil society. It was to be, in the first instance, in a considerable degree, a government of accommodation as well as a government of laws. Much was to be done by prudence, much by conciliation, much by firmness. Few who are not philosophical spectators can realize the difficult and delicate part which a man in my situation had to act. All see, and most admire, the glare which hovers round the external happiness of elevated office. To me there is nothing in it beyond the lustre which may be reflected from its connection with a power of promoting human felicity. In our progress towards political happiness my station is new, and, if I may use the expression, I walk on untrodden ground. There is scarcely an action the motive of which may not be subject to a double interpretation. There is scarcely any part of my conduct which may not hereafter be drawn into precedent. If, after all my humble but faithful endeavors to advance the felicity of my country and mankind, I may indulge a hope that my labors have not been altogether without success, it will be the only real compensation I can receive in the closing scenes of life."

There is nothing very stimulating to the imagination in this sober-ness of mind and calmness of utterance. The military conquerors and the saviors of society, with epigrammatic sayings, dramatic effects and rhyth-mic proclamations, are much more exciting and dazzle the fancy much better. But it is this seriousness of mind, coupled with intensity of pur-pose and grim persistence, which has made the English-speaking race spread over the world and carry successful government in its train. The personal empire of Napoleon had crumbled before he died an exile in St. Helena, but the work of Washington still endures. Just what that work was, and how it was achieved, is all that still remains to be considered.

The policies set on foot and carried through under the first federal administration were so brilliant and so successful that we are apt to for-get that months elapsed before the first of them was even announced. When Washington, on May 1, 1789, began his duties, there was absolutely nothing of the government of the United States in existence but a President and a Congress. The imperfect and broken machinery of the confederation still moved feebly, and performed some of the absolutely necessary functions of government. But the new organization had nothing to work with except these outworn remnants of a discarded system. There were no departments, and no arrangements for the collec-tion of revenue or the management of the postal service. A few scattered soldiers formed the army, and no navy existed. There were no funds and no financial resources. There were not even traditions and forms of gov-ernment, and, slight as these things may seem, settled methods of doing public business are essential to its prompt and proper transaction. These forms had to be devised and adopted first, and although they seem mat-ters of course now, after a century of use, they were the subject of much thought and of some sharp controversy in 1789. The manner in which the President was to be addressed caused some heated discussion even before the inauguration. America had but just emerged from the colonial condition, and the colonial habits were still unbroken. In private letters we find Washington referred to as "His Highness," and in some newspa-pers as "His Highness the President-General," while the Senate commit-tee reported in favor of addressing him as "His Highness the President of the United States and Protector of their Liberties." In the House, however, the democratic spirit was strong, there was a fierce attack upon the proposed titles, and that body ended by addressing Washington simply as the "President of the United States," which, as it happened, settled the question finally. Washington personally cared little for titles, although, as John Adams wrote to Mrs. Warren, he thought them appropriate to high office. But in this case he saw that there was a real danger lurking in the empty name, and so he was pleased by the decision of the House. Another matter was the relation between the President and the Senate. Should he communicate with them in writing or orally, being present during their deliberations as if they formed an executive council? It was promptly decided that nominations should be made in writing; but as to treaties, it was at first thought best that the President should deliver them to the Senate in person, and it was arranged with minute care where he should sit, beside the Vice-President, while the matter was under discussion. This arrangement, however, was abandoned after a single trial, and it was agreed that treaties, like nominations, should come with written messages.

Last and most important of all was the question of the mode of conduct and the etiquette to be established with regard to the President himself. In this, as in the matter of titles, Washington saw a real importance in what many persons might esteem only empty forms, and he proceeded with his customary thoroughness in dealing with the subject. What he did would be a precedent for the future as well as a target for present criticism, and he determined to devise a scheme which would resist attack, and be worthy to stand as an example for his successors. He therefore wrote to Madison: "The true medium, I conceive, must lie in pursuing such a course as will allow him (the President) time for all the official duties of his station. This should be the primary object. The next, to avoid as much as may be the charge of superciliousness, and seclusion from information, by too much reserve and too great a withdrawal of himself from company on the one hand, and the inconveniences, as well as a diminution of respectability, from too free an intercourse and too much familiarity on the other." This letter, with a set of queries, was also sent to the Vice-President, to Jay, and to Hamilton. They all agreed in the general views outlined by Washington. Adams, fresh from Europe, was inclined to surround the office, of which he justly had a lofty conception, with a good deal of ceremony, because he felt that these things were necessary in our relations with foreign nations. In the main, however, the advice of all who were consulted was in favor of keeping the nice line between too much reserve and too much familiarity, and this line, after all the advising, Washington of course drew for himself. He did it in this way. He decided that he would return no calls, and that he would receive no general visits except on specified days, and official visitors at fixed hours. The third point was in regard to dinner parties. The presidents of Congress hitherto had asked every one to dine, and had ended by keeping a sort of public table, to the waste of both time and dignity. Many persons, disgusted with this system, thought that the President ought not to ask anybody to dinner. But Washington, never given to extremes, decided that he would invite to dinner persons of official rank and strangers of distinction, but no one else, and that he would accept no invitations for himself. After a time he arranged to have a reception every Tuesday, from three to four in the afternoon, and Mrs. Washington held a similar levee on Fridays. These receptions, with a public dinner every week, were all the social entertainments for which the President had either time or health.

By these sensible and apparently unimportant arrangements, Washington managed to give free access to every one who was entitled to it, and yet preserved the dignity and reserve due to his office. It was one of the real although unmarked services which he rendered to the new government, and which contributed so much to its establishment, for it would have been very easy to have lowered the presidential office by a false idea of republican simplicity. It would have been equally easy to have made it odious by a cold seclusion on the one hand, or by pomp and ostentation on the other. With his usual good judgment and perfect taste, Washington steered between the opposing dangers, and yet notwithstanding the wisdom of his arrangements, and in spite of their simplicity, he did not escape calumny on account of them. One criticism was that at his reception every one stood, which was thought to savor of incipient monarchy. To this Washington replied, with the directness of which he was always capable, that it was not usual to sit on such occasions, and, if it were, he had no room large enough for the number of chairs that would be required, and that, as the whole thing was perfectly unceremonious, every one could come and go as he pleased. Fault was also found with the manner in which he bowed, an accusation to which he answered with an irony not untinged with bitterness and contempt: "That I have not been able to make bows to the taste of poor Colonel B. (who, by the by, I believe never saw one of them) is to be regretted, especially too, as, upon those occasions, they were indiscriminately bestowed, and the best I was master of. Would it not have been better to throw the veil of charity over them, ascribing their stiffness to the effects of age, or to the unskillfulness of my teacher, rather than to pride and dignity of office, which God knows has no charms for me?"

As party hostility developed, these attacks passed from the region of private conversation to the columns of newspapers and the declamation of mob orators, and an especial snarl was raised over the circumstance that at some public ball the President and Mrs. Washington were escorted to a sofa on a raised platform, and that guests passed before them and bowed. Much monarchy and aristocracy were perceived in this little matter, and Jefferson carefully set it down in that collection of withered slanders which he gave to an admiring posterity, after the grave had safely covered both him and those whom he feared and hated in his lifetime. This incident, however, was but an example of the political capital which was sought for in the conduct of the presidential office. The celebration of the birthday, the proposition to put Washington's head upon the coins, and many other similar trifles, were all twisted to the same purpose. The dynasty of Cleon has been a long one, so long that even the succession of the Popes seems temporary beside it, and it flourished in Washington's time as rankly as it did in Athens, or as it does to-day. The object of the assault varies, but the motives and the purpose are as old and as lasting as human nature. Envy and malice will always find a convenient shelter in pretended devotion to the public weal, and will seek revenge for their own lack of success by putting on the cloak of the tribune of the people, and perverting the noblest of offices to the basest uses.

But time sets all things even. The demagogues and the critics who assailed Washington's demeanor and behavior are forgotten, while the wise and simple customs which he established and framed for the great office that he honored, still prevail by virtue of their good sense. We part gladly with all remembrance of those bold defenders of liberty who saw in these slight forms forerunners of monarchy. We would even consent to drop into oblivion the precious legacy of Jefferson. But we will never part with the picture drawn by a loving hand of that stately figure, clad in black velvet, with the hand on the hilt of the sword, standing at one of Mrs. Washington's levees, and receiving with gentle and quiet dignity, full of kindliness but untinged by cheap familiarity, the crowd that came to pay their respects. It was well for the republic that at the threshold of its existence it had for President a man who, by the kindness of his heart, by his good sense, good manners, and fine breeding, gave to the office which he held and the government he founded the simple dignity which was part of himself and of his own high character.

Thus the forms and shows, important in their way, were dealt with, while behind them came the sterner realities of government, demanding regulation and settlement. At the outset Washington knew about the affairs of the government, especially for the last six years, only in a general way. He felt it to be his first duty, therefore, to familiarize himself with all these matters, and, although he was in the midst of the stir and bustle of a new government, he nevertheless sent for all the papers of each department of the confederation since the signature of the treaty of peace, went through them systematically, and made notes and summaries of their contents. This habit he continued throughout his presidency in dealing with all official documents. The natural result followed. He knew more at the start about the facts in each and every department of the public business than any other one man, and he continued to know more throughout his administration. In this method and this capacity for taking infinite pains is to be found a partial explanation at least of the easy mastery of affairs which he always showed, whether on the plantation, in the camp, or in the cabinet. It was in truth a striking instance of that "long patience" which the great French naturalist said was genius.

While he was thus regulating forms of business, and familiarizing himself with public questions, it became necessary to fix the manner of dealing with foreign powers. There were not many representatives of foreign nations present at the birth of the republic, but there was one who felt, and perhaps not without reason, that he was entitled to peculiar privileges. The Count de Moustier, minister of France, desired to have private access to the President, and even to discuss matters of business with him. Washington's reply to this demand was, in its way, a model. After saying that the only matter which could come up would relate to commerce, with which he was unfamiliar, he continued: "Every one, who has any knowledge of my manner of acting in public life, will be persuaded that I am not accustomed to impede the dispatch or frustrate the success of business by a ceremonious attention to idle forms. Any person of that description will also be satisfied that I should not readily consent to lose one of the most important functions of my office for the sake of preserving an imaginary dignity. But perhaps, if there are rules of proceeding which have originated from the wisdom of statesmen, and are sanctioned by the common consent of nations, it would not be prudent for a young state to dispense with them altogether, at least without some substantial cause for so doing. I have myself been induced to think, possibly from habits of experience, that in general the best mode of conducting negotiations, the detail and progress of which might be liable to accidental mistakes or unintentional misrepresentations, is by writing. This mode, if I was obliged by myself to negotiate with any one, I should still pursue. I have, however, been taught to believe that there is in most polished nations a system established with regard to the foreign as well as the other great departments, which, from the utility, the necessity, and the reason of the thing, provides that business should be digested and prepared by the heads of those departments."

The Count de Moustier hastened to excuse himself on the ground that he expressed himself badly in English, which was over-modest, for he expressed himself extremely well. He also explained and defended his original propositions by trying to show that they were reasonable and usual; but it was labor lost. Washington's letter was final, and the French minister knew it. The count was aware that he was dealing with a good soldier, but in statecraft he probably felt he had to do with a novice. His intention was to take advantage of the position of France, secure for her peculiar privileges, and put her in the attitude of patronizing inoffensively but effectively the new government founded by the people she had helped to free. He found himself turned aside quietly, almost deferentially, and yet so firmly and decidedly that there was no appeal. No nation, he discovered, was to have especial privileges. France was the good friend and ally of the United States, but she was an equal, not a superior. It was also fixed by this correspondence that the President, representing the sovereignty of the people, was to have the respect to which that sovereignty was entitled. The pomp and pageant of diplomacy in the old world were neither desired nor sought in America; yet the President was not to be approached in person, but through the proper cabinet officer, and all diplomatic communications after the fashion of civilized governments were to be in writing. Thus within a month France, and in consequence other nations, were quietly given to understand that the new republic was to be treated like other free and independent governments, and that there was to be nothing colonial or subservient in her attitude to foreign nations, whether those nations had been friends or foes in the past.

It required tact, firmness, and a sure judgment to establish proper relations with foreign ministers. But once done, it was done for all time. This was not the case with another and far more important class of people, whose relation to the new administration had to be determined at the very first hour of its existence. Indeed, before Washington left Mount Vernon he had begun to receive letters from persons who considered themselves peculiarly well fitted to serve the government in return for a small but certain salary. In a letter to Mrs. Wooster, for whom as the widow of an old soldier he felt the tenderest sympathy, he wrote soon after his arrival in New York: "As a public man acting only with reference to the public good, I must be allowed to decide upon all points of my duty, without consulting my private inclinations and wishes. I must be permitted, with the best lights I can obtain, and upon a general view of characters and circumstances, to nominate such persons alone to offices as in my judgment shall be the best qualified to discharge the functions of the departments to which they shall be appointed." This sentiment in varying forms has been declared since 1789 by many Presidents and many parties. Washington, however, lived up exactly to his declarations. At the same time he did not by any means attempt to act merely as an examining board.

Great political organizations, as we have known them since, did not exist at the beginning of the government, but there were nevertheless two parties, divided by the issue which had been settled by the adoption of the Constitution. Washington took, and purposed to take, his appointees so far as he could from those who had favored the Constitution and were friends of the new system. It is also clear that he made every effort to give the preference to the soldiers and officers of the army, toward whom his affectionate thought ever turned. Beyond this it can only be said that he was almost nervously anxious to avoid any appearance of personal feeling in making appointments, as was shown in the letter refusing to make his nephew Bushrod a district attorney, and that he, resented personal pressure of any kind. He preferred always to reach his conclusions so far as possible from a careful study of written testimony. These principles, rigidly adhered to, his own keen perception of character, and his knowledge of men, resulted in a series of appointments running through eight years which were really marvelously successful. The only rejection, outside the special case of John Rutledge, was that of Benjamin Fishbourn for naval officer of the port of Savannah, which was due apparently to the personal hostility of the Georgia senators. Washington, conscious of his own painstaking, was not a little provoked by this setting aside of an old soldier. He sent in a sharp message on the subject, pointing out the trouble he took to make sure of the fitness of an appointment, and intimated that the same effort would not come amiss in the Senate when they rejected one of his nominees. In view of the fact that it was a new government, the absence of mistakes in the appointments is quite extraordinary, and the value of such success can be realized by considering the disastrous consequences which would have come from inefficient officers or malfeasance in office when the great experiment was just put on trial, and was surrounded by doubters and critics ready and eager to pick flaws and find faults.

The general tone of the government and its reputation at widely scattered points depended largely on the persons appointed to the smaller executive offices. Important, however, as these were, the fate of the republic under the new Constitution was infinitely more involved in the men whom Washington called about him in his cabinet, to decide with him as to the policies which were to be begun, and on which the living vital government was to be founded. Congress, troubled about many things, and struggling with questions of revenue and taxation, managed in the course of the summer to establish and provide for three executive departments and for an attorney-general. To the selection of the men to fill these high offices Washington gave, of course, the most careful thought, and succeeded in forming a cabinet which, in its aggregate ability, never has been equaled in this country.

Edmund Randolph was appointed attorney-general. Losing his father at an early age, and entering the army, he had been watched over and protected by Washington with an almost paternal care, and at the time of his appointment he was one of the most conspicuous men in public life, as well as a leading lawyer at the bar of Virginia. He came from one of the oldest and strongest of the Virginian families, and had been governor of his State, and a leader in the constitutional convention, where he had introduced what was known as the Virginian plan. He had refused to sign the Constitution, but had come round finally to its support, largely through Washington's influence. There was then, and there can be now, no question as to Randolph's really fine talents, or as to his fitness for his post. His defect was a lack of force of character and strength of will, which was manifested by a certain timidity of action, and by an infirmity of purpose, such as had appeared in his course about the Constitution. He performed the duties of his office admirably, but in the decision of the momentous questions which came before the cabinet he showed an uncertainty of opinion which was felt by all his colleagues.*

Henry Knox of Massachusetts was head of the War Department under the confederacy, and was continued in office by Washington, who appointed him secretary of war under the new arrangement. It was a natural and excellent selection. Knox was a distinguished soldier, he had served well through the Revolution, and Washington was warmly attached to him. He was not a statesman by training or habit of mind, nor was he possessed of commanding talents. But he was an able man, sound in his views and diligent in his office, devoted to his chief and unswerving in his loyalty to the administration and all its measures. There was never any doubt as to the attitude of Henry Knox, and Washington found him as faithful and efficient in the cabinet as he had always been in the field.

Second in rank, but first in importance, was the secretaryship of the treasury. "Finance! Ah, my friend, all that remains of the American Revolution grounds there." So Gouverneur Morris had written to Jay. So might he have written again of the American Union, for the fate of the experiment rested at the outset on the Treasury Department. Yet there was probably less hesitation as to the proper man for this place than for any other. Washington no doubt would have been glad to give it to Robert Morris, whose great services in the Revolution he could never forget. But this could not be, and acting on his own judgment, fortified by that of Morris himself, he made Alexander Hamilton secretary of the treasury.

It is one of the familiar marks of greatness to know how to choose the right men to perform the tasks which no man, either in war or peace, can complete single-handed. Napoleon's marshals were conspicuous proofs of his genius, and Washington had a similar power of selection. The gen-

---

*This passage was written before the recent appearance of Mr. Conway's *Life of Randolph*. That ample biography, in my opinion, confirms the view of Randolph here given. If, in the light of this new material, I have erred at all, it is, I think, on the charitable side. Mr. Conway, in order to vindicate Randolph, has sacrificed so far as he could nearly every conspicuous public man of that period. From Washington, whom he charges with senility, down, there is hardly a man who ever crossed Randolph's path whom he has not assailed. Yet he presents no reason, so far as I can see, to alter the present opinion of Randolph.

erals whom he trusted were the best generals, the statesmen whom he consulted stand highest in history. He was fallible, as other mortals are fallible. He, too, had his Varus, and the time was coming when he could echo the bitter cry of the great emperor for his lost legions. But the mistakes were the exceptions. He chose with the sureness of a strong and penetrating mind, and the most signal example of this capacity was his secretary of the treasury. He knew Hamilton well. He had known him as his staff officer, active, accomplished, and efficient. He had seen him leave his side in a tempest of boyish rage, and he had watched him charging with splendid gallantry the Yorktown redoubts. He was familiar with Hamilton's extraordinary mastery of financial and political problems, and he had found him a powerful leader in the work of forming the Constitution. He understood Hamilton's strength, and he knew where his dangers lay. Now he called him to his cabinet, and gave into his hands the department on which the immediate success of the government hinged. It was a brilliant choice. The mark in his lifetime for all the assaults of his political opponents, the leader and the victim of the schism which rent his own party, Hamilton, after his death, was made the target for attack and reprobation by his political foes, who for nearly sixty years, with few intermissions, controlled the government. His work, however, could not be undone, and as passions have subsided his fame has proved to be of that highest and rarest kind which broadens and rises with the lapse of years, until in the light of history it overtops that of any of our statesmen, except of his own great chief and Abraham Lincoln. The work to which he was called was that of organizing a national government, and in the performance of this work he showed that he belonged to the highest type of constructive statesmen, and was one of the rare men who build, and whose building stands the test of time.

Last to be mentioned, but first in rank, was the Department of State. For this high place Washington chose Thomas Jefferson, who was then our minister in Paris, and who did not return to take up his official duties until the following March. Of the four cabinet offices, this was the only one where Washington proceeded entirely on public grounds. He took Jefferson on account of his wide reputation, his unquestioned ability, his standing before the country, and his experience in our foreign relations. With the other three there was a strong element of personal friendship and familiarity. With the secretary of state his intercourse had been, so far as we can judge, almost wholly of a public character, and, so far as can be inferred from an expression of some years before, the selection was made by Washington in deference simply to what he believed to be the public interest. The only allusion to Jefferson in all the printed volumes of correspondence prior to 1789 occurs in a letter to Robert Livingston, of January 8, 1783. He there said: "What office is Mr. Jefferson appointed to that he has, you say, lately accepted? If it is that of commissioner of peace, I hope he will arrive too late to have any hand in it." There is no indication that their personal relations were then or afterwards other than pleasant. Yet this brief sentence is a strong expression of distrust, and especially so from the fact that Washington was not at all given to criticising other people in his letters. What he distrusted was not Jefferson's ability, for that no man could doubt, still less his patriotism. But Washington read character well, and he felt that Jefferson might be lacking in the qualities of boldness and determination, so needful in a negotiation like that which resulted in the acknowledgment of our independence.

The truth was that the two men were radically different, and never could have been sympathetic. Washington was strong, direct, masculine, and at times fierce in anger. Jefferson was adroit, subtle, and feminine in his sensitiveness. Washington was essentially a fighting man, tamed by a stern self-control from the recklessness of his early days, but always a fighter. Jefferson was a lover of peace, given to quiet, hating quarrels and blood-shed, and at times timid in dealing with public questions. Washington was deliberate and conservative, after the fashion of his race. Jefferson was quick, impressionable, and always fascinated by new notions, even if they were somewhat fantastic. A thoroughly liberal and open-minded man, Washington never turned a deaf ear to any new suggestion, whether it was a public policy or a mechanical invention, but to all alike he gave careful consideration before he adopted them. To Jefferson, on the other hand, mere novelty had a peculiar charm, and he jumped at any device, either to govern a state or improve a plough, provided that it had the flavor of ingenuity. The two men might easily have thought the same concerning the republic, but they started from opposite poles, and no full communion of thought and feeling was possible between them. That Washington chose fitly from purely public and outside considerations can not be questioned, but he made a mistake when he put next to himself a man for whom he did not have the personal regard and sympathy which he felt for his other advisers. The necessary result finally came, after many troubles in the cabinet, in dislike and distrust, if not positive alienation.

Looking at the cabinet, however, as it stood in the beginning, we can only admire the wisdom of the selection and the high abilities which were thus brought together for the administration and construction of a great national government. It has always been the fashion to speak of this first cabinet as made up without reference to party, but the idea is a mistaken one from any point of view. Washington himself gave it color, for he felt very rightly that he was the choice of the whole people and not of a party. He wished to rise above party, and in fact to have no party, but a devotion of all to the good of the country. The time came when he sorrowed for and censured party bitterness and party strife, but it is to be observed that the party feeling which he most deplored was that which grew up against his own policies and his own administration. The fact was that Washington, who rose above party more than any other statesman in our history, was nevertheless, like most men of strong will and robust mind, and like all great political leaders, a party man, as we shall have occasion to see further on. It is true that his cabinet contained the chiefs and founders of two great schools of political thought, which have ever since divided the country; but when these parties were once fairly developed, the cabinet became a scene of conflict and went to pieces, only to be reformed on party lines. When it was first made up, the two parties of our subsequent history, with which we are familiar, did not exist, and it was in the administration of Washington that they were developed. Yet the cabinet of 1789 was, so far as there were parties, a partisan body. The only political struggle that we had had was over the

adoption of the Constitution. The parties of the first Congress were the
Federalists and the anti-Federalists, the friends and the enemies of the
Constitution. Among those who opposed the Constitution were many
able and distinguished men, but Washington did not invite Sam Adams,
or George Mason, or Patrick Henry, or George Clinton to enter his cabinet. On the contrary, he took only friends and supporters of the
Constitution. Hamilton was its most illustrious advocate. Randolph, after
some vacillation, had done very much to turn the wavering scale in
Virginia in its favor. Knox was its devoted friend; and Jefferson, although
he had carped at it and criticised it in his letters, was not known to have
done so, and was considered, and rightly considered, to be friendly to the
new system. In other words, the cabinet was made up exclusively of the
party of the Constitution, which was the victorious party of the moment.
This was of course wholly right, and Washington was too great and wise
a leader to have done anything else. The cabinet was formed with regard
to existing divisions, and, when those divisions changed, the cabinet
which gave birth to them changed too.

Outside the cabinet, the most weighty appointments were those of
the Supreme Court. No one then quite appreciated, probably, the vast
importance which this branch of the government was destined to assume,
or the great part it was to play in the history of the country and the development of our institutions. At the same time no one could fail to see that
much depended on the composition of the body which was to be the ultimate interpreter of the Constitution. The safety of the entire scheme
might easily have been imperiled by the selection of men as judges who
were lacking in ability or character. Washington chose with his wonted
sureness. At the head of the court he placed John Jay, one of the most distinguished of the public men of the day, who gave to the office at once
the impress of his own high character and spotless reputation. With him
were associated Wilson of Pennsylvania, Cushing of Massachusetts, Blair
of Virginia, Iredell of North Carolina, and Rutledge of South Carolina.
They were all able and well-known men, sound lawyers, and also, be it
noted, warm friends of the Constitution.

Thus the business of organizing the government in the first great and essential points was completed. It was the work of the President, and, anxious and arduous as it was, it is worth remembering, too, that it was done, and thoroughly done, in the midst of severe physical suffering. Just after the inauguration, Washington was laid up with an anthrax or carbuncle in his thigh, which brought him at one time very near death. For six weeks he could lie only on one side, endured the most constant and acute pain, and was almost incapable of motion. He referred to his illness at the time in a casual and perfectly simple way, and mind and will so prevailed over the bodily suffering that the great task of organizing the government was never suspended nor interrupted.

When the work was done and Congress had adjourned, Washington, feeling that he had earned a little rest and recreation, proceeded to carry out a purpose, which he had formed very early in his presidency, of visiting the Eastern States. This was the first part of a general plan which he had conceived of visiting while in office all portions of the Union. The personal appearance of the President, representing the whole people, would serve to bring home to the public mind the existence and reality of a central government, which to many if not to most persons in the outlying States seemed shadowy and distant. But General Washington was neither shadowy nor distant to any one. Every man, woman, and child had heard of and loved the leader of the Revolution. To his countrymen everywhere, his name meant political freedom and victory in battle; and when he came among them as the head of a new government, that government took on in some measure the character of its chief. His journey was a well-calculated appeal, not for himself but for his cause, to the warm human interest which a man readily excites, but which only gathers slowly around constitutions and forms of government. The world owes a good deal to the right kind of hero-worship, and the United States have been no exception.

The journey itself was uneventful, and was carried out with Washington's usual precision. It served its purpose, too, and brought out a popular enthusiasm which spoke well for the prospects of the federal government, and which was the first promise of the loyal support which New England gave to the President, as she had already given it to the general. In the succession of crowds and processions and celebrations which marked the public rejoicing, one incident of this journey stands out as still memorable, and possessed of real meaning. Mr. John Hancock was governor of Massachusetts. There is no need to dwell upon him. He was a man of slender abilities, large wealth, and ready patriotism, with a great sense of his own importance, and a fine taste for impressive display. Every external thing about him, from his handsome house and his Copley portrait to his imposing gout and his immortal signature, was showy and effective. He was governor of Massachusetts, and very proud of that proud old commonwealth as well as of her governor. Within her bounds he was the representative of her sovereignty, and he felt that deference was due to him from the President of the United States when they both stood on the soil of Massachusetts. He did not meet Washington on his arrival, and Washington thereupon did not dine with the governor as he had agreed to do. It looked a little stormy. Here was evidently a man with some new views as to the sovereignty of States and the standing of the union of States. It might have done for Governor Hancock to allow the President of Congress to pass out of Massachusetts without seeing its governor, and thereby learn a valuable lesson, but it would never do to have such a thing happen in the case of George Washington, no matter what office he might hold. A little after noon on Sunday, October 26, therefore, the governor wrote a note to the President, apologizing for not calling before, and asking if he might call in half an hour, even though it was at the hazard of his health. Washington answered at once, expressing his pleasure at the prospect of seeing his excellency, but begging him, with a touch of irony, not to do anything to endanger his health. So in half an hour Hancock appeared. Picturesque, even if defeated, he was borne upstairs on men's shoulders, swathed in flannels, and then and there made his call. The old house in Boston where this happened has had since then a series of successors, but the ground on which it stood has been duly remembered and commemorated. It is a more important spot than we are wont to think; for there it was settled, on that autumn Sunday, that the idea that the States were able to own and to bully the Union they had formed was dead, and that

the President of the new United States was henceforth to be regarded as
the official superior of every governor in the land. It was a mere question
of etiquette, nothing more. But how the general government would have
sunk in popular estimation if the President had not asserted, with perfect
dignity and yet entire firmness, its position! Men are governed very
largely by impressions, and Washington knew it. Hence his settling at
once and forever the question of precedence between the Union and the
States. Everywhere and at all times, according to his doctrine, the nation
was to be first.*

So the President traveled on to the North, and then back by another
road to New York, and that excellent bit of work in familiarizing the people with their federal government was accomplished. Meantime the
wheels had started, the machine was in motion, and the chief officers were
at their places. The preliminary work had been done, and the next step
was to determine what policies should be adopted, and to find out if the
new system could really perform the task for which it had been created.

---

*The most lately published contemporary account of this affair with Hancock can be found in
the *Magazine of American History*, June, 1888, p. 508, entitled "Incidents in the Life of John
Hancock, as related by Dorothy Quincy Hancock Scott (from the Diary of Gen. W. H. Sumner)."

CHAPTER XIV

DOMESTIC AFFAIRS

TO TRACE IN detail the events of Washington's administration would be to write the history of the country during that period. It is only possible here to show, without much regard to chronological sequence, the part of the President in developing the policy of the government at home, and his attitude toward each question as it arose. We are concerned here merely with the influence and effect of Washington in our history, and not with the history itself. What did he do, and what light do we get on the man himself from his words and deeds? These are the only questions that a brief study of a career so far-reaching can attempt to answer.

Congress came together for the first time with the government actually organized on January 4, 1790. On the day when the session opened, Washington drove down to the hall where the Congress met, alone in his own coach drawn by four horses. He was preceded by Colonel Humphreys and Major Jackson, mounted on his two white horses, while immediately behind came his chariot with his private secretaries, and Mr. Lewis on horseback. Then followed in their own coaches the chief justice and the secretaries of war and of the treasury. When the President reached the hall he was met at the entrance by the doorkeeper of the Congress, and was escorted to the Senate chamber. There he passed between the members of each branch, drawn up on either hand, and took his seat by the Vice-President. When order and silence were obtained, he rose and spoke to the assembled representatives of the people standing before him. Having concluded his speech, he bowed and withdrew with his suite as he had come. Jefferson killed this simple ceremonial, and substituted for it the written message, sent by a secretary and read by a clerk in the midst of talk and bustle, which is the form we have to-day. Jefferson's change was made, of course, in the name of liberty, and also because he was averse to public speaking. From the latter point of view, it was reasonable enough, but the ostensible cause was as hollow and meaningless as any of the French notions to which it was close akin. It is well for the head of the state to meet face to face the representatives of the same people who elected him. For more than a century this has been the practice in Massachusetts, to take a single instance, and liberty in that commonwealth has not been imperiled, nor has the State been obliged to ask Federal aid to secure to her a republican form of government because of her adherence to this ancient custom.

The forms adopted by Washington had the grave and simple dignity which marked all he did, and it was senseless to abandon what his faultless taste and patriotic feeling approved. Forms are in their way important things: they may conceal perils to liberty, or they may lend dignity and call forth respect to all that liberty holds most dear. The net result of all this business has been very curious. Jefferson's written message prevails; and yet at the same time we inaugurate our Presidents with a pomp and parade to which those of the dreaded Federalists seem poor and quiet, and which would make the hero of the message-in-writing fancy that the air was darkened by the shadows of monarchy and despotism. The author of the Declaration of Independence was a patriotic man and lover of freedom, but he who fought out the Revolution in the field was quite as safe a guardian of American liberty; and his clear mind was never confused by the fantasies of that Parisian liberty which confused facts with names, and ended in the Terror and the first Empire. The people of the United States to-day surround the first office of the land with a respect and dignity which they deem equal to the mighty sovereignty that it represents, and in this is to be found the genuine American feeling expressed by Washington in the plain and simple ceremonial which he adopted for his meetings with the Congress.

In this first speech, thus delivered, Washington indicated the subjects to which he wished Congress to direct their attention, and which in their development formed the policies of his administration. His first recommendation was to provide for the common defense by a proper military establishment. His last and most elaborate was in behalf of education, for which he invoked the aid of Congress and urged the foundation of a national university, a scheme he had much at heart, and to which he constantly returned. The history of these two recommendations is soon told. Provision was made for the army, inadequate enough, as Washington thought, but still without dispute, and such additional provision was afterwards made from time to time as the passing exigency of the moment demanded. For education nothing was done, and the national university has never advanced beyond the recommendation of the first President.

He also advised the adoption of a uniform standard of coinage, weights, and measures. In two years a mint was duly established after an able report from Hamilton, and out of his efforts and those of Jefferson came our decimal system. There was debate over the devices on the coins in which the ever-vigilant Jeffersonians scented monarchical dangers, but with this exception the country got its uniform coinage peacefully enough. The weights and measures did not fare so well. They obtained a long report from Jefferson, and a still longer and more learned disquisition from John Quincy Adams thirty years later. But that was all. We still use the rule of thumb systems inherited from our English ancestors, and Washington's uniform standard, except for the two reports, has gone no further than the national university.

Another recommendation to the effect that invention ought to be encouraged and protected bore fruit in this same year in patent and copyright laws, which became the foundation of our present system. The same good fortune befell the recommendation for a uniform rule for naturalization, and the law of 1790 was quietly enacted, no one then imagining that its alteration less than ten years later was destined to form part of a policy which, after a fierce struggle, settled the fate of parties and decided the control of the government. The post-office was also commended to the care of Congress, and for that, as for the army, provision was duly made, insufficient at the outset, but growing steadily from this small beginning, as it was called upon to meet the spread and increase of population.

Provision was also made gradually, and with much occasional conflict, for a diplomatic service such as the President advised. But this was merely the machinery to carry out our foreign policy on which, in a few years, our political history largely turned, and which will demand a chapter by itself.

A paragraph devoted to Indian affairs informed Congress that measures were on foot to establish pacific relations with our savage neighbors, but that it would be well to be prepared to use force. This brief sentence was the beginning of an important policy, which, in its consequences and effects, played a large part in the history of the next eight years.

These various matters thus disposed of, there remained only the request to the House to provide for the revenue and the public credit. From this came Hamilton's financial policy which created parties, and with it was interwoven in the body of the speech the general recommendation to make all proper effort for the advancement of manufactures, commerce, and agriculture.

The speech as a whole, short though it was, drew the outline of a vigorous system, which aimed at the establishment of a strong government with enlarged powers. It cut at a blow all ties between the new government and the feeble strivings of the dead confederation. It displayed a broad conception of the duties of the government under the Constitution, and in every paragraph it breathed the spirit of a robust nationality, calculated to touch the people directly in every State of the Union.

Before taking up the financial question, which became the great issue in our domestic affairs, it will be well to trace briefly the story of our relations with the Indians. The policy of the new administration in this respect was peculiarly Washington's own, and, although it affected more or less the general course of events at that period, it did not directly become the subject of party differences. The "Indian problem" is still with us, but it is now a very mild problem indeed. Within a few years, it is true, we have had Indian wars, conducted by the forces of the United States, and ever-recurring outbreaks between savages and frontiersmen. But it has been a very distant business. To the great mass of the American people it has been little more than interesting news, to be leisurely scanned in the newspaper without any sense of immediate and personal concern. Moreover, the popular conception of the Indian has for a long time been wildly inaccurate. We have known him in various capacities, as the innocent victim of corrupt agents and traders, and as the brutal robber and murderer with the vices and force of the Western frontiersman, but without any of the latter's redeeming virtues. Last and most important of all, we have known him as the rare hero and the conventional villain of romance, ranging from the admirable stories of Cooper to the last production of the "penny dreadful." The result has been to create in the public mind a being who probably never existed anywhere except in the popular imagination, and who certainly is not the North American Indian.

We are always loath to admit that our conceptions are formed by fiction, but in the case of people remote from our daily observation it plays in nine instances out of ten a leading part, and it has certainly done so here. In this way we have been provided with two types simple and well defined, which represent the abnormally good on the one hand and the inconceivably bad on the other. The Indian hero is a person of phenomenal nobility of character, and of an ability which would do credit to the training of a highly refined civilization. He is the product of the orator, the novelist, or the philanthropist, and has but slight and distant relation to facts. The usual type, however, and the one which has entered most largely into the popular mind, is the Indian villain. He is portrayed invariably as cunning, treacherous, cruel, and cowardly, without any relieving quality. In this there is of course much truth. As a matter of fact, Indians are cunning, treacherous, and cruel, but they are also bold fighters. The leading idea of the Indian that has come down from Cooper's time, and which depicts him as a "cowardly redskin," unable to stand for a moment against a white man in fair fight, is a complete delusion designed to flatter the superior race. It has been in a large measure dissipated by Parkman's masterly histories, but the ideas born of popular fiction die hard. They are due in part to the theory that cruelty implies cowardice, just as we say that a bully must be a coward, another mistaken bit of proverbial wisdom.

As a matter of fact, the records show that the North American Indian is one of the most remarkable savage warriors of whom we have any knowledge; and the number of white men killed for each Indian slain in war exhibits an astonishing disproportion of loss. Captain James Smith, for many years a captive, and who figured in most of the campaigns of the last century, estimated that fifty of our people were killed to one of theirs. This of course includes women and children; and yet even in the battle of the Big Kanawha, the Virginia riflemen, although they defeated the Indians with an inferior force, lost two to one, and a similar disproportion seems to have continued to the present day.

The Indian, moreover, not only fought well and to the death, if surrounded, but he had a discipline and plan of battle which were most effective for the wilderness. It seems probable that, if the experiment had been properly tried, the Indians might have been turned into better soldiers than the famous Sikhs; and the French, who used the red men skillfully, if without much discipline, found them formidable and effective allies. They cut off more than one English and American army, and the fact that they resorted to ambush and surprise does not detract from their exploits. It was a legitimate mode of warfare, and was used by them with terrible effect. They have fought more than one pitched battle against superior numbers when the victory hung long in the balance, and they have carried on guerrilla wars for years against overwhelming forces with extraordinary persistence and success. There is no savage, except the Zulu or Maori, who has begun to exhibit the natural fighting quality of the American Indian; and although the Zulu appears to have displayed greater dash, the Indian, by his mastery of the tactics of surprise, has shown a far better head. In a word, the Indian has always been a formidable savage, treacherous, cruel, and cunning to an extreme degree, no doubt, but a desperate and dogged fighter, with a natural instinct for war.

It must be remembered, too, that he was far more formidable in 1790 than he is to-day, with the ever-rising tide of civilized population flowing upon him and hemming him in. When the Constitution came into being, the Indians were pretty well out of the Atlantic States, but beyond the Alleghanies all was theirs, and they had the unbroken wilderness as their ally and their refuge. There they lay like a dark line on the near frontier, threatening war and pillage and severe check to the westward advance of our people. They were a serious matter to a new government, limited in resources and representing only three millions of people.

Fortunately the President was of all men best fitted to deal with this grave question, for he knew the Indians thoroughly. His earliest public service had been to negotiate with them, and from that time on he had been familiar with them in peace and in diplomacy, while he had fought with them in war over and over again. He was not in the least confused in his notions about them, but saw them, as he did most facts, exactly as they were. He had none of the false sentimentality about the noble and injured red man, which in later days has been at times highly mischievous, nor on the other hand did he take the purely brutal view of the fighting scout or backwoodsman. He knew the Indian as he was, and understood him as a dangerous, treacherous, fighting savage. Better than any one else he appreciated the difficulties of Indian warfare when an army had to be launched into the wilderness and cut off from a base of supplies. He was well aware, too, that the western tribes were a constant temptation to England and Spain on either border, and might be used against us with terrible effect. In taking up the question for solution, he believed first, as was his nature, in justice, and he resolved to push every pacific measure, and strive unremittingly by fair dealing and binding treaties to keep a peace which was of great moment to the young republic. But he also felt that pacific measures were an uncertain reliance, and that sharp, decisive blows were often the only means of maintaining peace and quiet on the frontier, and of warding off English and Spanish intrigue. This was the policy he indicated in the brief sentences of his first speech, and it only remains to see how he carried it out.

The outlook in regard to the Indians, when Washington assumed the presidency, was threatening enough. The Continental Congress had shown in this respect most honorable intention and some vigor, but their honest purposes had been in large measure thwarted by the action of the various States, which they were unable to control. In New York peace reigned, despite some grumbling; for the Six Nations had made a general treaty, and also two special treaties, not long before, which were on the whole just and satisfactory. At the same time a general treaty had been made with the western Indians, which modified some of the injustices of the treaties of 1785, and which were also fair and reasonable. In this treaty, however, the tribes of the Wabash were not included, and they therefore were engaged in war with the Kentucky people. Those hardy backwoodsmen were quick enough to retaliate, and they generally proceeded on the simple backwoods principle that tribal distinctions were futile, and that every Indian was an enemy. This view, it must be admitted, saved a good deal of thought, but it led the Kentuckians in their raids to kill many Indians who did not belong to the Wabash tribes, but to those protected by treaty. The result of this impartiality was, that, besides the chronic Wabash troubles, there was every probability that a general war with all the western and northwestern tribes might break out at any moment.

South of the Ohio, matters were even worse. The Choctaws, it is true, owing to their distance from our frontier settlements, were on excellent terms with our government. But the Cherokees had just been beaten and driven back by Sevier and his followers from the short-lived state of Franklin, and had taken refuge with the Creeks. These last were a formidable people. Not only were they good fighters, but they were also well armed, thanks to their alliance with the Spaniards, from whom they obtained not only countenance, but guns, ammunition, and supplies. They were led also by a chief of remarkable ability, a Scotch half-breed, educated at Charlestown, and named Alexander McGillivray. With a tribe so constituted and commanded, it was not difficult to bring on trouble, as soon proved to be the case. Georgia had claimed and seized certain lands under treaties which she alleged had been made, whereupon the Creeks denied the validity of these treaties and went to war, in which they were highly successful. The Georgians had already asked assistance from their neighbors, and they now demanded it from the new general government. Thereupon, under an act of Congress, Washington, appointed as commissioners to arrange the difficulties General Lincoln, Colonel Humphrey, and David Griffin of Virginia, all remote from the scene of conflict, and all judicious selections. The Creeks readily met the new commissioners, but when they found that no lands were to be given up, they declined to treat further, and said they would await a new negotiation.

Washington attributed this failure, and no doubt correctly, to the intrigues and influence of Spain. On the day the report of the commissioners went to Congress, he wrote to Governor Pinckney of South Carolina: "For my own part I am entirely persuaded that the present general government will endeavor to lay the foundations for its proceedings in national justice, faith, and honor. But should the government, after having attempted in vain every reasonable pacific measure, be obliged to have recourse to arms for the defense of its citizens, I am also of opinion that sound policy and good economy will point to a prompt and decisive effort, rather than to defensive and lingering operations." "Lingering" had been the curse of our Indian policy, and it was this above all things that Washington was determined to be rid of. Whether peace or war, there was to be quick and decisive action. He therefore, in this spirit, at once sent southward another commissioner, Colonel Willett, who very shrewdly succeeded in getting McGillivray and his chiefs to agree to accompany him to New York. Thither they accordingly came in due time, the Scotch half-breed and twenty-eight of his chiefs. They were entertained and well treated at the seat of government, and there, with Knox acting for the United States, they made a treaty which involved concessions on both sides. The Creeks gave up all claims to lands north and east of the Oconee, and the United States, under a recent general act regulating trade and intercourse with the Indians, gave up all lands south and west of the same river, and agreed to make the tribes an annual present. Then Washington gave them wampum and tobacco, and shook hands with them, and the chiefs went home. There was grumbling on both sides, especially among the

Georgians, but nevertheless the treaty held for a time at least, and there was peace.

Washington's policy of justice had succeeded, and the Indians got an idea of the power and fair dealing of the new government, which was of real value. More valuable still was the lesson to the people of the United States that this central government meant to deal justly with the Indians, and would try to prevent any single State from frustrating by bad faith the policy designed to benefit the whole country. Trouble soon began again in this direction, and in later days States inflated with state-right doctrines carried this resistance in Indian affairs to a much greater extent, and flouted the acts of the federal government. This, however, does not detract from the wisdom of the President, who inaugurated the policy of acting justly toward the Indians, and of overruling the selfish injustice of the State immediately affected. If the policy of justice and firmness adopted by Washington had never been abandoned, it would have been better for the honor and the interest both of the nation and the separate States.

The same pacific policy which had succeeded in the south was tried in the west and failed. The English, with their usual thoughtfulness, incited the Indians to claim the Ohio as their boundary, which meant war and murderous assaults on all our people traveling on the river. Retaliation, of course, followed, and in April, 1790, Colonel Harmar with a body of Kentucky militia invaded the Indian country, burned a deserted village, and returned without having accomplished anything substantial. The desultory warfare of murder and pillage went on for a time, and then Washington felt that the moment had come for the other branch of his policy. At all events there should be no lingering, and there should be action. Peaceful measures having failed, there should be war and a settlement in some fashion.

Accordingly, in the fall of 1790, soon after his successful Creek negotiation, he ordered out some three hundred regulars and eleven hundred militia from Pennsylvania and Kentucky, and sent them under Harmar into the Miami country. The expedition burned a village on the Scioto; and then Colonel Hardin, detached with some hundred and fifty men in pursuit of the Indians, was caught in an ambush and his regulars cut off, the militia running away apparently quite successfully. There upon Harmar retreated; but, changing his mind in a day or two, advanced again, and again sent out Hardin with a larger force than before. Then the advance was again surprised, and the regulars nearly all killed, while the militia, who stood their ground better this time, lost about a hundred men. The end was the repulse of the whites after a pretty savage fight. Then Harmar withdrew altogether, declaring, with a strange absence of humor, if of no more important quality, that he had won a victory. After reaching home, this mismanaged expedition caused much crimination and heart-burning, followed by courtsmartial on Hardin and Harmar, who were both acquitted, and by the resignation of the latter.

This defeat of course simply made worse the state of affairs in general, and the Six Nations, who had hitherto been quiet, became uneasy and were kept so by the ever-kind incitement of the English. Various mediations with these powerful tribes failed; but Colonel Pickering, appointed a special commissioner, managed at last to appease their discontents. To the southward also the Cherokees began to move and threaten, but were pacified by the exertions of Governor Blount of the Southwest Territory. Meantime an act had been passed to increase the army, and Arthur St. Clair was appointed major-general. Washington, who had been greatly disturbed by the failure of Harmar, was both angered and disheartened by the conduct of the States and of the frontier settlers. "Land-jobbing, the intermeddling of the States, and the disorderly conduct of the borderers, who were indifferent as to the killing of an Indian," were in his opinion the great obstacles in the way of success. Yet these very men who shot Indians at sight and plundered them of their lands, as well as the States immediately concerned, were the first to cry out for aid from the general government when a war, brought about usually by their own violation of the treaties of the United States, was upon them. On the other hand, the Indians themselves were warlike and quarrelsome, and they were spurred on by England and Spain in a way difficult to understand at the present day.

In all this perplexity, however, one thing was now clear to Washington.

There could not longer be any doubt that the western troubles must be put down vigorously and by the armed hand. Even while he was negotiating in the north and south, therefore, he threw himself heart and soul into the preparation of St. Clair's expedition, pushing forward all necessary arrangements, and planning the campaign with a care and foresight made possible by his military ability and by his experience as an Indian fighter. While the main army was thus getting ready, two lesser expeditions, one under Scott and one under Wilkinson, were sent into the Indian country; but beyond burning some deserted villages and killing a few stray savages both were fruitless.

At last all was ready. St. Clair had an interview with Washington, in which the whole plan of campaign was gone over, and especial warning given against ambuscades. He then took his departure at once for the west, and late in September left Cincinnati with some two thousand men. The plan of campaign was to build a line of forts, and accordingly one named Fort Hamilton was erected twenty-four miles north on the Miami, and then Fort Jefferson was built forty-four miles north of that point. Thence St. Clair pushed slowly on for twenty-nine miles until he reached the head-waters of the Wabash. He had been joined on the march by some Kentucky militia, who were disorderly and undisciplined. Sixty of them promptly deserted, and it became necessary to send a regiment after them to prevent their plundering the baggage trains. At the same time some Chickasaw auxiliaries, with the true rat instinct, deserted and went home. Nevertheless St. Clair kept on, and finally reached what proved to be his last camp, with about fourteen hundred men. The militia were on one side of the stream, the regulars on the other. At sunrise the next day the Indians surprised the militia, drove them back on the other camp, and shattered the first line of the regulars. The second line stood their ground, and a desperate fight ensued; but it was all in vain. The Indians charged up to the guns, and, though they were repulsed by the bayonet, St. Clair, who was ill in his tent, was at last forced to order a retreat. The retreat soon became a rout, and the broken army, leaving their artillery and throwing away their arms, fled back to Fort Jefferson, where they left their wounded, and hurried on to their starting-point at Fort Washington. It was Braddock over again. General Butler, the second in command, was killed on the field, while the total loss reached nine hundred men and fifty-nine officers, and of these six hundred were killed. The Indians do not appear to have numbered much more than a thousand. No excuse for such a disaster and such murderous slaughter is possible, for nothing but the grossest carelessness could have permitted a surprise of that nature upon an established camp. The troops, too, were not only surprised, but apparently utterly unprepared to fight, and the battle was merely a wild struggle for life.

Washington was above all things a soldier, and his heart was always with his armies whenever he had one in the field. In this case particularly he hoped much, for he looked to this powerful expedition to settle the Indian troubles for a time, and give room for that great western movement which always was in his thoughts. He therefore awaited reports from St. Clair with keen anxiety, but in this case the ill tidings did not attain their proverbial speed. The battle was fought on November 4, and it was not until the close of a December day that the officer carrying dispatches from the frontier reached Philadelphia. He rode at once to the President's house, and Washington was called out from dinner, where he had company. He remained away some time, and on returning to the table said nothing as to what he had heard, talked with every one at Mrs. Washington's reception afterwards, and gave no sign. Through all the weary evening he was as calm and courteous as ever. When the last guest had gone he walked up and down the room for a few minutes and then suddenly broke out: "It's all over St.—Clair's defeated—routed; the officers nearly all killed, the men by wholesale; the rout complete—too shocking to think of—and a surprise into the bargain." He paused and strode up and down the room; stopped again and burst forth in a torrent of indignant wrath: "Here on this very spot I took leave of him; I wished him success and honor; 'You have your instructions,' I said, 'from the secretary of war; I had a strict eye to them, and will add but one word— Beware of a surprise! I repeat it—*beware of a surprise!* You know how the Indians fight us.' He went off with that as my last solemn warning thrown into his ears. And yet, to suffer that army to be cut to pieces, hacked, butchered, tomahawked, by a surprise, the very thing I guarded him against! O God, O God, he's worse than a murderer! How can he answer it to his country! The blood of the slain is upon him, the cause of widows and orphans, the curse of Heaven!"

His secretary was appalled and silent, while Washington again strode fiercely up and down the room. Then he sat down, collected himself, and said, "This must not go beyond this room." Then a long silence. Then, "General St. Clair shall have justice. I looked hastily through the dispatches, saw the whole disaster, but not all the particulars; I will receive him without displeasure; I will hear him without prejudice; he shall have full justice." The description of this scene by an eye-witness has been in print for many years, and yet we find people who say that Washington was cold of heart and lacking in human sympathy. What could be more intensely human than this? What a warm heart is here, and what a lightning glimpse of a passionate nature bursting through silence into burning speech! Then comes the iron will which has mastered all the problems of his life. "He shall have full justice;" and St. Clair had justice. He had been an unfortunate choice, but as a Revolutionary soldier and governor of the Northwest Territory his selection had been natural. He had never been a successful general, for it was not in him to be so. Something he lacked, energy, decision, foresight, it matters not what. But at least he was brave. Broken by sickness, he had displayed the utmost personal courage on that stricken field; and for this Washington would always forgive much. He received the unfortunate general kindly. He could not order a court martial, for there were no officers of sufficient rank to form one; but he gave St. Clair every opportunity for vindication, and a committee of Congress investigated the campaign and exculpated the leader. His personal bravery saved him and his reputation, but nothing can alter the fact that the surprise was unpardonable and the disaster awful.

Immediate results of the St. Clair defeat were not so bad as might have been expected. Panic, of course, ran rampant along the frontier, reaching even to Pittsburg; but the Indians failed to follow up their advantage, and did not come. Still the alarm was there, and Pennsylvania and Virginia ordered troops to be raised, while Congress also took action.

Another increase of the army was ordered, with consequent increase of appropriation, so that this Indian victory entered at this point into the great current of the financial policy, and thus played its part in the events on which parties were dividing, and history was being made.

No matter what happened, however, there was to be neither lingering nor delay in this business. The President set to work at once to organize a fresh army, and fight out a settlement of the troubles. His first thought for a new commander was of Henry Lee of Virginia, but considerations of rank deterred him. He then selected and appointed Wayne, who recently had got into politics and been deprived, on a contested election, of his seat in the House. No little grumbling ensued over this appointment, especially in Virginia, but it was unheeded by the President, and its causes now are not very clear. The event proved the wisdom of the choice, as so often happened with Washington, and it is easy to see the reason for it. Wayne was one of the shining figures of our Revolution, appealing strongly to the imagination of posterity. He was not a great general in the highest sense, but he was a brilliant corps-commander, capable of daring feats of arms like the storming of Stony Point. He was capable also of dashing with heedless courage into desperate places, and incurring thereby defeat and consequent censure, but escaping entire ruin through the same quickness of action which had involved him in trouble. He was well fitted for the bold and rapid movement required in Indian warfare, and with him Washington put well-chosen subordinates, selected evidently for their fighting capacity, for he clearly was determined that this should be at all events a fighting campaign.

Wayne, after his appointment, betook himself to Pittsburg, and proceeded with characteristic energy to raise and organize his army, a work of no little difficulty because he wished to have picked men. Washington did all that could be done to help him, and at the same time pushed negotiations with admirable patience, but with very varying success. Kirkland brought chiefs of the Six Nations to Congress with good results, and the Cherokees were pacified by additional presents. On the other hand, the Creeks were restless, stirred up always by Spain, and two brave officers, sent to try for peace with the western tribes, were murdered in cold blood. Nevertheless, treaties were patched up with some of them, and a great council was held in the fall of 1792, the Six Nations acting as mediators, which resulted in a badly kept armistice, but in nothing of lasting value. The next year Congress passed a general act regulating trade and intercourse with the Indians, and Washington appointed yet another commission to visit the north-western tribes, more to satisfy public opinion than with any hope of peace. Indeed, these commissioners never succeeded in even meeting the Indians, who rejected in advance all proposals which would not concede the Ohio as the boundary. English influence, it was said, was at the bottom of this demand, and there seems to be little doubt that such was the case, for England and France were now at war, and England thereupon had redoubled her efforts to injure the United States by every sort of petty outrage both on sea and land. This masterly policy had perhaps reasons for its existence which pass beyond the average understanding, but, so far as any one can now discover, it seems to have had no possible motive except to feed an ancient grudge and drive the country into the arms of France. Carried on for a long time in secret, this Indian intrigue came to the surface in a speech made by Lord Dorchester to the western tribes, in which he prophesied a speedy rupture with the United States and urged his hearers to continue war. It is worth remembering that for five years, covertly or openly, England did her best to keep an Indian war with all that it implied alive upon our borders,—the borders of a friendly nation with whom she was at peace.

But while Washington persistently negotiated, he as persistently prepared to fight, not trusting over-much either the savages or the English. Wayne, with similar views, moved his army forward in the autumn of 1793 to a point six miles beyond Fort Jefferson, and then went into winter quarters. Early in the spring of 1794 he was in motion again and advanced to St. Clair's battlefield, where he built Fort Recovery, and where he was attacked by the Indians, whom he repulsed after two days' fighting. He then marched in an unexpected direction and struck the central villages at the junction of the Au Glaize and Maumee. The surprised savages fled, and Wayne burned their village, laid waste their extensive fields, and built Fort Defiance. To the Indians, who had retreated thirty miles down the Maumee to the shelter of a British post, he sent word that he was ready to treat. The reply came back asking for a delay of ten days; but Wayne at once advanced, and found the Indians prepared for battle near the English fort. The ground was unfavorable, especially for cavalry, but Wayne made good arrangements and attacked. The Indians gave way before the bayonet, and were completely routed, the American loss being only one hundred and seven men. The army was not averse to storming the English fort; but Wayne, with unusual caution, contented himself with a sharp correspondence with the commandant, and then withdrew after a most successful campaign. The neat year, strengthened by his victory and by the surrender of the British posts under the Jay treaty, Wayne made a treaty with the western tribes by which vast tracts of disputed territory were ceded to the United States, and peace was established in that long troubled region.

On the southern frontier there were no such fortunate results. While Washington was negotiating and fighting in the north and west, all his patient efforts were frustrated in the south by the conduct of Georgia. The borderers kept assailing the Indians, peaceful tribes being generally chosen for the purpose; and the State itself broke through and disregarded all treaties and all arrangements made by the United States. The result was constant disquiet and chronic war, with the usual accompaniments of fire, murder, and pillage.

On the whole, however, when Washington left the presidency, his Indian policy had been a marked success. In place of uncertainty and weakness, a definite general system had been adopted. The northern and western tribes had been beaten and pacified, and the southern incursions and disorders had been much checked. The British posts, the most dangerous centres of Indian intrigue, had been abandoned, and the great regions of the west and northwest had been opened to the tide of settlement. These results were due to a well-defined plan, and above all to the persistent vigor which pushed steadily forward to its object without swinging, as had been done before, between feverish and often misdirected activity on the one side and complete and feeble inaction on the other. They were achieved, too, amid many difficulties, for there was anything but a unanimous support of the government in its Indian affairs. The opposition grumbled at the expense, and said that money needlessly raised by taxation was squandered in Indian wars, while the great body of the people, living safely along the eastern coast, thought but little about the frontier. Some persons took the sentimental view and considered the government barbarous to make causeless war. Others believed that altogether too much of the public time and money were wasted in looking after outlying settlements. The borderers themselves, on the other hand, thought that the general government was in league with the savages, and broke through treaties, and destroyed so far as they could the national policy. St. Clair was hissed and jeered as he traveled home, but a wakeful opposition turned from the unsuccessful general to a vain attempt to prove that ambushed savages and sleeping sentries were due to a weak war department and a corrupt and inefficient treasury. The mass of moderate people, no doubt, desired tranquillity on the frontier, and sustained the President's labors for that end, but for the most part they were silent. The voices that Washington heard most loudly joined in a discordant chorus of disapproval around his Indian policy. No one understood that here was an important part of a scheme to build up a nation, to make all the movements of the United States broad and national, and to open the vast west to the people who were to make it theirs. Washington heard all the criticism and saw all the opposition, and still pressed forward to his goal, not attaining all he wished, but fighting in a very clear and manful spirit, and not laboring in vain.

The Indian question in its management touched, as has been seen, at various points our financial policy and our foreign relations, on which the history of the country really turned in those years. The latter had not risen to their later importance when the government began, but the former was knocking importunately at the door of Congress when it first assembled. The condition of affairs is soon told. The Revolution narrowly escaped shipwreck on the financial reefs, and the shaky government of the confederation had there gone to pieces. The country, as a political organism, was bankrupt. It owed sums of money, which were vast in amount for those days, both at home and abroad, and it could not pay these debts, nor was there any provision for them. All interest was in arrears, there were no means provided for meeting it, and the national credit everywhere was dishonored and gone. The continental currency had disappeared, and the circulating medium was represented by a confused jumble of foreign coins and worthless scrip. Many of the States were up to their eyes in schemes of inflation, paper money, and repudiation. There was no money in the treasury to pay the ordinary charges of government; there was no revenue and no policy for raising one, or for funding the debt. This picture is darkly drawn, but it is not exaggerated. That high spirit of public honor, which seventy-five years later rose above the ravages of war and the temptings of dishonesty to pay the debt and the interest, dollar for dollar in gold, seemed in 1789 to be wellnigh extinct. But it was not dead. It was confused and overclouded in the minds of the people, but it was still there, and it was strong, clear, and determined in Washington and those who followed him.

Congress grappled with the financial difficulties in the most courageous and honest way, but it struggled with them rather helplessly despite its good disposition. It could lay taxes in one way or another so as to get money, but this was plainly insufficient. It could not formulate a coherent policy, which was the one essential thing, nor could it settle the thousand and one perplexing questions which hedged the subject on every side. The members turned, therefore, with a sigh of relief to the new Secretary of the Treasury, asked him the questions which were troubling them, and having directed him to make various reports, adjourned.

The result is well known. The great statesman to whom the task was confided assumed it with the boldness and ease of conscious power, and when Congress reassembled it listened to the first report on the public credit. In that great state paper all the confusions disappeared, and in terse sentences an entire scheme for funding the debt, disposing of the worthless currency, and raising the necessary revenue came out clear and distinct, so that all men could comprehend it. The provision for the foreign debt passed without resistance. That for the domestic debt excited much debate, and also passed. Last came the assumption of the state debts, and over that there sprang up a fierce struggle. It was carried by a narrow majority, and then defeated by the votes of the North Carolina members, who had just taken their seats. Washington strongly favored this hotly contested measure. He defended it in a letter to David Stuart, and again to Jefferson, at a later time, when that statesman was trying to undermine Hamilton by wailing about a "corrupt squadron" in Congress. To Washington, assumption seemed as obviously just as it does to posterity. All the debts had been incurred in a common cause, he said, why should they not be cared for by the common government? He had no patience with the sectional argument that assumption was unfair, because some States got more out of it than others. Some States had suffered more than others, but all shared in the freedom that had been won.[*] He saw in it, moreover, as Hamilton had seen, something far more important than a mere provision for the debts and for the payment of money to this community or to that. Assumption was essentially a union measure. The other debts were incurred by the central government directly, but the state debts were incurred by the States for a common cause. If the United States assumed them, it showed to the people and to the world that there were no state lines when the interests of the whole country were involved. It was therefore a national measure, a breeder of national sentiment, a new bond to fasten the States to each other and to the Union. This was enough to assure Washington's hearty approval; but the measure was saved and carried finally by the famous arrangement between Hamilton and Jefferson, which took the capital to the Potomac and made the war debts of the States a part of the national debt. Washington was more than satisfied with this solution, for both sides of the agreement pleased him, and there was nothing in the compromise which meant sacrifice on his part. He rejoiced in the successful adoption of the great financial policy of his administration, and he was much pleased to have the capital, in which he was intensely interested, placed near to his own Mount Vernon, in the very region he would have selected if he had had the power of fixing it.

---

[*]Sparks, *Writings of Washington*, x. 98.

The next great step in the development of the financial policy was the establishment of the national bank, and on this there arose another bitter contest in Congress and in the newspapers. A sharp opposition had developed by this time, and the supporters of the Secretary of the Treasury became on their side correspondingly ardent. In this debate much stress was laid on the constitutional point that Congress had no power to charter a bank. Nevertheless, the bill passed and went to the President, with the constitutional doubts following it and pressed home in this last resort. As has been seen from his letters written just after the Philadelphia convention, Washington was not a blind worshiper of the Constitution which he had helped so largely to make; but he believed it would work, and every day confirmed his belief. He felt, moreover, that one great element of its lasting success lay in creating a genuine reverence for it among the people, and it was therefore of the utmost importance that this reverence should begin among those to whom the management of the government had been intrusted. For this reason he exercised a jealous care in everything touching the organic law of the Union, and he was peculiarly sensitive to constitutional objections to any given measure. In the case of the national bank, the objections were strongly as well as vigorously urged, and Washington paused, before signing, to the utmost limit of the time allowed. He turned to Jefferson and Randolph, both opposed to the bill, and asked them for their objections to its constitutionality. They gave him in response two able reports. These he sent to Hamilton, who returned them with that most masterly argument, in which he not only defended the bank charter, but vindicated, in a manner never afterwards surpassed, the new doctrine of the implied powers of the Constitution. With both sides thus before him, Washington considered the question, and signed the bill.

Rives, in his "Life of Madison," intimates that Washington had doubts even after signing, but of this there is no evidence of any weight. He was not a man who indulged in doubts after he had made up his mind and rendered a decision, and it was not in his nature to fret over what had been done and was past, whether in war or peace. The story that he was worried about his action in this instance arose from his delay in signing, and from the disappointment of those who had hoped much from his hesitation. This pause, however, was both natural and characteristic. Washington had approved Morris's bank policy in the Revolution, and remembered the service it rendered. He was familiar with Hamilton's views on the subject, and knew that they were the result of long study and careful thought. He must also have known that any financial policy devised by his Secretary of the Treasury would contain as an integral part a national bank. There can be no doubt that both the plan for the bank and the report which embodied it were submitted to him before they went in to Congress, but the violence of the objections raised there on constitutional grounds awakened his attention in a new direction. He saw at once the gravity of a question, which involved not merely the incorporation of a bank, but which opened up a new field of constitutional powers and constitutional construction. When such far-reaching results were involved he paused and reflected, and, as was always the case with him under such circumstances, listened to and examined all the arguments on both sides. This done he decided, and with his national feeling he could not have decided otherwise than he did. The doctrine of the implied powers of the Constitution was the greatest weapon possible for those whose leading thought was to develop the union of States into a great and imperial nation; and we may well believe that it was this feeling, and not merely faith in the bank as a financial engine, which led Washington to sign the bill. When he did so he assented to the charter of a national bank, but he also assented to the doctrine of the implied powers and gave to that far-reaching construction of the Constitution the great weight of his name and character. It was, perhaps, the most important single act of his presidency.

It is impossible here, even were it necessary, to follow Washington's action in regard to all the details which went to make up and to sustain Hamilton's policy, to which, as a whole, Washington gave his hearty approval and support. The revenue system, the public lands, the arrangement of loans, the mint, all alike met with his active concurrence. He was too great a man not to value rightly Hamilton's work, and the way in which that work brought order, credit, honor, and prosperity out of a chaos of debt and bankruptcy appealed peculiarly to his own love for method, organization, and sound business principles. He met every criticism on Hamilton's policy without concession, and defended it when it was attacked. To Hamilton's genius that policy must be credited, but it gained its success and strength largely from the firm support of Washington.

There are two matters, however, connected with the Treasury Department, which cannot be passed over in this general way. One was a policy reasoned out and published by Hamilton, but never during his lifetime put into the form of law in the broad and systematic manner which he desired. The other was a consequence of his financial policy as adopted, but which reached far beyond the bounds of financial arrangements. The first was the policy set forth in Hamilton's Report on Manufactures. The second was the enforcement of the excise and its results.

The defense of our commerce against foreign discriminations was approximate cause of the movement which resulted in the Constitution of the United States, and closely allied to it was the anxious wish to develop our internal resources and our domestic industry. This idea was not at all new. Sporadic attempts to start and carry on various industries had been made during the colonial period. They had all failed, either because the watchful mother-country took pains to stifle them, or because lack of capital and experience, in addition to foreign competition, killed them almost at their birth. The idea of developing American industries was generally diffused for the first time when the colonists strove to bring England to terms by non-intercourse acts. The Americans then thought that they could carry their points by making war upon the British pocket, and excluding English merchants from their markets. The next step, of course, was to supply their own markets themselves; and the nonintercourse agreements, which were economically prohibitory tariff acts, gave a fitful impulse to various simple industries. In the clash of arms this idea naturally dropped out of the popular mind, but it began to revive soon after the return of peace. The government of the confederation was too feeble to adopt any policy in this or any other matter, but in the first Congress the desire to develop American industries found expression. The first tariff was laid primarily to raise the revenue so sorely needed at that moment. But the effort to do this gave rise to a debate in which the policy of protection, strongly advocated by the Pennsylvanian members, was freely discussed. Nobody, however, at that time, had any comprehensive plan or general system, so that the efforts for protection were incoherent, and resulted only in certain special protective features in the tariff bill, and not in a broad and well-rounded measure. Still the protective idea was there; it was recognized in the preamble of the act, and the constitutionality of the policy was affirmed by the framers and contemporaries of the Constitution.

Hamilton, of course, watched all these movements intently. His guiding thought in all things was the creation of a great nation. For this he strove for national unity and national sentiment, and he saw of course that one essential condition of national greatness was industrial independence, in addition to the political independence already won. One of the greatest thinkers of the time on all matters of public finance and political economy, he perceived at once that the irregular attempts of Congress to encourage home industries could have at best but partial results. He saw that a system broad, just, and continental in its scope must take the place of the isolated industries which now and again obtained an uncertain protection under the haphazard measures of Congress. With these views and purposes he wrote and sent to Congress his Report on Manufactures. In that great state paper he made an argument in behalf of protection, as applied to the United States and to the development of home industries, which has never been overthrown. The system which he proposed was imperial in its range and national in its design, like everything that proceeded from Hamilton's mind. He argued, of course, with reference to existing economic conditions, and in behalf only of what he then sought,—industrial independence and the establishment and diversification of industries. The social side of the question, which to-day overshadows all others, was not visible a hundred years ago. The Report, however, bore no immediate fruit, and Hamilton had been in his grave for years before the country turned from this practice of accidental protection, and tried to replace it by a broad, coherent system as set forth by the great Secretary.

But although it had no result at the moment, the Report on Manufactures, which laid the foundation of the American protective system, and which has so powerfully influenced American political thought, was one of the very greatest events of Washington's administration. To trace its effects and history through the succeeding century would be wholly out of place here. All that concerns us is Washington's relation to this far-reaching policy of his Secretary. If we had not a word or a line on the subject from his pen, we should still know that the policy of Hamilton was his policy too, for Washington was the head of his own administration, and was responsible and meant to be responsible for all its acts and policies. With his keen foresight he saw the full import of the Report on Manufactures, and we may be sure that when it went forth it was with his full and cordial approval, and after that minute consideration which he gave to all public questions. But we are not left to inference. We have Washington's views and feelings on this matter set forth again and again, and they show that the principle of the Report on Manufactures was as near and dear to him, and as full of meaning, as it was to Hamilton.

Washington was brought up and had lived all his life under a system which came as near as possible to the ideal of the modern free-trader. The people of Virginia were devoted almost entirely to a single interest, tobacco-growing, that being the occupation in which they could most profitably engage. No legislative artifices had been employed to enable them to diversify their industries or to establish manufactures. They bought in the cheapest market every luxury and most of the necessities of life. British merchants supplied all their wants, carried their tobacco, and advanced them money. Cheap labor, a single staple with wide fluctuations of value, a credit system, entire dependence on foreigners, and absolute free trade according to the Manchester theories, should have produced an earthly paradise. As a matter of fact, the Virginia planters had little ready money and were deeply in debt. Bankruptcy, as has been already said, seems to have come to them about once in a generation.

The land, rapidly exhausted by tobacco, was prodigally wasted, and the general prosperity declined. Washington, with his strong sense and perfect business methods, personally escaped most of these evils, but he saw the mischief of the system all the more clearly. It was bad enough in his time, but he did not live to see Virginia with her wasted and exhausted lands stand still, while her sister States to the north passed her with giant strides in the race for wealth and population. He did not live to see her become, as a result of her colonial system, a mere breeder of slaves for the plantations of the Gulf States. But he saw enough, and the lesson taught him by the results of industrial dependence was well learned.

When the war came and he was carrying the terrible burden of the Revolution, he learned the same lesson in a new and more bitter way. Nothing went so near to wreck the American cause as lack of all the supplies by which war was carried on, for the United States produced little or nothing of what was then needed. The resources of the northern colonies were soon exhausted, and the South had none. Powder, cannon, muskets, clothing, medical stores, all were lacking, and the fate of the nation hung trembling in the balance on account of the dependence in which the colonies had been kept by the skillful policy of England. These were teachings that a lesser man than Washington would have taken to heart and pondered deeply. In the midst of the struggle he wrote to James Warren (March 31, 1779): "Let vigorous measures be adopted, . . . to punish speculators, forestallers, and extortioners, and, above all, to sink the money by heavy taxes, to promote public and private economy, and to *encourage manufactures*.* Measures of this sort, gone heartily into by the several States, would strike at once at the root of all our evils, and give the *coup de grace* to the British hope of subjugating this continent either by their arms or their acts."

To Lafayette he wrote in 1789: "Though I would not force the introduction of manufactures by extravagant encouragements and to the prejudice of agriculture, yet I conceive much might be done in that way by women, children, and others, without taking one really necessary hand

---

*The italics are mine.

from tilling the earth. Certain it is, great savings are already made in many articles of apparel, furniture, and consumption. Equally certain it is, that no diminution in agriculture has taken place at this time, when greater and more substantial improvements in manufactures are making than were ever before known in America."

In the same year he wrote to Governor Randolph, favoring bounties, the strongest form of protection; and this encouragement he wished to have given to that industry which a hundred years later has been held up as one of the least deserving of all that have received the assistance of legislation. He said in this letter: "From the original letter, which I forward herewith, your Excellency will comprehend the nature of a proposal for introdu-cing and establishing the woolen manufacture in the State of Virginia. In the present stage of population and agriculture, I do not pretend to determine how far that plan may be practicable and advisable; or, in case it should be deemed so, whether any or what public encouragement ought to be given to facilitate its execution. *I have, however, no doubt as to the good policy of increasing the number of sheep in every state.** By a little legislative encouragement the farmers of Connecticut have, in two years past, added one hundred thousand to their former stock. If a greater quantity of wool could be produced, and if the hands which are often in a manner idle could be employed in manufacturing it, a spirit of industry might be promoted, a great diminution might be made in the annual expenses of individual families, and the public would eventually be exceedingly benefited." The only hesitation is as to the time of applying the policy. There is no doubt as to the wisdom of the policy itself, of giving protection and encouragement in every proper legislative form to domestic industry.

In his first speech to Congress he recommended measures for the advancement of manufactures, having already affixed his signature to the bill which declared their encouragement to be one of its objects. At the same time he wrote, in reply to an address: "The promotion of domestic manufactures will, in my conception, be among the first consequences

---

*The italics are mine.

which may naturally be expected to flow from an energetic government." In 1791 he consulted Hamilton as to the advisability of urging Congress to offer bounties for the culture of cotton and hemp, his only doubts being as to the power of the general government in this respect, and as to the temper of the time in regard to such an expenditure of public money. The following year Hamilton's Report on Manufactures was given to the country, finally establishing the position of the administration as to our economic policy.

The general drift of legislation, although it was not systematized, followed the direction pointed out by the administration. But this did not satisfy Washington. In his speech to Congress, December 7, 1796, he said: "Congress has repeatedly, and not without success, directed their attention to the encouragement of manufactures. *The object is of too much consequence not to insure a continuance of their efforts in every way which shall appear eligible.*"* He then goes onto argue at some length that, although manufacturing on the public account is usually inexpedient, it should be established and carried on to supply all that was needed for the public force in time of war. This was his last address to Congress, and his last word on this matter was to approve the course of Congress in following the recommendation of his first speech. All his utterances and all his opinions on the subject were uniform. Washington had never been a student of public finance or political economy like Hamilton, and he lived before the days of the Manchester school and its new gospel of procuring heaven on earth by special methods of transacting the country's business. But Washington was a great man, a state-builder who fought wars and founded governments. He knew that nations were raised up and made great and efficient, and that civilization was advanced, not by *laissez aller* and *laissez faire*, but by much patient human striving. He had fought and conquered, and again he had fought and been defeated, and through all he had come to victory, and to certain conclusive results both in peace and war. He had not done this by sitting still and letting each man go his way, but by strong brain and strong will, and by much organization and

---

*The italics are mine.

compulsion. He had set his hand to the building of a nation. He had studied his country and understood it, and with calm, far-seeing eyes he had looked forward into the future of his people. Neither the study nor the outlook were vain, and both told him that political independence was only part of the work, and that national sentiment, independent thinking, and industrial independence also must be reached. The first two, time alone could bring. The last, wise laws could help to produce; and so he favored protection by legislation to American industry and manufactures, threw all his potent influence into the scale, and gave his support to the protective policy set forth by his Secretary.

Two matters connected with the treasury, I have said, deserved fuller consideration than a general review could give. The one just described, the policy of the Report on Manufactures, came, as has been seen, to no clear and immediate result. The other reached a very sharp and definite conclusion, not without great effect on the new government of the United States, both at the moment and in the future. When Hamilton "struck the rock of the national resources," the stream of revenue which he sought at the outset was that flowing from duties on imports, for this, in his theory, was not only the first source, but the best. He would fain have had it the only one; but the situation drove him forward. The assumption of the state debts, a part of the legacy of the Revolution, and the continuing and at first increasing expenses of unavoidable Indian wars, made additional revenue absolutely essential. He turned therefore to the excise on domestic spirits to furnish what was needed.

Washington approved assumption. It was a measure of honesty, it would raise the public credit, and above all, it was thoroughly national in its operation and results. The appropriations for Indian wars he of course approved, for their energetic prosecution was part of the vigorous policy toward our wild neighbors upon which he was so determined. It followed, of course, that he did not shrink from imposing the taxes thus made necessary; and to raise the money from domestic spirits seemed to him, under the existing exigency, to be what it was,—thoroughly proper and reasonable both in form and subject.

It would seem, however, that neither Washington nor Hamilton realized the unpopularity of this mode of getting revenue. The frontier settlers along the line of the Alleghanies in Pennsylvania, Virginia, and North Carolina, who distilled whiskey, were not very familiar, perhaps, with Johnson's dictionary, but they would have cordially accepted his definition of an excise. To them it was indeed a "hateful tax," and nothing else. In fact, the word was one disliked throughout the States, for it brought up evil memories, and excited much jealous hostility and prejudice. The first excise law, therefore, when it went into force, was the signal for a general outburst of opposition; and in the Alleghany region, as might have been expected, the resistance was immediate and most bitter. State legislatures passed resolutions, public meetings were held and more resolutions were passed, while in the wilder parts of the country threats of violence were freely uttered. All these murmurings and menaces came on the passage of the first bill in 1791. The administration, however, had no desire to precipitate an uncalled-for strife, and so the law was softened and amended in the following year, the tax being lowered and the most obnoxious features removed. The result was general acquiescence throughout most of the States, and renewed opposition in the western counties of Pennsylvania and North Carolina. In the former a meeting was held denouncing the law, pledging the people to "boycott" the officers, and hinting at forcible resistance. If the people engaged in this business had stopped to consider the men with whom they had to deal, they would have been saved a great deal of suffering and humiliation. The President and his Secretary of the Treasury were not men who could be frightened by opposition or violent speeches. But angry frontiersmen, stirred up by demagogues, are not given to much reflection, and they meant to have their own way.

Washington was quite clear in his policy from the beginning. He was ready to make every proper concession, but when this was done he meant on his side to have his own way, which was the way of law and order and good government. He wrote to Hamilton in August, 1792: "If, after these regulations are in operation, opposition to the due exercise of the collection is still experienced, and peaceable procedure is no longer effectual, the public interests and my duty will make it necessary to enforce the laws respecting this matter; and however disagreeable this would be to me, it must nevertheless take place."

Meantime the disorders went on, and the officers were insulted and thwarted in the execution of their duty. Washington's next letter (September 7) has a touch of anger. He hated disorder and riot anywhere, but he was disgusted when they came from the very people for whose defense the Indian war was pushed and the excise made necessary. He approved of Hamilton's sending out an officer to examine into the survey, and said: "If, notwithstanding, opposition is still given to the due execution of the law, I have no hesitation in declaring, if the evidence of it is clear and unequivocal, that I shall, however reluctantly I exercise them, exert all the legal powers with which the executive is invested to check so daring and unwarrantable a spirit. It is my duty to see the laws executed. To permit them to be trampled upon with impunity would be repugnant to it; nor can the government longer remain a passive spectator of the contempt with which they are treated. Forbearance, under a hope that the inhabitants of that survey would recover from the delirium and folly into which they were plunged, seems to have had no other effect than to increase the disorder."

A few weeks later he issued a proclamation, declaring formally and publicly what he had already said in private. He warned the people engaged in resistance to the law that the law would be enforced, and exhorted them to desist. The proclamation was effective in the south, and the opposition died out in North Carolina. Not so in Pennsylvania. There the Scotch-Irish borderers who lived in the western counties were bent on having their way. A brave, self-willed, hot-headed, turbulent people, they were going to have their fight out. They had ridden roughshod over the Quaker and German government in Pennsylvania before this, and they no doubt thought they could do the same with this new government of the United States. They merely made a mistake about the man at the head of the government; nothing more than that. Such mistakes have been made before. The Paris mob, for example, made a similar blunder on the 13th Vendémiaire, when Bonaparte settled matters by the famous whiff of grape-shot. There is some excuse for the error of our

Scotch-Irish borderers in their past experience, more excuse still in the drift of other events that touched all men just then with the madness of France, and gave birth to certain democratic societies which applauded any resistance to law, even if the cause was no nobler than a whiskey still.

Perhaps, too, the Pennsylvanians were encouraged by the moderation and deliberate movement of the government. A lull came after the proclamation of 1792. Then every effort was made to settle the troubles by civil processes and by personal negotiation, but all proved vain. The disturbances went on increasing for two years, until law was at an end in the insurgent counties. The mails were stopped and robbed, there were violence, bloodshed, rioting, attacks on the officers of the United States, and meetings threatening still worse things.

Meanwhile Washington had waited and watched, and bided his time. He felt now that the moment had come when, if ever, public opinion must be with him, and that the hour had arrived when he must put his fortune to the touch, and "try if it were current gold indeed." On August 7 he issued a second proclamation, setting forth the outrages committed, and announcing his power to call out the militia, and his intention to do so if unconditional submission did not follow at once. As he wrote to a friend three days later: "Actual rebellion exists against the laws of the United States." On the crucial point, however, he felt safe. He was confident that all the public opinion worth having was now on his side, and that the people were ready to stand by the government. The quick and unconditional submission did not come, and on September 25 he issued a third proclamation, reciting the facts and calling out the militia of New Jersey, Pennsylvania, Maryland, and Virginia.

Washington had judged rightly. The States responded, and the troops came to the number of fifteen thousand, for he was in the habit of doing things thoroughly, and meant to have an overwhelming force. To Governor Lee of Virginia the command of the combined forces was intrusted. "I am perfectly in sentiment with you, that the business we are drawn out upon should be effectually executed, and that the daring and factious spirit which threatens to overturn the laws and to subvert the Constitution ought to be subdued." Thus he wrote to Morgan, while the commissioners from the insurgents were politely received, and told that the march of the troops could not be countermanded. Washington would fain have gone himself, in command of the army, but he felt that he could not leave the seat of government for so long a time with propriety. He went as far as Bedford with the troops, and then parted from them. When he took leave, he wrote a letter to Lee, to be read to the army, in which he said: "No citizen of the United States can ever be engaged in a service more important to their country. It is nothing less than to consolidate and to preserve the blessings of that revolution which at much expense of blood and treasure constituted us a free and independent nation." Thus admonished, the army marched, Hamilton going with them in characteristic fashion to the end. They did their work thoroughly. The insurrection disappeared, and resistance dropped suddenly out of sight. The Scotch-Irish of the border, with all their love of fighting, found too late that they were dealing with a power very different from that of their own State. The ringleaders of the insurrection were arrested and tried by civil process, the disorders ceased, law reigned once more, and the "hateful tax" was duly paid and collected.

The "Whiskey Rebellion" has never received due weight in the history of the United States. Its story has been told in the utmost detail, but its details are unimportant. As a fact, however, it is full of meaning, and this meaning has been too much overlooked. That this should be so, is not to be wondered at, for everything has conspired to make it seem, after a century has gone by, both mean and trivial. Its very name suggests ridicule and contempt, and it collapsed so utterly that people laughed at it and despised it. Its leaders, with the exception of Gallatin, were cheap and talkative persons of little worth, and the cause itself was neither noble, romantic, nor inspiriting. Nevertheless, it was a dangerous and formidable business, for it was the first direct challenge to the new government. It was the first clear utterance of the stern question asked of every people striving to live as a nation, Have you a right to live? Have you a government able to fight and to endure? Have you men ready to take up the challenge? These questions were put by rough frontier settlers, and put in the name and for the sake of distilling whiskey unvexed by law.

But they were there, they had to be answered, and on the reply the existence of the government was at stake. If it failed, all was over. If the States did not respond to this first demand, that they should put down disorder and dissension within the borders of one of their number, the experiment had failed. It came, as it almost always does come, to one man to make the answer. That man took up the challenge. He did not move too soon. He waited with unerring judgment, as Lincoln waited with the Proclamation of Emancipation, until he had gathered public opinion behind him by his firmness and moderation. Then he struck, and struck so hard that the whole fabric of insurrection and riot fell helplessly to pieces, and wiseacres looked on and laughed, and thought it had been but a slight matter after all. The action of the government vindicated the right of the United States to live, because they had proved themselves able to keep order. It showed to the American people that their government was a reality of force and power. If it had gone wrong, the history of the United States would not have differed widely from that of the confederation. No mistake was made, and people regarded the whole thing as an insignificant incident, and historians treat it as an episode. There could be no greater tribute to the strong and silent man who did the work and bore the stress of waiting for nearly five years. He did his duty so well and so completely that it seems nothing now, and yet the crushing of that insurrection in the western counties of Pennsylvania was one of the turning-points in a nation's life.

CHAPTER XV

FOREIGN RELATIONS

OUR PRESENT RELATIONS with foreign nations fill as a rule but a slight place in American politics, and excite generally only a languid interest, not nearly so much as their importance deserves. We have separated ourselves so completely from the affairs of other people that it is difficult to realize how commanding and disproportionate a place they occupied when the government was founded. We were then a new nation, and our attitude toward the rest of the world was wholly undefined. There was, therefore, among the American people much anxiety to discover what that attitude would be, for the unknown is always full of interest. Moreover, Europe was still our neighbor, for England, France, and Spain were all upon our borders, and had large territorial interests in the northern half of the New World. Within fifteen years we had been colonies, and all our politics, except those which were purely local and provincial, had been the politics of Europe; for during the eighteenth century we had been drawn into and had played a part in every European complication, and every European war in which England had the slightest share. Thus the American people came to consider themselves a part of the European system, and looked to Europe for their politics, which was a habit of thought both natural and congenial to colonists. We ceased to be colonists when the Treaty of Paris was signed; but treaties, although they settle boundaries and divide nations, do not change customs and habits of thought by a few strokes of the pen. The free and independent people of the United States, as there has already been occasion to point out, when they set out to govern themselves under their new Constitution, were still dominated by colonial ideas and prejudices. They felt, no doubt, that the new system would put them in a more respectable attitude toward the other nations of the earth. But this was probably the only definite popular notion on the subject. What our actual relations with other nations should be, was something wholly vague, and very varying ideas were entertained about it by communities and by individuals, according to their various prejudices, opinions, and interests.

The one idea, however, that the American people did not have on this subject was, that they should hold themselves entirely aloof from the politics of the Old World, and have with other nations outside the Americas no relations except those born of commerce. It had not occurred to them that they should march steadily forward on a course which would drive out European governments, and sever the connections of those governments with the North American continent. After a century's familiarity, this policy looks so simple and obvious that it is difficult to believe that our forefathers could even have considered any other seriously; but in 1789 it was so strange that no one dreamed of it, except perhaps a few thinkers speculating on the future of the infant nation. It was something so novel that when it was propounded it struck the people like a sudden shock of electricity. It was so broad, so national, so thoroughly American, that men still struggling in the fetters of colonial thought could not comprehend it. But there was one man to whom it was neither strange nor speculative. To Washington it was not a vague idea, but a well-defined system, which he had been long maturing in his mind.

Before he had been chosen President, he wrote to Sir Edward Newenham: "I hope the United States of America will be able to keep disengaged from the labyrinth of European politics and wars; and that before long they will, by the adoption of a good national government, have become respectable in the eyes of the world, so that none of the maritime powers, especially none of those who hold possessions in the New World or the West Indies, shall presume to treat them with insult or contempt. It should be the policy of the United States to administer to their wants without being engaged in their quarrels. And it is not in the power of the proudest and most polite people on earth to prevent us from becoming a great, a respectable, and a commercial nation if we shall continue united and faithful to ourselves." This plain statement shows his fixed belief that in an absolute breaking with the political affairs of other peoples lay the most important part of the work which was to make us a nation in spirit and in truth. He carried this belief with him when he took up the Presidency, and it was the chief burden of the last words of counsel which he gave to his countrymen when he retired to private life. To have begun and carried on to a firm establishment this policy of a separation from Europe would have required time, skill, and patience even under the calmest and most favorable conditions. But it was the fate of the new government to be born just on the eve of the French Revolution. The United States were at once caught up and tossed by the waves of that terrific storm, and it was in the midst of that awful hurly-burly, when the misdeeds of centuries of wrong-doing were brought to an account, that Washington opened and developed his foreign policy. It was a great task, and the manner of its performance deserves much and serious consideration.

His first act in foreign affairs, on entering the Presidency, was to make the minister of France understand that the government of the United States was to be treated with due formality and respect. His second was to examine the whole mass of foreign correspondence collected in the State Department of the confederation, and he did this, as has been said, pencil in hand, making notes and abstracts as he went. It was well worth doing, for he learned much, and from this laborious study and thorough knowledge certain facts became apparent, for the most part of a hard and unpleasant nature. First, he saw that England, taking advantage of our failure to fulfill completely our obligations under the treaty, had openly violated hers, and continued to hold the fortified posts along the northwestern and western borders. Here was a dangerous thorn which pricked sharply, for the posts in British hands offered constant temptations to Indian risings, and threatened war both with the savages and with Great Britain. Further west still, Spain held the Mississippi, closed navigation, and intrigued to separate our western settlers from the Union. No immediate danger lay here, but still peril and need of close watching, for the Mississippi was never to slip out of our power. The mighty river and the great region through which it flows were important features in that empire which Washington foresaw. His plan was that we should get them by binding the settlers beyond the Alleghanies to the old States with roads, canals, and trade, and then trust to those hardy pioneers to keep the river and its valley for themselves and their country. All that was needed for this were time, and vigilant firmness with Spain.

Beyond the sea were the West India Islands, the home of a commerce long carried on by the colonies and of much profit to them, especially to those of New England. This trade was now hampered by England, and was soon to be still further blocked, and thereby become the cause of much bickering and ill-will.

Across the ocean we maintained with the Barbary States the relations usual between brigands and victims, and we tried to make treaties with them, and really paid tribute to them, as was the fashion in dealing with those pirates at that period. With Holland, Sweden, and Prussia we had commercial treaties, and the Dutch sent a minister to the United States. With France alone were our relations close. She had been our ally, and we had formed with her a treaty of alliance and a treaty of commerce, as well as a consular convention, which we were at this time engaged in revising. To most of the nations of the world, however, we were simply an unknown quantity, an unconsidered trifle. The only people who really knew anything about us were the English, with whom we had fought, and from whom we had separated; the French, who had helped us to win our independence; and the Dutch, from whom we had borrowed money. Even these nations, with so many reasons for intelligent and profitable interest in the new republic, failed, not unnaturally, to see the possibilities shut up in the wild American continent.

To the young nation just starting thus unnoticed and unheeded, Washington believed that honorable peace was essential, if a firm establishment of the new government, and of a respectable and respected position in the eyes of the world, was ever to be attained; and it was toward England, therefore, as the source of most probable trouble, that Washington turned to begin his foreign policy. The return of John Adams had left us without a minister at London, and England had sent no representative to the United States. The President, therefore, authorized Gouverneur Morris, who was going abroad on private business, to sound the English government informally as to an exchange of ministers, the complete execution of the treaty of peace, and the negotiation of a commercial treaty. The mission was one of inquiry, and was born of good and generous feelings as well as of broad and wise views of public policy. "It is in my opinion very important," he wrote to Morris, "that we avoid errors in our system of policy respecting Great Britain; and this can only be done by forming a right judgment of their disposition and views."

What was the response to these fair and sensible suggestions? On the first point the assent was ready enough; but on the other two, which looked to the carrying out of the treaty and the making of a treaty of commerce, there was no satisfaction. Morris, who was as high-spirited as he was able, was irritated by the indifference and hardly concealed insolence shown to him and his business. It was the fit beginning of the conduct by which England for nearly a century has succeeded in alienating the good-will of the people of the United States. Such a policy was neither generous nor intelligent, and politically it was a gross blunder. Washington, however, was too great a man to be disturbed by the bad temper and narrow ideas of English ministers. After his fashion he persevered in what he knew to be right and for his country's interest, and in due time a diplomatic representation was established, while later still, in the midst of difficulties of which he little dreamed at the outset, he carried through a treaty that removed the existing grievances. In a word, he kept the peace, and it lasted long enough to give the United States the breathing space they so much needed at the beginning of their history.

The greatest perils in our foreign relations came, as it happened, from another quarter, where peace seemed most secure, and where no man looked for trouble. The government of the United States and the French revolution began almost together, and it is one of the strangest facts of history that the nation which helped so powerfully to give freedom to

America brought the results of that freedom into the gravest peril by its own struggle for liberty. When the great movement in France began, it was hailed in this country with general applause, and with a sympathy as hearty as it was genuine, for every one felt that France was now to gain all the blessings of free government with which America was familiar. Our glorious example, it was clear, was destined to change the world, and monarchies and despotisms were to disappear. There was to be a new political birth for all the nations, and the reign of peace and good-will was to come at once upon the earth at the hands of liberated peoples freely governing themselves. It was a natural delusion, and a kindly one. History, in the modern sense, was still unwritten, and men did not then understand that the force and character of a revolution are determined by the duration and intensity of the tyranny and misgovernment which have preceded and caused it. The vast benefit destined to flow from the French revolution was to come many years after all those who saw it begin were in their graves, but at the moment it was expected to arrive immediately, and in a form widely different from that which, in the slow process of time, it ultimately assumed. Moreover, Americans did not realize that the well-ordered liberty of the English-speaking race was something unknown and inconceivable to the French.

There were a few Americans who were never deceived for a moment, even by their hopes. Hamilton, who "divined Europe," as Talleyrand said, and Gouverneur Morris, studying the situation on the spot with keen and practical observation, soon apprehended the truth, while others more or less quickly followed in their wake. But Washington, whom no one ever credited with divination, and who never crossed the Atlantic, saw the realities of the thing sooner, and looked more deeply into the future than anybody else. No man lived more loyal than he, or more true to the duties of gratitude; but he looked upon the world of facts with vision never dimmed nor dazzled, and watched in silence, while others slept and dreamed. Let us follow his letters for a moment. In October, 1789, in the first flush of hope and sympathy, he wrote to Morris: "The revolution which has been effected in France is of so wonderful a nature that the mind can hardly realize the fact. If it ends as our last accounts to the first of August predict, that nation will be the most powerful and happy in Europe; but I fear though it has gone triumphantly through the first paroxysm, it is not the last it has to encounter before matters are finally settled. In a word, the revolution is of too great magnitude to be effected in so short a space, and with the loss of so little blood. . . . To forbear running from one extreme to another is no easy matter; and should this be the case, rocks and shelves, not visible at present, may wreck the vessel, and give a higher-toned despotism than the one which existed before."

Seven years afterwards, reviewing his opinions in respect to France, he wrote to Pickering: "My conduct in public and private life, as it relates to the important struggle in which the latter is engaged, has been uniform from the commencement of it, and may be summed up in a few words: that I have always wished well to the French revolution; that I have always given it as my decided opinion that no nation had a right to intermeddle in the internal concerns of another; that every one had a right to form and adopt whatever government they liked best to live under themselves; and that if this country could, consistently with its engagements, maintain a strict neutrality and thereby preserve peace, it was bound to do so by motives of policy, interest, and every other consideration that ought to actuate a people situated as we are, already deeply in debt, and in a convalescent state from the struggle we have been engaged in ourselves."

Thus prepared, Washington waited and saw his cautious predictions verified, and the revolution rush headlong from one extreme to another. He also saw the flames spread beyond the borders of France, changing and dividing public opinion everywhere; and he knew it was only a question of time how soon the new nation, at whose head he stood, would be affected. Histories and biographies which treat of that period, as a rule convey the idea that the foreign policy of our first administration dealt with the complications that arose as they came upon us. Nothing could be further from the truth, for the general policy was matured at the outset, as has been seen in the letter to Newenham, and the occasions for its application were sure to come sooner or later, in one form or another.

Washington was not surprised by the presence of the perils that he feared, and danger only made him more set on carrying out the policy upon which he had long since determined. In July, 1791, he wrote to Morris: "I trust we shall never so far lose sight of our own interest and happiness as to become unnecessarily a party to these political disputes. Our local situation enables us to maintain that state with respect to them which otherwise could not, perhaps, be preserved by human wisdom." He followed this up with a strong and concise argument as to the advantage and necessity of this policy, showing a complete grasp of the subject, which came from long and patient thought.

All his firmness and knowledge were needed, for the position was most trying. With every ship that brought news of the extraordinary doings in Europe, the applause which greeted the early uprisings of Paris grew less general. The wise, the prudent, the conservative, cooled gradually at first, and then more quickly in their admiration of the French; but in the beginning, this deepening and increasing hostility to the revolution kept silence. It was popular to be the friend of France, and highly unpopular to be anything else. But when excesses multiplied and blood flowed, when religion tottered and the foundations of society were shaken, this silence was broken. Discussion took the place of harmonious congratulation, and it soon became apparent that there was to be a sharp and bitter division of public opinion, growing out of the affairs of France. It was necessary for the government to maintain a friendly yet cautious attitude toward our former ally, and not endanger the stability of the Union and the dignity of the country by giving to the French sympathizers any good ground for accusing them of ingratitude, or of lukewarmness toward the cause of human rights. That a time would soon come when decisive action must be taken, Washington saw plainly enough; and when that moment arrived, the risk of fierce party divisions on a question of foreign politics could not be avoided. Meantime domestic bitterness on these matters was to be repressed and delayed, and yet in so doing no step was to be taken which would involve the country in any inconsistency, or compel a change of position when the crisis was actually reached. The policy of separating the United States from all foreign politics is usually dated from what is called the neutrality proclamation; but the theory, as has been pointed out, was clear and well defined in Washington's mind when he entered upon the presidency. The outlines were marked out and pursued in practice long before the outbreak of war between France and England put his system to the touch. In everything he said or wrote, whether in public or private, his tone toward France was so friendly that her most zealous supporter could not take offense, and at the same time it was so absolutely guarded that the country was committed to nothing which could hamper it in the future. The course of the administration as a whole, and its substantive acts as well, were in harmony with the tone of expression used by the President; for Washington, it may be repeated, was the head of his own administration, a fact which the biographers of the very able men who surrounded him are too prone to overlook. In this case he was not only the leader, but the work was peculiarly his own, and a few extracts from his letters will show the completeness of his policy and the firmness with which he followed it whenever occasion came.

To Lafayette he wrote in July, 1791, a letter full of sympathy, but with an undertone of warning none the less significant because it was veiled. Coming to a point where there was an intimation of trouble between the two countries, he said: "The decrees of the National Assembly respecting our tobacco and oil do not appear to be very pleasing to the people of this country; but I do not presume that any hasty measures will be adopted in consequence thereof; for we have never entertained a doubt of the friendly disposition of the French nation toward us, and are therefore persuaded that, if they have done anything which seems to bear hard upon us at a time when the Assembly must have been occupied in very important matters, and which, perhaps, would not allow time for a due consideration of the subject, they will in the moment of calm deliberation alter it and do what is right."

The unfriendly act was noted, so that Lafayette would understand that no tame submission was intended, and yet no resentment was expressed. The same tone can be noticed in a widely different direction. Washington foresaw that the troubles in France, sooner or later, would involve her in war with England. The United States, as the former allies of the French, were certain to attract the attention of the mother country, and so he watched on that side also with equal caution. England, if possible, was to be made to understand that the American policy was not dictated by anything but the interests and the dignity of the United States, and their resolve to hold aloof from European complications. In June, 1792, he wrote to Morris: "One thing, however, I must not pass over in silence, lest you should infer from it that Mr. D. had authority for reporting that the United States had asked the mediation of Great Britain to bring about a peace between them and the Indians. You may be fully assured, sir, that such mediation never was asked, that the asking of it

LE MARQUIS DE LA FAYETTE
Marechal de Camp.

never was in contemplation, and I think I might go further and say that it not only never will be asked, but would be rejected if offered. The United States will never have occasion, I hope, to ask for the interposition of that power, or any other, to establish peace within their own territory."

Here is again the same note, always so true and clear, that the United States are not colonies but an independent nation. So far as it was in the power of the President, this was something which should be heard by all men, even at the risk of much reiteration. It was a fact not understood at home and not recognized abroad, but Washington proposed to insist upon it so far as in him lay, until it was both understood and admitted.

Meantime the flames were ever spreading from Paris, consuming and threatening to consume the heaped up rubbish of centuries, and also burning up many other more valuable things, as is the way with great fires when they get beyond control. Many persons were interested in the things of worth now threatened with destruction, and many others in the rubbish and the tyrannous abuses. It was clear that war of a wide and far-reaching kind could not be long put off. In March, 1793, Washington wrote: "All our late accounts from Europe hold up the expectation of a general war in that quarter. For the sake of humanity, I hope such an event will not take place. But if it should, I trust that we shall have too just a sense of our own interest to originate any cause that may involve us in it."

Even while he wrote, the general war that he anticipated, the war between France and England, had come. The news reached him at Mount Vernon, and in the letter to Jefferson announcing his immediate departure for Philadelphia he said: "War having actually commenced between France and Great Britain, it behooves the government of this country to use every means in its power to prevent the citizens thereof from embroiling us with either of those powers, by endeavoring to main-tain a strict neutrality. I therefore require that you will give the subject mature consideration, that such measures as shall be deemed most likely to effect this desirable purpose may be adopted without delay." These instructions were written on April 12, and on the 18th Washington was in Philadelphia, and had sent out a series of questions to be considered by his cabinet and answered on the following day. After much discussion, it was unanimously agreed to issue a proclamation of neutrality, to receive the new French minister, and not to convene Congress in extra session. The remaining questions were put over for further consideration.

Hamilton framed the questions, say the historians; Randolph drafted the proclamation, says his biographer, in a very instructive and fresh discussion of the relations between the Secretary of State and the Attorney General. It is interesting to know what share the President's advisers took when he consulted them on this momentous question, but the leading idea was his own. When the moment came, the policy long meditated and matured was put in force. The world was told that a new power had come into being, which meant to hold aloof from Europe, and which took no interest in the balance of power or the fate of dynasties, but looked only to the welfare of its own people and to the conquest and mastery of a continent as its allotted tasks. The policy declared by the proclamation was purely American in its conception, and severed the colonial tradition at a stroke. In the din then prevailing among civilized men, it was but little heeded, and even at home it was almost totally misunderstood; yet nevertheless it did its work. For twenty-five years afterward the American people slowly advanced toward the ground then taken, until the ideas of the neutrality proclamation received their final acceptance and extension at the hands of the younger Adams, in the promulgation of the Monroe doctrine. The shaping of this policy which was then launched was a great work of far-sighted and native statesmanship, and it was preëminently the work of the President himself.

Moreover, it did not stop here. A circular to the officers of the customs provided for securing notice of infractions of the law, and the task of enforcing the principles laid down in the proclamation began. As it happened, the theory of neutrality was destined at once to receive rude tests of its soundness in practice. The new French minister was landing on our shores, and beginning his brief career in this country, while the proclamation was going from town to town and telling the people, in sharp and unaccustomed tones, that they were Americans and not colonists, and must govern themselves accordingly.

Everything, in fact, seemed to conspire to make the path of the new policy rough and thorny. In the excitement of the time a large portion of the population regarded it as a party measure aimed against our beloved allies, while, to make the situation worse, France on one side and England on the other proceeded, as if deliberately, to do everything in their power to render neutrality impossible, and to drive us into war with some one.

The new minister, Genet, could not have been better chosen, if the special errand for which he had been employed had been to make trouble. Light-headed and vain, with but little ability and a vast store of unintelligent zeal, the whirl of the French revolution flung him on our shores, where he had a glorious chance for mischief. This opportunity he at once seized. As soon as he landed he proceeded to arm privateers at Charleston. Thence he took his way north, and the enthusiastic popular acclaim which everywhere greeted his arrival almost crazed him, and drew forth a series of high-flown and most injudicious speeches. By the time he reached Philadelphia, and before he had presented his credentials, he had induced enough violations of neutrality, and sown the seeds of enough trouble, to embarrass our government for months to come.

Washington had written to Governor Lee on May 6: "I foresaw in the moment information of that event (the war) came to me, the necessity for announcing the disposition of this country towards the belligerent powers, and the propriety of restraining, as far as a proclamation would do it, our citizens from taking part in that contest. . . . The affairs of France would seem to me to be in the highest paroxysm of disorder; not so much from the presence of foreign enemies, for in the cause of liberty this ought to be fuel to the fire of a patriot soldier and to increase his ardor, but because those in whose hands the government is intrusted are ready to tear each other to pieces, and will more than probably prove the worst foes the country has."

He easily foresaw the moment of trial, when he would be forced to the declaration of his policy, which was so momentous for the United States, and he also understood the condition of affairs at Paris, and the probable tendencies and proximate results of the Revolution. It was evident that the great social convulsion had brought forth men of genius and force, and had maddened them with the lust of blood and power. But it was less easy to foresee, what was equally natural, that the revolution would also throw to the surface men who had neither genius nor force, but who were as wild and dangerous as their betters. No one, surely, could have been prepared to meet in the person of the minister of a great nation such a feather-headed mischief-maker as Genet.

In everything relating to France Washington had observed the utmost caution, and his friendliness had been all the more marked because he had felt obliged to be guarded. He had exercised this care even in personal matters, and had refrained, so far as possible, from seeing the *émigrés* who had begun to come to this country. Such men as the Vicomte de Noailles had been referred to the State Department, and in many cases the maintenance of this attitude had tried his feelings severely, for the exiles were not infrequently men who had fought or sympathized with us in our day of conflict. Now came the new minister of the republic, a being apparently devoid of training or manners. Before he had been received, or had appeared at the seat of government, before he had even taken possession of his predecessor's papers, he had behaved in a way which would not have been inappropriate to a Roman governor of a conquered province. He had ordered the French consuls to act as admiralty courts, he had armed cruisers, enlisted and commissioned American citizens, and had seen the vessels of a power with which the United States were at peace captured in American waters, and condemned in the States by French consular courts. Three weeks before Genet's audience Jefferson had a memorial from the British minister, justly complaining of the injuries done his country under cover of our flag; and while the government was considering this pleasant incident, Genet was faring gayly northward, fêted and caressed, cheered and applauded, the subject of ovations and receptions everywhere. At Philadelphia he was received by a great concourse of citizens, called together by the guns of the very privateer that had violated our neutrality, and led by provincial persons, who thought it fine to name themselves "citizen" Smith and "citizen" Brown, because that particular folly was the fashion in France. A day was passed in receiving addresses, and then Genet was presented to the President.

A stranger contrast could not easily have been found even in that strange time, and two men more utterly unlike probably never faced each other as representatives of two great nations. In the difference between them the philosopher may find, perhaps, some explanation of the difference in the character and results of the revolutions which came so near together in the two countries. Nothing, moreover, could well be conceived more distasteful to Washington than the Frenchman's conduct except the Frenchman himself. There was about the man and his performances everything most calculated to bring one of those gusts of passionate contempt which now and again had made things unpleasant for some one who had failed in sense, decency, and duty. This was impossible to a President, but nevertheless his self-restraint from the beginning to the end of his intercourse with Genet was very remarkable in a man of his temperament. At their first interview his demeanor may have been a little colder than usual, and the dignified reserve somewhat more marked, but there was no trace of any feeling. His manner, nevertheless, chilled Genet and came upon him like a cold bath after the warm atmosphere of popular plaudits and turgid addresses. He went away grumbling, and complained that he had seen medallions of the Capets on the walls of the President's room.

But although Washington was calm and polite, he was also watchful and prepared, as he had good reason to be, for Genet immediately began, in addition to his wild public utterances, to pour in notes upon the State Department. He demanded money; he announced in florid style the opening of the French ports; he wrote that he was ready to make a new treaty; and finally he filed an answer to the complaints of the British minister. His arguments were wretched, but they seemed to weigh with Jefferson, although not with the President; and meantime the dragon's teeth which he had plentifully sown began to come up and bear an abundant harvest. More prizes were made by his cruisers, and after many remonstrances one was ordered away, and two Americans whom Genet had enlisted were indicted. Genet declared that this was an act which his pen almost refused to state; but still it was done, and the administration pushed on and ordered the seizure of privateers fitting in American ports. Governor Clinton made a good beginning with one at New York, and in hot haste Genet wrote another note more furious and impertinent than any he had yet sent. He was answered civilly, and the work of stopping the sale of prizes went on.

Meantime the opposition were not idle. The French sympathizers bestirred themselves, and attacks began to be made even on the President himself. The popular noise and clamor were all against the administration, but the support of it was really growing stronger, although the President and his secretaries could not see it. Jefferson, on whom the conduct of foreign affairs rested, was uneasy and wavering. He wrote able letters, as he was directed, but held, it is to be feared, quite different language in his conversations with Genet. Randolph argued and hesitated, while Hamilton, backed by Knox, was filled with wrath and wished more decisive measures. Still, as we look at it now across a century, we can observe that the policy went calmly forward, consistent and unchecked. The French minister was held back, privateers were stopped, the English minister's complaints were answered, every effort was made for exact justice, and neutrality was preserved. It was hard and trying work, especially to a man of strong temper and fighting propensities. Still it was done, and toward the end of June Washington went for a little rest to Mount Vernon.

Then came a sudden explosion. One July morning the rumor ran through Philadelphia that the *Little Sarah*, a prize of the French man-of-war, was fitting out as a privateer. The reaction in favor of the administration was beginning, and men, indignant at the proceeding, carried the news to Governor Mifflin, and also to the Secretary of State. Great disturbance of mind thereupon ensued to these two gentlemen, who were both much interested in France and the rights of man. The brig would not sail before the arrival of the President, said the Secretary of State. Still the arming went on apace, and then came movements on the part of the governor. Dallas, Secretary of State for Pennsylvania, went at midnight to expostulate with Genet, who burst into a passion, and declared that the vessel should sail. This defiance roused the governor, and a company of militia marched to the vessel and took possession. Greatly excited, Jefferson went next morning to Genet, who very honestly declined to promise to detain the vessel, but said that she would not be ready to sail until Wednesday. This announcement, which was distinctly not a promise, the Secretary of State chose to accept as such, and as he was very far from being a fool, he did so either from timidity, or from a very unworthy political preference for another nation's interests to the dignity of his own country. At all events, he had the troops withdrawn, and the *Little Sarah*, now rejoicing in the name of the Petit Democrat, dropped down to Chester. Hamilton and Knox, being neither afraid nor un-American, were for putting a battery on Mud Island and sinking the privateer if she attempted to go by. Great saving of trouble and bloodshed would have been accomplished by the setting up of this battery and the sinking of this vessel, for it would have informed the world that though the United States were weak and young, they were ready nevertheless to fight as a nation, a fact which we subsequently were obliged to prove by a three years' war.

Jefferson, however, opposed decisive measures, and while the cabinet wrangled, Washington, hurrying back from Mount Vernon, reached Philadelphia. He was full of just anger at what had been done and left undone. Jefferson, feeling uneasy, had gone to the country, where he was fond of making a retreat at unpleasant moments, and Washington at once wrote him a letter, which could not have been very agreeable to the discoverer of diplomatic promises in a refusal to give any. "What," said the President, "is to be done in the case of the *Little Sarah*, now at Chester? Is the minister of the French Republic to set the acts of this government at defiance *with impunity?* and then threaten the executive with an appeal to the people? What must the world think of such conduct, and of the government of the United States in submitting to it?" Then came a demand for an immediate opinion.

To the tender feelings of the Secretary of State, who had not been considering the affair from an American standpoint, this must have seemed a violent and almost a coarse way of treating the "great republic," and he replied that the French minister had assured him that the vessel would not sail until the President reached a decision. Having got the vessel to Chester, however, by telling the truth, Genet now changed his tack. He lied about detaining her, and she went to sea. This performance filled the cup of Washington's disgust almost to overflowing, for he had what Jefferson seems to have totally lost at this juncture—a keen national feeling, and it was touched to the quick. The truth was, that in all this business Jefferson was thinking too much of France and of the cause of human liberty in Paris, while Washington thought of the United States alone. The result was the escape of the vessel, owing to Washington's absence, and the consequent humiliation to the government. To refrain from ordering Genet out of the country at once required a strong effort of self-control; but he wished to keep the peace as long as possible, and he proposed to get rid of him speedily but decorously. He resolved also that no more such outrages should be committed through his absence, and the consequent differences among his advisers. He continued, of course, to consult his cabinet, but he took the immediate control, more definitely even than before, into his own hands. On July 25 he wrote to Jefferson, whose vigor at this critical time he evidently doubted: "As the letter of the minister of the Republic of France, dated the 22d of June, lies yet unanswered, and as the official conduct of that gentleman, relative to the affairs of this government, will have to undergo a very serious consideration, . . . in order to decide upon measures proper to be taken thereupon, it is my desire that all the letters to and from that minister may be ready to be laid before me, the heads of departments, and the attorney-general, whom I shall advise with on the occasion." He also saw to it that better precautions should be taken by the officers of the customs to prevent similar attempts to break neutrality, and set the administration and the laws of the country at defiance.

The cabinet consultations soon bore good fruit, and Genet's recall was determined on during the first days of August. There was some discussion over the manner of requesting the recall, but the terms were made gentle by Jefferson, to the disgust of the Secretary of the Treasury and the Secretary of War, who desired direct methods and stronger language. As

finally toned up and agreed upon by the President and cabinet, the document was sufficiently vigorous to annoy Genet, and led to bitter reproaches
addressed to his friend in the State Department. Then there was question
about publishing the correspondence, and again Jefferson intervened in
behalf of mildness. The substantive fact, however, was settled, and the let
ter asking Genet's recall, as desired by Washington, went in due time,
and in the following February came a successor. Genet, however, did not
go back to his native land, for he preferred to remain here and save his
head, valueless as that article would seem to have been. He spent the rest
of his days in America, married, harmless, and quite obscure. His noise
and fireworks were soon over, and one wonders now how he could ever
have made as much flare and explosion as he did.

But even while his recall was being decided, before he knew of it
himself, and long before his successor came, Genet's folly produced more
trouble than ever, and his insolence rose to a higher pitch. The arming of
privateers had been checked, but the consuls continued to arrogate powers which no self-respecting nation could permit, and for some gross
offense Washington revoked the *ex-equatur* of Duplaine, consul at Boston.
An insolent note from Genet thereupon declared that the President had
overstepped his authority, and that he should appeal to the sovereign
State of Massachusetts. Next there was riot and the attempted murder of
a man from St. Domingo who was accused by the refugees. Then it
began to get abroad that Genet had threatened to appeal from the
President to the people, and frantic denials ensued from all the opposition press; whereupon a card appeared from John Jay and Rufus King,
which stated that they were authority for the story and believed it.
Apologies now took the place of denial, and were backed by ferocious
attacks on the signers of the card. Unluckily, intelligent people seemed
to put faith in Jay and King rather than in the opposition newspapers, and
the tide, which had turned some time before, now ran faster every
moment against the French. To make it flow with overwhelming force
and rapidity was reserved for Genet himself who was furious at the Jay
card, and wrote to the President, demanding a denial of the statement
which it contained. A cool note informed him that the President did not

consider it proper or material to make denials, and pointed out to him that he must address his communications to the State Department. This correspondence was published, and the mass of the people were at last aroused, and turned from Genet in disgust. The leaders tried vainly to separate the minister from his country, and Genet himself frothed and foamed, demanded that Randolph should sue Jay and King for libel, and declared that America was no longer free. This sad statement had little effect. Washington had triumphed completely, and without haste but with perfect firmness had brought the people round to his side as that of the national dignity and honor.

The victory had been won at no little cost to Washington himself in the way of self-control. He had been irritated and angered at every step, so much so that he even referred in a letter to Richard Henry Lee to the trial of temper to which he had been put, a bit of personal allusion in which he rarely indulged. "The specimens you have seen," he wrote, "of Mr. Genet's sentiments and conduct in the gazettes form a small part only of the aggregate. But you can judge from them to what test the temper of the executive has been put in its various transactions with this gentleman. It is probable that the whole will be exhibited to public view in the course of the next session of Congress. Delicacy towards his nation has restrained the doing of it hitherto. The best that can be said of this agent is, that he is entirely unfit for the mission on which he is employed; unless (which I hope is not the case), contrary to the express and unequivocal declaration of his country made through himself, it is meant to involve ours in all the horrors of a European war."

But there was another side to the neutrality question even more full of difficulties and unpopularity, which began to open just as the worst of the contests with Genet was being brought to a successful close. Genet had not confined his efforts to the seaboard, nor been content with civic banquets, privateers, rioting, and insolent notes to the government. He had fitted out ships, and he intended also to levy armies. With this end in view he had sent his agents through the south and west to raise men in order to invade the Floridas on the one hand and seize New Orleans on the other. To conceive of such a performance by a foreign minister on the soil of the United States, requires an effort of the imagination to-day almost equal to that which would be necessary for an acceptance of the reality of the Arabian nights. It brings home with startling clearness not merely the crazy insolence of Genet, but a painful sense of the manner in which we were regarded by the nations of Europe. Still worse is the fact that they had good reason for their view. The imbecility of the confederation had bred contempt, and it was now seen that we were still so wholly provincial that a large part of the people was not only ready to condone but even to defend the conduct of the minister who engaged in such work. Worst of all, the people among whom the French agents went received their propositions with much pleasure. In South Carolina, where it was said five thousand men had been enlisted, there was sufficient self-respect to stop the precious scheme. The assembly arrested certain persons and ordered an inquiry, which came to nothing; but the effect of their action was sufficient. In Kentucky, on the other hand, the authorities would not interfere. The people there were always quite ready for a march against New Orleans, and that it did not proceed was due to Genet's inability to get money; for the governor declined to meddle, and the democratic society of Lexington demanded war. Matters looked so serious that the cavalry was sent to Kentucky, and the rest of the army wintered in Ohio. It was actually necessary to teach the American people by the presence of the troops of the United States that they must not enroll themselves in the army of a foreign minister.

Nothing can show more strikingly than this the almost inconceivable difficulties with which the President was contending. To develop a policy of wise and dignified neutrality, and to impress it upon the world, was a great enough task in itself. But Washington was obliged to impress it also upon his own people, and to teach them that they must have a policy of their own toward other nations. He had to carry this through in the teeth of an opposition so utterly colonial that it could not grasp the idea of having any policy but that which, from sympathy or hate, they took from foreigners. Beyond the mountains, he had to bring this home to men to whom American nationality was such a dead letter that they were willing to defy their own government, throw off their allegiance, and enlist for an offensive war under the banners of a crazy French Girondist. It is neither easy nor pleasant to carry out a new foreign policy in time of general war, with one's own people united in its support; but when the foreign divisions are repeated at home, the task is enhanced in difficulty a thousandfold. Nevertheless, there was the work to do, and the President faced it. He dealt with Genet, he prevailed in public opinion on the seaboard, and in some fashion he maintained order west of the mountains.

Washington also saw, as we can see now very plainly, that, wrong and unpatriotic as the Kentucky attitude was, there was still an excuse for it. Those bold pioneers, to whom the country owes so much, had very substantial grievances. They knew nothing of the laws of nations, and did not yet realize that they had a country and a nationality; but they had the instincts of all great conquering races. They looked upon the Mississippi and felt that it was of right theirs, and that it must belong to the vast empire which they were winning from the wilderness. They saw the mighty river held and controlled by Spaniards, and they were harassed and interfered with by Spanish officials, whom they both hated and despised. To men of their mould and training there was but one solution conceivable. They must fight the Spaniard, and drive him from the land forever. Their purposes were quite right, but their methods were faulty. Washington, born to a life of adventure and backwoods conquest, had a good deal of real sympathy with these men, for he knew them to be in the main right, and his ultimate purposes were the same as theirs. But he had a nation in his charge to whom peace was precious. To have the backwoodsmen of Kentucky go down the river and harry the Spaniards out of the country, as their descendants afterwards harried the Mexicans out of Texas, would have been a refreshing sight, but it would have interfered sadly with the nation which was rising on the Atlantic seaboard, and of which Kentucky was a part. War was to be avoided, and above all a war into which we should have been dragged as the vassal of France; so Washington intended to wait, and he managed to make the Kentuckians wait too, a process by no means agreeable to that enterprising people.

His own policy about the Mississippi, which has already been described, never wavered. He meant to have the great river, for his ideas of the empire of the future were quite as extended as those of the pioneers, and much more definite, but his way of getting it was to build up the Atlantic States and bind them, with their established resources, to the settlers over the mountains. This done, time would do the rest; and the sequel showed that he was right. A little more than a year after he came to the presidency he wrote to Lafayette: "Gradually recovering from the distresses in which the war left us, patiently advancing in our task of civil government, unentangled in the crooked politics of Europe, *wanting scarcely anything but the free navigation of the Mississippi, which we must have, and as certainly shall have, if we remain a nation*,"* etc.

Time and peace, sufficient for the upbuilding of the nation, that is the theme everywhere. Yet he knew that a sacrifice of everything for peace was the surest road both to war and ruin. Peace must be kept; yet war was still the last resort, and he was ready to go to war with the Spaniards, as with the Indians, if all else failed. But he did not mean to have all else fail, nor did he mean to submit to Spanish insolence and exactions. The grievances of the pioneers of the West were to be removed, if possible, by treaty, and if that way was impossible, then by fighting.

Carmichael, who had been minister at Madrid under the confederation, had been continued there by the new government. But while the intrigues of Spain to detach Kentucky, and the interference and exactions of Spanish officials, went on, our negotiation for the settlement of our rights to the navigation of the Mississippi halted. Tired of this inaction, Washington, late in 1791, united William Short, our minister to Holland, in a commission with Carmichael, to open a fresh and special negotiation as to the Mississippi, and at the same time a confidential agent was sent to Florida to seek some arrangements with the governor as to fugitive slaves, a matter of burning interest to the planters on the border. The joint commission bore no fruit, and the troubles in the West increased. Fostered by Genet, they came near bringing on war and detaching the western settlements from the Union, so that it was clearly necessary to take more vigorous measures.

---

*The italics are mine.

Accordingly, in 1794, after Genet had been dismissed, Washington sent Thomas Pinckney, who for some years had been minister in London, on a special treaty-making mission to Madrid. The first results were vexatious and unpromising enough, and Pinckney wrote at the outset that he had had two interviews with the Duke de Alcudia, but to no purpose. It was the old game of delay, he said, with inquiries as to why we had not replied to propositions, which in fact never had been made. Even what Pinckney wrote, unsatisfactory as it was, could not be wholly made out, for some passages were in a cipher to which the State Department had no key. Washington wrote to Pickering, then acting as Secretary of State: "A kind of fatality seems to have pursued this negotiation, and, in short, all our concerns with Spain, from the appointment of Mr. Carmichael, under the new government, as minister to that country, to the present day. . . . Enough, however, appears already to show the temper and policy of the Spanish court, and its undignified conduct as it respects themselves, and insulting as it relates to us; and I fear it will prove that the late treaty of peace with France portends nothing favorable to these United States." Washington's patience had been sorely tried by the delays and shifty evasions of Spain, but he was now on the brink of success, just as he concluded that negotiation was hopeless.

He had made a good choice in Thomas Pinckney, better even than he knew. Triumphing over all obstacles, with persistence, boldness, and good management, Pinckney made a treaty and brought it home with him. Still more remarkable was the fact that it was an extremely good treaty, and conceded all we asked. By it the Florida boundary was settled, and the free navigation of the Mississippi was obtained. We also gained the right to a place of deposit at New Orleans, a pledge to leave the Indians alone, a commercial agreement modeled on that with France, and a board of arbitration to settle American claims. All this Pinckney obtained, not as the representative of a great and powerful state, but as the envoy of a new nation, distant, unknown, disliked, and embroiled in various complications with other powers. Our history can show very few diplomatic achievements to be compared with this, for it was brilliant in execution, and complete and valuable in result. Yet it has passed into history almost unnoticed, and both the treaty and its maker have been singularly and most unjustly neglected. Even the accurate and painstaking Hildreth omits the date and circumstances of Pinckney's appointment, while the last elaborate history of the United States scarcely alludes to the matter, and finds no place in its index for the name of its author. It was in fact one of the best pieces of work done during Washington's administration, and perfected its policy on a most difficult and essential point. It is high time that justice were done to the gallant soldier and accomplished diplomatist who conducted the negotiation and rendered such a solid service to his country. Thomas Pinckney, who really did something, who did work worth doing and without many words, has been forgotten, while many of his contemporaries, who simply made a noise, are freshly remembered in the pages of history.

There was, however, another nation out on our western and northern border more difficult to deal with than Spain; and in this quarter there was less evasion and delay, but more arrogance and bad temper. It was to England that Washington turned first when he took up the presidency, and it was in her control of the western posts and her influence among the Indian tribes that he saw the greatest dangers to the continental movement of our people. Morris, as we have seen, sounded the British government with but little success. Still they promised to send a minister, and in due time Mr. George Hammond arrived in that capacity, and opened a long and somewhat fruitless correspondence with the Secretary of State on the various matters of difference existing between the two countries. This interchange of letters went on peaceably and somewhat monotonously for many months, and then suddenly became very vivid and animated. This was the effect of the arrival of Genet; and at this point begins the long series of mistakes made by Great Britain in her dealings with the United States.

The principle of the declaration of neutrality could be easily upheld on broad political grounds, but technically its defense was by no means so simple. By the treaty of commerce with France we were bound to admit her privateers and prizes to our ports; and here, as any one could see, and as the sequel amply proved, was a fertile source of dangerous complications. Then by the treaty of alliance we guaranteed to France her West Indian possessions, binding ourselves to aid her in their defense; and a proclamation of neutrality when France was actually at war with a great naval power was an immediate and obvious limitation upon this guarantee. Hamilton argued that while France had an undoubted right to change her government, the treaty applied to a totally different state of affairs, and was therefore in suspense. He also argued that we were not bound in case of offensive war, and that this war was offensive. Jefferson and Randolph held that the treaties were as binding and as much in force now as they had ever been; but they both assented to the proclamation of neutrality. There can be little question that on the general legal principle Jefferson and Randolph were right. Hamilton's argument was ingenious and very fine-spun. But when he made the point about the character of the war as relieving us from the guarantee, he was unanswerable; and this of itself was a sufficient ground. He went beyond it in order to make his reasoning fit existing conditions consistently and throughout, and then it was that his position became untenable.

In reality the French revolution was showing itself so wholly abnormal and was so rapid in its changes, that as a matter of practical statesmanship it was worse than idle even to suppose that previous treaties, made with an established government, were in force with this ever-shifting thing which the revolution had brought forth. Still the general doctrine as to the binding force of treaties remained unaltered, and this conflict between fact and principle was what constituted the great difficulty in the way of Washington and Hamilton. The latter met it with one clever and adroit argument which it was difficult to sustain, and avoided it with a second, which was narrower, but at the same time sound and all-sufficient, as to the character of the war. Jefferson and Randolph stood by the general principle, but abandoned it in practice under pressure of imperious facts, as men generally do, while France herself soon removed all technical difficulties by abrogating by her measures the treaty of commerce, an act which relieved us of any further obligations and justified Hamilton's position. But in the beginning this was not known, and yet action was none the less necessary.

The result was right, and Washington had his way, which it must be confessed he had fully determined on before his cabinet supplied him with technical arguments.

All these points must have been plain enough to Hammond and the English ministry. They could not see the full scope of the neutrality policy in its national meaning, and they very naturally failed to perceive that it marked the rise of a new power wholly disconnected from Europe, to which their own views were confined. But they were quite able to understand the immediate aspect of the case. They saw Washington adopt and carry out a policy of dignified impartiality; they were well able to value rightly the technical objections which stood in his path, and they could see also that this policy was at the outset very unpopular in America. The remembrance of old injuries and of the war for independence was still fresh, and the hatred of England was well nigh universal in the United States. On the other hand, a lively sense of gratitude to France, and a sympathy with the objects of the revolution, made affection for that country uniform and general. The easy and popular course was for our government to range itself more or less directly with the French, and the refusal to do so was bold and in the highest degree creditable to the administration. It was, moreover, an important advantage to England that the United States should not ally themselves with her enemy, for next to herself, the Americans were the great seafaring people of the world, and were in a position to ravage her commerce, and, aided by France, to break up her West Indian possessions. If the United States had followed the natural prejudices of the time and had espoused the cause of France, it would have been wise and right for England to attack them and break them down if possible. But when, from a sense of national dignity and of fair dealing, the United States stood apart from the conflict and placed their former foe on the same footing as their friend and ancient ally, a very small allowance of good sense would have led the British ministry to encourage them in so doing. By favorable treatment, and by a friendly and conciliatory policy, they should have helped Washington in his struggle against popular prejudices, and endeavored by so doing to keep the United States neutral, and lead them, if possible, to their side; but with

a fatuity almost incomprehensible they pursued an almost exactly opposite course. By similar conduct England had brought on the war for independence, which ended in the division of her empire. In precisely the
same way she now proceeded to make it as arduous as possible for
Washington to maintain neutrality, and thereby played directly into the
hands of the party that supported France. The true policy demanded no
sacrifices on the part of Great Britain. Civility and consideration in her
dealings, and a careful abstention from wanton aggression and insult,
were all-sufficient. But England disliked us, as was quite natural; she did
not wish us to thrive and prosper, and she knew that we were weak and
not in a position to enter upon an offensive war.

As soon as it became known that Genet's privateers, manned by seamen enlisted in our ports, were preying on British commerce, and that
the French man-of-war L'Ambuscade had taken an English vessel, The
Grange, within the capes of the Delaware, Hammond filed a memorial in
regard to these incidents. In so doing he was of course quite right, and
the government responded immediately, and proceeded in good faith to
make every effort to repair these breaches of neutrality, and to redress
the wrongs suffered by Great Britain. Hammond, however, instead of
doing all in his power, not merely to gain his own ends, but to make it
easy for our government to satisfy him, assumed at once a disagreeable
tone with a strong flavor of bullying, which was not calculated to conciliate the statesmen with whom he was dealing. It was a small matter
enough, but unfortunately it was an indication of what was to come.

On November 6, 1793, a British order in council was passed, but not
immediately published, directing the seizure of all vessels carrying the
produce of the French islands, or loaded with provisions for the use of
the French colonies. The object of the order was to destroy all neutral
trade, and it was aimed particularly at the commerce of the United States.
The moment selected for its adoption was when the troubles with Genet
had culminated, when we were on the point of getting rid of that very
objectionable person, and when we had proved that we meant to maintain an honest and a real neutrality. It was as well calculated as any move
could have been to drive us back into the arms of France, yet the man-

ner of executing the order was far worse than the order itself. Our merchantmen and traders had been quick to take advantage of the opening of the French ports, and they had gone in swarms to the French islands. Now, without a word of warning, their vessels were seized by the cruisers of a nation with which we were supposed to be at peace. Every petty governor of an English island sat as a judge in admiralty. Many of them were corrupt, all were unfit for the duty, and our vessels were condemned and pillaged. The crews were made prisoners, and in many cases thrown into loathsome and unhealthy places of confinement, while the ships were left to rot in the harbors. The tale of the outrages and miseries thus inflicted on citizens of the United States without any warning, and by a nation considered to be at peace with us, fills an American with shame and anger even to-day. If our people remonstrated, they were told that England meant to have no neutrals, and that six of their frigates could blockade our coast. A course of kind treatment would have made us the friends of Great Britain, but the experiment was not even tried. The truth was that we were weak, and this was not only a misfortune but apparently an unpardonable sin. England could not conquer us, but she could harry our coasts, and let loose her Indians on our borders; and we had no navy with which to retaliate. She meant that there should be no neutrals, and so adopted a policy which would make us the active ally of France. It was no answer to say, what was perfectly true, that French privateers preyed upon our commerce with that fine indifference to rights and treaties which characterized the governments of the Revolution. If both sides maltreated us, the natural course was to unite with the power to which we at least owed a debt of gratitude.

About the same time a speech was reported from Quebec, in which Lord Dorchester told the Indians that they should soon take the war-path for England against the United States. Lord Grenville denied in Parliament, and subsequently to Jay, that the ministry had ever taken any step to incite the Indians against the United States, and the authenticity of Lord Dorchester's utterances has been questioned in later days; but it was not disavowed at the time, even by Hammond in a sharp correspondence which he held on that and other topics with Randolph. The speech, as is now known and proved, was probably made, whether it was authorized or not, and it was universally accepted at the moment as both true and authoritative.

This menace of desolating savage war in the West, in addition to the unquestioned outrages to our seamen, the loss of our ships, and the destruction of our commerce, with consequent ruin to all our seaboard towns, led to a general outburst of indignation from men of all parties, and Congress began to prepare for war. Many of the methods suggested were feeble and inadequate, but there could be no doubt of either the spirit or intentions which dictated them. News that an order of January 8, 1794, modified that of November 6, and confined the seizure to vessels carrying French property, and reports that some of our vessels were being restored, moderated the movements of Congress, but it was nevertheless evident that a resolution cutting off commercial intercourse with Great Britain would soon pass. In the existing state of things such a step in all probability meant war, and Washington was thus brought face to face with the most serious problem of his administration. It did not take him unawares, nor find him unprepared, for he had anticipated the situation, and his mind was made up. He had no intention of letting the country drift into war without a great effort to prevent it, and the time for that effort had now come. As in the case of Spain, he was resolved to send a special envoy to make a treaty. His first choice for this important mission was Hamilton, which, like most of his selections, would have been the best choice that could have been made. Hamilton, however, was so conspicuous as the great leader of the party which supported both the foreign and domestic policy of the administration, and he was so hated by the opposition, that a loud outcry was at once raised against his appointment. At that particular juncture it was very important that the envoy should depart with as much general good-will and public confidence as possible, so Hamilton sacrificed himself to this necessity, and withdrew his name voluntarily. His withdrawal was a mistake, but it was a wholly natural one under the circumstances. Washington then made the next best choice, and appointed John Jay, who was a man of most spotless character, honorable, high-minded, and skilled in public affairs. He was chief justice of the United States, and that fact gave additional weight to the mission. The only point in which he fell behind Hamilton was in aggressiveness of character, and this negotiation demanded, not merely firmness and tact, which Jay had in abundance, but a boldness verging on audacity. The immediate purpose, however, was answered, and Jay set forth on his journey with much good feeling toward himself, and with a very solemn sense among the people of the gravity of his undertaking. Washington himself saw Jay depart with many misgivings, and the act of sending such a mission at all was very trying to him, for the conduct of England galled him to the quick. He had long suspected Great Britain, as well as Spain, of inciting the Indians secretly to assail our settlements, and knowing as he did the character of savage warfare, and feeling deeply the bloodshed and expense of our Indian wars, he cherished a profound dislike for those who could be capable of promoting such misery to the injury of a friendly and civilized nation. As England became more and more hostile, he made up his mind that she was bent on attacking us, and in March, 1794, he wrote to Governor Clinton that he had no doubts as to the authenticity of Lord Dorchester's speech, and that he believed England intended war. He therefore urged the governor to inquire carefully into the state of feeling in Canada, and as to the military strength of the country, especially on the border. He put no trust in the disclaimers of the ministry when he saw the long familiar signs of hostile intrigue among the Indians, and he was quite determined that, if war should come, all the suffering should not be on one side.

This belief in the coming of war, however, only strengthened him in his well-matured plans to leave nothing undone to prevent it. It was in this spirit that he despatched the special mission, although his first letter to Jay shows that he had no very strong hopes of peace, and that his upper-most thoughts were of the wrongs which had been perpetrated, and of the perils which hung over the border. He did not wish the commissioner to mince matters at all. "There does not remain a doubt," he wrote, "in the mind of any well-informed person in this country, not shut against conviction, that all the difficulties we encounter with the Indians, their hostilities, the murder of helpless women and innocent children along our frontiers, result from the conduct of the agents of Great Britain in this country. . . . Can it be expected, I ask, so long as these things are known in the United States, or at least firmly believed, and suffered with impunity by Great Britain, that there ever will or can be any cordiality between the two countries? I answer, No. And I will undertake, without the gift of prophecy, to predict that it will be impossible to keep this country in a state of amity with Great Britain long, if the posts are not surrendered. A knowledge of these being my sentiments would have little weight, I am persuaded, with the British administration, and perhaps not with the nation, in effecting the measure; but both may rest satisfied that, if they want to be in peace with this country, and to enjoy the benefits of its trade, to give up the posts is the only road to it. Withholding them, and the consequences we feel at present continuing, war will be inevitable."

Jay meantime had been well received in England. Lord Grenville expressed the most friendly feelings, and every desire that the negotiation might succeed. Jay was also received at court, where he was said to have kissed the queen's hand, a crime, so the opposition declared, for which his lips ought to have been blistered to the bone, a difficult and by no means common form of punishment. Receptions, dinner parties, and a ready welcome everywhere, did not, however, make a treaty. When it came to business, the English did not differ materially from their neighbors whom Canning satirized.

> The fault of the Dutch
> Is giving too little and asking too much.

So the Americans now found it with Lord Grenville. There were many subjects of dispute, some dangerous, and all requiring settlement for the benefit of both countries. Boundaries, negro claims, and British debts were easily disposed of by reference to boards of arbitration. Two others, awkward and threatening, but not immediately pressing, were the impressment of British seamen, real or pretended, from American ships, and the exclusion of American vessels from the trade of the British West Indies. The latter circumstance was no doubt disagreeable to us, and deprived us of profit; but it is difficult to see what right we had to complain of it, for the ports of the British West Indies belonged to Great Britain, and if she chose to close them to us, or anybody else, she was quite within her rights. At all events, Lord Grenville declined to let us in, except in a very limited way and under most onerous conditions. The right of search and the right of impressment were simply the rights of the powerful over the weak. England wanted to get seamen where she could for her navy; and so long as she could violate our flag and carry off as recruits any able-bodied seaman who spoke English, she meant to do it. It was worse than idle to negotiate about it. When we should be ready and willing to fight we could settle that question, but not before. In due time we were ready to fight. England defeated us in various battles, ravaged our coasts, and burned our capital; while we whipped her frigates and lake flotillas, and repulsed her Peninsula veterans with heavy slaughter at New Orleans. Impressment was not mentioned in the treaty which concluded that war, but it ended at that time. The English are a brave and combative people, but rather than get into wars with nations that will fight, and fight hard, they will desist from wanton and illegal aggressions, in which they do not differ greatly from the rest of mankind; and so the practical abandonment of impressment came with the war of 1812. The fact was officially stated by Webster, not many years later, when he announced that the flag covered and protected all those who lived or traded under it.

But in 1794 impressment was a negotiable question, because we were not ready to go to war about it then and there. So Jay, wisely enough, allowed this especial form of bullying to drift aside, along with the exclusion from the West India trade, and addressed himself to the two points which it was essential to have settled at that particular moment. These questions were: the retention of the western posts, and neutral rights at sea. In return for the agreement on our part to pay the British debts, as determined by arbitration, England agreed to surrender the posts on June 1, 1796. There was to be mutual reciprocity in inland trade on the North American continent; but coastwise, while we opened all our harbors and rivers to the British, they shut us out from theirs in the colonies and the territory of the Hudson's Bay Company. In the eighteen articles, limited in duration to two years after the conclusion of the existing war, a treaty of commerce was practically formed and neutral rights dealt with. We were to be admitted to British ports in Europe and the East Indies on terms of equality with British vessels, but we were refused admission to the East Indian coasting trade, and to that between East India and Europe. We gained the right to trade to the West Indies, but only on condition that we should give up the transportation from America to Europe of any of the principal products of the colonies. These were enumerated, and besides sugar, molasses, coffee, and cocoa, included cotton, which had just become an export from the southern States, and which already promised to assume the importance that it afterwards reached. The vexed questions of privateers, prizes, and contraband of war were also settled and determined.

The treaty as a whole was not a very brilliant one for the United States, but its treatment was far worse than its deserts, and it was received with such a universal outburst of indignation that even to this day it has never freed itself from the bad name it then acquired. Nobody, not even its supporters, liked it, and yet it may be doubted whether anything materially better was possible at the time. The admirers of Hamilton, from that day to this, have believed that if he had been sent, his boldness, ability, and force would have wrung better terms from England. This is not at all improbable; but that they would have been materially improved, even by Hamilton, does not seem very likely. The treaty, in reality, was by no means bad; on the contrary, it had many good points. It disposed satisfactorily and fairly of all the minor questions which were vexatious and threatening to the peaceful relation of the two countries. It settled the British debts, gave us the western posts, which was a matter of the utmost importance, and arranged the disputed and thorny question of neutral rights, for the time being at least. It left impressment totally unsettled, simply because we were still too weak to be ready to fight England profitably on that theme. It opened to us the West Indian ports, which was the matter most nearly affecting our interests and our pockets, but it did so under limitations and concessions which were excessive and even humiliating. We were obliged to pay a price far too high for this coveted privilege, and it was on this point that the controversy finally hinged.

The treaty reached Philadelphia on March 7. Nothing was said of its arrival, which does not seem to have been known to any one but the President and Randolph, who had meantime succeeded Jefferson as Secretary of State. Three months later, on June 8, the Senate was called together in special session, and the treaty was laid before them. Washington did not like it and never changed his feeling in that respect, but he had made up his mind upon full reflection to accept it; and the Senate, after most careful consideration, voted by exactly the necessary two thirds to ratify it, provided that the objectionable West Indian article could be modified. On no terms could we consent to forego the exportation of cotton, and it is difficult to see how the Senate could have taken any other ground upon this point. Their action, however, opened some delicate questions. Washington wrote to Randolph: "First, is or is not that resolution intended to be the final act of the Senate; or do they expect that the new article which is proposed shall be submitted to them before the treaty takes effect? Secondly, does or does not the Constitution permit the President to ratify the treaty, without submitting the new article, after it shall be agreed to by the British King, to the Senate for their further advice and consent?"

These questions were carefully considered, and Washington had made up his mind to ratify conditionally on the modification of the West Indian article, when news arrived which caused him to suspend action. England, having made the treaty, and before any news could have been received of our attitude in regard to it, took steps to render its ratification both difficult and offensive, if not impossible. The mode adopted was to renew the "provision order," as it was called, which directed the seizure of all vessels carrying food products to France, and thus give to the Jay treaty the interpretation it was designed to avoid, that provisions could be declared contraband at the pleasure of one of the belligerents. It was a stupid thing to do, for if England desired to have peace with us, as her making the treaty indicated, she should not have renewed the

most irritating of all her past performances before we had had opportunity even to sign and ratify. Washington, on hearing of this move,
withheld his signature, bade Randolph prepare a strong memorial
against the provision order, and then betook himself to Mount Vernon on
some urgent private business.

Before he started, however, the storm of popular rage had begun to
break. Bache had the substance of the treaty in the "Aurora" on June 29,
and Mr. Stevens Thomson Mason, senator from Virginia, was so pained
by some slight inaccuracies in this version that he wrote Mr. Bache a
note, and sent him a copy of the treaty despite the injunction of secrecy
by which he as a senator was bound. Mr. Mason gained great present
glory by this frank breach of promise, and curiously enough this single
discreditable act is the only thing that keeps his name and memory alive
in history. All that he achieved at the moment was to hurry the inevitable
disclosure of the contents of a treaty which no one desired to conceal,
except in deference to official form. Mason's note and copy of the treaty,
made up into a pamphlet, were issued from Bache's press on July 2, and
hundreds of copies were soon being carried by eager riders north and
south throughout the Union.

Everywhere, as the treaty traveled, the popular wrath was kindled.
The first explosion came in Boston, Federalist Boston, devoted beyond
any other town in the country to Washington and his administration.
There was a town meeting in Faneuil Hall, violent speeches were made,
and a committee was appointed to draw up a memorial to the President
against ratification. This remonstrance was despatched at once by special
messenger, who seemed to carry the torch of Malise instead of a set of dry
resolutions. Everywhere the anger and indignation flamed forth. The
ground had been carefully prepared, for, ever since Jay sailed, the partisans of the French had been denouncing him and his mission, predict-
ing failure, and, in one case at least, burning him in effigy before it was
known whether he had done anything at all. As soon as the news spread
that the treaty had actually arrived, the attacks were multiplied in number and grew ever more bitter as the Senate consulted. The popular
mind was so worked up that in Boston a British vessel had been burned

on suspicion that she was a privateer, while in New York there had been street fights and rioting because of an insult to a French flag. In such a state of feeling, artificially stimulated and ingeniously misled, the most brilliant diplomatic triumph would have had but slight chance of approval. Jay's moderate achievement was better than his enemies expected, but it was sufficient for their purpose, and the popular fury blazed up and ran through the country, like a whirlwind of fire over the parched prairie. Everywhere the example of Boston was followed, meetings were held, committees appointed, and memorials against the treaty sent to the President. In New York Hamilton was stoned when he attempted to speak in favor of ratification; and less illustrious persons, who ventured to differ from the crowd, were ducked and otherwise maltreated. Jay was hanged and burned in effigy in every way that imagination could devise, and copies of his treaty suffered the same fate at the hands of the hangman. Feeling ran highest in the larger towns where there was a mob, but even some of the smaller places and those most Federal in their politics were carried away. The excitement seems also to have been confined for the most part to the seaboard, but after all that was where the bulk of the population lived. The crowd, moreover, was not led by obscure agitators or by violent and irresponsible partisans. The Livingstons in New York, Rodney in Delaware, Gadsden and the Rutledges in South Carolina, were some of the men who guided the meetings and denounced the treaty. On the other hand, the friends and supporters of the administration appeared stunned, and for weeks no opposition to the popular movement except that attempted by Hamilton was apparent. Even the administration was divided, for Randolph was as hostile to the treaty as it was possible for a man of his temperament to be.

The crisis was indeed a serious one. There have been worse in our history, but this was one of the gravest; and never did a President stand, so far as any one could see, so utterly alone. With his own party silenced and even divided, with the opposition rampant, and with popular excitement at fever heat, Washington was left to take his course alone and unsupported. It was the severest trial of his political life, but he met it, as he met the reverses of 1776, calmly and without flinching. He was always

glad to have advice and suggestions. No man ever sought them or benefited from them more than he; yet no man ever lived so little dependent
on others and so perfectly capable of standing alone as Washington. After
the Senate had acted, he made up his mind to conditional ratification. He
withheld his signature on hearing of the provision order, and was ready to
sign as soon as that order was withdrawn. Whether he would make its
withdrawal another condition of his signature he had not determined
when he left Philadelphia for Mount Vernon, and on his arrival he wrote
to Randolph: "The conditional ratification (if the late order, which we
have heard of, respecting provision vessels is not in operation) may, on all
fit occasions, be spoken of as my determination. Unless, from anything
you have heard or met with since I left you, it should be thought more
advisable to communicate further with me on the subject, my opinion
respecting the treaty is the same now that it was, namely, not favorable to
it; but that it is better to ratify it in the manner the Senate have advised,
and with the reservation already mentioned, than to suffer matters to
remain as they are, unsettled." He had already received the Boston resolutions, and had sent them to his cabinet for their consideration. He did
not for a moment underrate their importance, and he saw that they were
the harbingers of others of like character, although he could not yet estimate the full violence of the storm of popular disapprobation. On July 28
he sent his answer to the selectmen of Boston, and it is such an important
paper that it must be given in full. It was as follows:—

UNITED STATES, *28th of July*, 1795.

GENTLEMEN: In every act of my administration I have
sought the happiness of my fellow-citizens. My system for
the attainment of this object has uniformly been to overlook
all personal, local, and partial considerations; to contemplate
the United States as one great whole; to confide that sudden
impressions, and erroneous, would yield to candid reflections; and to consult only the substantial and permanent
interests of our country.

Nor have I departed from this line of conduct on the

occasion which has produced the resolutions contained in your letter of the 13th inst.

Without a predilection for my own judgment, I have weighed with attention every argument which has at any time been brought into view. But the Constitution is the guide which I never can abandon. It has assigned to the President the power of making treaties with the advice and consent of the Senate. It was doubtless supposed that these two branches of government would combine, without passion and with the best means of information, those facts and principles upon which the success of our foreign relations will always depend; that they ought not to substitute for their own convictions the opinions of others, or to seek truth through any channel but that of a temperate and well-informed investigation.

Under this persuasion, I have resolved on the manner of executing the duty before me. To the high responsibility attached to it, I fully submit; and you, gentlemen, are at liberty to make these sentiments known as the grounds of my procedure. While I feel the most lively gratitude for the many instances of approbation from my country, I can no otherwise deserve it than by obeying the dictates of my conscience. With due respect, I am, etc.

It will be noticed that this letter is dated "The United States, 28th of July," which is, I think, the only instance of the sort to be found in his letters. In all his vast correspondence there possibly may be other cases in which he used this method of dating, but one cannot help feeling that on this occasion at least it had a particular significance. It was not George Washington writing from Mount Vernon, but the President, who represented the whole country, pointing out to the people of Boston that the day of small things and of local considerations had gone by. This letter served also as a model for many others. The Boston address had a multitude of successors, and they were all answered in the same strain.

Washington was not a man to underrate popular feeling, for he knew that the strongest bulwark of the government was in sound public opinion. On the other hand, he was one of the rare men who could distinguish between a temporary excitement, no matter how universal, and an abiding sentiment. In this case he quietly resisted the noisy popular demand, believing that the sober second thought of the people would surely be with him; but at the same time the outcry against the treaty, while it could not make him waver in his determination to do what he believed to be right, caused him deep anxiety. The day after he sent his answer to Boston he wrote to Randolph:—

> I view the opposition which the treaty is receiving from the meetings in different parts of the Union in a very serious light; not because there is more weight in any of the objections which are made to it than was foreseen at first, for there is none in some of them, and gross misrepresentations in others; nor as it respects myself personally, for this shall have no influence on my conduct, plainly perceiving, and I am accordingly preparing my mind for it, the obloquy which disappointment and malice are collecting to heap upon me. But I am alarmed at the effect it may have on and the advantage the French government may be disposed to make of, the spirit which is at work to cherish a belief in them that the treaty is calculated to favor Great Britain at their expense. . . . To sum the whole up in a few words I have never, since I have been in the administration of the government, seen a crisis, which, in my judgment, has been so pregnant with interesting events, nor one from which more is to be apprehended, whether viewed on one side or the other.

He already felt that it might be necessary for him to return to Philadelphia at any moment; and, writing to Randolph to this effect two days later, he said:—

To be wise and temperate, as well as firm, the present crisis most eminently calls for. There is too much reason to believe, from the pains which have been taken before, at, and since the advice of the Senate respecting the treaty, that the prejudices against it are more extensive than is generally imagined. This I have lately understood to be the case in this quarter from men who are of no party, but well-disposed to the present administration. Nor should it be otherwise, when no stone has been left unturned that could impress on the minds of the people the most arrant misrepresentation of facts; that their rights have not only been *neglected*, but absolutely *sold*; that there are no reciprocal advantages in the treaty; that the benefits are all on the side of Great Britain; and, what seems to have had more weight with them than all the rest, and to have been most pressed, that the treaty is made with the design to oppress the French, in open violation of our treaty with that nation, and contrary, too, to every principle of gratitude and sound policy. In time, when passion shall have yielded to sober reason, the current may possibly turn; but, in the mean while, this government, in relation to France and England, may be compared to a ship between the rocks of Scylla and Charybdis. If the treaty is ratified, partisans of the French, or rather of war and confusion, will excite them to hostile measures, or at least to unfriendly sentiments; if it is not, there is no foreseeing all the consequences which may follow, as it respects Great Britain.

It is not to be inferred from hence that I am disposed to quit the ground I have taken, unless circumstances more imperious than have yet come to my knowledge should compel it; for there is but one straight course, and that is to seek truth, and pursue it steadily. But these things are mentioned to show that a close investigation of the subject is more than ever necessary, and that there are strong evidences of the necessity of the most circumspect conduct in carrying the determination of government into effect, with prudence, as it respects our own people, and with every exertion to produce a change for the better from Great Britain.

The memorial seems well designed to answer the end proposed, and by the time it is revised and new-dressed, you will probably (either in the resolutions which are or will be handed to me, or in the newspaper publications, which you promise to be attentive to) have seen all the objections against the treaty which have any real force in them, and which may be fit subjects for representation in a memorial, or in the instructions, or both. But how much longer the presentation of the memorial can be delayed without exciting unpleasant sensations here, or involving serious evils elsewhere, you, who are at the scene of information and action, can decide better than I. In a matter, however, so interesting and pregnant with consequences as this treaty, there ought to be no precipitation; but on the contrary, every step should be explored before it is taken, and every word weighed before it is uttered or delivered in writing.

The form of the ratification requires more diplomatic experience and legal knowledge than I possess, or have the means of acquiring at this place, and therefore I shall say nothing about it.

Three days later, on August 3, he wrote again to Randolph to say that the mails had been delayed, and that he had not received the Baltimore resolutions. He then continued:—

The like may be expected from Richmond, a meeting having been had there also, at which Mr. Wythe, it is said, was seated as moderator; by chance more than design, it is added. A queer chance this for the chancellor of the state.

All these things do not shake my determination with respect to the proposed ratifications, nor will they, unless something more imperious and unknown to me should, in the judgment of yourself and the gentlemen with you, make it advisable for me to pause.

A few days later Washington was recalled by a letter from Randolph, and also by a private note from Pickering, which said, mysteriously, that there was a "special reason" for his immediate return. He had been expecting to be recalled at any moment, and he now hastened to Philadelphia, reaching there on August 11. He little dreamed, however, of what had led his two secretaries, one ignorantly and the other wittingly, to hasten his return. On the very day when he dated his letter to the selectmen of Boston as from the United States, the British minister placed in the hands of Mr. Wolcott, the Secretary of the Treasury, an intercepted letter from Fauchet, the French minister, to his own government. This dispatch, bearing the number 10, had come into the possession of Mr. Hammond by a series of accidents; but the British government and its representatives were quick to perceive that the chances of the sea had thrown into their hands a prize of much more value than many French merchantmen. The dispatch thus rescued from the water, where its bearer had cast it, was filled with a long and somewhat imaginative dissertation on political parties in the United States, and with an account of the whiskey rebellion. It also gave the substance of some conversations held by the writer with the Secretary of State. This is not the place, nor would space serve, to examine the details of this famous dispatch, with reference to the American statesman whom it incriminated. On its face it showed that Randolph had held conversations with the French minister which no American Secretary of State ought to have held with any representative of a foreign government, and it appeared further that the most obvious interpretation of certain sentences, in view of the readiness of man to think ill of his neighbor, was that Randolph had suggested corrupt practices. Such was the document, implicating in a most serious way the character of his chief cabinet officer, which Pickering and Wolcott placed in Washington's hands on his arrival in Philadelphia.

Mr. Conway, in his biography of Randolph, devotes many pages to explaining what now followed. His explanations show, certainly, a most refined ingenuity, and form the most elaborate discussion of this incident that has ever appeared. All this effort and ingenuity are needless, however, unless the object be to prove that Randolph was wholly without fault, which is an impossible task. There was nothing complicated about the affair, and nothing strange about the President's course, if we confine ourselves to the plain facts and the order of their occurrence.

Before the treaty went to the Senate, Washington made up his mind to sign it, and when the Senate ratified conditionally, he still adhered to his former opinion. Then came the news of the provision order, and thereupon he paused and withheld his signature, at the same time ordering a memorial against the order to be prepared. But there is no evidence whatever that he changed his mind, or that he had determined to make his signature conditional upon the revocation of the order. To argue that he had is, in fact, misrepresentation. In the letter of July 22, on which so much stress was laid afterwards by Randolph, Washington said that his intention to ratify conditionally was to be announced, if the provision order was not in operation. Put in the converse form, his intention was not to be announced if the order was in operation; but this is very different from saying that his intention had altered, and that he would not sign unless the order was revoked. This last idea was Randolph's, but not Washington's. Indeed, in the very next lines of the same letter he said expressly that his opinion had not changed, that he did not like the treaty, but that it was best to ratify. It is a fair inference, no doubt, that he was considering whether he should change his intention and make his signature conditional; but if this was the case, it is sure beyond a peradventure that his original opinion was only confirmed as the days went by.

He examined with the utmost care all the remonstrances and addresses that were poured in upon him, and found few solid objections, and none that he had not already weighed and disposed of. On July 31 he wrote to Randolph that it was not to be inferred that he was disposed to quit his ground unless more imperious circumstances than had yet come to his knowledge should compel him to do so. The provision order was of course within his knowledge, and therefore had not led him to change his mind. On August 3 he wrote even more strongly that nothing had come to his knowledge to shake his determination. In his letter to Randolph of October 21, giving him full liberty to have and publish everything he desired for his vindication, Washington said: "You know that it was my determination to ratify before submission to the Senate; that the doubts which arose proceeded from the provision order." Doubts are mentioned here, and not changes of intention. If he had changed his mind at any time he would have said so, for he was neither timid nor dishonest, but as a matter of fact he never had changed his mind. He came to Philadelphia with his mind made up to ratify, and that being the case, it was clear that further delay would be wrong and impolitic. The surest way to check the popular excitement and rally the friends of the administration was to act. Suspense fostered opposition more than ratification, for most people accept the inevitable when the deed is done.

The Fauchet letter, therefore, although its revelations astounded and grieved him, had no effect upon his action, which would have been the same in any event; for he had said over and over again that he had not changed his first opinion. In the letter to Randolph, just quoted, he also said: "And finally you know the grounds on which my ultimate decision was taken, as the same were expressed to you, the other secretaries of departments, and the late attorney general, after a thorough investigation of the subject in all the aspects in which it could be placed." As the Fauchet letter was not disclosed to Randolph until after the treaty had been signed, it was impossible that it should have been one of the grounds of the President's decision, for Washington said to him, "You knew the grounds." If we are to suppose that the Fauchet letter had anything to do with the ratification so far as the President himself was concerned, we must, in the face of this letter, set Washington down as a deliberate liar, which is so wholly impossible that it disposes at once of the theory that he was driven into signing by a clever British intrigue.

Here as elsewhere the simple and obvious explanation is the true one, although the whole matter is sufficiently plain on the mere narration of facts. The treaty was a great public question, to be decided on its merits, and the only new point raised by the Fauchet dispatch was how to deal with Randolph himself at this particular juncture. To have shown the letter to him at once would have been to break the cabinet, with the treaty unsigned. It would have resulted in much delay, extending to weeks, unless the President was ready to have an acting secretary sign both treaty and memorial; and it would have added during the continued suspense a fresh subject of excitement to the popular mind. Washington's duty plainly was to carry out his policy and bring the matter to an immediate conclusion, and, as was his custom, he did his duty. If, as Mr. Conway thinks, the Fauchet letter was what compelled the ratification, Washington would have given it to the world at once, and then, having by this means discredited the opposition and roused a feeling against the French, would have signed the treaty. England, of course, had taken advantage of this letter, and equally of course her minister and his influence were against Randolph, who was thought to be unfriendly. Hammond intrigued with our public men just as all the French ministers did. It is humiliating that such should have been the case, but it was due to our recent escape from a colonial condition, and to the way in which we allowed our politics to turn on foreign affairs. Having made up his mind to ratify and end the question, Washington very properly kept silence as to the Fauchet letter until the work was done. To do this, it was necessary of course that he should make no change in his personal attitude toward Randolph, nor was he obliged to do so, for he was too just a man to assume Randolph's guilt until his defense had been made. The ratification was brought before the cabinet at once. There was a sharp discussion, in which it appeared that Randolph had advanced a good deal in his hostility to the treaty, a fact not tending to make the Fauchet business look better; and then ratification was voted, and a memorial against the provision order was adopted. On August 18 the treaty was signed, and on the 19th, Washington, in the presence of his cabinet, placed the Fauchet letter in Randolph's hands. Randolph read it, made some comments, and asked time to offer suitable explanations. He then withdrew, and in a few hours sent in his resignation.

There would be no need, so far as Washington is concerned, to say more on this unfortunate affair of the Secretary of State, were it not for the recent statements made by Randolph's biographer. In order to clear his hero, Mr. Conway represents that Washington, knowing Randolph to be innocent, sacrificed him in great anguish of heart to an imperious political necessity, while the fact was, that nobody sacrificed Randolph except himself. He was represented in a dispatch written by the French minister in a light which, as Washington said, gave rise to strong suspicions; a moderate statement in which every candid man who knew anything about the matter has agreed from that day to this. According to Fauchet, Randolph not only had held conversations wholly unbecoming his position, but on the same authority he was represented to have asked for money. That the Secretary of State was corrupt, no one who knew him, as Jefferson said, for one moment believed. Whether he disposed of this charge or not, it was plain to his friends, as it is to posterity, that Randolph was a perfectly honorable man. But neither his own vindication nor that of his biographer have in the least palliated or even touched the real error which he committed.

As Secretary of State, the head of the cabinet, and in charge of our foreign relations, he had, according to Fauchet's dispatch and to his own admissions, entered into relations with a foreign minister which ought to have been as impossible as they were discreditable to an American statesman. That Fauchet believed that Randolph deceived him did not affect the merits of the case, nor, if true, did it excuse Randolph, especially as everybody with whom he was brought into close contact seems at some time or other to have had doubts of his sincerity. As a matter of fact, Randolph could find no defense except to attack Washington and discuss our foreign relations, and his biographer has followed the same line. What was it then that Washington had actually done which called for assault? He had been put in possession of an official document which on its face implicated his Secretary of State in the intrigues of a foreign minister, and suggested that he was open to corruption. These were the views which the public, having no personal knowledge of Randolph, would be sure to take, and as a matter of fact actually took, when the affair became known. There was a great international question to be settled, and settled without delay. This was done in a week, during which time Washington kept silent, as his public duty required. The moment the treaty was signed he handed Fauchet's dispatch to Randolph and asked for an explanation. None knew of the dispatch except the cabinet officers, through whom it had necessarily come. Washington did not prejudge the case; he did not dismiss Randolph with any mark of displeasure, as he would have been quite justified in doing. He simply asked for explanation, and threw open his own correspondence and the archives of the department, so that Randolph might have every opportunity for defense. It is difficult to see how Washington could have done less in dealing with Randolph, or in what way he could have shown greater consideration.

Randolph resigned of his own motion, and then cried out against Washington because he had been obliged to pay the penalty of his own errors. When it is considered that Washington did absolutely nothing to Randolph except to hand him Fauchet's dispatch and accept his consequent resignation, the talk about Randolph's forgiving him becomes simply ludicrous. Randolph saw his own error, was angry with himself, and, like the rest of humanity, proceeded to vent his anger on somebody else, but unfortunately he had the bad taste to turn at the outset to the newspapers. Like Mr. Snodgrass, he took off his coat in public and announced in a loud voice that he was going to begin. The President's only response was to open the archives and bid him publish everything he desired. Randolph then wrote the President a private letter, which was angry and impertinent; "full of innuendoes," said the recipient. Washington drafted a sharp reply, and then out of pure kindness withheld it, and let the private letter drop into silence, whither the bulky "Vindication," which vindicated nobody, soon followed it. The fact was, that Washington treated Randolph with great kindness and forbearance. He had known him long; he was fond of him on his own account as well as his father's; he appreciated Randolph's talents; but he knew on reading that dispatch, if he had never guessed it before, that Randolph, although honest and clever, and certainly not bad, was a dangerously weak man. Others among our public men had put themselves into relations with foreign representatives which it is now intolerable to contemplate, but Randolph, besides being found out at the moment, had, after the fashion of weak natures, gone further and shown more feebleness than any one else had. Washington's conduct was so perfectly simple, and the facts of the case were so plain, that it would seem impossible to complicate them. The contemporary verdict was harsh, crushing, and unjust in many respects to Randolph. The verdict of posterity, which is both gentler and fairer to the secretary, will certainly at the same time sustain Washington's course at every point as sensible, direct, and proper.

Only one question remains which demands a word before tracing briefly the subsequent fate of the Jay treaty, and that is, to know exactly why the President signed it. The answer is fortunately not difficult. There was a choice of evils. When Washington determined to send a special envoy, he said: "My objects are, to prevent a war, if justice can be obtained by fair and strong representations (to be made by a special envoy) of the injuries which this country has sustained from Great Britain in various ways; to put it into a complete state of military defense; and to provide eventually such measures for execution as seem to be now pending in Congress, if negotiation in a reasonable time proves unsuccessful." From these views he never varied. The treaty was not a perfect one, but it had good features and was probably, as has been said, the best that could then be obtained. It settled some vexed questions, and it gave us time. If the United States could only have time without making undue sacrifice, they could pass beyond the stage when a foreign war with its consequent suffering and debt would endanger our national existence. If they could only have time to grow into a nation, there would be no difficulty in settling all their disputes with other people satisfactorily, either by war or negotiation. But if the national bonds were loosened, then all was lost. It was in this spirit that Washington signed the Jay treaty; and although there was much in it that he did not like, and although men were bitterly divided about the ratification, a dispassionate posterity has come to believe that he was right at the most difficult if not the most perilous crisis in his career.

The signature of the treaty, however, did not put an end to the attacks upon it, or upon the action of the Senate and the Executive.

Nevertheless, it turned the tide, and, as Washington foresaw, brought out a strong movement in its favor. Hamilton began the work by the publication of the letters of "Camillus." The opposition newspapers sneered, but after Jefferson had read a few numbers he begged Madison in alarm to answer them. His fears were well grounded, for the letters were reprinted in newspapers throughout the country, and their powerful and temperate arguments made converts and strengthened the friends of the administration everywhere. The approaching surrender of the posts gratified the western people when they at last stopped to think about it. The obnoxious provision order was revoked, and the traders and merchants found that security and commerce even under unpleasant restrictions were a great deal better than the uncertainty and the vexatious hostilities to which they had before been exposed. Those who had been silent, although friendly to the policy of the government, now began to meet in their turn and send addresses to Congress; for in the House of Representatives the last battle was to be fought.

That body came together under the impression of the agitation and excitement which had been going on all through the summer. There was a little wrangling at the opening over the terms to be employed in the answer to the President's message, and then the House relapsed into quiet, awaiting the formal announcement of the treaty. At last the treaty arrived with the addition of the suspending article, and the President proclaimed it to be the law of the land, and sent a copy to the House. Livingston, of New York, at once moved a resolution, asking the President to send in all the papers relating to the negotiation, and boldly placed the motion on the ground that the House was vested with a discretionary power as to carrying the treaty into execution. On this principle the debate went on for three weeks, and then the resolution passed by 62 to 37. A great constitutional question was thus raised, for there was no pretense that the papers were really needed, inasmuch as committees had seen them all, and they contained practically nothing which was not already known.

Washington took the request into consideration, and asked his cabinet whether the House had the right, as set forth in the resolutions, to call for the papers, and if not, whether it was expedient to furnish them. Both questions were unanimously answered in the negative. The inquiry was largely formal, and Washington had no real doubts on the point involved. He wrote to Hamilton: "I had from the first moment, and from the fullest conviction in my own mind, resolved *to resist the principle*, which was evidently intended to be established by the call of the House of Representatives; and only deliberated on the manner in which this could be done with the least bad consequences." His only question was as to the method of resistance, and he finally decided to refuse absolutely, and did so in a message setting forth his reasons. He said that the intention of the constitutional convention was known to him, and that they had intended to vest the treaty-making power exclusively in the Executive and Senate. On that principle he had acted, and in that belief foreign nations had negotiated, and the House had hitherto acquiesced. He declared further that the assent of the House was not necessary to the validity of treaties; that they had all necessary information; and "as it is essential to the due administration of the government that the boundaries fixed by the Constitution should be preserved, a just regard to the Constitution and to the duty of my office, under all the circumstances of this case, forbid a compliance with your request." The question was a difficult one, but there could be no doubt as to Washington's opinion, and the weight of authority has sustained his view. From the practical and political side there can be little question that his position was extremely sound. In a letter to Carrington he gave the reasons for his action, and no better statement of the argument in a general way has ever been made. He wrote:—

> No candid man in the least degree acquainted with the progress of this business will believe for a moment that the ostensible dispute was about papers, or whether the British treaty was a good one or a bad one, but whether there should be a treaty at all without the concurrence of the House of Representatives. This was striking at once, and that boldly, too, at the fundamental principles of the Constitution; and,

if it were established, would render the treaty-making power not only a nullity, but such an absolute absurdity as to reflect disgrace on the framers of it. For will any one suppose that they who framed, or those who adopted, that instrument ever intended to give the power to the President and Senate to make treaties, and, declaring that when made and ratified they should be the supreme law of the land, would in the same breath place it in the power of the House of Representatives to fix their vote on them, unless apparent marks of fraud or corruption (which in equity would set aside any contract) accompanied the measure, or such striking evidence of national injury attended their adoption as to make a war or any other evil preferable? Every unbiased mind will answer in the negative.

What the source and what the object of all this struggle is, I submit to my fellow-citizens. Charity would lead me to hope that the motives to it would be pure. Suspicions, however, speak a different language, and my tongue for the present shall be silent.

No man who has ever held high office in this country had a more real deference for the popular will than Washington. But he also had always a keen sensitiveness to the dignity and the prerogatives of the office which he happened to hold, whether it was that of president or general of the armies. This arose from no personal feeling, for he was too great a man ever to worry about his own dignity; but he esteemed the great offices to which he was called to be trusts, which were to suffer no injury while in his hands. He regarded the attempt of the House of Representatives to demand the papers as a matter of right as an encroachment on the rights of the Executive Department, and he therefore resisted it at once, and after his usual fashion left no one in any doubt as to his views. So far as the President was concerned, the struggle ended here; but it was continued for some time longer in the House, where the debate went on for a fortnight, with the hostile majority surely and steadily declining. The current out-doors ran more and more strongly every day in favor of the administration, until at last the contest ended with Ames's great speech, and then the resolution to carry out the treaty prevailed. Washington's policy had triumphed, and was accepted by the country.

The Jay treaty and its ratification had, however, other results than mere domestic conflicts. Spain, acting under French influence, threatened to rescind the Pinckney treaty which had just been made so advantageously to the United States; but, like most Spanish performances at that time, these threats evaporated in words, and the Mississippi remained open. With France, however, the case was very different. Our demand for the recall of Genet had been met by a counter-demand for the recall of Morris, to which, of course, we were obliged to accede, and the question as to the latter's successor was a difficult and important one. Washington himself had been perfectly satisfied with the conduct of Morris, but he was also aware that the known dislike of that brilliant diplomatist to the revolutionary methods then dominant in Paris had seriously complicated our relations with France. He wished by all fair means to keep France in good humor, and he therefore determined that Morris's successor should be a man whose friendship toward the French republic was well known: His first choice was Madison, which would have answered admirably, for Madison was preëminently a safe man. Very unluckily, however, Madison either could not or would not go, and the President's final choice was by no means equally good.

It was, of course, most desirable that the new minister should be *persona grata* to the republic, but it was vastly more important that he should be in cordial sympathy with the administration at home, for no administration ought ever to select for a foreign mission, especially at a critical moment, any one outside the ranks of its own supporters. This was the mistake which Washington, from the best of motives, now committed by appointing James Monroe to be minister to France. It is one of the puzzles of our history to reconcile the respectable and commonplace gentleman, who for two terms as President of the United States had less opposition than ever fell to the lot of any other man in that office, with the violent, unscrupulous, and extremely light-headed politician who figured as senator from Virginia and minister to France at the close of the last century. Monroe at the time of his appointment had distinguished himself chiefly by his extreme opposition to the administration, and by his intrigues against Hamilton, which were so dishonestly conducted that they ultimately compelled the publication of the "Reynolds Pamphlet," a sore trial to its author, and a lasting blot on the fame of the enemy who made the publication necessary. From such a man loyalty to the President who appointed him was hardly to be expected. But there was no reason to suppose that he would lose his head, and forget that he was an American, and not a French citizen.

Monroe reached Paris in the summer of 1794. He was publicly received by the Convention, made an undignified and florid speech, received the national embrace from the president of the Convention, and then effected an exchange of flags with more embracings and addresses. But when he came to ask redress for the wrongs committed against our merchants, he got no satisfaction. So far as he was concerned, this appears to have been a matter of indifference, for he at once occupied himself with the French proposition that we should lend France five millions of dollars, and France in return was to see to it that we obtained control of the Spanish possessions in North America. Monroe fell in with this precious scheme to make the United States a dependency of France, and received as a reward vast promises as to what the great republic would do for us. Meantime he regarded with suspicion Jay's movements in England, and endeavored to obtain information, if not control, of that negotiation. In this he completely failed; but he led the French government to believe, first, that the English treaty would not be made, then that it would not be ratified, and finally that the House would not make the appropriations necessary to carry it into effect; and all the time he was compromising his own government by his absurd efforts to involve it in an offensive alliance with France. The upshot of it all was that he was disowned at home, discredited in France, and brought our relations with that nation into a state of dangerous complication, without obtaining any redress for our injuries.

Washington at first, little as he liked the theatrical performances with

which Monroe opened his mission, wrote about him with great moderation to Jay, who was naturally much annoyed by the manner in which
Monroe had tried to interfere with his negotiations. Six months later,
however, Washington saw only too plainly that he had been mistaken in
his minister to France. He wrote to Randolph on July 24, 1795: "The
conduct of Mr. Monroe is of a piece with that of the other; and one can
scarcely forbear thinking that these acts are part of a premeditated system to embarrass the executive government." When it became clear that
Monroe had omitted to explain properly our reasons for treating with
England, that he had held out hopes to the French government which
were totally unauthorized, that he had brought on a renewal of the hostilities of that government, and that he had placed us in all ways in the
most unenviable light, Washington recalled him, and appointed Charles
Cotesworth Pinckney in his place. By this time too he was thoroughly
disgusted with Monroe's performances, and in his letter to Pinckney, on
July 8, 1796, offering him the appointment to Paris, he said: "It is a fact
too notorious to be denied that the greatest embarrassments under which
the administration of this government labors proceed from the counter-
action of people among ourselves, who are more disposed to promote the
views of another nation than to establish a national character of their own;
and that, unless the virtuous and independent men of this country will
come forward, it is not difficult to predict the consequences. Such is my
decided opinion." He felt, as he wrote to Hamilton at the close of his
administration, that "the conduct of France towards this country is,
according to my ideas of it, outrageous beyond conception; not to be war-
ranted by her treaty with us, by the law of nations, by any principle of justice, or even by a regard to decent appearances." This was after we had
begun to reap the humiliations which Monroe's folly had prepared for us,
and it is easy to understand that Washington regarded their author with
anything but satisfaction or approval.

The culprit himself took a very different view, came home presently
in great wrath, and proceeded to pose as a martyr and compile a vindication, which he entitled "A View of the Conduct of the Executive," and
which surpassed in bulk any of the vindications in which that period of

our history was prolific. It was published after Washington had retired to private life, and did not much disturb his serenity. In a letter to Nicholas, on March 8, 1798, he said: "If the executive is chargeable with 'premeditating the destruction of Mr. Monroe in his appointment, because he was the *centre* around which the Republican party rallied in the Senate' (a circumstance quite new to me), it is to be hoped he will give it credit for its lenity toward that gentleman in having designated several others, not of the Senate, as victims to this office *before* the sacrifice of Mr. Monroe was even had in contemplation. As this must be some consolation to him and his friends, I hope they will embrace it."

Washington apparently did not think Monroe was worthy of anything more serious than a little sarcasm, and he was quite content, as he said, to leave the book to the tribunal to which the author himself had appealed. He read the book, however, with care, and in his methodical way he appended a number of notes, which are worth consideration by all persons interested in the character of Washington. They are especially to be commended to those who think that he was merely good and wise and solemn, for it would be difficult to find a better piece of destructive criticism, or a more ready and thorough knowledge of complicated foreign relations, than are contained in these brief notes. His own opinion of Monroe is concisely stated in one of them. Referring to one of that gentleman's statements he said: "For this there is no better proof than his own opinion; whilst there is abundant evidence of his being a mere tool in the hands of the French government, cajoled and led away always by unmeaning assurances of friendship." With this brief comment we may leave the Monroe incident. His appointment was a mistake, and increased existing complications, which were not finally settled until the next administration.

Monroe's recall was the last act, however, in the long contest of the Jay treaty, and it was also, as it happened, the last important act in Washington's foreign policy. That policy has been traced here in its various branches, but it is worth while to look at it as a whole before leaving it, in order to see just what the President aimed at and just what he effected. The guiding principle, which had been with him from the day when he took command of the army at Cambridge, was to make the United States independent. The war had achieved this so far as our connection with England was concerned, but it still remained to prove to the world that we were an independent nation in fact as well as in name. For this the neutrality policy was adopted and carried out. We were not only to cease from dependence on the nations of Europe, but we were to go on our own way with a policy of our own wholly apart from them. It was also necessary to lift up our own politics, to detach our minds from those of other nations, and to make us truly Americans. All this Washington's policy did so far as it was possible to do it in the time given to him. A new generation had to come upon the stage before our politics were finally taken out of colonialism and made national and American, but the idea was that of the first President. It was the foresight and the courage of Washington which at the outset placed the United States in their relations with foreign nations on the ground of a firm, independent, and American policy.

His foreign policy had, however, some immediate practical results which were of vast importance. In December, 1795, he wrote to Morris: "It is well known that peace has been (to borrow a modern phrase) the order of the day with me since the disturbances in Europe first commenced. My policy has been, and will continue to be while I have the honor to remain in the administration, to maintain friendly terms with, but to be independent of, all the nations of the earth; to share in the broils of none; to fulfill our own engagements; to supply the wants and be carriers for them all; being thoroughly convinced that it is our policy and interest to do so. Nothing short of self-respect and that justice which is essential to a national character ought to involve us in war; for sure I am, if this country is preserved in tranquillity twenty years longer, it may bid defiance in a just cause to any power whatever; such in that time would be its population, wealth, and resources."

He wanted time, but he wanted space also for his country; and if we look for a moment at the results of his foreign policy we see clearly how he got both. The time gained by peace without any humiliating concessions is plain enough. If we look a little further and a little deeper, we can

see how he compassed his other object. The true and the first mission of
the American people was, in Washington's theory, the conquest of the
continent which stretched away wild and silent behind them, for in that
direction lay the sure road to national greatness. The first step was to
bind by interest, trade, and habit of communication the Atlantic States
with the settlements beyond the mountains, and for this he had planned
canals and highways in the days of the confederation. The next step was
to remove every obstacle which fettered the march of American settlement; and for this he rolled back the Indian tribes, patiently negotiated
with Spain until the Mississippi was opened, and at great personal sacrifice and trial signed the Jay treaty, and obtained the surrender of the
British posts. When Washington went out of office, the way was open to
the western movement; the dangers of disintegration by reason of foreign
intrigues on the frontier were removed; peace had been maintained; and
the national sentiment had had opportunity for rapid growth. France had
discovered that, although she had been our ally, we were not her depen-
dants; other nations had been brought to perceive that the United States
meant to have a foreign policy all its own; and the American people were
taught that their first duty was to be Americans and nothing else. There
is no need to comment on or to praise the greatness of a policy with such
objects and results as these. The mere summary is enough, and it speaks
for itself and for its author in a way which makes words needless.

CHAPTER XVI

WASHINGTON AS A PARTY MAN

WASHINGTON WAS NOT chosen to office by a political party; he considered parties to be perilous things, and he entered the presidency determined to have nothing to do with them. Yet, as has already been pointed out, he took the members of his cabinet entirely from one of the two parties which then existed, and which had been produced by the divisions over the Constitution and its adoption. To this charge he would no doubt have replied that the parties caused by the constitutional differences had ceased to exist when that instrument went into operation, and that it was to be supposed that all men were then united in support of the government. Accepting this view of it, it only remains to see how he fared when new and purely political parties, as was inevitable, sprang into active life.

Whatever his own opinions may have been as to parties and party-strife, Washington was under no delusions in regard either to human nature or to himself, and he had no expectation that everything he said or did would meet with universal approbation. He well knew that there would be dissatisfaction, and no man ever took high office with a mind more ready to bear criticism and to profit by it. Three months after his inauguration he wrote to his friend David Stuart: "I should like to be informed of the public opinion of both men and measures, and of none more than myself; not so much of what may be thought commendable parts, if any, of my conduct, as of those which are conceived to be of a different complexion. The man who means to commit no wrong will never

375

be guilty of enormities; consequently he can never be unwilling to learn what are ascribed to him as foibles. If they are really such, the knowledge of them in a well-disposed mind will go halfway towards a reform. If they are not errors, he can explain and justify the motives of his actions." This readiness to hear criticism and this watching of public opinion were characteristic, for his one desire was to know the truth and never deceive himself. His journey through New England in the autumn of that year, his visit to Rhode Island a year later, and his trip through the southern States in the spring of 1791, had a double motive. He wished to bring home to the people the existence and the character of the new government by his appearance among them as its representative; and he desired also to learn from his own observation, and from inquiries made on the spot, what the people thought of the administration and its policies, and of the doings of Congress. He was a keen observer and a good gatherer of information; for he was patient and persistent, and had that best of all gifts for getting at public opinion, an absolute and cheerful readiness to listen to advice from any one. His travels all had the same result. In the South as in New England he found that the people were pleased with the new government, and contented with the prosperity which began at once to flow from the adoption of a stable national system.

More credit, if anything, was given to it than it really deserved; for, as he had written to Lafayette before the Constitution went into effect, "Many blessings will be attributed to our new government which are now taking their rise from that industry and frugality into which the people have been forced from necessity." Whether this were true or not, the new government was entitled to the benefit of all accidents, and Washington's correct conclusion was that the great body of the people were heartily with him and his administration. But he was also quite aware that all the criticism was not friendly, and as the measures of the government one by one passed Congress, he saw divisions of sentiment appear, slight at first, but deepening and hardening with each successive contest. Indeed, he had not been in office a year when he wrote a long letter to Stuart deploring the sectionalism which had begun to show itself. The South was complaining that everything was done in the interest of the northern and eastern States, and against this idea Washington argued with great force. He was especially severe on the unreasonable and childish character of such grievances, and he attributed the feeling in certain States largely to the outcries of persons who had come home disappointed in some personal matter from the seat of government. "It is to be lamented," he said, "that the editors of the different gazettes in the Union do not more generally and more correctly (instead of stuffing their papers with scurrility and nonsensical declamation, which few would read if they were apprised of the contents) publish the debates in Congress on all great national questions. And this, with no uncommon pains, every one of them might do." Washington evidently believed that there was no serious danger of the people going wrong if they were only fully informed. But the able editors of that day no doubt felt that they and their correspondents were better fitted to enlighten the public than any one else could be, and there is no evidence that any of them ever followed the President's suggestion.

The jealousies and the divisions in Congress, which Washington watched with hearty dislike on account of their sectional character, began, as is well known, with the financial measures of the Treasury. As time went on they became steadily more marked and better defined, and at last they spread to the cabinet. Jefferson had returned to take his place as Secretary of State after an absence of many years, and during that time he had necessarily dropped out of the course of home politics. He came back with a very moderate liking for the Constitution, and an intention undoubtedly to do his best as a member of the cabinet. His first and most natural impulse, of course, was to fall in with the administration of which he was a part; and so completely did he do this that it was at his table that the famous bargain was made which assumed the state debts and took the capital to the banks of the Potomac.

Exactly what led to the first breach between Jefferson and Hamilton, whose financial policy was then in the full tide of success, is not now very easy to determine. Jefferson's action was probably due to a mixture of motives and a variety of causes, as is generally the case with men, even when they are founders of the democratic party. In the first place,

Jefferson very soon discovered that Hamilton was looked upon as the leader in the cabinet and in the policies of the administration, and this fact excited a very natural jealousy on his part, because he was the official head of the President's advisers. In the second place, it was inevitable that Jefferson should dislike Hamilton, for there never were two men more unlike in character and in their ways of looking at things. Hamilton was bold, direct, imperious, and masculine; he went straight to his mark, and if he encountered opposition he either rode over it or broke it down. When Jefferson met with opposition he went round it or undermined it; he was adroit, flexible, and extremely averse to open fighting. There was also good ground for a genuine difference of opinion between the two secretaries in regard to the policy of the government. Jefferson was a thorough representative of the great democratic movement of the time. At bottom his democracy was of the sensible, practical American type, but he had come home badly bitten by many of the wild notions which at that moment pervaded Paris. A man of much less insight than Jefferson would have had no difficulty in perceiving that Hamilton and his friends were not in sympathy with these ideas. They hoped for the establishment of a republic, but they desired for it a highly energetic and centralized government not devoid of aristocratic tendencies. This fundamental difference of opinion, increased as it was by personal jealousies, soon put Jefferson, therefore, into an attitude of hostility to the men who were then guiding the policy of the government. The new administration had been so successful that there was at first practically no party of opposition, and the task before Jefferson involved the creation of a party, the formulation of principles, and the definition of issues, with appropriate shibboleths for popular consumption. Jefferson knew that Hamilton and all who fought with him were as sincerely in favor of a republic as he himself was; but his unerring genius in political management told him that he could never raise a party or make a party-cry out of the statement that, while he favored a democratic republic, the men to whom he was opposed preferred one of a more aristocratic caste. It was necessary to have something much more highly seasoned than this. So he took the ground that his opponents were monarchists, bent on establishing a monarchy in this country, and were backed by a "corrupt squadron" in Congress in the pay of the Treasury. This was of course utter nonsense, but it served its purpose admirably. Jefferson, indeed, shouted these cries so much that he almost came to believe in them himself, and sympathetic writers to this day repeat them as if they had reality instead of having been mere noise to frighten the unwary. The prime object of it all was to make the great leaders odious by connecting them in the popular mind with the royal government that had been overthrown.

Jefferson's first move was a covert one. In the spring of 1791 he received Thomas Paine's "Rights of Man," and straightway sent the pamphlet to the printer with a note of approbation reflecting upon John Adams. The pamphlet promptly appeared in a reprint with the note prefixed. It made much stir, and the published approval of the Secretary of State excited a great deal of criticism, much of which was very hostile. Jefferson thereupon expressed extreme surprise that his note had been printed, and on the plea of explaining the matter wrote to Washington a letter, in which he declared that his friend Mr. Adams, for whom he had a most cordial esteem, was an apostate to hereditary monarchy and nobility. He further described his old friend as a political heretic and as the bellwether Davila, upon whom and whose writings Mr. Adams had recently been publishing some discourses. It is but fair to say that no more ingenious attack on the Vice-President could have been made, but the purpose of it was simply to arrest the public attention for the real struggle which was to follow.

The true object of all these movements was to rally a party and break down Jefferson's great colleague in the cabinet. The "Rights of Man" served to start the discussion; and the next step was to bring on from New York Philip Freneau, a verse-writer and journalist, and make him translating clerk in the State Department, and editor of an opposition newspaper known as the "National Gazette." The new journal proceeded to do its work after the fashion of the time. It teemed with abuse not only of Hamilton and Adams and all the supporters of the treasury measures, denouncing them as "monarchists," "aristocrats," and "a corrupt squadron," but it even began a series of coarse assaults upon the

President himself. Jefferson, of course, denied that he had anything to do with the writing in the newspaper, and Freneau made oath at the time that the Secretary wrote nothing; but in his old age he declared that Jefferson wrote or dictated all the most abusive articles, and he showed a file of the "Gazette" with these articles marked. Strict veracity was not the strongest characteristic of either Freneau or Jefferson, and it is really of but little consequence whether Freneau was lying in his old age or in the prime of life. The undoubted facts of the case are enough to fix the responsibility upon Jefferson, where it belongs. The editor of a newspaper devoted to abusing the administration was brought to Philadelphia by the Secretary of State, was given a place in his department, and was his confidential friend. Jefferson himself took advantage of his position to gather material for attacks upon his chief, and upon his colleagues, to whom he was bound to be loyal by every rule which dictates the conduct of honorable men. He did not, moreover, content himself with this outside work. It has been too much overlooked that Jefferson, in addition to forming a party and organizing attacks upon the Secretary of the Treasury and his friends, sought in the first instance to break down Hamilton in the cabinet, to deprive him of the confidence of Washington, and by driving him from the administration to get control himself. At no time did Jefferson ever understand Washington, but he knew him well enough to be quite aware that he would never give up a friend like Hamilton on account of any newspaper attacks. He therefore took a more insidious method.

Knowing that Washington was in the habit of consulting with old friends at home of all shades of opinion in regard to public affairs, he contrived through their agency to have his own charges against Hamilton laid before the President. He also, to make perfectly sure, wrote himself to Washington, candidly setting forth outside criticism, and his letter took the form of a well-arranged indictment of the Treasury measures. This method had the advantage of assailing Hamilton without incurring any responsibility, and the charges were skilfully formulated and ingeniously constructed to raise in the mind of the reader every possible suspicion. At this point Washington comes for the first time into the famous contro-

versy from which our two great political parties were born. He did exactly
what Jefferson would not have done, sent the charges all duly formulated
to Hamilton, and asked him his opinion about them. As the accusations
thus made against the policies of the government and the Secretary of
the Treasury were all mere wind of the "monarchist" and "corrupt
squadron" order, Hamilton disposed of them with very little difficulty.
The whole proceeding, if Jefferson was aware of it at the time, must have
been a great disappointment to him. But his mistake was the natural error
of an ingenious man wasting his efforts on one of great directness and
perfect simplicity of character. Hamilton's answer was what Washington
undoubtedly expected. He knew the hollowness of the attack, but none
the less he was made anxious by it as an indication of the serious party
divisions rising about him. This, however, was but the beginning, and he
was soon to have much more direct evidence of the grave nature of a
political conflict, which he then could not bring himself to believe was
irrepressible.

Hamilton, on his side, was not the most patient of men, and although
he bore the attacks of Freneau for some time in silence he finally retali-
ated. He did not get any one to do his fighting for him, but under a thin
disguise proceeded to answer in Fenno's newspaper the abuse of the
"National Gazette." He was the best political writer in the country, and
when he struck, his blows told. Jefferson winced and cried out under the
punishment, but it would have been more dignified in Hamilton to have
kept out of the newspapers. Still there was the fight. It had gone from the
cabinet to the press, and the public knew that the two principal secretaries were at swords' points and were marshaling behind them strong
political forces. The point had been reached where the President was
compelled to interfere unless he wished his administration to be thoroughly discredited by the bitter and open conflicts of its members.

He wrote to both secretaries in a grave and almost pathetic tone of
remonstrance, urging them to abandon their quarrel, and, sinking minor
differences, to work with him for the success of the Constitution to which
they were both devoted. Each man replied after his fashion. Hamilton's
letter was short and straightforward. He could not profess to have

changed his opinion as to the conduct or purpose of his colleague, but he regretted the strife which had arisen, and promised to do all that was in his power to allay it by ceasing from further attacks. Jefferson wrote at great length, controverting Hamilton's published letters in a way which showed that he was still smarting from the well-aimed shafts. He also contrived to make his own defense the vehicle for a renewal of all his accusations against the Treasury, and he wound up by saying that he looked forward to retirement with the longing of "a wave-worn mariner," and that he should reserve any further fighting that he had to do until he was out of office. Soon after he followed this letter with another, containing a collection of extracts from his own correspondence while in Paris, to show his devotion to the Constitution. One is irresistibly reminded by all this of the Player Queen—"The lady protests too much, methinks." Washington had not accused Jefferson of lack of loyalty to the Constitution, indeed he had made no accusations against him of any kind; but Jefferson knew that his own position was a false one, and he could not refrain from taking a defensive tone. Washington, in his reply, said that he needed no proofs of Jefferson's fidelity to the Constitution, and reiterated his earnest desire for an accommodation of all differences. "I will frankly and solemnly declare," he said, "that I believe the views of both of you to be pure and well-meant, and that experience only will decide with respect to the salutariness of the measures which are the subjects of dispute. . . . I could, and indeed was about to, add more on this interesting subject, but will forbear, at least for the present, after expressing a wish that the cup which has been presented to us may not be snatched from our lips by a discordance of action, when I am persuaded there is no discordance in your views."

The difficulty was that there was not only discordance in the views of the two secretaries, but a fundamental political difference, extending throughout the people, which they typified. The accommodation of views and the support of the Constitution could only mean a support of Washington's administration and its measures. Those measures not only had the President's approval, but they were in many respects peculiarly his own, and in them he rightly saw the success and maintenance of the

Constitution. But, unfortunately for the interests of harmony, these measures were either devised or ardently sustained by the Secretary of the Treasury. They were not the measures of the Secretary of State, and received from him either lukewarm support or active, if furtive, hostility. The only peace possible was in Jefferson's giving in his entire adherence to the policies of Washington and Hamilton, which were radically opposed to his own. In one word, a real, profound, and inevitable party division had come, and it had found the opposing chiefs side by side in the cabinet.

Against this conclusion Washington struggled hard. He had come in as the representative and by the votes of the whole people, and he shrank from any step which would seem to make him lean on a party for support in his administration. He had made up his cabinet with what he very justly considered the strongest material. He believed that a breaking up of the cabinet or a change in its membership would be an injury to the cause of good government, and he was so entirely single-minded in his own views and wishes, that, with all his knowledge of human nature, he found it difficult to understand how any one could differ from him materially. Moreover, having started with the firm intention of governing without party, he determined, with his usual persistence, to carry it through, if it were possible. When party feeling had once developed, and division had sprung up between the two principal officers of his cabinet, no greater risk could have been run than that which Washington took in refusing to make the changes which were necessary to render the administration harmonious. With any lesser man, such a perilous experiment would have failed and brought with it disastrous consequences. There is no greater proof of the force of his will and the weight and strength of his character than the fact that he held in his cabinet Jefferson and Hamilton, despite their hatred for each other and each other's principles, and that he not only prevented any harm, but actually drew great results from the talents of each of them. Yet, with all his strength of grasp, this ill-assorted combination could not last, although Washington resisted the inevitable in a surprising way, and he even begged Jefferson to remain when the impossibility of doing so had become quite clear to that gentleman.

The remonstrance in regard to the Freneau matter had but a temporary effect. Hamilton stopped his attacks, it is true; but Jefferson did not
discontinue his; and he set on foot a movement which was designed to
destroy his rival's public and private reputation. Hamilton met this attack
in Congress, where he refuted it signally; and although the ostensible
movers were members of the House, the defeat recoiled on the Secretary
of State. Having failed in Congress and before the public to ruin his
opponent, and having failed equally to shake Washington's confidence in
Hamilton or the latter's influence in the administration, Jefferson made
up his mind that the cabinet was no longer the place for him. He became
more than ever satisfied that he was a "wave-worn mariner," and after
some hesitation he finally resigned and transferred his political operations to another field. A year later Hamilton, from very different reasons
of a purely private character, followed him.

Meantime many events had occurred which all tended to show the
growing intensity of party divisions, and which were not without their
effect upon the mind of the President. In 1792 it became necessary to
consider the question of the approaching election, and all elements
united in urging upon Washington the absolute necessity of accepting
the presidency a second time. Hamilton and the Federalists, of course,
desired Washington's reëlection, because they regarded him as their
leader, as the friend and supporter of their measures, and as the great bulwark of the government. Jefferson, who was equally urgent, felt that in
the unformed condition of his own party the withdrawal of Washington,
in addition to its injury to the general welfare, would leave his incoherent forces at the mercy of an avowed and thorough-going Federalist
administration.

So it came about that Washington received another unanimous election. He had no great longing for public office, but at this time he seems
to have been not without a desire to continue President, in order that he
might carry his measures to completion. In the unanimity of the choice
he took a perfectly natural pleasure, for besides the personal satisfaction,
he could not but feel that it greatly strengthened his hands in doing the
work which he had at heart. On January 20, 1793, he wrote to Henry Lee:

"A mind must be insensible, indeed, not to be gratefully impressed by so distinguished and honorable a testimony of public approbation and confidence; and as I suffered my name to be contemplated on this occasion, it is more than probable that I should, for a moment, have experienced chagrin if my reëlection had not been by a pretty respectable vote. But to say I feel pleasure from the prospect of commencing another tour of duty would be a departure from the truth." Some time was still to pass before Washington, either by word or deed, would acknowledge himself to be the chief or even a member of a party; but before he entered the presidency a second time, he had no manner of doubt that a party existed which was opposed to him and to all his measures.

The establishment of the government and the treasury measures had very quickly rallied a strong party, which kept the name that it had adopted while fighting the battles of the Constitution. They were known in their own day, and have been known ever since to history, as the Federalists. The opposition, composed chiefly of those who had resisted the adoption of the Constitution, were discredited at the very start by the success of the union and the new government. When Jefferson took hold of them they were disorganized and even nameless, having no better appellation than that of "Anti-Federalists." In the process of time their great chief gave them a name, a set of principles, a war-cry, an organization, and at last an overwhelming victory. They began to take on something like form and coherence in resisting Hamilton's financial measures; but the success of his policy was so dazzling that they were rather cowed by it, and were left by their defeat little better off in the way of discipline than before. The French Revolution and its consequences, including a war with England, gave them a much better opportunity. It is melancholy to think that American parties should have entered upon their first struggle purely on questions of foreign politics. The only explanation is to repeat that we were still colonists in all but name and allegiance, and it was Washington's task not only to establish a dignified and independent policy of his own abroad, but to beat down colonial politics at home.

In the first burst of rejoicing over the uprising of the French people, no divisions were apparent; but the arrival of Genet was the signal for their beginning. The extraordinary spectacle was then presented of an American party arrayed against the administration under the lead of the French minister, and with the strong, although covert sympathy of the Secretary of State. The popular feeling in fact was so strongly with France that the new party seemed on the surface to have almost universal support. The firm attitude of the administration and Washington's unyielding adherence to his policy of neutrality gave them their first serious check, but also embittered their attacks. In the first three years of the government almost every one refrained from attacking Washington personally. The unlimited love and respect in which he was held were the principal causes of this moderation, but even those opponents who were not influenced by feelings of respect were restrained by a wholesome prudence from bringing upon themselves the odium of being enemies of the President.

The fiction that the king could do no wrong was carried to the last extreme by the Long Parliament when they made war on Charles in order to remove him from evil counselors. It was, no doubt, the exercise of a wise conservatism in that instance; but in the United States, and in the ordinary condition of politics, such a position was of course untenable. The President was responsible for his cabinet and for the measures of his administration, and it was impossible to separate them long, even when the chief magistrate was so great and so well-beloved as Washington. Freneau, editing his newspaper from the office of the Secretary of State, seems to have been the first to break the line. He passed speedily from attacks on measures to attacks on men, and among the latter he soon included the President. Washington had had too much experience of slander and abuse during the revolutionary war to be worried by them. But Freneau took pains to send him copies of his newspapers, a piece of impertinence which apparently led to a little vigorous denunciation, the account of which seems probable, although our only authority is in Jefferson's "Ana." As the attacks went on and were extended, and when Bache joined in with the "Aurora," Washington was not long in coming to the unpleasant conclusion that all this opposition proceeded from a well-formed plan, and was the work of a party which designed to break down his measures and ruin his administration. All statesmen intrusted in a representative system with the work of government are naturally prone to think that their opponents are also the enemies of the public welfare, and Washington was no exception to the rule. Such an opinion is indeed unavoidable, for a public man must have faith that his own measures are the best for the country, and if he did not, he would be but a faint-hearted representative, unfit to govern and unable to lead. History has agreed with Washington in his view of the work of his administration, and has set it down as essential to the right and successful foundation of the government. It is not to be wondered at that at the moment Washington should regard a party swayed by the French minister and seeking to involve us in war as unpatriotic and dangerous. He even thought that one probable solution of Genet's conduct was that he was the tool and not the leader of the party which sustained him. In fact, his general view of the opposition was marked by that perfect clearness which was characteristic of all his opinions when he had fully formed them. In July, 1793, he wrote to Henry Lee:—

"That there are in this as well as in all other countries, discontented characters, I well know; as also that these characters are actuated by very different views: some good, from an opinion that the general measures of the government are impure; some bad, and, if I might be allowed to use so harsh an expression, diabolical, inasmuch as they are not only meant to impede the measures of that government generally, but more especially, as a great means toward the accomplishment of it, to destroy the confidence which it is necessary for the people to place, until they have unequivocal proof of demerit, in their public servants. In this light I consider myself whilst I am an occupant of office; and if they were to go further and call me their slave during this period, I would not dispute the point.

"But in what will this abuse terminate? For the result, as it respects myself, I care not; for I have a consolation within that no earthly efforts can deprive me of, and that is, that neither ambition nor interested motives have influenced my conduct. The arrows of malevolence, therefore, however barbed and well pointed, never can reach the most vulnerable part of me; though, whilst I am up as a *mark*, they will be continually aimed. The publications in Freneau's and Bache's papers are outrages on common decency, and they progress in that style in proportion as their pieces are treated with contempt, and are passed by in silence by those at whom they are aimed. The tendency of them, however, is too obvious to be mistaken by men of cool and dispassionate minds, and, in my opinion, ought to alarm them, because it is difficult to prescribe bounds to the effect."

He was not much given, however, to talking about his assailants. If he said anything, it was usually only in the way of contemptuous sarcasm, as when he wrote to Morris: "The affairs of this country *cannot go amiss*. There are *so many watchful guardians of them*, and such *infallible guides*, that one is at no loss for a director at every turn. But of these matters I shall say little." If these attacks had any effect on him, it was only to make him more determined in carrying out his purposes. In the first skirmish, which ended in the recall of Genet, he not only prevailed, but the French minister's audacity especially in venturing to appeal to the people against their President, demoralized the opposition and brought public opinion round to the side of the administration with an overwhelming force.

Genet's mischief, however, did not end with him. He had sown the seeds of many troubles, and among others the idea of societies on the model of the famous Jacobin Club of Paris. That American citizens should have so little self-respect as to borrow the political jargon and ape the political manners of Paris was sad enough. To put on red caps, drink confusion to tyrants, sing *Ça ira*, and call each other "citizen," was foolish to the verge of idiocy, but it was at least harmless. When, however, they began to form "democratic societies" on the model of the Jacobins, for the defense of liberty against a government which the people themselves had made, they ceased to be fatuous and became mischievous. These societies, senseless imitations of French examples, and having no real cause to defend liberty, became simply party organizations, with a strong tendency to foster license and disorder. Washington regarded them with unmixed disgust, for he attributed to them the agitation and discontent of the settlers beyond the mountains, which threatened to embroil us with Spain, and he believed also that the much more serious matter of the whiskey rebellion was their doing. After having exhausted every reasonable means of concession and compromise, and having concentrated the best public opinion of the country behind him, he resolved to put down this "rebellion" with a strong hand, and he wrote to Henry Lee, just as he was preparing to take the last step: "It is with equal pride and satisfaction I add that, as far as my information extends, this insurrection is viewed with universal indignation and abhorrence, except by those who have never missed an opportunity, by side-blows or otherwise, to attack the general government; and even among these there is not a spirit hardy enough yet openly to justify the daring infractions of law and order; but by palliatives they are attempting to suspend all proceedings against the insurgents, until Congress shall have decided on the case, thereby intending to gain time, and, if possible, to make the evil more extensive, more formidable, and, of course, more difficult to counteract and subdue.

"I consider this insurrection as the first formidable fruit of the democratic societies, brought forth, I believe, too prematurely for their own views, which may contribute to the annihilation of them."

The insurrection vanished on the advance of the forces of the United States. It had been formidable enough to alarm all conservative people, and its inglorious end left the opposition, which had given it a certain encouragement, much discredited. This matter being settled, Washington determined to strike next at what he considered the chief sources of the evil, the clubs, which, to use his own words, "were instituted for the express purpose of poisoning the minds of the people of this country, and making them discontented with the government." Accordingly, in his speech to the next Congress he denounced the democratic societies. After tracing the course of the whiskey rebellion, he said:—

> And when in the calm moments of reflection they [the citizens of the United States] shall have traced the origin and progress of the insurrection, let them determine whether it has not been fomented by combinations of men, who,

careless of consequences, and disregarding the unerring truth, that those who rouse cannot always appease a civil convulsion, have disseminated, from an ignorance or perversion of facts, suspicions, jealousies, and accusations of the whole government.

The opposition both in Congress and in the newspapers shrieked loudly over this plain speaking; but when Washington struck a blow, it was usually well timed, and the present instance was no exception. Coming immediately after the failure of the insurrection, and the triumph of the government, this strong expression of the President's disapproval had a fatal effect upon the democratic societies. They withered away with the rapidity of weeds when their roots have been skillfully cut.

After this, even if Washington still refused to consider himself the head of a party, the opposition no longer had any doubts on that point. They not only regarded him as the chief of the Federalists, but also, and with perfect justice, as their own most dangerous enemy, and the man who had dealt them and their cause the most deadly blows. Whatever restraint they may have hitherto placed upon themselves in dealing with him personally, they now abandoned, and the opportunity for open war soon came to them in the vexed question of the British treaty, where they occupied much better ground than in the Genet affair, and commanded much more popular sympathy. Their orators did not hesitate to say that the conduct of the President in this affair had been improper and monarchical, and that he ought to be impeached. After the treaty was signed, the "Aurora" declared that the President had violated the Constitution, and made a treaty with a nation abhorred by our people; that he answered the respectful remonstrances of Boston and New York as if he were the omnipotent director of a seraglio, and had thundered contempt upon the people with as much confidence as if he sat upon the throne of "Industan."

All these remarks and many more of like tenor have been gathered together and very picturesquely arranged by Mr. McMaster, in whose volumes they may be studied with advantage by any one who has doubts as to Washington's political position. It is not probable that the writer of the brilliant diatribe just quoted had any very distinct idea about either seraglios or "Industan," but he, and others of like mind, probably took pleasure in the words, as did the old woman who always loved to hear Mesopotamia mentioned. Other persons, however, were more definite in their statements. John Beckley, who had once been clerk of the House, writing under the very opposite signature of "A Calm Observer," declared that Washington had been overdrawing his salary in defiance of law, and had actually stolen in this way $4,750. Such being the case, the "Calm Observer" very naturally inquired: "What will posterity say of the man who has done this thing? Will it not say that the mask of political hypocrisy has been worn by Cæsar, by Cromwell, and by Washington?" Another patriot, also of the Democratic party, declared that the President had been false to a republican government. He said that Washington maintained the seclusion of a monk and the supercilious distance of a tyrant; and that the concealing carriage drawn by supernumerary horses expressed the will of the President, and defined the loyal duty of the people.

The support of Genet, the democratic societies, and now this concerted and bitter opposition to the Jay treaty, convinced Washington, if conviction were needed, that he could carry on his administration only by the help of those who were thoroughly in sympathy with his policy and purposes. When Jefferson left the State Department, the President promoted Randolph, and put Bradford, a Federalist, in the place of Attorney-General. When Hamilton left the Treasury, Oliver Wolcott, Hamilton's right-hand man, and the staunchest of party men, was given the position thus left vacant. If Randolph had remained in the cabinet, he would have become a Federalist. Like all men disposed to turn, when he was compelled to jump he sprang far, as was shown by his signing the treaty and memorial, both of which he strongly disapproved. He was quite ready to fall in with the rest of the cabinet, but on account of the Fauchet dispatch he resigned. Then Washington, after offering the portfolio to several persons known to be in hearty sympathy with him, took the risk of giving it to Timothy Pickering, who was by no means a safe leader, rather than take any chance of getting another adviser who was not entirely of his own way of thinking. At the same time he gave the

secretaryship of war to James McHenry, a most devoted personal friend
and follower. He still held back from calling himself a party chief, but he
had discovered, as William of Orange discovered, that he could not,
even with his iron will and lofty intent, overcome the impossible, alter
human nature, or carry on a successful government under a representative system, without the assistance of a party. He stated his conclusion
with his wonted plainness in a letter to Pickering written in September,
1795, in the midst of the struggle over the treaty. "I shall not," he said,
"whilst I have the honor to administer the government, bring a man into
any office of consequence knowingly, whose political tenets are adverse
to the measures which the general government are pursuing; for this, in
my opinion, would be a sort of political suicide. That it would embarrass
its movements is most certain." A terser statement of the doctrine of
party government it would be difficult to find, and in the conduct of
Monroe and the course of the opposition journals Washington had ample
proofs of the soundness of his theory.

If he had needed to be strengthened in his determination, his opponents furnished the requisite aid. In February, 1796, the House refused
to adjourn on his birthday for half an hour, in order to go and pay him
their respects, as had been the pleasant custom up to that time. The
Democrats of that day were in no confusion of mind as to the party to
which Washington belonged, and they did not hesitate to put this deliberate slight upon him in order to mark their dislike. This was not the
utterance of a newspaper editor, but the well-considered act of the representatives of a party in Congress. Party feeling, indeed, could hardly
have gone further; and this single incident is sufficient to dispel the
pleasing delusion that party strife and bitterness are the product of modern days, and of more advanced forms of political organization.

Yet despite all these attacks there can be no doubt that Washington's
hold upon the masses of the people was substantially unshaken. They
would have gladly seen him assume the presidency for the third time, and
if the test had been made, thousands of men who gave their votes to the
opposition would have still supported him for the greatest office in their
gift. But this time Washington would not yield to the wishes of his friends

or of the country. He felt that he had done his work and earned the rest and the privacy for which he longed above all earthly things. In September, 1796, he published his farewell address, and no man ever left a nobler political testament. Through much tribulation he had done his great part in establishing the government of the Union, which might easily have come to naught without his commanding influence. He had imparted to it the dignity of his own great character. He had sustained the splendid financial policy of Hamilton. He had struck a fatal blow at the colonial spirit in our politics, and had lifted up our foreign policy to a plane worthy of an independent nation. He had stricken off the fetters which impeded the march of western settlement, and without loss of honor had gained time to enable our institutions to harden and become strong. He had made peace with our most dangerous enemies, and, except in the case of France, where there were perilous complications to be solved by his successor, he left the United States in far better and more honorable relations with the rest of the world than even the most sanguine would have dared to hope when the Constitution was formed. Now from the heights of great achievement he turned to say farewell to the people whom he so much loved, and whom he had so greatly served. Every word was instinct with the purest and wisest patriotism. "Be united," he said; "be Americans. The name which belongs to you, in your national capacity, must exalt the just pride of patriotism more than any appellation derived from local discriminations. Let there be no sectionalism, no North, South, East or West; you are all dependent one on another, and should be one in union. Beware of attacks, open or covert, upon the Constitution. Beware of the baneful effects of party spirit and of the ruin to which its extremes must lead. Do not encourage party spirit, but use every effort to mitigate and assuage it. Keep the departments of government separate, promote education, cherish the public credit, avoid debt. Observe justice and good faith toward all nations; have neither passionate hatreds nor passionate attachments to any; and be independent politically of all. In one word, be a nation, be Americans, and be true to yourselves."

His admonitions were received by the people at large with profound respect, and sank deep into the public mind. As the generations have come and gone, the farewell address has grown dearer to the hearts of the people, and the children and the children's children of those to whom it was addressed have turned to it in all times and known that there was no room for error in following its counsel.

Yet at the moment, notwithstanding the general sadness at Washington's retirement and the deep regard for his last words of advice, the opposition was so thoroughly hostile that they seized on the address itself as a theme for renewed attack upon its author. "His character," said one Democrat, "can only be respectable while it is not known; he is arbitrary, avaricious, ostentatious; without skill as a soldier, he has crept into fame by the places he has held. His financial measures burdened the many to enrich the few. History will tear the pages devoted to his praise. France and his country gave him fame, and they will take that fame away." "His glory has dissolved in mist," said another writer, "and he has sunk from the high level of Solon or Lycurgus to the mean rank of a Dutch Stadtholder or a Venetian Doge. Posterity will look in vain for any marks of wisdom in his administration."

To thoughtful persons these observations are not without a curious interest, as showing that even the wisest of men may be in error. The distinguished Democrat who uttered these remarks has been forgotten, and the page of history on which Washington's name was inscribed is still untorn. The passage of the address, however, which gave the most offense, as Mr. McMaster points out, was, as might have been expected from the colonial condition of our politics, that which declared it to be our true policy "to steer clear of permanent alliances with any portion of the foreign world." This, it was held, simply meant that, having made a treaty with England, we were to be stopped from making one with France. Another distinguished editor declared that the fare-well address came from the meanest of motives; that the President knew he could not be reëlected because the Republicans would have united to supersede him with Adams, who had the simplicity of a Republican, while Washington had the ostentation of an Eastern Pasha, and it was in order to save himself from this humiliation that he had cunningly resigned.

When Washington met his last Congress, William Giles of Virginia took the opportunity afforded by the usual answer to the President's speech to assail him personally. It would be of course a gross injustice to suppose that a coarse political ruffian like Giles really represented the Democratic party. But he represented the extreme wing, and after he had declared in his place that Washington was neither wise nor patriotic, and that his retirement was anything but a calamity, he got twelve of his party friends to sustain his sentiments by voting with him. The press was even more unbridled, and it was said in the "Aurora" at this time that Washington had debauched and deceived the nation, and that his administration had shown that the mask of patriotism may be worn to conceal the foulest dangers to the liberties of the people. Over and over again it was said by these writers that he had betrayed France and was the slave of England.

This charge of being a British sympathizer was the only one of all the abuse heaped upon him by the opposition that Washington seems really to have resented. In August, 1794, when this slander first started from the prolific source of all attacks against the government, he wrote to Henry Lee: "With respect to the words said to have been uttered by Mr. Jefferson, they would be enigmatical to those who are acquainted with the characters about me, unless supposed to be spoken ironically; and in that case they are too injurious to me, and have too little foundation in truth, to be ascribed to him. There could not be the trace of doubt in his mind of predilection in mine toward Great Britain or her politics, unless, which I do not believe, he has set me down as one of the most deceitful and uncandid men living; because, not only in private conversations between ourselves on this subject, but in my meetings with the confidential servants of the public, he has heard me often, when occasions presented themselves, express very different sentiments, with an energy that could not be mistaken by any one present.

"Having determined, as far as lay within the power of the executive, to keep this country in a state of neutrality, I have made my public conduct accord with the system; and whilst so acting as a public character, consistency and propriety as a private man forbid those intemperate expressions in favor of one nation, or to the prejudice of another, which may have wedged themselves in, and, I will venture to add, to the embarrassment of government, without producing any good to the country."

He had shown by his acts as well as by his words his real friendship for France, such as a proper sense of gratitude required. As has been already pointed out, rather than run the risk of seeming to reflect in the slightest degree upon the government of the French republic, he had refused even to receive distinguished *émigrés* like Noailles, Liancourt, and Talleyrand.* He was so scrupulous in this respect that he actually did violence to his own strong desires in not taking into his house at once the son of Lafayette; and when it became necessary to choose a successor to Morris, his anxiety was so great to select some one agreeable to France that he took such an avowed opponent of his administration as Monroe.

On the other hand, he had never lost the strong feeling of hostility toward England which he, above all men, had felt during the Revolution. The conduct of England, when he was seeking an honorable peace with her, tried his patience severely. He wrote to Morris in 1795: "I give you these details (and if you should again converse with Lord Grenville on the subject, you are at liberty, unofficially, to mention them, or any of them, according to circumstances), as evidences of the unpolitic conduct (for so it strikes me) of the British government towards these United States; that it may be seen how difficult it has been for the executive, under such an accumulation of irritating circumstances, to maintain the ground of neutrality which had been taken; and at a time when the remembrance of the aid we had received from France in the Revolution was fresh in every mind, and while the partisans of that country were continually contrasting the affections of *that* people with the unfriendly disposition of the *British government*. And that, too, as I have observed before, while *their own* sufferings during the war with the latter had not been forgotten." The one man in the country who above all others had the highest conception of American nationality, who was the first to seek to lift up our politics from the low level of colonialism, who was the

---

*See the Letter to the Due de Liancourt explaining the reasons for his not being received by the President. (Sparks, xi. 161.)

author of the neutrality policy, had reason to resent the bitter irony of an attack which represented him as a British sympathizer. The truth is, that the only foreign party at that time was that which identified itself with France, and which was the party of Jefferson and the opposition. The Federalists and the administration under the lead of Washington and Hamilton were determined that the government should be American and not French, and this in the eyes of their opponents was equivalent to being in the control of England. In after years, when the Federalists fell from power and declined into the position of a factious minority, they became British sympathizers, and as thoroughly colonial in their politics as the party of Jefferson had been. If they had had the wisdom of their better days they would then have made themselves the champions of the American idea, and would have led the country in the determined effort to free itself once for all from colonial politics, even if they were obliged to fight somebody to accomplish it. They proved unequal to the task, and it fell to a younger generation led by Henry Clay and his contemporaries to sweep Federalist and Jeffersonian republican alike, with their French and British politics, out of existence. In so doing the younger generation did but complete the work of Washington, for he it was who first trod the path and marked the way for a true American policy in the midst of men who could not understand his purposes.

Bitter and violent as had been the attacks upon Washington while he held office, they were as nothing compared to the shout of fierce exultation which went up from the opposition journals when he finally retired from the presidency. One extract will serve as an example of the general tone of the opposition journals throughout the country. It is to be found in the "Aurora" of March 6, 1797:—

> "Lord, now lettest Thou Thy servant depart in peace," was the pious ejaculation of a pious man who beheld a flood of happiness rushing in upon mankind. If ever there was a time that would license the reiteration of the ejaculation, that time has now arrived, for the man who is the source of all the misfortunes of our country is this day reduced to a level with

his fellow-citizens, and is no longer possessed of power to multiply evils upon the United States. If ever there was a period for rejoicing, this is the moment. Every heart in unison with the freedom and happiness of the people ought to beat high with exultation that the name of Washington ceases from this day to give currency to political insults, and to legalize corruption. A new era is now opening upon us, an era which promises much to the people, for public measures must now stand upon their own merits, and nefarious projects can no longer be supported by a name. When a retrospect has been taken of the Washingtonian administration for eight years, it is a subject of the greatest astonishment that a single individual should have cankered the principles of republicanism in an enlightened people just emerged from the gulf of despotism, and should have carried his designs against the public liberty so far as to have put in jeopardy its very existence. Such, however, are the facts, and with these staring us in the face, the day ought to be a JUBILEE in the United States.

This was not the outburst of a single malevolent spirit. The article was copied and imitated in New York and Boston, and wherever the party that called Jefferson leader had a representative among the newspapers. It is not probable that stuff of this sort gave Washington himself a moment's anxiety, for he knew too well what he had done, and he was too sure of his own hold upon the hearts of the people, to be in the least disturbed by the attacks of hostile editors. But the extracts are of interest as showing that the opposition party of that time, the party organized and led by Jefferson, regarded Washington as their worst enemy, and assailed him and slandered him to the utmost. They even went so far as to borrow materials from the enemies of the country with whom we had lately been at war, by publishing the forged letters attributed to Washington, and circulated by the British in 1777, in order to discredit the American general. One of Washington's last acts, on March 3, 1797, was to file in the

State Department a solemn declaration that these letters, then republished by an American political party, were base forgeries, of English origin in a time of war. His own view of this performance is given in a letter to Benjamin Walker, in which he said: "Amongst other attempts, . . . spurious letters, known at the time of their first publication (I believe in the year 1777) to be forgeries, are (or extracts from them) brought forward with the highest emblazoning of which they are susceptible, with a view to attach principles to me which every action of my life has given the lie to. But that is no stumbling-block with the editors of these papers and their supporters."

Two or three extracts from private letters will show how Washington regarded the course of the opposition, and the interpretation he put upon their attacks. After sketching in a letter to David Stuart the general course of the hostilities toward his administration, he said: "This not working so well as was expected, from a supposition that there was too much confidence in, and perhaps personal regard for, the present chief magistrate and his politics, the batteries have lately been leveled against him particularly and personally. Although he is soon to become a private citizen, his opinions are knocked down, and his character reduced as low as they are capable of sinking it, even by resorting to absolute falsehoods." Again he said, just before leaving office: "To misrepresent my motives, to reprobate my politics, and to weaken the confidence which has been reposed in my administration, are objects which cannot be relinquished by those who will be satisfied with nothing short of a change in our political system." He at least labored under no misapprehension after eight years of trial as to the position or purposes of the party which had fought him and his administration, and which had savagely denounced his measures at every step, and with ever-increasing violence.

Having defined the attitude of the opposition, we can now consider that of Washington himself after he had retired from office, and no longer felt restrained by the circumstances of his election to the presidency from openly declaring his views, or publicly identifying himself with a political party. He rightly regarded the administration of Mr. Adams as a continuation of his own, and he gave to it a cordial support. He was equally clear and determined in his distrust and dislike of the opposition. Not long before leaving office he had written a letter to Jefferson, which, while it exonerated that gentleman from being the author of certain peculiarly malicious attacks, showed very plainly that the writer completely understood the position occupied by his former secretary. It was a letter which must have been most unpleasant reading for the person to whom it was addressed. A year later he wrote to John Nicholas in regard to Jefferson: "Nothing short of the evidence you have adduced, corroborative of intimations which I had received long before through another channel, could have shaken my belief in the sincerity of a friendship which I had conceived was possessed for me by the person to whom you allude." There was no doubt in his mind now as to Jefferson's conduct, and he knew at last that he had been his foe even when a member of his political household.

When the time came to fill the offices in the provisional army made necessary by the menace of war with France, Washington wrote to the President that he ought to have generals who were men of activity, energy, health, and "sound politics," carrying apparently his suspicion of the opposition even to disbelieving in them as soldiers. He repeated the same idea in a letter to McHenry, in which he said: "I do not conceive that a desirable set could be formed from the old generals, some having never displayed any talent for enterprise, and others having shown a general opposition to the government, or predilection to French measures, be their present conduct what it may."

When the question arose in regard to the relative rank of the major-generals, Washington said to Knox: "No doubt remained in my mind that Colonel Hamilton was designated second in command (and first, if I should decline an acceptance) by the Federal characters of Congress; whence alone anything like a public sentiment relative thereto could be deduced." He was quite clear that there was no use in looking beyond the confines of the Federal party for any public sentiment worth considering. He had serious doubts also as to the advisability of having the opponents of the government in the army, and wrote to McHenry on September 30, 1798, that brawlers against the government in certain parts of Virginia had suddenly become silent and were seeking commissions in the army. "The motives ascribed to them are that in such a situation they would endeavor to divide and contaminate the army by artful and seditious discourses, and perhaps at a critical moment bring on confusion. What weight to give to these conjectures you can judge as well as I. But as there will be characters enough of an opposite description who are ready to receive appointments, circumspection is necessary. Finding the resentment of the people at the conduct of France too strong to be resisted, they have in appearance adopted their sentiments, and pretend that, notwithstanding the misconduct of the government has brought it upon us, yet if an invasion should take place, it will be found that *they* will be among the first to defend it. This is their story at all elections and election meetings, and told in many instances with effect." He wrote again in the same strain to McHenry, on October 21: "Possibly no injustice would be done, if I were to proceed a step further, and give it as an opinion that most of the candidates [for the army] brought forward by the opposition members possess sentiments similar to their own, and might poison the army by disseminating them, if they were appointed." In this period of danger, when the country was on the verge of war, the attitude of the opposition gave Washington much food for thought because it appeared to him so false and unpatriotic. In a letter to Lafayette, written on Christmas day, 1798, he gave the following brief sketch of the opposition: "A party exists in the United States, formed by a combination of causes, which opposed the government in all its measures, and are determined, as all their conduct evinces, by clogging its wheels indirectly to change the nature of it, and to subvert the Constitution. The friends of government, who are anxious to maintain its neutrality and to preserve the country in peace, and adopt measures to secure these objects, are charged by them as being monarchists, aristocrats, and infractors of the Constitution, which according to their interpretation of it would be a mere cipher. They arrogated to themselves . . . the sole merit of being the friends of France, when in fact they had no more regard for that nation than for the Grand Turk, further than their own views were promoted by it; denouncing those who differed in opinion (those principles are purely

American and whose sole view was to observe a strict neutrality) as acting under British influence, and being directed by her counsels, or as being her pensioners."

Shortly before this sharp definition was written, an incident had occurred which had given Washington an opportunity of impressing his views directly and personally upon a distinguished leader of the opposite party. Dr. Logan of Philadelphia, under the promptings of Jefferson, as was commonly supposed, had gone on a volunteer mission to Paris for the purpose of bringing about peace between the two republics. He had apparently a fixed idea that there was something very monstrous in our having any differences with France, and being somewhat of a busybody, although a most worthy man, he felt called upon to settle the international complications which were then puzzling the brains and trying the patience of the ablest men in America. It is needless to say that his mission was not a success, and he was eventually so unmercifully ridiculed by the Federalist editors that he published a long pamphlet in his own defense. Upon his return, however, he seems to have been not a little pleased with himself, and he took occasion to call upon Washington, who was then in Philadelphia on business. It would be difficult to conceive anything more distasteful to Washington than such a mission as Logan's, or that he could have a more hearty contempt for any one than for a meddler of this description, who by his interference might help to bring his country into contempt. He was sufficiently impressed, however, by Dr. Logan's call to draw up a memorandum, which gave a very realistic and amusing account of it. It may be surmised that when Washington wished to be cold in his manner, he was capable of being very freezing, and he was not very apt at concealing his emotions when he found himself in the presence of any one whom he disliked and disapproved. The memorandum is as follows:—

> *Tuesday, November* 13, 1798.—Mr. Lear, my secretary, being from our lodgings on business, one of my servants came into the room where I was writing and informed me that a gentleman in the parlor below desired to see me; no name was

sent up. In a few minutes I went down, and found the Rev. Dr. Blackwell and Dr. Logan there. I advanced towards and gave my hand to the former; the latter did the same towards me. I was backward in giving mine. He, possibly supposing from hence that I did not recollect him, said his name was Logan. Finally, in a very cold manner, and with an air of marked indifference, I gave him my hand and asked *Dr. Blackwell to be seated*; the other *took* a seat at the same time. I addressed *all* my conversation to Dr. Blackwell; the other all his to me, to which I only gave negative or affirmative answers as laconically as I could, except asking him how Mrs. Logan did. He seemed disposed to be very polite, and while Dr. Blackwell and myself were conversing on the late calamitous fever, offered me an asylum at his house, if it should return or I thought myself in any danger in the city, and two or three rooms, by way of accommodation. I thanked him slightly, observing there would be no call for it.

About this time Dr. Blackwell took his leave. We all rose from our seats, and I moved a few paces toward the door of the room, expecting the other would follow and take his leave also.

The worthy Quaker, however, was not to be got rid of so easily. He literally stood his ground, and went on talking of a number of things, chiefly about Lafayette and his family, and an interview with Mr. Murray, our minister in Holland. Washington, meanwhile, stood facing him, and to use his own words, "showed the utmost inattention," while his visitor described his journey to Paris. Finally Logan said that his purpose in going to France was to ameliorate the condition of our relations with that country. "This," said Washington, "drew my attention more pointedly to what he was saying and induced me to remark that there was something very singular in this; that *he*, who could only be viewed as a private character, unarmed with proper powers, and presumptively unknown in France, should suppose he could effect what three gentlemen of the first respectability in our country, especially charged under the authority of the government, were unable to do." One is not surprised to be then told that Dr. Logan seemed a little confounded at this observation; but he recovered himself, and went on to say that only five persons knew of his going, and that his letters from Mr. Jefferson and Mr. McKean obtained for him an interview with M. Merlin, president of the Directory, who had been most friendly in his expressions. To this Washington replied with some very severe strictures on the conduct of France; and the conversation, which must by this time have become a little strained, soon after came to an end. One cannot help feeling a good deal of sympathy for the excellent doctor, although he was certainly a busybody and, one would naturally infer, a bore as well. It would have been, however, a pity to have lost this memorandum, and there is every reason to regret that Washington did not oftener exercise his evident powers for realistic reporting. Nothing, moreover, could bring out better his thorough contempt for the opposition and their attitude toward France than this interview with the volunteer commissioner.

There were, however, much more serious movements made by the Democratic party than well-meant and meddling attempts to make peace with France. This was the year of the Kentucky and Virginia resolutions, the first note of that disunion sentiment which was destined one day to involve the country in civil war and be fought out on a hundred battlefields. Washington, with his love for the Union and for nationality ever uppermost in his heart, was quick to take alarm, and it cut him especially to think that a movement which he esteemed at once desperate and wicked should emanate from his own State, and as we now know, and as he perhaps suspected, from a great Virginian whom he had once trusted. He straightway set himself to oppose this movement with all his might, and he summoned to his aid that other great Virginian who in his early days had been the first to rouse the people against oppression, and who now in his old age, in response to Washington's appeal, came again into the forefront in behalf of the Constitution and the union of the States. The letter which Washington wrote to Patrick Henry on this occasion is one of the most important that he ever penned, but there is room to quote only a single passage here.

At such a crisis as this, when everything dear and valuable to us is assailed, when this party hangs upon the wheels of government as a dead weight, opposing every measure that is calculated for defense and self-preservation, abetting the nefarious views of another nation upon our rights, preferring, as long as they dare contend openly against the spirit and resentment of the people, the interest of France to the welfare of their own country, justifying the former at the expense of the latter; when every act of their own government is tortured, by constructions they will not bear, into attempts to infringe and trample upon the Constitution with a view to introduce monarchy; when the most unceasing and the purest exertions which were making to maintain a neutrality . . . are charged with being measures calculated to favor Great Britain at the expense of France, and all those who had any agency in it are accused of being under the influence of the former and her pensioners; when measures are systematically and pertinaciously pursued, which must eventually dissolve the Union or produce coercion; I say, when these things have become so obvious, ought characters who are best able to rescue their country from the pending evil to remain at home? . . .

Vain will it be to look for peace and happiness, or for the security of liberty or property, if civil discord should ensue. And what else can result from the policy of those among us, who, by all the measures in their power, are driving matters to extremity, if they cannot be counteracted effectually? The views of men can only be known, or guessed at, by their words or actions. Can those of the *leaders* of opposition be mistaken, then, if judged by this rule? That they are followed by numbers, who are unacquainted with their designs and suspect as little the tendency of their principles, I am fully persuaded. But if their conduct is viewed with indifference, if there are activity and misrepresentations on one side and supineness on the other, their numbers accumulated by intriguing and discontented foreigners under proscription, who were at war with their own government, and the greater part of them with *all* governments, they will increase, and nothing short of omniscience can foretell the consequences.

It would have been difficult to draw a severer indictment of the opposition party than that given in this letter, but there is one other letter even more striking in its contents, without which no account of the relation of Washington to the two great parties which sprang up under his administration would be complete. It was addressed to Governor Trumbull of Connecticut, was written on July 21, 1799, less than six months before his death, and although printed, has been hidden away in the appendix to the "Life of Benjamin Silliman." Governor Trumbull, who bore the name and filled the office of Washington's old revolutionary friend, had written to the general, as many other Federalists were writing at that time, urging him to come forward and stand once more for the presidency, that he might heal the dissensions in his own party and save the country from the impending disaster of Jefferson's election. That Washington refused all these requests is of course well known, but his reasons as stated to Trumbull are of great interest:

> I come now, my dear sir, to pay particular attention to that part of your letter which respects myself.
>
> I remember well the conversation which you allude to. I have not forgot the answer I gave you. In my judgment it applies with as much force *now* as *then*; nay, more, because at that time the line between the parties was not so clearly drawn, and the views of the opposition so clearly developed as they are at present. Of course allowing your observation (as it respects myself) to be well founded, personal influence would be of no avail.
>
> Let that party set up a broomstick, and call it a true son of liberty, —a democrat,—or give it any other epithet that

will suit their purpose, and it will command their votes *in toto!* * Will not the Federalists meet, or rather defend, their cause on the opposite ground? Surely they must, or they will discover a want of policy, indicative of weakness and pregnant of mischief, which cannot be admitted. Wherein, then, would lie the difference between the present gentleman in office and myself?

It would be matter of grave regret to me if I could believe that a serious thought was turned toward me as his successor, not only as it respects my ardent wishes to pass through the vale of life in retirement, undisturbed in the remnant of the days I have to sojourn here, unless called upon to defend my country (which every citizen is bound to do); but on public grounds also; for although I have abundant cause to be thankful for the good health with which I am blessed, yet I am not insensible to my declination in other respects. It would be criminal, therefore, in me, although it should be the wish of my countrymen and I could be elected, to accept an office under this conviction which another would discharge with more ability; and this, too, at a time when I am thoroughly convinced I should not draw a *single* vote from the anti-Federal side, and of course should stand upon no other ground *than any other Federal character*† well supported; and when I should become a mark for the shafts of envenomed malice and the basest calumny to fire at,—when I should be charged not only with irresolution but with concealed ambition, which waits only an occasion to blaze out, and, in short, with dotage and imbecility.

All this, I grant, ought to be like dust in the balance, when put in competition with a *great* public good, when the accomplishment of it is apparent. But, as no problem is better

* "As an analysis of this position, look to the pending election of governor in Pennsylvania."
†These italics are mine.

defined in my mind than that principle, not men, is now, and will be, the object of contention; and that I could not obtain a solitary vote from that party; *that any other respectable Federal character could receive the same suffrages that I should*;* that at my time of life (verging towards threescore and ten) I should expose myself without rendering any essential service to my country, or answering the end contemplated; prudence on my part must avert any attempt of the well-meant but mistaken views of my friends to introduce me again into the chair of government.

It does not fall within the scope of this biography to attempt to portray the history or weigh the merits of the two parties which came into existence at the close of the last century, and which, under varying names, have divided the people of the United States ever since. But it is essential here to define the relation of Washington toward them because one hears it constantly said and sees it as constantly written down, that Washington belonged to no party, which is perhaps a natural, but is certainly a complete misconception. Washington came to the presidency by a unanimous vote. He had in his mind very strongly the idea of the framers of the Constitution that the President, by the method of his election and by his independence of the other departments of government, was to be above and beyond party, and the representative of the whole people. In addition to this he was so absorbed by the great conception which he had of the future of the country, and was so confident of the purity and rectitude of his own purposes, that he was loath to think that party divisions could arise while he held the chief magistracy. It was not long before he was undeceived on this point, and he soon found that party divisions sprang up from the measures of his own administration. Nevertheless, he clung to his determination to govern without the assistance of a party as such. When this, too, became impossible, he still felt that the unanimity of his election required that he should not declare

---

*These italics are mine.

himself to be the head of a party; but he had become thoroughly convinced that under the representative system of the Constitution party government could not be avoided. In his farewell address he warned the people against the excesses of that party spirit which he deplored; but he did not suggest that it could be extinguished. Being a wise and far-seeing man, he saw that if party government was an evil, it also was under a free representative system, and in the present condition of human nature a necessary evil, furnishing the only machinery by which public affairs could be carried on.

In a time of deep political excitement and strong party feeling, Washington was the last man in the world not to be decidedly on one side or the other. He was possessed of too much sense, force, and virility to be content to hold himself aloof and croak over the wickedness of people, who were trying to do something, even if they did not always try in the most perfect way. He was himself preëminently a doer of deeds, and not a critic or a phrase-maker, and we can read very distinctly in the extracts which have been brought together in this chapter what he thought on party and public questions. He was opposed to the party which had resisted all the great measures of his administration from the foundation of the government of the United States. They had assailed and maligned him and his ministers, and he regarded them as political enemies. He believed in the principles of that party which had supported the financial policy of Hamilton and his own policy of neutrality toward foreign nations. He was opposed to the party which introduced the interests of France as the leading issue of American politics, and which embodied the doctrines of nullification and separatism in the resolutions of Kentucky and Virginia. In one word, Washington, in policies and politics, was an American and a Nationalist; and the National and American party, from 1789 to 1801, was the Federalist party. It may be added that it was the only party which, at that precise time, could claim those qualities. While he remained in the presidency he would not declare himself to be of any party; but as soon as this fetter was removed, he declared himself freely after his fashion, expressing in words what he had formerly only expressed in action. His feelings warmed and strengthened as the controversy with France deepened, and as the attitude of the opposition became more un-American and leaned more and more to separatism. They culminated at last in the eloquent letter to Patrick Henry, and in the carefully weighed words with which he tells Trumbull that he can hope for no more votes than "any other Federal character."

CHAPTER XVII

THE LAST YEARS

WASHINGTON HAD ENTERED upon the presidency with the utmost reluctance, and at the sacrifice of all he considered pleasantest and best in life. He took it and held it for eight years from a sense of duty, and with no desire to retain it beyond that which every man feels who wishes to finish a great work that he has undertaken. He looked forward to the approaching end of his second term with a feeling of intense relief, and compared himself to the wearied traveler who sees the resting-place where he is at length to have repose. On March 3 he gave a farewell dinner to the President and Vice-President elect, the foreign ministers and their wives, and other distinguished persons, from one of whom we learn that it was a very pleasant and lively gathering. When the cloth was removed Washington filled his glass and said: "Ladies and gentlemen, this is the last time I shall drink your health as a public man. I do it with sincerity, wishing you all possible happiness." The company did not take the same cheerful view as their host of this leave-taking. There was a pause in the gayety, some of the ladies shed tears, and the little incident only served to show the warm affection felt for Washington by every one who came in close contact with him.

The next day the last official ceremonies were performed. After Jefferson had taken the oath as Vice-President and had proceeded with the Senate to the House of Representatives, which was densely crowded, Washington entered and was received with cheers and shouts, the waving

411

of handkerchiefs, and an enthusiasm which seemed to know no bounds. Mr. Adams followed him almost immediately and delivered his inaugural address, in which he paid a stately compliment to the great virtues of his predecessor. It was the setting and not the rising sun, however, that drew the attention of the multitude, and as Washington left the hall there was a wild rush from the galleries to the corridors and then into the streets to see him pass. He took off his hat and bowed to the people, but they followed him even to his own door, where he turned once more and, unable to speak, waved to them a silent farewell.

In the evening of the same day a great banquet was given to him by the merchants of Philadelphia, and when he entered the band played "Washington's March," and a series of emblematic paintings were disclosed, the chief of which represented the ex-President at Mount Vernon surrounded by the allegorical figures then so fashionable. After the festivities Washington lingered for a few days in Philadelphia to settle various private matters and then started for home. Whether he was going or coming, whether he was about to take the great office of President or retire to the privacy of Mount Vernon, the same popular enthusiasm greeted him. When he was really brought in contact with the people, the clamors of the opposition press and the attacks of the Jeffersonian editors all faded away and were forgotten. On March 12 he reached Baltimore, and the local newspaper of the next day said:

> Last evening arrived in this city, on his way to Mount Vernon, the illustrious object of veneration and gratitude, GEORGE WASHINGTON. His excellency was accompanied by his lady and Miss Custis, and by the son of the unfortunate Lafayette and his preceptor. At a distance from the city, he was met by a crowd of citizens, on horse and foot, who thronged the road to greet him, and by a detachment from Captain Hollingsworth's troop, who escorted him in through as great a concourse of people as Baltimore ever witnessed. On alighting at the Fountain Inn, the general was saluted with reiterated and thundering huzzas from the spectators.

His excellency, with the companions of his journey, leaves
town, we understand, this morning.

Thus with the cheers and the acclamations still ringing in his ears he
came home again to Mount Vernon, where he found at once plenty of
occupation, which in some form was always a necessity to him. An
absence of eight years had not improved the property. On April 3 he
wrote to McHenry: "I find myself in the situation nearly of a new beginner; for, although I have not houses to build (except one, which I must
erect for the accommodation and security of my military, civil, and private papers, which are voluminous and may be interesting), yet I have
scarcely anything else about me that does not require considerable
repairs. In a word, I am already surrounded by joiners, masons, and
painters; and such is my anxiety to get out of their hands, that I have
scarcely a room to put a friend into or to sit in myself without the music
of hammers or the odoriferous scent of paint." He easily dropped back
into the round of country duties and pleasures, and the care of farms and
plantations, which had always had for him so much attraction. "To make
and sell a little flour annually," he wrote to Wolcott, "to repair houses
going fast to ruin, to build one for the security of my papers of a public
nature, will constitute employment for the few years I have to remain on
this terrestrial globe." Again he said to McHenry: "You are at the source
of information, and can find many things to relate, while I have nothing
to say that would either inform or amuse a secretary of war at
Philadelphia. I might tell him that I begin my diurnal course with the
sun; that if my hirelings are not in their places by that time I send them
messages of sorrow for their indisposition; that having put these wheels
in motion I examine the state of things further; that the more they are
probed the deeper I find the wounds which my buildings have sustained
by an absence and neglect of eight years; that by the time I have accomplished these matters breakfast (a little after seven o'clock, about the
time I presume that you are taking leave of Mrs. McHenry) is ready; that
this being over I mount my horse and ride round my farms, which employs
me until it is time to dress for dinner, at which I rarely miss seeing strange

faces, come, as they say, out of respect for me. Pray, would not the word curiosity answer as well? And how different this from having a few social friends at a cheerful board. The usual time of sitting at table, a walk, and tea bring me within the dawn of candle-light; previous to which, if not prevented by company, I resolve that as soon as the glimmering taper supplies the place of the great luminary I will retire to my writing-table and acknowledge the letters I have received; that when the lights are brought I feel tired and disinclined to engage in this work, conceiving that the next night will do as well. The next night comes and with it the same causes for postponement, and so on. Having given you the history of a day, it will serve for a year, and I am persuaded you will not require a second edition of it. But it may strike you that in this detail no mention is made of any portion of time allotted for reading. The remark would be just, for I have not looked into a book since I came home; nor shall I be able to do it until I have discharged my workmen; probably not before the nights grow longer, when possibly I may be looking in Doomsday book."

There is not much that can be added to his own concise description of the simple life he led at home. The rest and quiet were very pleasant, but still there was a touch of sadness in his words. The long interval of absence made the changes which time had wrought stand out more vividly than if they had come one by one in the course of daily life at home. Washington looked on the ruins of Belvoir, and sighed to think of the many happy hours he had passed with the Fairfaxes, now gone from the land forever. Other old friends had been taken away by death, and the gaps were not filled by the new faces of which he speaks to McHenry. Indeed, the crowd of visitors coming to Mount Vernon from all parts of his own country and of the world, whether they came from respect or curiosity, brought a good deal of weariness to a man tired with the cares of state and longing for absolute repose. Yet he would not close his doors to any one, for the Virginian sense of hospitality, always peculiarly strong in him, forbade such action. To relieve himself, therefore, in this respect, he sent for his nephew Lawrence Lewis, who took the social burden from his shoulders. But although the visitors tired him when he felt responsible for their pleasure, he did not shut himself up now any more than at any other time in self-contemplation. He was constantly thinking of others; and the education of his nephews, the care of young Lafayette until he should return to France, as well as the happy love-match of Nellie Custis and his nephew, supplied the human interest without which he was never happy.

Before we trace his connection with public affairs in these closing years, let us take one look at him, through the eyes of a disinterested but keen observer. John Bernard, an English actor, who had come to this country in the year when Washington left the presidency, was playing an engagement with his company at Annapolis, in 1798. One day he mounted his horse and rode down below Alexandria, to pay a visit to an acquaintance who lived on the banks of the Potomac. When he was returning, a chaise in front of him, containing a man and a young woman, was overturned, and the occupants were thrown out. As Bernard rode to the scene of the accident, another horseman galloped up from the opposite direction. The two riders dismounted, found that the driver was not hurt, and succeeded in restoring the young woman to consciousness; an event which was marked, Bernard tells us, by a volley of invectives addressed to her unfortunate husband. "The horse," continues Bernard, "was now on his legs, but the vehicle still prostrate, heavy in its frame, and laden with at least half a ton of luggage. My fellow-helper set me an example of activity in relieving it of the internal weight; and when all was clear, we grasped the wheel between us, and to the peril of our spinal columns righted the conveyance. The horse was then put in, and we lent a hand to help up the luggage. All this helping, hauling, and lifting occu pied at least half an hour, under a meridian sun, in the middle of July, which fairly boiled the perspiration out of our foreheads." The possessor of the chaise beguiled the labor by a full personal history of himself and his wife, and when the work was done invited the two Samaritans to go with him to Alexandria, and take a drop of "something sociable." This being declined, the couple mounted into the chaise and drove on. "Then," says Bernard, "my companion, after an exclamation at the heat, offered very courteously to dust my coat, a favor the return of which enabled me to take deliberate survey of his person. He was a tall, erect, well-made man, evidently advanced in years, but who appeared to have retained all the vigor and elasticity resulting from a life of temperance and exercise. His dress was a blue coat buttoned to his chin, and buckskin breeches. Though the instant he took off his hat I could not avoid the recognition of familiar lineaments, which indeed I was in the habit of seeing on every sign-post and over every fireplace, still I failed to identify him, and to my surprise I found that I was an object of equal speculation in his eyes." The actor evidently did not have the royal gift of remembering faces, but the stranger possessed that quality, for after a moment's pause he said, "Mr. Bernard, I believe," and mentioned the occasion on which he had seen him play in Philadelphia. He then asked Bernard to go home with him for a couple of hours' rest, and pointed out the house in the distance. At last Bernard knew to whom he was speaking. "'Mount Vernon!' I exclaimed; and then drawing back with a stare of wonder, 'Have I the honor of addressing General Washington?' With a smile whose expression of benevolence I have rarely seen equaled, he offered his hand and replied: 'An odd sort of introduction, Mr. Bernard; but I am pleased to find you can play so active a part in private, and without a prompter.'" So they rode on together to the house and had a chat, to which we must recur further on.

There is no contemporary narrative of which I am aware that shows Washington to us more clearly than this little adventure with Bernard, for it is in the common affairs of daily life that men come nearest to each other, and the same rule holds good in history. We know Washington much better from these few lines of description left by a chance acquaintance on the road than we do from volumes of state papers. It is such a pleasant story, too. There is the great man, retired from the world, still handsome and imposing in his old age, with the strong and ready hand to succor those who had fallen by the wayside; there are the genuine hospitality, the perfect manners, and the well-turned little sentence with which he complimented the actor, put him at his ease, and asked him to his house. Nothing can well be added to the picture of Washington as we see him here, not long before the end of all things came. We must break off, however, from the quiet charm of home life, and turn again briefly to the affairs of state. Let us, therefore, leave these two riding along the road together in the warm Virginia sunshine to the house which has since become one of the Meccas of humanity, in memory of the man who once dwelt in it.

The highly prized retirement to Mount Vernon did not now, more than at any previous time, separate Washington from the affairs of the country. He continued to take a keen interest in all that went on, to correspond with his friends, and to use his influence for what he thought wisest and best for the general welfare. These were stirring times, too, and the progress of events brought him to take a more active part than he had ever expected to play again; for France, having failed, thanks to his policy, to draw us either by fair words or trickery from our independent and neutral position, determined, apparently, to try the effect of force and ill usage. Pinckney, sent out as minister, had been rebuffed; and then Adams, with the cordial support of the country, had made another effort for peace by sending Pinckney, Marshall, and Gerry as a special commission. The history of that commission is one of the best known episodes in our history. Our envoys were insulted, asked for bribes, and browbeaten, until the two who retained a proper sense of their own and their country's dignity took their passports and departed. The publication of the famous X, Y, Z letters, which displayed the conduct of France, roused a storm of righteous indignation from one end of the United States to the other. The party of France and of the opposition bent before the storm, and the Federalists were at last all-powerful. A cry for war went up from every corner, and Congress provided rapidly for the formation of an army and the beginning of a navy.

Then the whole country turned, as a matter of course, to one man to stand at the head of the national forces of the United States, and Adams wrote to Washington, urging him to take command of the provisional army. To any other appeal to come forward Washington would have been deaf, but he could never refuse a call to arms. He wrote to Adams on July 4, 1798: "In case of *actual invasion* by a formidable force, I certainly should not intrench myself under the cover of age or retirement, if my services should be required by my country to assist in repelling it." He agreed, therefore, to take command of the army, provided that he should not be called into active service except in the case of actual hostilities, and that he should have the appointment of the general's staff. To these terms Adams of course acceded. But out of the apparently simple condition relating to the appointment of officers there grew a very serious trouble. There were to be three major-generals, the first of them to have also the rank of inspector-general, and to be the virtual commander-in-chief until the army was actually called into the field. For these places, Washington after much reflection selected Hamilton, Pinckney, and Knox, in the order named, and in doing so he very wisely went on the general principle that the army was to be organized *de novo*, without reference to prior service. Apart from personal and political jealousies, nothing could have been more proper and more sound than this arrangement; but at this point the President's dislike of Hamilton got beyond control, and he made up his mind to reverse the order, and send in Knox's name first. The Federalist leaders were of course utterly disgusted by this attempt to set Hamilton aside, which was certainly ill-judged, and which proved to be the beginning of the dissensions that ended in the ruin of the Federalist party. After every effort, therefore, to move Adams had failed, Pickering and others, including Hamilton himself, appealed to Washington. At a distance from the scene of action, and unfamiliar with the growth of differences within the party, Washington was not only surprised, but annoyed by the President's conduct. In addition to the evils which he believed would result in a military way from this change, he felt that the conditions which he had made had been violated, and that he had not been treated fairly. He therefore wrote to the President with his wonted plainness, on September 25, and pointed out that his stipulations had not been complied with, that the change of order among the major-generals was thoroughly wrong, and that the President's meddling with the inferior appointments had been hurtful and injudicious. His views were expressed in the most courteous way, although with an undertone of severe disapproval. There was no mistaking the meaning of the letter, however, and Adams, bold man and President as he was, gave way at once. Mr. Adams thought at the time that there had been about this matter of the major-generals too much intrigue, by which Washington had been deceived and he himself made a victim; but there seems no good reason to take this view of it, for there is no indication whatever that Washington did not know and understand the facts; and it was on the facts that he made his decision, and not on the methods by which they were conveyed to him. The propriety of the decision will hardly now be questioned, although it did not tend to make the relations between the ex-President and his suc-

cessor very cordial. They had always a great respect for each other, but not much sympathy, for they differed too widely in temperament. Even if Washington would have permitted it, it would have been impossible for the President to have quarreled with him, but at the same time he felt not a little awkwardness in dealing with his successor, and was inclined to think that that gentleman did not show him all the respect that was due. He wrote to McHenry on October 1: "As no mode is yet adopted by the President by which the battalion officers are to be appointed, and as I think I stand on very precarious ground in my relation to him, I am not over-zealous in taking *unauthorized* steps when those that I thought *were authorized* are not likely to meet with much respect."

There was, however, another consequence of this affair which gave Washington much more pain than any differences with the President. His old friend and companion in arms, General Knox, was profoundly hurt at the decision which placed Hamilton at the head of the army. One cannot be surprised at Knox's feelings, for he had been a distinguished officer, and had outranked both Hamilton and Pinckney. He felt that he ought to command the army, and that he was quite capable of doing so; and he did not relish being told in this official manner that he had grown old, and that the time had come for younger and abler men to pass beyond him. The archbishop in "Gil Blas" is one of the most universal types of human nature that we have. Nobody feels kindly to the monitor who points out the failings which time has brought, and we are all inclined to dismiss him with every wish that he may fare well and have a little more taste. Poor Knox could not dismiss his Gil Blas, and he felt the unpleasant admonition all the more bitterly from the fact that the blow was dealt by the two men whom he most loved and admired. Hamilton wrote him the best and most graceful of letters, but failed to soothe him; and Washington was no more fortunate. He tried with the utmost kindliness, and in his most courteous manner, to soften the disappointment, and to show Knox how convincing were the reasons for his action. But the case was not one where argument could be of avail, and when Knox persisted in his refusal to take the place assigned him, Washington, with all his sympathy, was perfectly frank in expressing his views.

In a second letter, complaining of the injustice with which he had been treated, Knox intimated that he would be willing to serve on the personal staff of the commander-in-chief. This was all very well; but much as Washington grieved for his old friend's disappointment, there was to be no misunderstanding in the matter. He wrote Knox on October 21: "After having expressed these sentiments with the frankness of undisguised friendship, it is hardly necessary to add that, if you should finally decline the appointment of major-general, there is none to whom I would give a more decided preference as an aide-de-camp, the offer of which is highly flattering, honorable, and grateful to my feelings, and for which I entertain a high sense. But, my dear General Knox, and here again I speak to you in a language of candor and friendship, examine well your mind upon this subject. Do not unite yourself to the suite of a man whom you may consider as the primary cause of what you call a degradation, with unpleasant sensations. This, while it was gnawing upon you, would, if I should come to the knowledge of it, make me unhappy; as my first wish would be that my military family and the whole army should consider themselves a band of brothers, willing and ready to die for each other."

Knox would not serve; and his ill temper, irritated still further by the apparent preference of the President and by the talk of his immediate circle, prevailed. On the other hand, Pinckney, one of the most generous and patriotic of men, accepted service at once without a syllable of complaint on the score that he had ranked Hamilton in the former war. It was with these two, therefore, that Washington carried on the work of organizing the provisional army. Despite his determination to remain in retirement until called to the field, his desire for perfection in any work that he undertook brought him out, and he gave much time and attention not only to the general questions which were raised, but to the details of the business, and on November 10, he addressed a series of inquiries, both general and particular, to Hamilton and Pinckney. These inquiries covered the whole scope of possible events, probable military operations, and the formation of the army. They were written in Philadelphia, whither he had gone, and where he passed a month with the two major-generals in the discussion of plans and measures. The result of their conferences was an elaborate and masterly report on army organization drawn up by Hamilton, upon whom, throughout this period of impending war, the brunt of the work fell.

Careful and painstaking, however, as Washington was in the matter of appointments and organization, dealing with them as if he was about to take the field at the head of the army, there was never a moment when he felt that there was danger of actual war. He had studied foreign affairs and the conditions of Europe too well to be much deceived about them, and least of all in regard to France. He felt from the beginning that the moment we displayed a proper spirit, began to arm, and fought one or two French ships successfully, that France would leave off bullying and abusing us, and make a satisfactory peace. The declared adherent of the maxim that to prepare for war was the most effectual means of preserving peace, he felt that never was it more important to carry out this doctrine than now; and it was for this reason that he labored so hard and gave so much thought to army organization at a time when he felt more than ever the need of repose, and shrank from the least semblance of a return to public life. In all his long career there was never a better instance of his devoted patriotism than his coming forward in this way at the sacrifice of every personal wish after his retirement from the presidency.

Yet, although he closely watched the course of politics, and gave, as has been said, a cordial support to the administration, his sympathies were rather with the opponents of the President within the ranks of their common party. The conduct of Gerry, who had been Adams's personal selection for a commissioner, was very distasteful to Washington, and was very far from exciting in his mind the approval which it drew from Mr. Adams. He wrote to Pickering on October 18: "With respect to Mr. Gerry, his own character and public satisfaction require better evidence than his letter to the minister of foreign relations to prove the propriety of his conduct during his envoyship." He did not believe that we were to have war with France, but he was very confident that a bold and somewhat uncompromising attitude was the best one for the country, and that above all we should not palter with France after the affronts to which we had been subjected. When President Adams, therefore, made his sudden change of policy by nominating Murray as a special envoy, Washington, despite his desire for peace, was by no means enthusiastic in his approval of the methods by which it was sought. The President wrote him announcing the appointment of Murray, and Washington acknowledged the letter and the information without any comment. He saw, of course, that as the President had seen fit to take the step he must be sustained, and he wrote to Murray to impress upon him the gravity of the mission with which he was intrusted; but he had serious doubts as to the success of such a mission under such conditions, and when delays occurred he was not without hopes of a final abandonment. The day after his letter to Murray he wrote to Hamilton: "I was surprised at the *measure*, how much more so at the manner of it! This business seems to have commenced in an evil hour, and under unfavorable auspices. I wish mischief may not tread in all its steps, and be the final result of the measure. A wide door was open, through which a retreat might have been made from the first *faux pas*, the shutting of which, to those who are not behind the curtain and are as little acquainted with the secrets of the cabinet as I am, is, from the present aspect of European affairs, quite incomprehensible." He hoped but little good from the mission, although it had his fervent wishes for its success, expressed repeatedly in letters to members of the cabinet; and while he was full of apprehension, he had a firm faith that all would end well.

For this anxiety, indeed, there was abundant reason. A violent change of policy toward France, the disorders occasioned by political dissensions at home, and the sudden appearance of the deadly doctrine of nullification, all combined to excite alarm in the mind of a man who looked as far into the future and as deep beneath the surface of things as did Washington. It was then that he urged Patrick Henry to reenter public life, and exerted his own influence wherever he could to check the separatist movement set on foot by Jefferson. He was deeply disturbed, too, by the tendencies of the times in other directions. The delirium of the French Revolution was not confined to France. Her soldiers bore with them the new doctrines, while far beyond the utmost reach of her armies flew the ideas engendered in the fevered air of Paris. Wherever they alighted they touched men and stung them to madness, and the madness that they bred was not confined to those who believed the new gospel, but was shared equally by those who resisted and loathed it. Burke, in his way, was as much crazed as Camille Desmoulins, and it seemed impossible for people living in the midst of that terrific convulsion of society to retain their judgment. Nowhere ought men to have been better able to withstand the contagion of the revolution than in America, and yet even here it produced the same results as in countries nearly affected by it. The party of opposition to the government became first ludicrous and then dangerous, in their wild admiration and senseless imitation of ideas and practices as utterly alien to the people of the United States as cannibalism or fire-worship. Then the Federalists, on their side, fell beneath the spell. The overthrow of religion, society, property, and morals, which they beheld in Paris, seemed to them to be threatening their own country, and they became as extreme as their opponents in the exactly opposite direction. Federalist divines came to look upon Jefferson, the most timid and prudent of men, as a Marat or Robespierre, ready to reproduce the excesses of his prototypes; while Pickering, Wolcott, and all their friends in public life regarded themselves as engaged in a struggle for the preservation of order and society and of all that they held most dear. They were in the habit of comparing French principles to a pestilence, and the French republic to a raging tiger. Even Hamilton was so moved as to believe that the United States were on the verge of anarchy, and he laid down his life at last in a senseless duel because he thought that his refusal to fight would disable him for leading the forces of order when the final crash came.

Washington, with his strong, calm judgment and his penetrating vision, was less affected than any of those who had followed and sustained him; but he was by no means untouched, and if we try to put ourselves in his place, his views seem far from unreasonable. He had at the outset wished well to the great movement in France, although even then he doubted its final success. Very soon, however, doubts changed to suspicions, and suspicions to conviction. As he saw the French revolution move on in its inevitable path, he came to hate and dread its deeds, its policies, and its doctrines. To a man of his temper it could not have been otherwise, for license and disorder were above all things detestable to him. They were the immediate fruits of the French revolution, and when he saw a party devoted to France preaching the same ideas in the United States, he could not but feel that there was a real and practical danger confronting the country. This was why he felt that we needed an energetic policy, and it was on this account that he distrusted the President's renewed effort for peace. The course of the opposition, as he saw it, threatened not merely the existence of the Union, but wittingly or unwittingly struck at the very foundations of society. His anxiety did not make him violent, as was the case with lesser men, but it convinced him of the necessity of strong measures, and he was not a man to shrink from vigorous action. He was quite prepared to do all that could be done to maintain the authority of the government, which he considered equivalent to the protection of society, and for this reason he approved of the Alien and Sedition acts.

In the process of time these two famous laws have come to be universally condemned, and those who have not questioned their constitutionality have declared them wrong, inexpedient and impolitic, and the immediate cause of the overthrow of the party responsible for them. Everybody has made haste to disown them, and there has been a general effort on the part of Federalist sympathizers to throw the blame for them on persons unknown. Biographers, especially, have tried zealously to clear the skirts of their heroes from any connection with these obnoxious acts; but the truth is, that, whether right or wrong, wise or unwise, these laws had the entire support of the ruling party from the President down. Hamilton, who objected to the first draft because it was needlessly violent, approved the purpose and principle of the legislation; and Washington was no exception to the general rule. He was calm about it, but his approbation was none the less distinct, and he took pains to circulate a sound argument, when he met with one, in justification of the Alien and Sedition acts.* In November, 1798, Alexander Spotswood wrote to him, asking his judgment on those laws. As the writer announced himself

---

*See letter to Bushrod Washington, Sparks, vi. p. 387.

to be thoroughly convinced of their unconstitutionality, Washington, with a little sarcasm, declined to enter into argument with him. "But," he continued, "I will take the liberty of advising such as are not 'thoroughly convinced,' and whose minds are yet open to conviction, to read the pieces and hear the arguments which have been adduced in favor of, as well as those against, the constitutionality and expediency of those laws, before they decide and consider to what lengths a certain description of men in our country have already driven, and seem resolved further to drive matters, and then ask themselves if it is not time and expedient to resort to protecting laws against aliens (for citizens, you certainly know, are not affected by that law), who acknowledge no allegiance to this country, and in many instances are sent among us, as there is the best circumstantial evidence to prove, for the express purpose of poisoning the minds of our people and sowing dissensions among them, in order to alienate their affections from the government of their choice, thereby endeavoring to dissolve the Union, and of course the fair and happy prospects which are unfolding to our view from the Revolution."

With these strong and decided feelings as to the proper policy to be adopted, and with such grave apprehensions as to the outcome of existing difficulties, Washington was deeply distressed by the divisions which he saw springing up among the Federalists. From his point of view it was bad enough to have the people of the country divided into two great parties; but that one of those parties, that which was devoted to the maintenance of order and the preservation of the Union, should be torn by internal dissensions, seemed to him almost inconceivable. He regarded the conduct of the party and of its leaders with quite as much indignation as sorrow, for it seemed to him that they were unpatriotic and false to their trust in permitting for a moment these personal factions which could have but one result. He wrote to Trumbull on August 30, 1799: —

"It is too interesting not to be again repeated, that if principles instead of men are not the steady pursuit of the Federalists, their cause will soon be at an end; if these are pursued they will not divide at the next election of President; if they do divide on so *important* a point, it would be dangerous to trust them on any other,—and none except those who might be solicitous to fill the chair of government would do it."*

He was a true prophet, but he did not live to see the verification of his predictions, which would have been to him a source of so much grief. In the midst of his anxieties about public affairs, and of the quiet, homely interests which made the days at Mount Vernon so pleasant, the end suddenly came. There was no more forewarning than if he had been struck down by accident or violence. He had always been a man of great physical vigor, and although he had had one or two acute and dangerous illnesses arising from mental strain and much overwork, there is no indication that he had any organic disease, and since his retirement from the presidency he had been better than for many years. There was not only no sign of breaking up, but he appeared full of health and activity, and led his usual wholesome outdoor life with keen enjoyment.

The morning of December 12 was overcast. He wrote to Hamilton warmly approving the scheme for a military academy; and having finished this, which was probably the last letter he ever wrote, he mounted his horse and rode off for his usual round of duties. He noted in his diary, where he always described the weather with methodical exactness, that it began to snow about one o'clock, soon after to hail, and then turned to a settled cold rain. He stayed out notwithstanding for about two hours, and then came back to the house and franked his letters. Mr. Lear noticed that his hair was damp with snow, and expressed a fear that he had got wet; but the General said no, that his coat had kept him dry, and sat down to dinner without changing his clothes. The next morning snow was still falling so that he did not ride, and he complained of a slight sore throat, but nevertheless went out in the afternoon to mark some trees that were to be cut down. His hoarseness increased toward night, yet still he made light of it, and read the newspapers and chatted with Mrs. Washington during the evening.

When he went to bed Mr. Lear urged him to take something for his

*Life of Silliman, vol. ii. p. 385.

cold. "No," he replied, "you know I never take anything for a cold. Let it go as it came." In the night he had a severe chill, followed by difficulty in breathing; and between two and three in the morning he awoke Mrs. Washington, but would not allow her to get up and call a servant lest she should take cold. At daybreak Mr. Lear was summoned, and found Washington breathing with difficulty and hardly able to speak. Dr. Craik, the friend and companion of many years, was sent for at once, and meantime the General was bled slightly by one of the overseers. A futile effort was also made to gargle his throat, and external applications were tried without affording relief. Dr. Craik arrived between eight and nine o'clock with two other physicians, when other remedies were tried and the patient was bled again, all without avail. About half-past four he called Mrs. Washington to his bedside and asked her to get two wills from his desk. She did so, and after looking them over he ordered one to be destroyed and gave her the other to keep. He then said to Lear, speaking with the utmost difficulty, but saying what he had to say with characteristic determination and clearness: "I find I am going; my breath cannot last long. I believed from the first that the disorder would prove fatal. Do you arrange and record all my late military letters and papers. Arrange my accounts and settle my books, as you know more about them than any one else; and let Mr. Rawlins finish recording my other letters, which he has begun." He then asked if Lear recollected anything which it was essential for him to do, as he had but a very short time to continue with them. Lear replied that he could recollect nothing, but that he hoped the end was not so near. Washington smiled, and said that he certainly was dying, and that as it was the debt which we must all pay, he looked to the event with perfect resignation.

The disease which was killing him was acute œdematous laryngitis,[*] which is as simple as it is rare and fatal,[†] and he was being slowly strangled to death by the closing of the throat. He bore the suffering, which

---

[*] It was called at the time a quinsy.

[†] See Memoir on *The Last Sickness of Washington*, by James Jackson, M.D. In response to an inquiry as to the modern treatment of this disease, the late Dr. F. H. Hooper of Boston, well known as an authority on diseases of the throat, wrote me: "Washington's physicians are not to

must have been intense, with his usual calm self-control, but as the afternoon wore on the keen distress and the difficulty of breathing made him
restless. From time to time Mr. Lear tried to raise him and make his position easier. The General said, "I fear I fatigue you too much;" and again,
on being assured to the contrary, "Well, it is a debt we must pay to each
other, and I hope when you want aid of this kind you will find it." He was
courteous and thoughtful of others to the last, and told his servant, who
had been standing all day in attendance upon him, to sit down. To Dr.
Craik he said: "I die hard, but I am not afraid to go. I believed from my
first attack that I should not survive it. My breath cannot last long."
When a little later the other physicians came in and assisted him to sit up,
he said: "I feel I am going. I thank you for your attentions, but I pray you
will take no more trouble about me. Let me go off quietly. I cannot last
long." He lay there for some hours longer, restless and suffering, but
utterly uncomplaining, taking such remedies as the physicians ordered in
silence. About ten o'clock he spoke again to Lear, although it required a
most desperate effort to do so. "I am just going," he said. "Have me
decently buried, and do not let my body be put into the vault in less than
three days after I am dead." Lear bowed, and Washington said, "Do you
understand me?" Lear answered, "Yes." " 'Tis well," he said, and with
these last words again fell silent. A little later he felt his own pulse, and,
as he was counting the strokes, Lear saw his countenance change. His
hand dropped back from the wrist he had been holding, and all was over.
The end had come. Washington was dead. He died as he had lived, simply and bravely, without parade and without affectation. The last duties

---

be criticised for their treatment, for they acted according to their best light and knowledge. To
treat such a case in such a manner in the year 1889 would be little short of criminal. At the present time the physicians would use the laryngoscope and look and see what the trouble was.
(The laryngoscope has only been used since 1857.) In this disease the function most interfered
with is breathing. The one thing which saves a patient in this disease is a *timely tracheotomy.* (I
doubt if tracheotomy had ever been performed in Virginia in Washington's time.) Washington
ought to have been tracheotomized, or rather that is the way cases are saved to-day. No one
would think of antimony, calomel, or bleeding now. The point is to let in the air, and not to let
out the blood. After tracheotomy has been performed, the œdema and swelling of the larynx
subside in three to six days. The tracheotomy tube is then removed, and respiration goes on
again through the natural channels."

were done, the last words said, the last trials borne with the quiet fitness, the gracious dignity, that even the gathering mists of the supreme hour could neither dim nor tarnish. He had faced life with a calm, high, victorious spirit. So did he face death and the unknown when Fate knocked at the door.

CHAPTER XVIII

GEORGE WASHINGTON

THIS LAST CHAPTER cannot begin more fitly than by quoting again the words of Mr. McMaster: "George Washington is an unknown man." Mr. McMaster might have added that to no man in our history has greater injustice of a certain kind been done, or more misunderstanding been meted out, than to Washington, and although this sounds like the merest paradox, it is nevertheless true. From the hour when the door of the tomb at Mount Vernon closed behind his coffin to the present instant, the chorus of praise and eulogy has never ceased, but has swelled deeper and louder with each succeeding year. He has been set apart high above all other men, and reverenced with the unquestioning veneration accorded only to the leaders of mankind and the founders of nations; and in this very devotion lies one secret at least of the fact that, while all men have praised Washington, comparatively few have understood him. He has been lifted high up into a lonely greatness, and unconsciously put outside the range of human sympathy. He has been accepted as a being as nearly perfect as it is given to man to be, but our warm personal interest has been reserved for other and lesser men who seemed to be nearer to us in their virtues and their errors alike. Such isolation, lofty though it be, is perilous and leads to grievous misunderstandings. From it has come the widespread idea that Washington was cold, and as devoid of human sympathies as he was free from the common failings of humanity.

Of this there will be something to say presently, but meantime there is another more prolific source of error in regard to Washington to be considered. Men who are loudly proclaimed to be faultless always excite a certain kind of resentment. It is a dangerous eminence for any one to occupy. The temples of Greece are in ruins, and her marvelous literature is little more than a collection of fragments, but the feelings of the citizens who exiled Aristides because they were weary of hearing him called "just," exist still, unchanged and unchangeable. Washington has not only been called "just," but he has had every other good quality attributed to him by countless biographers and eulogists with an almost painful iteration, and the natural result has followed. Many persons have felt the sense of fatigue which the Athenians expressed practically by their oyster shells, and have been led to cast doubts on Washington's perfection as the only consolation for their own sense of injury. Then, again, Washington's fame has been so overshadowing, and his greatness so immutable, that he has been very inconvenient to the admirers and the biographers of other distinguished men. From these two sources, from the general jealousy of the classic Greek variety, and the particular jealousy born of the necessities of some other hero, much adverse and misleading criticism has come. It has never been a safe or popular amusement to assail Washington directly, and this course usually has been shunned; but although the attacks have been veiled they have none the less existed, and they have been all the more dangerous because they were insidious.

In his lifetime Washington had his enemies and detractors in abundance. During the Revolution he was abused and intrigued against, thwarted and belittled, to a point which posterity in general scarcely realizes. Final and conclusive victory brought an end to this, and he passed to the presidency amid a general acclaim. Then the attacks began again. Their character has been shown in a previous chapter, but they were of no real moment except as illustrations of the existence and meaning of party divisions. The ravings of Bache and Freneau, and the coarse insults of Giles, were all totally unimportant in themselves. They merely define the purposes and character of the party which opposed Washington, and but for him would be forgotten. Among his eminent contemporaries, Jefferson and Pickering, bitterly opposed in all things else, have left memoranda and letters reflecting upon the abilities of their former chief. Jefferson disliked him because he blocked his path, but with habitual caution he never proceeded beyond a covert sneer implying that Washington's mental powers, at no time very great, were impaired by age during his presidency, and that he was easily deceived by practised intriguers. Pickering, with more boldness, set Washington down as commonplace, not original in his thought, and vastly inferior to Hamilton, apparently because he was not violent, and did not make up his mind before he knew the facts.

Adverse contemporary criticism, however, is slight in amount and vague in character; it can be readily dismissed, and it has in no case weight enough to demand much consideration. Modern criticism of the same kind has been even less direct, but is much more serious and cannot be lightly passed over. It invariably proceeds by negations setting out with an apparently complete acceptance of Washington's greatness, and then assailing him by telling us what he was not. Few persons who have not given this matter a careful study realize how far criticism of this sort has gone, and there is indeed no better way of learning what Washington really was than by examining the various negations which tell us what he was not.

Let us take the gravest first. It has been confidently asserted that Washington was not an American in anything but the technical sense. This idea is more diffused than, perhaps, would be generally supposed, and it has also been formally set down in print, in which we are more fortunate than in many other instances where the accusation has not got beyond the elusive condition of loose talk.

In that most noble poem, the "Commemoration Ode," Mr. Lowell speaks of Lincoln as "the first American." The poet's winged words fly far, and find a resting-place in many minds. This idea has become widespread, and has recently found fuller expression in Mr. Clarence King's prefatory note to the great life of Lincoln by Hay and Nicolay.* Mr. King says: "Abraham Lincoln was the first American to reach the lonely height

---

*Mr. Matthew Arnold, and more recently Professor Goldwin Smith, have both spoken of Washington as an Englishman. I do not mention this to discredit the statements of Mr. Lowell or Mr. King, but merely to indicate how far this mistaken idea has traveled.

of immortal fame. Before him, within the narrow compass of our history, were but two preëminent names,—Columbus the discoverer, and Washington the founder; the one an Italian seer, the other an English country gentleman. In a narrow sense, of course, Washington was an American. . . . For all that he was English in his nature, habits, moral standards, and social theories; in short, in all points which, aside from mere geographical position, make up a man, he was as thorough-going a British colonial gentleman as one could find anywhere beneath the Union Jack. The genuine American of Lincoln's type came later. . . . George Washington, an English commoner, vanquished George, an English king."

In order to point his sentence and prove his first postulate, Mr. King is obliged not only to dispose of Washington, but to introduce Columbus, who never was imagined in the wildest fantasy to be an American, and to omit Franklin. The omission of itself is fatal to Mr. King's case. Franklin has certainly a "preëminent name." He has, too, "immortal fame," although of course of a widely different character from that of either Washington or Lincoln, but he was a great man in the broad sense of a worldwide reputation. Yet no one has ever ventured to call Benjamin Franklin an Englishman. He was a colonial American, of course, but he was as intensely an American as any man who has lived on this continent before or since. A man of the people, he was American by the character of his genius, by his versatility, the vivacity of his intellect, and his mental dexterity. In his abilities, his virtues, and his defects he was an American, and so plainly one as to be beyond the reach of doubt or question. There were others of that period, too, who were as genuine Americans as Franklin or Lincoln. Such were Jonathan Edwards, the peculiar product of New England Calvinism; Patrick Henry, who first broke down colonial lines to declare himself an American; Samuel Adams, the great forerunner of the race of American politicians; Thomas Jefferson, the idol of American democracy. These and many others Mr. King might exclude on the ground that they did not reach the lonely height of immortal fame. But Franklin is enough. Unless one is prepared to set Franklin down as an Englishman, which would be as reasonable as to say that Daniel Webster was a fine example of the Slavic race, it must be admitted that it was possible for the thirteen colonies to produce in the eighteenth century a genuine American who won immortal fame. If they could produce one of one type, they could produce a second of another type, and there was, therefore, nothing inherently impossible in existing conditions to prevent Washington from being an American.

Lincoln was undoubtedly the first great American of his type, but that is not the only type of American. It is one which, as bodied forth in Abraham Lincoln, commands the love and veneration of the people of the United States, and the admiration of the world wherever his name is known. To the noble and towering greatness of his mind and character it does not add one hair's breadth to say that he was the first American, or that he was of a common or uncommon type. Greatness like Lincoln's is far beyond such qualifications, and least of all is it necessary to his fame to push Washington from his birthright. To say that George Washington, an English commoner, vanquished George, an English king, is clever and picturesque, but like many other pleasing antitheses it is painfully inaccurate. Allegiance does not make race or nationality. The Hindoos are subjects of Victoria, but they are not Englishmen.

Franklin shows that it was possible to produce a most genuine American of unquestioned greatness in the eighteenth century, and with all possible deference to Mr. Lowell and Mr. King, I venture the assertion that George Washington was as genuine an American as Lincoln or Franklin. He was an American of the eighteenth and not of the nineteenth century, but he was none the less an American. I will go further. Washington was not only an American of a pure and noble type, but he was the first thorough American in the broad, national sense, as distinct from the colonial American of his time.

After all, what is it to be an American? Surely it does not consist in the number of generations merely which separate the individual from his forefathers who first settled here. Washington was fourth in descent from the first American of his name, while Lincoln was in the sixth generation. This difference certainly constitutes no real distinction. There are people to-day, not many luckily, whose families have been here for two hundred and fifty years, and who are as utterly un-American as it is possible to be, while there are others, whose fathers were immigrants, who are as intensely American as any one can desire or imagine. In a new country, peopled in two hundred and fifty years by immigrants from the Old World and their descendants, the process of Americanization is not limited by any hard and fast rules as to time and generations, but is altogether a matter of individual and race temperament. The production of the well-defined American types and of the fixed national characteristics which now exist has been going on during all that period, but in any special instance the type to which a given man belongs must be settled by special study and examination.

Washington belonged to the English-speaking race. So did Lincoln. Both sprang from the splendid stock which was formed during centuries from a mixture of the Celtic, Teutonic, Scandinavian, and Norman peoples, and which is known to the world as English. Both, so far as we can tell, had nothing but English blood, as it would be commonly called, in their veins, and both were of that part of the English race which emigrated to America, where it has been the principal factor in the development of the new people called Americans. They were men of English race, modified and changed in the fourth and sixth generations by the new country, the new conditions, and the new life, and by the contact and admixture of other races. Lincoln, a very great man, one who has reached "immortal fame," was clearly an American of a type that the Old World cannot show, or at least has not produced. The idea of many persons in regard to Washington seems to be, that he was a great man of a type which the Old World, or, to be more exact, which England, had produced. One hears it often said that Washington was simply an American Hampden. Such a comparison is an easy method of description, nothing more. Hampden is memorable among men, not for his abilities, which there is no reason to suppose were very extraordinary, but for his devoted and unselfish patriotism, his courage, his honor, and his pure and lofty spirit. He embodied what his country-men believe to be the moral qualities of their race in their finest flower, and no nation, be it said, could have a nobler ideal. Washington was conspicuous for the same qualities, exhibited in like fashion. Is there a single one of the essential attributes of Hampden that Lincoln also did not possess? Was he not an unselfish and devoted patriot, pure in heart, gentle of spirit, high of honor, brave, merciful, and temperate? Did he not lay down his life for his country in the box at Ford's Theatre as ungrudgingly as Hampden offered his in the smoke of battle upon Chalgrove field? Surely we must answer Yes. In other words, these three men all had the great moral attributes which are the characteristics of the English race in its highest and purest development on either side of the Atlantic. Yet no one has ever called Lincoln an American Hampden simply because Hampden and Washington were men of ancient family, members of an aristocracy by birth, and Lincoln was not. This is the distinction between them; and how vain it is, in the light of their lives and deeds, which make all pedigrees and social ranks look so poor and worthless! The differences among them are trivial, the resemblances deep and lasting.

I have followed out this comparison because it illustrates perfectly the entirely superficial character of the reasons which have led men to speak of Washington as an English country gentleman. It has been said that he was English in his habits, moral standards, and social theories, which has an important sound, but which for the most part comes down to a question of dress and manners. He wore black velvet and powdered hair, knee-breeches and diamond buckles, which are certainly not American fashions to-day. But they were American fashions in the last century, and every man wore them who could afford to, no matter what his origin. Let it be remembered, however, that Washington also wore the hunting-shirt and fringed leggins of the backwoodsman, and that it was he who introduced this purely American dress into the army as a uniform.

His manners likewise were those of the century in which he lived, formal and stately, and of course colored by his own temperament. His moral standards were those of a high-minded, honorable man. Are we ready to say that they were not American? Did they differ in any vital point from those of Lincoln? His social theories were simple in the extreme. He neither overvalued nor underrated social conventions, for he knew that they were a part of the fabric of civilized society, not vitally important and yet not wholly trivial. He was a member of an aristocracy, it is true, both by birth and situation. There was a recognized social aristocracy in every colony before the Revolution, for the drum-beat of the great democratic march had not then sounded. In the northern colonies it was never strong, and in New England it was especially weak, for the governments and people there were essentially democratic, although they hardly recognized it themselves. In Virginia and the southern colonies, on the other hand, there was a vigorous aristocracy resting on the permanent foundation of slavery. Where slaves are there must be masters, and where there are masters there are aristocrats; but it was an American and not an English aristocracy. Lineage and family had weight in the south as in the north, but that which put a man undeniably in the ruling class was the ownership of black slaves and the possession of a white skin. This aristocracy lasted with its faults and its virtues until it perished in the shock of civil war, when its foundation of human slavery was torn from under it. From the slave-holding aristocracy of Virginia came, with the exception of Patrick Henry, all the great men of that State who did so much for American freedom, and who rendered such imperishable service to the republic in law, in politics, and in war. From this aristocracy came Marshall, and Mason, and Madison, the Lees, the Randolphs, the Harrisons, and the rest. From it came also Thomas Jefferson, the hero of American democracy; and to it was added Patrick Henry, not by lineage or slave-holding, but by virtue of his brilliant abilities, and because he, too, was an aristocrat by the immutable division of race. It was this aristocracy into which Washington was born, and amid which he was brought up. To say that it colored his feelings and habits is simply to say that he was human; but to urge that it made him un-American is to exclude at once from the ranks of Americans all the great men given to the country by the South. Washington, in fact, was less affected by his surroundings, and rose above them more quickly, than any other man of his day, because he was the greatest man of his time, with a splendid breadth of vision.

When he first went among the New England troops at the siege of Boston, the rough, democratic ways of the people jarred upon him, and offended especially his military instincts, for he was not only a Virginian but he was a great soldier, and military discipline is essentially aristocratic. These volunteer soldiers, called together from the plough and the fishing-smack, were free and independent men, unaccustomed to any rule but their own, and they had still to learn the first rudiments of military service. To Washington, soldiers who elected and deposed their officers, and who went home when they felt that they had a right to do so, seemed well-nigh useless and quite incomprehensible. They angered him and tried his patience almost beyond endurance, and he spoke of them at the outset in harsh terms by no means wholly unwarranted. But they were part of his problem, and he studied them. He was a soldier, but not an aristocrat wrapped up in immutable prejudices, and he learned to know these men, and they came to love, obey, and follow him with an intelligent devotion far better than anything born of mere discipline. Before the year was out, he wrote to Lund Washington praising the New England troops in the highest terms, and at the close of the war he said that practically the whole army then was composed of New England soldiers. They stayed by him to the end, and as they were steadfast in war so they remained in peace. He trusted and confided in New England, and her sturdy democracy gave him a loyal and unflinching support to the day of his death.

This openness of mind and superiority to prejudice were American in the truest and best sense; but Washington showed the same qualities in private life and toward individuals which he displayed in regard to communities. He was free, of course, from the cheap claptrap which abuses the name of democracy by saying that birth, breeding, and education are undemocratic, and therefore to be reckoned against a man. He valued these qualities rightly, but he looked to see what a man was and not who he was, which is true democracy. The two men who were perhaps nearest to his affections were Knox and Hamilton. One was a Boston bookseller, who rose to distinction by bravery and good service, and the other was a young adventurer from the West Indies, without either family or money at his back. It was the same with much humbler persons. He never failed, on his way to Philadelphia, to stop at Wilmington and have a chat with one Captain O'Flinn, who kept a tavern and had been a

Revolutionary soldier; and this was but a single instance among many of like character. Any soldier of the Revolution was always sure of a welcome at the hands of his old commander. Eminent statesmen, especially of the opposition, often found his manner cold, but no old soldier ever complained of it, no servant ever left him, and the country people about Mount Vernon loved him as a neighbor and friend, and not as the distant great man of the army and the presidency.

He believed thoroughly in popular government. One does not find in his letters the bitter references to democracy and to the populace which can be discovered in the writings of so many of his party friends, legacies of pre-revolutionary ideas inflamed by hatred of Parisian mobs. He always spoke of the people at large with a simple respect, because he knew that the future of the United States was in their hands and not in that of any class, and because he believed that they would fulfill their mission. The French Revolution never carried him away, and when it bred anarchy and bloodshed he became hostile to French influence, because license and disorder were above all things hateful to him. Yet he did not lose his balance in the other direction, as was the case with so many of his friends. He resisted and opposed French ideas and French democracy, so admired and so loudly preached by Jefferson and his followers, because he esteemed them perilous to the country. But there is not a word to indicate that he did not think that such dangers would be finally overcome, even if at the cost of much suffering, by the sane sense and ingrained conservatism of the American people. Other men talked more noisily about the people, but no one trusted them in the best sense more than Washington, and his only fear was that evils might come from their being misled by false lights.

Once more, what is it to be an American? Putting aside all the outer shows of dress and manners, social customs and physical peculiarities, is it not to believe in America and in the American people? Is it not to have an abiding and moving faith in the future and in the destiny of America?—something above and beyond the patriotism and love which every man whose soul is not dead within him feels for the land of his birth? Is it not to be national and not sectional, independent and not colonial? Is it not to have a high conception of what this great new country should be, and to follow out that ideal with loyalty and truth?

Has any man in our history fulfilled these conditions more perfectly and completely than George Washington? Has any man ever lived who served the American people more faithfully, or with a higher and truer conception of the destiny and possibilities of the country? Born of an old and distinguished family, he found himself, when a boy just out of school, dependent on his mother, and with an inheritance that promised him more acres than shillings. He did not seek to live along upon what he could get from the estate, and still less did he feel that it was only possible for him to enter one of the learned professions. Had he been an Englishman in fact or in feeling, he would have felt very naturally the force of the limitations imposed by his social position. But being an American, his one idea was to earn his living honestly, because it was the creed of his country that earning an honest living is the most creditable thing a man can do. Boy as he was, he went out manfully into the world to win with his own hands the money which would make him self-supporting and independent. His business as a surveyor took him into the wilderness, and there he learned that the first great work before the American people was to be the conquest of the continent. He dropped the surveyor's rod and chain to negotiate with the savages, and then took up the sword to fight them and the French, so that the New World might be secured to the English-speaking race. A more purely American training cannot be imagined. It was not the education of universities or of courts, but that of hard-earned personal independence, won in the backwoods and by frontier fighting. Thus trained, he gave the prime of his manhood to leading the Revolution which made his country free, and his riper years to building up that independent nationality without which freedom would have been utterly vain.

He was the first to rise above all colonial or state lines, and grasp firmly the conception of a nation to be formed from the thirteen jarring colonies. The necessity of national action in the army was of course at once apparent to him, although not to others; but he carried the same broad views into widely different fields, where at the time they wholly escaped notice. It was Washington, oppressed by a thousand cares, who in the early days of the Revolution saw the need of Federal courts for admiralty cases and for other purposes. It was he who suggested this scheme, years before any one even dreamed of the Constitution; and from the special committees of Congress, formed for this object in accordance with this advice, came, in the process of time, the Federal judiciary of the United States.* Even in that early dawn of the Revolution, Washington had clear in his own mind the need of a continental system for war, diplomacy, finance, and law, and he worked steadily to bring this policy to fulfilment.

When the war was over, the thought that engaged his mind most was of the best means to give room for expansion, and to open up the unconquered continent to the forerunners of a mighty army of settlers. For this purpose all his projects for roads, canals, and surveys were formed and forced into, public notice. He looked beyond the limits of the Atlantic colonies. His vision went far over the barriers of the Alleghanies; and where others saw thirteen infant States backed by the wilderness, he beheld the germs of a great empire. While striving thus to lay the West open to the march of the settler, he threw himself into the great struggle, where Hamilton and Madison, and all who "thought continentally," were laboring for that union without which all else was worse than futile.

From the presidency of the convention that formed the Constitution, he went to the presidency of the government which that convention brought into being; and in all that followed, the one guiding thought was to clear the way for the advance of the people, and to make that people and their government independent in thought, in policy, and in character, as the Revolution had made them independent politically. The same spirit which led him to write during the war that our battles must be fought and our victories won by Americans, if victory and independence were to be won at all, or to have any real and solid worth, pervaded his whole administration. We see it in his Indian policy, which was directed not only to pacifying the tribes, but to putting it out of their power to

---

*See the very interesting memoir on this subject by the Hon. J. C. Bancroft Davis.

arrest or even delay western settlement. We see it in his attitude toward foreign ministers, and in his watchful persistence in regard to the Mississippi, which ended in our securing the navigation of the great river. We see it again in his anxious desire to keep peace until we had passed the point where war might bring a dissolution; and how real that danger was, and how clear and just his perception of it, is shown by the Kentucky and Virginia Resolutions and by the separatist movement in New England during the later war of 1812. Even in 1812 the national existence was menaced, but the danger would have proved fatal if it had come twenty years earlier, with parties divided by their sympathies with contending foreign nations. It was for the sake of the Union that Washington was so patient with France, and faced so quietly the storm of indignation aroused by the Jay treaty.

In his whole foreign policy, which was so peculiarly his own, the American spirit was his pole star; and of all the attacks made upon him, the only one which really tried his soul was the accusation that he was influenced by foreign predilections. The blind injustice, which would not comprehend that his one purpose was to be American and to make the people and the government American, touched him more deeply than anything else. As party strife grew keener over the issues raised by the war between France and England, and as French politics and French ideas became more popular, his feelings found more frequent utterance, and it is interesting to see how this man, who, we are now told, was an English country gentleman, wrote and felt on this matter in very trying times. Let us remember, as we listen to him now in his own defense, that he was an extremely honest man, silent for the most part in doing his work, but when he spoke meaning every word he said, and saying exactly what he meant. This was the way in which be wrote to Patrick Henry in October, 1795, when he offered him the secretaryship of State:—

> My ardent desire is, and my aim has been as far as depended upon the executive department, to comply strictly with all our engagements, foreign and domestic; but to keep the United States free from political connection with every

other country, to see them independent of all and under the influence of none. In a word, I want an *American* character, that the powers of Europe may be convinced that we act for *ourselves*, and not for others. This, in my judgment, is the only way to be respected abroad and happy at home; and not, by becoming partisans of Great Britain or France, create dissensions, disturb the public tranquillity, and destroy, perhaps forever, the cement which binds the Union.

Not quite a year later, when the Jay treaty was still agitating the public mind in regard to our relations with France, he wrote to Pickering:—

The Executive has a plain road to pursue, namely, to fulfill all the engagements which duty requires; be influenced beyond this by none of the contending parties; maintain a strict neutrality unless obliged by imperious circumstances to depart from it; do justice to all, and never forget that we are Americans, the remembrance of which will convince us that we ought not to be French or English.

After leaving the presidency, when our difficulties with France seemed to be thickening, and the sky looked very dark, he wrote to a friend saying that he firmly believed that all would come out well, and then added: "To me this is so demonstrable, that not a particle of doubt could dwell on my mind relative thereto, if our citizens would advocate their own cause, instead of that of any other nation under the sun; that is, if, instead of being Frenchmen or Englishmen in politics they would be Americans, indignant at every attempt of either or any other powers to establish an influence in our councils or presume to sow the seeds of discord or disunion among us."

A few days later he wrote to Thomas Pinckney: "It remains to be seen whether our country will stand upon independent ground, or be directed in its political concerns by any other nation. A little time will show who are its true friends, or, what is synonymous, who are true Americans."

But this eager desire for a true Americanism did not stop at our foreign policy, or our domestic politics. He wished it to enter into every part of the life and thought of the people, and when it was proposed to bring over the entire staff of a Genevan university to take charge of a national university here, he threw his influence against it, expressing grave doubts as to the advantage of importing an entire "seminary of foreigners," for the purpose of American education. The letter on this subject, which was addressed to John Adams, then continued:—

> My opinion with respect to emigration is that except of useful mechanics, and some particular descriptions of men or professions, there is no need of encouragement; while the policy or advantage of its taking place in a body (I mean the settling of them in a body) may be much questioned; for by so doing they retain the language, habits, and principles, good or bad, which they bring with them. Whereas by an intermixture with our people, they or their descendants get assimilated to our customs, measures, and laws; in a word, soon become one people.

He had this thought so constantly in his mind that it found expression in his will, in the clause bequeathing certain property for the foundation of a university in the District of Columbia. "I proceed," he said, "after this recital for the more correct understanding of the case, to declare that it has always been a source of serious regret with me to see the youth of these United States sent to foreign countries for the purposes of education, often before their minds were formed, or they had imbibed any adequate ideas of the happiness of their own; contracting too frequently not only habits of dissipation and extravagance, but *principles unfriendly to republican government and to the true and genuine liberties of mankind*, which thereafter are rarely overcome; for these reasons it has been my ardent wish to see a plan devised on a liberal scale, which would have a tendency to spread systematic ideas through all parts of this rising empire, thereby to do away with local attachments and state prejudices, as far as the nature of things would or indeed ought to admit, from our national councils."

Were these the words of an English country gentleman, who chanced to be born in one of England's colonies? Persons of the English country gentleman pattern at that time were for the most part loyalists; excellent people, very likely, but not of the Washington type. Their hopes and ideals, their policies and their beliefs were in the mother country, not here. The faith, the hope, the thought, of Washington were all in the United States. His one purpose was to make America independent in thought and action, and he strove day and night to build up a nation. He labored unceasingly to lay the foundations of the great empire which, with almost prophetic vision, he saw beyond the mountains, by opening the way for the western movement. His foreign policy was a declaration to the world of a new national existence, and he strained every nerve to lift our politics from the colonial condition of foreign issues. He wished all immigration to be absorbed and moulded here, so that we might be one people, one in speech and in political faith. His last words, given to the world after the grave had closed over him, were a solemn plea for a home training for the youth of the Republic, so that all men might think as Americans, untainted by foreign ideas, and rise above all local prejudices. He did not believe that mere material development was the only or the highest goal; for he knew that the true greatness of a nation was moral and intellectual, and his last thoughts were for the upbuilding of character and intelligence. He was never a braggart, and mere boasting about his country as about himself was utterly repugnant to him. He never hesitated to censure what he believed to be wrong, but he addressed his criticisms to his countrymen in order to lead them to better things, and did not indulge in them in order to express his own discontent, or to amuse or curry favor with foreigners. In a word, he loved his country, and had an abiding faith in its future and in its people, upon whom his most earnest thoughts and loftiest aspirations were centred. No higher, purer, or more thorough Americanism than his could be imagined. It was a conception far in advance of the time, possible only to a powerful mind, capable of lifting itself out of existing conditions and alien influences, so that it might look with undazzled gaze upon the distant future. The first American in the broad national sense, there has never been a man more thoroughly and truly American than Washington. It will be a sorry day when we consent to take that noble figure from "the forefront of the nation's life," and rank George Washington as anything but an American of Americans, instinct with the ideas, as he was devoted to the fortunes of the New World which gave him birth.

There is another class of critics who have attacked Washington from another side. These are the gentlemen who find him in the way of their own heroes. Washington was a man of decided opinions about men as well as measures, and he was extremely positive. He had his enemies as well as his friends, his likes and his dislikes, strong and clear, according to his nature. The respect which he commanded in his life has lasted unimpaired since his death, and it is an awkward thing for the biographers of some of his contemporaries to know that Washington opposed, distrusted, or disliked their heroes. Therefore, in one way or another they have gone round a stumbling-block which they could not remove. The commonest method is to eliminate Washington by representing him vaguely as the great man with whom every one agreed, who belonged to no party, and favored all; then he is pushed quietly aside. Evils and wrong-doing existed under his administration from the opposition point of view, but they were the work of his ministers and of wicked advisers. The king could do no wrong, and this pleasant theory, which is untrue in fact, amounts to saying that Washington had no opinions, but was simply a grand and imposing figure-head. The only ground for it which is even suggested is that he sought advice, that he used other men's ideas, and that he made up his mind slowly. All this is true, and these very qualities help to show his greatness, for only small minds mistake their relations with the universe, and confuse their finite powers with omniscience. The great man, who sees facts and reads the future, uses other men, knows the bounds of possibility in action, can decide instantly if need be, but leaves rash conclusions to those who are incapable of reaching any others. In reality there never was a man who had more definite and vigorous opinions than Washington, and the responsibility which he bore he never shifted to other shoulders. The work of the Revolution and the presidency, whether good or bad, was his own, and he was ready to stand or fall by it.

There is a still further extension of the idea that Washington represented all parties and all views, and had neither party nor opinions of his own. This theory is to the effect that he was great by character alone, but that in other respects he did not rise above the level of dignified commonplace. Such, for instance, is apparently the view of Mr. Parton, who in a clever essay discusses in philosophical fashion the possible advantages arising from the success attained by mere character, as in the case of Washington. Mr. Parton points his theory by that last incident of counting the pulse as death drew nigh. How characteristic, he exclaims, of the methodical, commonplace man, is such an act. It was not common, be it said, even were it commonplace. It was certainly a very simple action, but rare enough so far as we know on the every-day deathbed, or in the supreme hour of dying greatness, and it was wholly free from that affectation which Dr. Johnson thought almost inseparable from the last solemn moment. Irregularity is not proof of genius any more than method, and of the two, the latter is the surer companion of greatness. The last hour of Washington showed that calm, collected courage which had never failed in war or peace; and so far it was proof of character. But was it not something more? The commonplace action of counting the pulse was in reality profoundly characteristic, for it was the last exhibition of the determined purpose to know the truth, and grasp the fact. Death was upon him; he would know the fact. He had looked facts in the face all his life, and when the mists gathered, he would face them still.

High and splendid character, great moral qualities for after-ages to admire, he had beyond any man of modern times. But to suppose that in other respects he belonged to the ranks of mediocrity is not only a contradiction in terms, but utterly false. It was not character that fought the Trenton campaign and carried the revolution to victory. It was military genius. It was not character that read the future of America and created our foreign policy. It was statesmanship of the highest order. Without the great moral qualities which he possessed, his career would not have been possible; but it would have been quite as impossible if the intellect had not equaled the character. There is no need to argue the truism that Washington was a great man, for that is universally admitted. But it is vary needful that his greatness should be rightly understood, and the right understanding of it is by no means universal. His character has been exalted at the expense of his intellect, and his goodness has been so much insisted upon both by admirers and critics that we are in danger of forgetting that he had a great mind as well as high moral worth.

This false attitude both of praise and criticism has been so persisted in that if we accept the premises we are forced to the conclusion that Washington was actually dull, while with much more openness it is asserted that he was cold and at times even harsh. "In the mean time," says Mr. McMaster, "Washington was deprived of the services of the only two men his cold heart ever really loved." "A Cromwell with the juice squeezed out," says Carlyle somewhere, in his rough and summary fashion. Are these judgments correct? Was Washington really, with all his greatness, dull and cold? He was a great general and a great President, first in war and first in peace and all that, says our caviler, but his relaxation was in farm accounts, and his business war and politics. He could plan a campaign, preserve a dignified manner, and conduct an administration, but he could write nothing more entertaining than a state paper or a military report. He gave himself up to great affairs, he was hardly human, and he shunned the graces, the wit, and all the salt of life, and passed them by on the other side.

That Washington was serious and earnest cannot be doubted, for no man could have done what he did and been otherwise. He had little time for the lighter sides of life, and he never exerted himself to say brilliant and striking things. He was not a maker of phrases and proclamations, and the quality of the charlatan, so often found in men of the highest genius, was utterly lacking in him. He never talked or acted with an eye to dramatic effect, and this is one reason for the notion that he was dull and dry; for the world dearly loves a little charlatanism, and is never happier than in being brilliantly duped. But was he therefore really dull and juiceless, unlovable and unloving? Responsibility came upon him when a boy, and he was hardly of age when he was carrying in his hands the defense of his colony and the heavy burden of other human lives. Experience like this makes a man who is good for anything sober; but sobriety is not dullness, and if we look a little below the surface we find the ready refutation of such an idea. In his letters and even in the silent diaries we detect the keenest observation. He looked at the country, as he traveled, with the eye of the soldier and the farmer, and mastered its features and read its meaning with rapid and certain glance. It was not to him a mere panorama of fields and woods, of rivers and mountains. He saw the beauties of nature and the opportunities of the farmer, the trader, or the manufacturer wherever his gaze rested. He gathered in the same way the statistics of the people and of their various industries. In the West Indies, on the Virginian frontier, in his journeys when he was President, he read the story of all he saw as he would have read a book, and brought it home with him for use.

In the same way he read and understood men, and had that power of choosing among them which is essential in its highest form to the great soldier or statesman. His selection never erred unless in a rare instance like that of Monroe, forced on him by political exigencies, or when the man of his choice would not serve. Congress chose Gates for the southern campaign, but Washington selected Greene, in whom he saw great military ability before any one else realized it. He took Hamilton, young and unknown, from the captaincy of an artillery company, and placed him on his personal staff. He bore with Hamilton's outbreak of temper, kept him ever in his confidence, and finally gave him the opportunity to prove himself the most brilliant of American statesmen. In the crowd of foreign volunteers, the men whom he especially selected and trusted were Lafayette and Steuben, each in his way of real value to the service. Even more remarkable than the ability to recognize great talent was his capacity to weigh and value with a nice exactness the worth of men who did not rise to the level of greatness. There is a recently published letter, too long for quotation here, in which he gives his opinions of all the leading officers of the Revolution,* and each one shows the most remarkable insight, as well

---

*Magazine of American History, vol. iii., 1879, p. 81.

as a sharp definiteness of outline that indicates complete mastery. These compact judgments were so sound that even the lapse of a century and all the study of historians and biographers find nothing in their keen analysis to alter and little to add. He did not expect to discover genius everywhere, or to find a marshal's baton in every knapsack, but he used men according to their value and possibilities, which is quite as essential as the preliminary work of selection. His military staff illustrated this faculty admirably. Every man, after a few trials and changes, fitted his place and did his particular task better than any one else could have done it. Colonel Meade, loyal and gallant, a good soldier and planter, said that Hamilton did the headwork of Washington's staff and he the riding. When the war was drawing to a close, Washington said one day to Hamilton, "You must go to the Bar, which you can reach in six months." Then turning to Meade, "Friend Dick, you must go to your plantation; you will make a good farmer, and an honest foreman of the grand jury."* The prediction was exactly fulfilled, with all that it implied, in both cases. But let it not be supposed that there was any touch of contempt in the advice to Meade. On the contrary, there was a little warmer affection, if anything, for he honored success in any honest pursuit, especially in farming, which he himself loved. But he distinguished the two men perfectly, and he knew what each was and what each meant. It seems little to say, but if we stop to think of it, this power to read men aright and see the truth in them and about them is a power more precious than any other bestowed by the kindest of fairy godmothers. The lame devil of Le Sage looked into the secrets of life through the roofs of houses, and much did he find of the secret story of humanity. But the great man looking with truth and kindliness into men's natures, and reading their characters and abilities in their words and acts, has a higher and better power than that attributed to the wandering sprite, for such a man holds in his hand the surest key to success. Washington, quiet and always on the watch, after the fashion of silent greatness, studied untiringly the ever recurring human problems, and his just conclusions were powerful factors in the great result. He was slow, when he had plenty of time, in adopting a policy or plan, or in settling a public question, but he read men very quickly. He was never under any delusion as to Lee, Gates, Conway, or any of the rest who engaged against him because they were restless from the first under the suspicion that he knew them thoroughly. Arnold deceived him because his treason was utterly inconceivable to Washington, and because his remarkable gallantry excused his many faults. But with this exception it may be safely said that Washington was never misled as to men, either

---

Memoir of Rt. Rev. William Meade, by Philip Slaughter, D.D., p. 7.

as general or President. His instruments were not invariably the best and sometimes failed him, but they were always the best he could get, and he knew their defects and ran the inevitable risks with his eyes open. Such sure and rapid judgments of men and their capabilities were possible only to a man of keen perception and accurate observation, neither of which is characteristic of a slow or commonplace mind.

These qualities were, of course, gifts of nature, improved and developed by the training of a life of action on a great scale. He had received, indeed, little teaching except that of experience, and the world of war and politics had been to him both school and college. His education had been limited in the extreme, scarcely going, beyond the most rudimentary branches except in mathematics, and this is very apparent in his early letters. He seems always to have written a handsome hand and to have been good at figures, but his spelling at the outset was far from perfect, and his style, although vigorous, was abrupt and rough. He felt this himself, took great pains to correct his faults in this respect, and succeeded, as he did in most things. Mr. Sparks has produced a false impression in this matter by smoothing and amending in very extensive fashion all the earlier letters, so as to give an appearance of uniformity throughout the correspondence; a process which not only destroyed much of the vigor and force of the early writings, but made them somewhat unnatural. The surveyor and frontier soldier wrote very differently from the general of the army and the President of the United States, and the improvements of Mr. Sparks only served to hide the real man.*

---

*These facts in regard to Washington's early letters, and to his correspondence generally, were first brought to public attention by the Reed letters, and by the controversy between Mr. Sparks and Lord Mahon. They have, of course, been long familiar to students of the original manuscripts. The full extent, however, of the changes made by Mr. Sparks, and of the mischief he wrought, and of the injustice thus done both to his hero and to posterity, has but lately been made known generally by the new edition of Washington's papers which have been published, under the supervision of Mr. W. C. Ford. Washington himself, when he undertook to arrange his military and state papers after his retirement from the presidency, began to correct the style of some of his earlier letters. This was natural enough, and he had a right to do what he pleased with his own, even if he thereby injured the material of the future historian and biographer. But he did not proceed far in his work, and the fact that he corrected a few of his own letters gave Mr. Sparks no right whatever to enter upon a wholesale revision.

If Washington had been of coarse fibre and heavy mind, this lack of education would have troubled him but little. His great success in that case would have served only to convince him of the uselessness of education except for inferior persons, who could not get along in the world without artificial aids. As it was, he never ceased to regret his deficiency in this respect, and when Humphreys urged him to prepare a history or memoirs of the war, he replied: "In a former letter I informed you, my dear Humphreys, that if I had talent for it, I have not leisure to turn my thoughts to commentaries. A consciousness of a defective education and a certainty of a want of time unfit me for such an undertaking." He was misled by his own modesty as to his capacity, but his strong feeling as to his lack of schooling haunted and troubled him always, although it did not make him either indifferent or bitter. He only admired more that which he himself had missed. He regarded education, and especially the higher forms, with an almost pathetic reverence, and its advancement was never absent from his thoughts. When he was made chancellor of the college of William and Mary, he was more deeply pleased than by any honor ever conferred upon him, and he accepted the position with a diffidence and a seriousness which were touching in such a man. In the same spirit he gave money to the Alexandria Academy, and every scheme to promote public education in Virginia had his eager support. His interest was not confined by state lines, for there was nothing so near his heart as the foundation of a national university. He urged its establishment upon Congress over and over again, and, as has been seen, left money in his will for its endowment.

All his sympathies and tastes were those of a man of refined mind, and of a lover of scholarship and sound learning. Naturally a very modest man, and utterly devoid of any pretense, he underrated, as a matter of fact, his own accomplishments. He distrusted himself so much that he always turned to Hamilton, both during the Revolution and afterwards, as well as in the preparation of the farewell address, to aid him in clothing his thoughts in a proper dress, which he felt himself unable to give them. His tendency was to be too diffuse and too involved, but as a rule his style was sufficiently clear, and he could express himself with nervous force when the occasion demanded, and with a genuine and stately eloquence when he was deeply moved, as in the farewell to Congress at the close of the war. It is not a little remarkable that in his letters after the first years there is nothing to betray any lack of early training. They are the letters, not of a scholar or a literary man, but of an educated gentleman; and although he seldom indulged in similes or allusions, when he did so they were apt and correct. This was due to his perfect sanity of mind, and to his aversion to all display or to any attempt to shine in borrowed plumage. He never undertook to speak or write on any subject, or to make any reference, which he did not understand. He was a lover of books, collected a library, and read always as much as his crowded life would permit. When he was at Newburgh, at the close of the war, he wrote to Colonel Smith in New York to send him the following books:—

> Charles the XIIth of Sweden.
> Lewis the XVth, 2 vols.
> History of the Life and Reign of the Czar Peter the Great.
> Campaigns of Marshal Turenne.
> Locke on the Human Understanding.
> Robertson's History of America, 2 vols.
> Robertson's History of Charles V.
> Voltaire's Letters.
> Life of Gustavus Adolphus.
> Sully's Memoirs.
> Goldsmith's Natural History.
> Mildman on Trees.
> Vertot's Revolution of Rome, 3 vols. ⎫ If they are in
> Vertot's Revolution of Portugal, 3 vols. ⎭ estimation.
> If there is a good Bookseller's shop in the City, I would thank you for sending me a catalogue of the Books and their prices that I may choose such as I want.

His tastes ran to history and to works treating of war or agriculture, as is indicated both by this list and some earlier ones. It is not probable that he gave so much attention to lighter literature, although he wrote verses in his youth, and by an occasional allusion in his letters he seems to have been familiar with some of the great works of the imagination, like "Don Quixote."*

He never freed himself from the self-distrust caused by his profound sense of his own deficiencies in education, on the one hand, and his deep reverence for learning, on the other. He had fought the Revolution, which opened the way for a new nation, and was at the height of his fame when he wrote to the French officers, who begged him to visit France, that he was "too old to learn French or to talk with ladies;" and it was this feeling in a large measure which kept him from ever being a maker of phrases or a sayer of brilliant things. In other words, the fact that he was modest and sensitive has been the chief cause of his being thought dull and cold. This idea, moreover, is wholly that of posterity, for there is not the slightest indication on the part of any contemporary that Washington could not talk well and did not appear to great advantage in society. It is posterity, looking with natural weariness at endless volumes of official letters with all the angles smoothed off by the editorial plane, that has come to suspect him of being dull in mind and heavy in wit. His contemporaries knew him to be dignified and often found him stern, but they never for a moment considered him stupid, or thought him a man at whom the shafts of wit could be shot with impunity. They were fully conscious that he was as able to hold his own in conversation as he was in the cabinet or in the field; and we can easily see the justice of contemporary opinion if we take the trouble to break through the official bark and get at the real man who wrote the letters. In many cases we find that he could employ irony and sarcasm with real force, and his powers of description, even if stilted at times, were vigorous and effective. All these qualities come out strongly in his letters, if carefully read, and his private correspondence in particular shows a keenness and point which the formalities of public intercourse veiled generally from view. We are fortunate in having the account of a disinterested and acute observer of the manner

---

*At his death the appraisers of the estate found 863 volumes in his library, besides a great number of pamphlets, magazines, and maps. This was a large collection of books for those days, and showed that the possessor, although purely a man of affairs, loved reading and had literary tastes.

in which Washington impressed a casual acquaintance in conversation. The actor Bernard, whom we have already quoted, and whom we left with Washington at the gates of Mount Vernon, gives us the following vivid picture of what ensued:—

> In conversation his face had not much variety of expression. A look of thoughtfulness was given by the compression of the mouth and the indentations of the brow (suggesting an habitual conflict with, and mastery over, passion), which did not seem so much to disdain a sympathy with trivialities as to be incapable of denoting them. Nor had his voice, so far as I could discover in our quiet talk, much change or richness of intonation, but he always spoke with earnestness, and his eyes (glorious conductors of the light within) burned with a steady fire which no one could mistake for mere affability; they were one grand expression of the well-known line: "I am a man, and interested in all that concerns humanity." In one hour and a half's conversation he touched on every topic that I brought before him with an even current of good sense, if he embellished it with little wit or verbal elegance. He spoke like a man who had felt as much as he had reflected, and reflected more than he had spoken; like one who had looked upon society rather in the mass than in detail, and who regarded the happiness of America but as the first link in a series of universal victories; for his full faith in the power of those results of civil liberty which he saw all around him led him to foresee that it would, erelong, prevail in other countries, and that the social millennium of Europe would usher in the political. When I mentioned to him the difference I perceived between the inhabitants of New England and of the Southern States, he remarked: "I esteem those people greatly; they are the stamina of the Union and its greatest benefactors. They are continually spreading themselves too, to settle and enlighten less favored quarters.

Dr. Franklin is a New Englander." When I remarked that his observations were flattering to my country, he replied, with great good-humor, "Yes, yes, Mr. Bernard, but I consider your country the cradle of free principles, not their armchair. Liberty in England is a sort of idol; people are bred up in the belief and love of it, but see little of its doings. They walk about freely, but then it is between high walls; and the error of its government was in supposing that after a portion of their subjects had crossed the sea to live upon a common, they would permit their friends at home to build up those walls about them." A black coming in at this moment with a jug of spring water, I could not repress a smile, which the general at once interpreted. "This may seem a contradiction," he continued, "but I think you must perceive that it is neither a crime nor an absurdity. When we profess, as our fundamental principle, that liberty is the inalienable right of every man, we do not include madmen or idiots; liberty in their hands would become a scourge. Till the mind of the slave has been educated to perceive what are the obligations of a state of freedom, and not confound a man's with a brute's, the gift would insure its abuse. We might as well be asked to pull down our old warehouses before trade has increased to demand enlarged new ones. Both houses and slaves were bequeathed to us by Europeans, and time alone can change them; an event, sir, which, you may believe me, no man desires more heartily than I do. Not only do I pray for it, on the score of human dignity, but I can already foresee that nothing but the rooting out of slavery can perpetuate the existence of our Union, by consolidating it in a common bond of principle."

I now referred to the pleasant hours I had passed in Philadelphia, and my agreeable surprise at finding there so many men of talent, at which his face lit up vividly. "I am glad to hear you, sir, who are an Englishman, say so, because you must now perceive how ungenerous are the assertions people are always making on your side of the water. One gentleman, of high literary standing,—I allude to the Abbé Raynal,—has demanded whether America has yet produced one great poet, statesman, or philosopher. The question shows anything but observation, because it is easy to perceive the causes which have combined to render the genius of this country scientific rather than imaginative. And, in this respect, America has surely furnished her quota. Franklin, Rittenhouse, and Rush are no mean names, to which, without shame, I may append those of Jefferson and Adams, as politicians; while I am told that the works of President Edwards of Rhode Island are a text-book in polemics in many European colleges."

Of the replies which I made to his inquiries respecting England, he listened to none with so much interest as to those which described the character of my royal patron, the Prince of Wales. "He holds out every promise," remarked the general, "of a brilliant career. He has been well educated by *events*, and I doubt not that, in his time, England will receive the benefit of her child's emancipation. She is at present bent double, and has to walk with crutches; but her offspring may teach her the secret of regaining strength, erectness, and independence." In reference to my own pursuits he repeated the sentiments of Franklin. He feared the country was too poor to be a patron of the drama, and that only arts of a practical nature would for some time be esteemed. The stage he considered to be an indispensable resource for settled society, and a chief refiner; not merely interesting as a comment on the history of social happiness by its exhibition of manners, but an agent of good as a school for poetry, in holding up to honor the noblest principles. "I am too old and too far removed," he added, "to seek for or require this pleasure myself, but the cause is not to droop on my account. There's my friend Mr. Jefferson has time and taste; he goes always to the play, and I'll introduce you to him," a promise which he kept, and which proved to me the source of the greatest benefit and pleasure.

This is by far the best account of Washington in the ordinary converse of daily life that has come down to us. The narrator belonged to the race who live by amusing their fellow-beings, and are in consequence quick to notice peculiarities and highly susceptible to being bored. Bernard, after the first interest of seeing a very eminent man had worn off, would never have lingered for an hour and a half of chat and then gone away reluctantly if his host had been either dull of speech or cold and forbidding of manner. It is evident that Washington talked well, easily, and simply, ranging widely over varied topics with a sure touch, and that he drew from the ample resources of a well-stored and reflective mind. The scraps of conversation which Bernard preserves are interesting and above the average of ordinary talk, without manifesting any attempt to be either brilliant or striking, and it is also apparent that Washington had the art of putting his guest entirely at his ease by his own pleasant and friendly manner. He had picked up the English actor on the road, liked his readiness to be helpful (always an attraction to him in any one), found him well-mannered and intelligent, and brought him home to rest and chat in the pleasant summer afternoon. To Bernard he was simply the plain Virginia gentleman, with a liberal and cultivated interest in men and things, and not a trace of oppressive and conscious greatness about him. It is to be suspected that he was by no means equally genial to the herd of sight-seers who pursued him in his retirement, but in this meeting he appeared as he must always have appeared to his family and friends.

We get the same idea from the scattered allusions that we have to Washington in private life. Although silent and reserved as to himself, he was by no means averse to society, and in his own house all his guests, both great and small, felt at their ease with him, although with no temptation to be familiar. We know from more than one account that the dinners at the presidential house, as well as at Mount Vernon, were always agreeable. It was his wont to sit at table after the cloth was removed sipping a glass of wine and eating nuts, of which he was very fond, while he listened to the conversation and caused it to flow easily, not so much by what he said as by the kindly smile and ready sympathy which made all feel at home. We can gather an idea also of the charm which he had in the informal intercourse of daily life from some of his letters on trifling matters. Here is a little note written to Mrs. Stockton in acknowledgment of a pastoral poem which she had sent him:—

> MOUNT VERNON, February 18, 1784.
>
> DEAR MADAM: The intemperate weather and very great care which the post riders take of themselves prevented your letter of the 4th of last month from reaching my hands till the 10th of this. I was then in the very act of setting off on a visit to my aged mother, from whence I am just returned. These reasons I beg leave to offer as an apology for my silence until now.
>
> It would be a pity indeed, my dear madam, if the muses should be restrained in you; it is only to be regretted that the hero of your poetical talents is not more deserving their lays. I cannot, however, from motives of pure delicacy (because I happen to be the principal character in your Pastoral) withhold my encomiums on the performance; for I think the easy, simple, and beautiful strain with which the dialogue is supported does great justice to your genius; and will not only secure Lucinda and Amista from wits and critics, but draw from them, however unwillingly, their highest plaudits; if they can relish the praises that are given, as they must admire the manner of bestowing them.
>
> Mrs. Washington, equally sensible with myself of the honor you have done her, joins me in most affectionate compliments to yourself, and the young ladies and gentlemen of your family.
>
> With sentiments of esteem, regard and respect, I have the honor to be ___ ___

This is not a matter of "great pith or moment," but it shows how pleasantly he could acknowledge a civility. The turn of the sentences smacks of the formality of the time. They sound a little labored, perhaps, to modern ears, but they were graceful according to the standard of his day, and they have a gentle courtesy which can never be out of fashion.

He had the power also of paying a compliment in an impressive and really splendid manner whenever he felt it to be deserved. When Charles Thomson, who for fifteen years had been the honored secretary of the Continental Congress, wrote to announce his retirement, Washington replied: "The present age does so much justice to the unsullied reputation with which you have always conducted yourself in the execution of the duties of your office, and posterity will find your name so honorably connected with the verification of such a multitude of astonishing facts, that my single suffrage would add little to the illustration of your merits. Yet I cannot withhold any just testimonial in favor of so old, so faithful, and so able a public officer, which might tend to soothe his mind in the shades of retirement. Accept, then, this serious declaration, that your services have been important, as your patriotism was distinguished; and enjoy that best of all rewards, the consciousness of having done your duty well."

Dull men do not write in this fashion. It is one thing to pay a handsome compliment, although even that is not by itself easy, but to give it in addition the note of sincerity which alone makes it of real value demands both art and good feeling. Let us take one more example of this sort before we drop the subject. When the French officers were leaving America Washington wrote to De Chastellux to bid him farewell. "Our good friend, the Marquis of Lafayette," he said, "prepared me, long before I had the honor to see you, for those impressions of esteem which opportunities and your own benevolent mind have since improved into a deep and lasting friendship; a friendship which neither time nor distance can eradicate. I can truly say that never in my life have I parted with a man to whom my soul clave more sincerely than it did to you. My warmest wishes will attend you in your voyage across the Atlantic to the rewards of a generous prince, the arms of affectionate friends; and be assured that it will be one of my highest gratifications to keep up a regular intercourse with you by letter."

These letters exhibit not only the grace and point born of intelligence, but also the best of manners; by which I mean private manners, not those of the public man, of which there will be something to say hereafter. The attraction of Washington's society as a private gentleman lay in his good sense, breadth of knowledge, and good manners. Now the essence of good manners of the highest and most genuine kind is good feeling, which is thoughtful of others, and which is impossible to a cold, bard, or insensible nature. Such manners as we see in Washington's private letters and private life would have been strange offspring from the cold heart attributed to him by Mr. McMaster. In justice to Mr. McMaster, however, be it said, the charge is not a new one. It has been hinted at and spoken of elsewhere, and many persons have suspected that such was the case from the well-meant efforts of what may be called the cherry-tree school to elevate Washington's character by depicting him as a soulless, bloodless prig. The blundering efforts of the latter need not be noticed, but the reflections of serious critics cannot be passed by. The theory of the cold heart and the unfeeling nature seems to proceed in this wise. Washington was silent and reserved, he did not wear his heart upon his sleeve for daws to peck at, therefore he was cold; just as if mere noise and chatter had any relation to warm affections. He would take no salary from Congress, says Mr. McMaster, in fine antithesis, but he exacted his due from the family of the poor mason. This has an unpleasant sound, and suggests the man who is generous in public, and hard and grasping in private. Mr. McMaster in this sentence, however, whether intentionally or not, is not quite accurate in his facts, and conveys by his mode of statement an entirely false impression. The story to which he refers is given by Parkinson, who wrote a book about his experiences in America in 1798–1800. Parkinson had the story from one General Stone, and it was to this effect:* A room was plastered at Mount Vernon on one occasion, and was paid for during the owner's absence. When Washington

*Parkinson's *Tour in America*, 1798–1800, 437 and ff.

returned he examined the work and had it measured, as was his habit. It then appeared that an error had been made, and that fifteen shillings too much had been paid. Meantime the plasterer had died. His widow married again, and her second husband advertised in the newspapers that he was prepared to pay the debts of his predecessor and collect all moneys due him. Thereupon Washington put in his claim, which was paid as a matter of course. He did not extort the debt from the family of the poor mason, but collected it from the second husband of the widow, in response to a voluntary advertisement. It was very careful and even close dealing, but it was neither harsh nor unjust, and the writer who has preserved the story would be not a little surprised at the interpretation that has been put upon it, for he cited it, as he expressly says, merely to illustrate the extraordinary regularity and method to which he attributed much of Washington's success.

Parkinson, in this same connection, tells several other stories, vague in origin, and sounding like mere gossip, but still worthy of consideration. According to one of them, Washington maintained a public ferry, which was customary among the planters, and the public paid regular tolls for its use. On one occasion General Stone, the authority for the previous anecdote, crossed the ferry and offered a moidore in payment. The ferryman objected to receiving it, on the ground that it was short weight, but Stone insisted, and it was finally accepted. On being given to Washington it was weighed, and being found three half-pence short, the ferryman was ordered to collect the balance due. On another occasion a tenant could not make the exact change in paying his rent, and Washington would not accept the money until the tenant went to Alexandria and brought back the precise sum. There is, however, still another anecdote, which completes this series, and which shows a different application of the same rule. Washington, in traveling, was in the habit of paying at inns the same for his servants as for himself. An innkeeper once charged him three shillings and ninepence for himself, and three shillings for his servant. Thereupon Washington sent for his host, said that his servant ate as much as he, and insisted on paying the additional ninepence.

This extreme exactness in money matters, down even to the most trifling sums, was no doubt a foible, but it is well to observe that it was not a foible which sought only a selfish advantage, for the rule which he applied to others he applied also to himself. He meant to have his due, no matter how trivial, and he meant also that others should have theirs. In trifles, as in greater things, he was scrupulously just, and although he was always generous and ready to give, he insisted rigidly on what was justly his. A gift was one thing, a business transaction was another. The man himself who told these very stories was a good example of the kindliness which went hand in hand with this exactness in business affairs. Parkinson was an Englishman, of great narrowness of mind, who came out here to be a farmer, failed, and went home to write a book in denunciation of the country. America never had a more hostile critic. According to this profound observer, there was no good land in America, and no possibility of successful agriculture. The horses were bad, the cattle were bad, and sheep-raising was impossible. There was no game, the fish and oysters were poor and watery, and no one could ever hope in this wretchedly barren land for either wealth or comfort. It was a country fit only for the reception of convicts, and the castoff mistress of an Englishman made a good wife for an American. A person who held such views as these was not likely to be biased in favor of anything American, and his evidence as to Washington may be safely trusted as not likely to be unduly favorable. He tells us that on his arrival at Mount Vernon, with letters of introduction, he was kindly received; that this hospitality was never relaxed; and that the general lent him money. He was at least grateful, and these are his last words as to Washington:—

> To me he appeared a mild, friendly man, in company rather reserved, in private speaking with candor. His behavior to me was such that I shall ever revere his name.
>
> General Washington lived a great man, and died the same.
>
> I am of opinion that the general never knowingly did anything wrong, but did to all men as he would they should do to him.

Evidently he appeared to Mr. Parkinson kindly and generous, as well as exactly just. It is well to have the truth about Washington, and nothing but the truth. Yet in escaping from the falsehoods of the eulogist and the myth-maker, let us beware of those which spring from the reaction against the current and accepted views. I have quoted the Parkinson stories at length, because they enforce this point admirably. No *a priori* theory is safe, and to assume that Washington must have committed grave errors and been guilty of mean actions because they are common to humanity, and have not been admitted in his case, is just as misleading as to assume, as is usually done, that he was absolutely perfect and without fault.

Let it be admitted that Washington, ever ready to pay his own dues, was strict, and sometimes severe, in demanding them of others; but let it be also remembered, this is the worst that can be said. He was always ready to overlook faults of omission or commission; he would pardon easily mismanagement or extravagance on his estate or in his household; but he had no mercy for anything that savored of ingratitude, treachery, or dishonesty, and he carried this same feeling into public as well as private affairs. No officer who had bravely done his best had anything to fear in defeat from Washington's anger. He was never unjust, and he was always kind to misfortune or mistake, but to the coward or the traitor he was entirely unforgiving. This it was which made Arnold's treason so bitter to him. Not only had he been deceived, but the country as well as himself had been most basely betrayed; and for this reason he was relentless to Andre, whom it is said he never saw, living or dead. The young Englishman had taken part in a wretched piece of treachery, and for the sake of the country, and as a warning to traitors, Washington would not spare him. He would never have ordered a political prisoner to be taken out and shot in a ditch, after the fashion of Napoleon; nor would he have dealt with any people as the Duke of Cumberland dealt with the clansmen after Culloden. Such performances would have seemed to him wanton as well as cruel, and he was too wise and too humane a man to be either. Indian atrocities, for instance, with which he was familiar, never led him to retaliate in kind. But he was perfectly prepared to exact the extremest penalty by just and recognized methods; and had it not been for the urgent entreaties of his friends, he would have sent Asgill to the scaffold, repugnant as it was to his feelings, because he felt that the murder of Huddy was a crime for which the English army was responsible, and which demanded a just and striking vengeance. He was, it may be freely confessed, of anything but a tame nature. There was a good deal of Berserker in his make-up, and he was fierce in his anger when he believed that a great wrong had been done. But because he was stern and unrelenting when he felt that justice and his duty required him to be so, no more proves that he had a cold heart than does the fact that he was silent, dignified, and reserved. Cold-blooded men are not fierce in seeking to redress the wrongs of others, nor are the fluent of speech the only kind and generous members of the human family.

Washington's whole life, indeed, contradicts the charge that he was cold of heart and sluggish of feeling. The man who wrote as he did in his extreme youth, when Indians were harrying the frontier where he commanded, was not lacking in humanity or sympathy; and such as he then was he remained to the end of his life. A soldier by instinct and experience, he never grew indifferent to the miseries of war. Human suffering always appealed to him and moved him deeply, and when it was wantonly inflicted stirred him to anger and to the desire for the wild justice of revenge.

The goodness and kindness of man's heart, however, are much more truly shown in the little details of life than in the great matters which affect classes or communities. Washington was considerate and helpful to all men, and if he was ever cold and distant in his manner, it was to the great, and not to the poor or humble. As has been indicated by his recognition of the actor Bernard, he had in high degree the royal gift of remembering names and faces. When he was at Senator Dalton's house in Newburyport, on his New England tour of 1789, he met an old servant whom he had not seen since the French war, thirty years before. He knew the man at once, spoke to him, and welcomed him. So it was with the old soldiers of the Revolution, who were always sure of a welcome, and, if he had ever seen them, of a recognition. No man ever turned from his presence wounded by a cold forgetfulness. When he was at Ipswich, on this same journey, Mr. Cleaveland, the minister of the town, was presented to him. As he approached, hat in hand, Washington said, "Put on your hat, parson, and I will shake hands with you." "I cannot wear my hat in your presence, general," was the reply, "when I think of what you have done for this country." "You did as much as I." "No, no," protested the parson. "Yes," said Washington, "you did what you could, and I've done no more." What a gracious, kindly courtesy is this, and not without the salt of wit! Does it not show the perfection of good manners which deals with all men for what they are, and is full of a warm sympathy born of a good heart? He was criticised for coldness and accused of monarchical leanings, because, at Mrs. Washington's receptions and his own public levees, he stood, dressed in black velvet, with one hand on the hilt of his sword and the other behind his back, and shook hands with no one, although he talked with all. He did this because he thought it became the President of the United States upon state occasions, and his sense of the dignity of his office was always paramount. But away from forms and ceremonies, with the old servant or the old soldier, or the country parson, his hand was never behind his back, and his manners were those of a great but simple gentleman, and came straight from a kind heart, full of sympathy and good feeling.

He was, too, the most hospitable of men in the best sense, and his house was always open to all who came. When he was away during the war or the presidency, his instructions to his agents were to keep up the hospitality of Mount Vernon, just as if he had been there himself; and he was especially careful in directing that, if there were general distress, poor persons of the neighborhood should have help from his kitchen or his granaries.

His own more immediate hospitality was of the same kind. He always entertained in the most liberal manner, both as general and President, and in a style which he thought befitted the station he occupied. But apart from all this, his table, whether at home or abroad, was never without its guest. "Dine with us," he wrote to Lear on July 31, 1797, "or we shall do what we have not done for twenty years, dine alone." The real hospitality which opens the door and spreads the board for the friend or stranger, admitting them to the family without form or ceremony, was his also. "My manner of living is plain," he wrote to a friend after the Revolution; "I do not mean to be put out of it. A glass of wine and a bit of mutton are always ready; and such as will be content to partake of them are always welcome. Those who expect more will be disappointed, but no change will be effected by it." Genuine hospitality as unstinted as it was sincere was not characteristic of a cold man, or of one who sought to avoid his fellows. It is one of the lighter graces of life, perhaps, but when it comes freely and simply, and not as a vehicle for the display or the aggrandizement of its dispenser, it is not without a meaning to the student of character.

Washington was not much given to professions of friendship, nor was he one of the great men who keep a circle of intimates and sometimes of flatterers about them. He was extremely independent of the world and perfectly self-sufficing, but it is a mistake to suppose that because he unbosomed himself to scarcely any one, and had the loneliness of greatness and of high responsibilities, he was therefore without friends. He had as many friends as usually fall to the lot of any man; and although he laid bare his inmost heart to none, some were very close and all were very dear to him. In war and politics, as has already been said, the two men who came nearest to him were Hamilton and Knox, and his diary shows that when he was President he consulted with them nearly every day wholly apart from the regular cabinet meetings. They were the two advisers who were friends as well as secretaries, and who followed and sustained him as a matter of affection as much as politics. At home his neighbor, George Mason, although they came to differ, was a strong friend whom he liked and respected, and whose opinion, whether favorable or adverse, he always sought. His feeling to Patrick Henry was much deeper than mere political or official acquaintance, and the lovable qualities of the brilliant orator, clear even now across the gulf of a century, were evidently strongly felt by Washington. They differed about the Constitution, but Washington was eager at a later day to have Henry by his side in the cabinet, and in the last years they stood shoulder to shoulder in defense of the Union with a personal sympathy deeper than any born of a mere similarity of opinion. Henry Lee, the son of his old sweetheart, he loved with a tender and peculiar affection. He watched over him and helped him, rejoiced in the dashing gallantry which made him famous as Light-horse Harry, and, when he had won civil as well as military distinction, trusted him and counseled with him. Dr. Craik, the companion of his youth and his life-long physician, was always a dear and close friend, and the regard between the two is very pleasant to look at, as we see it glancing out here and there in the midst of state papers and official cases. For the officers of the army he had a peculiarly warm feeling, and he had among them many close friends, like Carrington of Virginia, and Charles Cotesworth Pinckney of South Carolina. His immediate staff he regarded with especial affection, and it is worthy of notice that they all not only admired their great chief, but followed him with a personal devotion which is not a little curious if Washington was cold of heart and distant of manner in the intimate association of a military family.

This feeling for his soldiers and his officers extended also to those civilians who had stood by him and the army, and who had labored for victory in all those trying years. Such a one was old Governor Trumbull, "Brother Jonathan," who never failed to respond when a call was made for men and money, and upon whose friendship and advice Washington always leaned. Such, too, were Robert and Gouverneur Morris. The sacrifices and energy of the one and the zeal and brilliant abilities of the other endeared both to him, and his friendship for them never wavered when misfortune overtook the elder, and when the younger was driven by malice, both foreign and domestic, from the place he had filled so well. Another, again, of this kind was Franklin. In the dark days of the old French war, Washington had seen displayed for the first time the force and tact of Franklin, which alone obtained the necessary wagons and enabled Braddock's army to move. The early impression thus obtained was never lost, and Franklin's patriotism, his sympathy for the general and the army in the Revolution, as well as the stanch support he gave them, aroused in Washington a sense of obligation and friendship of the sincerest kind. In proportion as he loathed ingratitude was he grateful himself. He loved Franklin for his friendship and support, he admired him for his successful diplomacy, and he reverenced him for his scientific attainments. The only American whose fame could for a moment come in competition with his own, he regarded the old philosopher with affectionate veneration, and when, after his own fashion, and not at all after the fashion of the time, he arrived in Philadelphia on the exact day set for the Constitutional Convention, his first act was to call upon Dr. Franklin and pay his respects to him. The courtesy and kindliness of this little act on the part of a man who had come to the town in the midst of shouting crowds, with joy bells ringing above his head, speak well for the simple, honest heart that dictated it.

After all, it may be said that a passing civility of this sort involved but little trouble, and was more a matter of good-breeding than anything else. Let us look, then, at another and widely different case. Of all the men whom the fortunes of war brought across Washington's path there was none who became dearer to him than Lafayette, for the generous, high-spirited young Frenchman, full of fresh enthusiasm and brave as a lion, appealed at once to Washington's heart. He quickly admitted him to his confidence, and the excellent service of Lafayette in the field, together with his invaluable help in securing the French alliance, deepened and strengthened the sympathy and affection which were entirely reciprocal. After Lafayette departed, a constant correspondence was maintained; and when the Bastille fell, it was to Washington that Lafayette sent its key, which still hangs on the wall of Mt. Vernon. As Lafayette rose rapidly to the dangerous heights of revolutionary leadership, he had at every step Washington's advice and sympathy. Then the tide turned; he fell headlong from power, and brought up in an Austrian prison. From that moment Washington spared no pains to help his unhappy friend, although his own position was one of extreme difficulty. Lafayette was not only the proscribed exile of one country, but also the political prisoner of another, and the President could not compromise the United States at that critical moment by showing too much interest in the fate of his unhappy friend. He nevertheless went to the very edge of prudence in trying to save him, and the ministers of the United States were instructed to use every private effort to secure Lafayette's release, or at least the mitigation of his confinement. All these attempts failed, but Washington was more successful in other directions. He sent money to Madame de Lafayette, who was absolutely beggared at the moment, and represented to her that it was in settlement of an account which he owed the marquis. When Lafayette's son and his own namesake came to this country for an asylum, he had him cared for in Boston and New York by his personal friends; George Cabot in the one case, and Hamilton in the other. As soon as public affairs made it proper for him to do it, he took the lad into his own household, treated him like a son, and kept him near him until events permitted the boy to return to Europe and rejoin his father. The sufferings and dangers of Lafayette and his family were indeed a source of great unhappiness to Washington, and we have the authority of Bradford, his attorney-general, that when the President attempted to talk about Lafayette he was so much affected that he shed tears, a very rare exhibition of emotion in a man so intensely reserved.

Absence had as little effect upon his memory of old friends as misfortune. The latter stimulated recollection, and the former could not dim it. He found time, in the very heat and fire of war and revolution, to write to Bryan Fairfax lamenting the death of "the good old lord" whose house had been open to him, and whose hand had ever helped him when he was a young and unknown man just beginning his career. When he returned to Mount Vernon after the presidency, full of years and honors, one of his first acts was to write to Mrs. Fairfax in England to assure her of his lasting remembrance, and to breathe a sigh over the changes time had brought, and over the by-gone years when they had been young together.

The loyalty of nature which made his remembrance of old friends so real and lasting found expression also in the thoughtfulness which he showed toward casual acquaintances, and this was especially the case when he had received attention or service at any one's hands, or when he felt that he was able to give pleasure by a slight effort on his own part. A little incident which occurred during the first year of his presidency illustrates this trait in his character very well. Uxbridge was one among the many places where he stopped on his New England tour, and when he got to Hartford he wrote to Mr. Taft, who had been his host in the former town, and who evidently cherished for him a very keen admiration, the following note:—

NOVEMBER 8, 1789.

SIR: Being informed that you have given my name to one of your sons, and called another after Mrs. Washington's family, and being moreover very much pleased with the modest and innocent looks of your two daughters, Patty and Polly, I do for these reasons send each of these girls a piece of chintz; and to Patty, who bears the name of Mrs. Washington, and who waited more upon us than Polly did, I send five guineas, with which she may buy herself any little ornament she may want, or she may dispose of them in any other manner more agreeable to herself. As I do not give these things with a view to having it talked of, or even to its being known, the less there is said about the matter the better you will please me; but, that I may be sure the chintz and money have got safe to hand, let Patty, who I dare say is equal to it, write me a line informing me thereof, directed to "The President of the United States at New York." I wish you and your family well, and am, [etc.]

Let us turn now from friendship to nearer and closer relations. Washington was not only too reserved, but he had too much true senti-ment, to leave his correspondence with Mrs. Washington behind him; for he knew that his vast collection of papers would become the material of history, and he had no mind that strangers should look into the sacred recesses of his private life. Only one letter to Mrs. Washington apparently has survived. It is simple and full of affection, as one would expect, and tells, as well as many volumes could, of the happy relations between hus-band and wife. Washington had many love affairs in his youth, but he proved in the end a constant lover. His wife was a high-bred, intelligent woman, simple and dignified in her manners, efficient in all ways to be the helpmate of her husband in the high places to which he was called. No shadow ever rested on their married life, and when the end came Mrs. Washington only said, "All is over now. I shall soon follow him." She could not conceive of life without the presence of the unchanging love and noble character which had been by her side so long.

Children were denied to Washington, but although this was a disappointment it did not chill him nor narrow his sympathies, as is so often the case. He took to his heart his wife's children as if they were his own. He watched over them and cared for them, and their deaths caused him the deepest sorrow. He afterwards adopted his wife's two grandchildren, and watched over them, too, in the same way. In the midst of all the cares of the presidency, Washington found time always to write to George Custis, a boy at school or at college; while Nellie Custis was as dear to him as his own daughter, and her marriage a source of the most affectionate interest. Indeed, it is evident from various little anecdotes that he was much less strict with these children than was Mrs. Washington, and much more disposed to condone faults. Certain it is that they loved him tenderly, and in a way that only long years of loving-kindness could have made possible.

He showed the same feeling to all his own kindred. His mother was ever the object of the most loyal affection, and even at the head of the armies he would turn aside to visit her with the same respect and devotion as when he was a mere boy. He was ever mindful of his brothers and sisters, and their fortunes. None of them were ever forgotten, and he was especially kind to the children of those who had been least fortunate and most needed his help. He educated and counseled his favorite nephew Bushrod, and did the same for the sons of George Steptoe Washington. Nothing is pleasanter than to read in the midst of official papers the long letters in which he gave these boys great store of wise and kindly advice, guided their education, strove to form their characters, and traced for them the honorable careers which he wished them to pursue. Very few men who had risen to the heights reached by Washington would have found time, in the midst of engrossing cares, to write such letters as he wrote to friends and kinsmen. A kind heart prompted them, but they were much more than merely kind, for when Washington undertook to do anything he did it thoroughly. Whether it was a treaty with England, the education of a boy, or the service of a friend, he gave it his best thought and his utmost care. Where those he loved were concerned, he was never too busy to think of them, and he spared no pains to help them; censuring faults where they existed, and giving praise in generous manner where praise was due.

To any one who carefully studies his life, it is evident that Washington was as warm-hearted and affectionate as he was great in character and ability, and that he was so without noise or pretense. This really only amounts to saying that he was a well-balanced man, and yet even this cannot be said without admitting still another quality. The sanest of all senses is the sense of humor, and the nature in which it is wholly lacking cannot be thoroughly rounded and complete. Humor is not the most lofty of qualities, but it is one of the most essential, and it is generally assumed that Washington was very deficient in humor. This idea has arisen from a hasty consideration of the subject, and from a superficial conception of humor itself. To utter jests, or to say or write witty, brilliant, or amusing things, no doubt implies the possession of humor, but they are not the whole of it, for a man may have a fine sense of humor, and yet never make a joke nor utter a sarcasm. The distinction between humor and the want of it lies much deeper than word of mouth. The man without a sense of humor is sure to make a certain number of solemn blunders. They may be in matters of importance or in the merest trifles, but they are blunders none the less, and come from insensibility to the incongruous, the ludicrous, or the impossible. It may be said that common sense suffices to avoid these pitfalls, but this is really begging the question, inasmuch as common sense of a high order amounting almost to genius cannot exist without humor, for humor is the root and foundation of common sense. Let us apply this test to Washington and we shall find that there never was a man who made fewer mistakes than he, down even to matters of the smallest detail. Search his career from beginning to end, and there is not a solemn blunder to be found in it. He was attacked and assailed both as general and President, but he was never laughed at. In other words, he had a sense of humor which made it impossible for him to blunder solemnly, or to do or say anything which ridicule could touch.

It is not, however, necessary to leave his possession of a sense of humor to inference from his career and his freedom from blunders. That he had humor strong, sane, and abundant is susceptible of much more direct proof; and the idea that he was lacking in this respect arose undoubtedly from the gravity of demeanor which was characteristic of the man. He had assumed the heavy responsibilities of an important military command in the French war at an age when most men are just leaving college and beginning to study a profession. This of itself sobered him, and added to his natural quiet and reserve, so that in estimating him in after-life this early and severe discipline at a most impressionable age ought never to be overlooked, for it had a very marked effect upon his character.

He was not perhaps exactly joyous or gay of nature, but he had a contented and happy disposition, and, like all robust, well-balanced men, he possessed strong animal spirits and a keen sense of enjoyment. He loved a wild, open-air life, and was devoted to rough out-door sports. He liked to wrestle and run, to shoot, ride or dance, and to engage in all trials of skill and strength, for which his great muscular development suited him admirably. With such tastes, it followed almost as a matter of course that he loved laughter and fun. Good, hearty, country fun, a ludicrous mishap, a practical joke, all merriment of a simple, honest kind, were highly congenial to him, especially in his youth and early manhood. Here is the way, for example, in which he described in his diary a ball he attended in 1760: "In a convenient room, detached for the purpose, abounded great plenty of bread and butter, some biscuits, with tea and coffee which the drinkers of could not distinguish from hot water sweetened. Be it remembered that pocket handkerchiefs served the purposes of tablecloths, and that no apologies were made for them. I shall therefore distinguish this ball by the style and title of the bread-and-butter ball." The wit is not brilliant, but there was a good hearty laugh in the young man who jots down this little memorandum in his diary.

The years after the French war were happy years, free from care and full of simple pleasures. Then came the Revolution, bringing with it a burden such as has seldom been laid upon any man, and the seriousness bred by earlier experiences came back with tenfold force. The popular saying was that Washington never smiled during the war, and, roughly speaking, this was quite true. In all those years of danger and trial, inasmuch as he was a man big of heart and brain, he had the gravity and the sadness born of responsibility, and the suffering sure to come to an unselfish mind. It was at this time that he began to be most closely observed of men, and hence came the idea that he never laughed, and therefore was a being devoid of humor, the most sympathetic of gifts. But as a matter of fact, the old sense of fun never left him. It would come to his aid at the most serious moments, just as an endless flow of stories brought relief to Lincoln and carried him round many jagged corners. With Washington it was hearty, laughing mirth at some ludicrous incident. Putnam riding into Cambridge with an old woman clinging behind him; Greene searching for his wig while it was on his head; a young braggart flung over the head of an unbroken colt; or a good, rollicking story from Colonel Scammel or Major Fairlie, —all these would delight Washington, and send him off into peals of inextinguishable laughter. It was ever the old, hearty love of fun born of animal spirits, which never left him, and which would always break out on sufficient provocation. Mr. Parton would have us believe that this was all, and that the commonplace hero whom he describes never rose above the level of the humor conveyed by grinning through a horse-collar. Even admitting the truth of this, a real love of honest fun and of a hearty laugh is a kindly quality that all men like.

But was this all? Is it quite true that Washington had only a love of boisterous fun, and nothing else? It is worth looking a little deeper than the current stories of the camp to find out, and yet one of these very camp-stories raises at once a strong suspicion that Mr. Parton's conclusion in this regard, like so many conclusions about Washington, is unfounded. When General Lee took the oath of allegiance to the United States, he remarked, in making abjuration of his former allegiance, that he was perfectly ready to abjure the king, but could not bring himself to abjure the Prince of Wales, at which bit of irony Washington was greatly amused. The wit of the remark is a little cold to-day, but at the moment, accompanying as it did a solemn act of abjuration, it was keen enough. Washington himself, moreover, was perfectly capable of good-natured banter. Colonel Humphreys challenged him one day to jump over a hedge. Washington, always ready to accept a challenge where riding was concerned, told the colonel to go on. Humphreys put his horse at the hedge, cleared it, and landed in a quagmire on the other side up to his horse's girths; whereupon Washington rode up, stopped, and looking blandly at his struggling friend, remarked, "Ah, colonel, you are too deep for me." "Take care," he wrote to young Custis, when he sent him money for his college gown, "not to buy without advice; otherwise you may be more distinguished by your folly than your dress."

We find in his letters here and there a good-natured raillery, and jesting, which show a sense of humor that goes beyond the limits of mere fun and horseplay. Here is a letter he wrote toward the close of the war, asking some ladies to dine with him in his quarters at West Point:

WEST POINT, August 16, 1779.
DEAR DOCTOR: I have asked Mrs. Cochran and Mrs. Livingston to dine with me to-morrow; but ought I not to apprise you of their fare? As I hate deception, even where imagination is concerned, I will.

It is needless to premise that my table is large enough to hold the ladies: of this they had ocular demonstration yester-day. To say how it is usually covered is rather more essential, and this shall be the purport of my letter.

Since my arrival at this happy spot, we have had a ham, sometimes a shoulder of bacon, to grace the head of the table. A piece of roast beef adorns the foot, and a small dish of green beans—almost imperceptible—decorates the cen-tre. When the cook has a mind to cut a figure,—and this I presume he will attempt to-morrow,—we have two beefsteak pies, or dishes of crabs, in addition, one on each side of the centre dish, dividing the space, and reducing the distance between dish and dish to about six feet, which without them would be nearly twelve feet apart. Of late he has had the surprising luck to discover that apples will make pies; and it is a question if, amidst the violence of his efforts, we do not get one of apples instead of having both of beef.

If the ladies can put up with such entertainment, and submit to partake of it on plates once tin, but now iron, not become so by the labor of hard scouring, I shall be happy to see them.

We may be sure that the ladies found their dinner a pleasant one, and that the writer of the note was neither a stiff nor unsocial host. A much more charming letter is one to Nellie Custis, on the occasion of her first ball. It is too long for quotation, but it is a model of affectionate wisdom tinged with a gentle humor, and designed to guide a young girl just beginning the world of society.

Here, however, is another extract from a letter to Madame de Lafayette, of rather more serious purport, but in the same strain, and full of a simple and, as we should call it, an old-fashioned grace. He was replying to an invitation to visit France, which he felt obliged to decline. After giving his reasons, he said: "This, my dear Marchioness (indulge the freedom), is not the case with you. You have youth (and, if you should incline to leave your children, you can leave them with all the advantages of education), and must have a curiosity to see the country, young, rude, and uncultivated as it is, for the liberties of which your husband has fought, bled, and acquired much glory, where everybody admires, everybody, loves him. Come, then, let me entreat you, and call my cottage your home; for your own doors do not open to you with more readiness than mine would. You will see the plain manner in which we live, and meet with rustic civility; and you shall taste the simplicity of rural life. It will diversify the scene, and may give you a higher relish for the gayeties of the court when you return to Versailles."

There is also apparent in many of his letters a vein of worldly wisdom, shrewd but kindly, too gentle to be called cynical, and yet touched with the humor which reads and appreciates the foibles of humanity. Of an officer who grumbled at disappointments during the war he wrote: "General McIntosh is only experiencing upon a small scale what I have had an ample share of upon a large one; and must, as I have been obliged to do in a variety of instances, yield to necessity; that is, to use a vulgar phrase, 'shape his coat according to his cloth,' or in other words, if he cannot do as he wishes, he must do what he can." The philosophy is homely and common enough, but the manner in which the reproof was administered shows kindly tact, one of the most difficult of arts. Here is another passage, touching on something outside the range of war and politics. He was writing to Lund Washington in regard to Mrs. Washington's daughter-in-law, Mrs. Custis, who was contemplating a second marriage. "For my own part," he said, "I never did, nor do I believe I ever shall, give advice to a woman who is setting out on a matrimonial voyage: first, because I never could advise one to marry without her own consent; and secondly, because I know it is to no purpose to advise her to refrain when she has obtained it. A woman very rarely asks an opinion or requires advice on such an occasion till her resolution is formed; and then it is with the hope and expectation of obtaining a sanction, not that she means to be governed by your disapprobation, that she applies. In a word, the plain English of the application may be summed up in these words: 'I wish you to think as I do; but if unhappily you differ from me in opinion, my heart, I must confess, is fixed, and I have gone too far *now* to retract.' "

In the same spirit, but this time with a lurking smile at himself, did he write to the secretary of Congress for his commission: "If my commission is not necessary for the files of Congress, I should be glad to have it deposited among my own papers. It may serve *my grandchildren*, some fifty or a hundred years hence, for a theme to ruminate upon, if *they* should be contemplatively disposed."

He knew human nature well, and had a smile for its little weaknesses when they came to his mind. It was this same human sympathy which made him also love amusements of all sorts; but he was as little their slave as their enemy. No man ever carried great burdens with a higher or more serious spirit, but his cares never made him forbidding, nor rendered him impatient of the pleasure of others. He liked to amuse himself, and knew the value of a change of thought and scene, and he was always ready, when duty permitted, for a chat. He liked to take a comfortable seat and have his talk out, and he had the talent so rare in great men of being a good and appreciative listener. We hear of him playing cards at Tappan during the war, and he was always fond of a game in the evening, realizing the force of Talleyrand's remark to the despiser of cards: "*Quelle triste vieillesse vous vous préparez.*" In 1779 it is recorded that at a party he danced for three hours with Mrs. Greene without sitting down or resting, which speaks well for the health and spirits both of the lady and the gentleman. Even after Yorktown, he was ready to walk a minuet at a ball, and to the end he liked to see young people dance, as he had danced himself in his youth. As has been seen from his treatment of Bernard, he liked the theatre and the actors, and when he was in Philadelphia he was a constant attendant at the play, as he had been ever since he went to see "George Barnwell" in the Barbadoes. His love of horses stayed with him to the last. He not only rode and drove and trained horses,* but he enjoyed the sport of the race-course. He was probably aware, like the Shah of Persia who declined to go to the Derby, that one horse could run faster than another, but nevertheless he liked to see them run, and we hear of him, after he had reached the presidency, acting as judge at a race, and seeing his own colt Magnolia beaten, which he no doubt considered the next best thing to winning.

He had, indeed, in all ways a thoroughly well-balanced mind and temper. In great affairs he knew how to spare himself the details to which others could attend as well as he, and yet he was in no wise a despiser of small things. Before the Revolution, there was a warm discussion in the

---

*The Marquis de Chastelleux speaks of the perfect training of Washington's saddle horses, and says the general broke them himself. He adds "He (the general) is an excellent and bold horseman, leaping the highest fences and going extremely quick, without standing upon his stirrups, bearing on the bridle or letting his horse run wild; circumstances which our young men look upon as so essential a part of English horsemanship, that they would rather break a leg or an arm than renounce them."

Truro parish as to the proper site for the Pohick Church. Washington and George Mason led respectively the opposing forces, and each confidently asserted that the site he preferred was the most convenient for the largest number of parishioners. Finally, after much debate and no conclusion, Washington appeared at a vestry meeting with a collection of statistics. He had measured the distance from each proposed site to the house of each parishioner, and found, as he declared, that his site was nearer to more people than the other. It is needless to add that he carried his point, and that the spot he desired for the church was the one chosen.

The fact was that, if he confided a task of any sort to another, he let it go on without meddling; but if he undertook anything himself, he did it with the utmost thoroughness, and there is much success in this capacity to take pains even in small things. He managed his plantations entirely himself when he was at home, and did it well. He knew the qualities of each field, and the rotation of its crops. No improvement in agriculture and no ingenious invention escaped his attention, although he was not to be carried away by mere novelty, which had such a fascination for his ex-secretary at Monticello. Every resource of his estate was turned to good use, and his flour and tobacco commanded absolute confidence with his brand upon them. He followed in the same painstaking way all his business affairs, and his accounts, all in his own hand, are wonderfully minute and accurate. He was very exact in all business as well as very shrewd at a bargain, and the tradition is that his neighbors considered the general a formidable man in a horse-trade, that most difficult of transactions. Parkinson mentions that everything purchased or brought to the house was weighed, measured, or counted, generally in the presence of the master himself. Some of his letters to Lear, his private secretary, show that he looked after his china and servants, the packing and removal of his furniture with great minuteness. To some persons this appears evidence of a petty mind in a great man, but to those who reflect a little more deeply it will occur that this accuracy and care in trifles were the same qualities which kept the American army together, and enabled their owner to arrive on time and in full preparation at Yorktown and Trenton. The worst that can be said is that from his love of perfection and completeness he may in this respect have wasted time and strength, but his untiring industry and his capacity for work were so great that he accomplished so far as we can see all this drudgery without ever neglecting in the least more important duties. It was a satisfaction to him to do it; for he was methodical and exact to the last degree, and he was never happy unless he held everything in which he was concerned easily within his grasp.

He had the same attention to details in external things, and he wished everything about him to be of the best, if not "express'd in fancy." He had the handsomest carriages and the finest horses always in his stables. It was necessary that the furniture of his house should be as good as could be procured, and he was most particular in regard to it. When he was preparing as President to move to Philadelphia, he made the most searching inquiries as to horses, stables, servants, schools for young Custis, and everything affecting the household. He sent at the same time most minute directions to his agents as to the furniture of his house, touching upon everything, down to the color of the curtains and the form of his winecoolers. He had a like feeling in regard to dress. His fancy for handsome and appropriate dress in his youth has already been alluded to, but he never ceased to take an interest in it; and in a letter to McHenry, written in the last year of his life, he discusses with great care the details of the uniform to be prescribed for himself as commander-in-chief of the new army. It would be a mistake, of course, to infer that he was a dandy, or that he gave to dress and furniture the importance set upon them by shallow minds. He simply valued them rightly, and enjoyed the good things of this world. He had the best possible taste and the keenest sense of what was appropriate, and it was this good taste and sense of fitness which saved him from blundering in trifles, as much as his ability and his sense of humor preserved him from error in the conduct of great affairs.

The value of all this to the country he served cannot be too often reiterated, for ridicule was a real danger to the Revolutionary cause when it started. The raw levies, headed by volunteer officers from the shop, the plough, the work-bench, or the trading vessel, despite their patriotism and the nobility of their cause, could easily have been made subjects of derision, a perilous enemy to all new undertakings. Men prefer to be shot at, if they are taken seriously, rather than to be laughed at and made objects of contempt. The same principle holds true of a revolution seeking the sympathy of a hostile world. When Washington drew his sword beneath the Cambridge elm and put himself at the head of the American army, effective ridicule became impossible, for the dignity of the cause was seen in that of its leader. The British generals soon found that they not only had a dangerous enemy to encounter, but that they were dealing with a man whose pride in his country and whose own sense of self-respect reduced any assumption of personal superiority on their part to speedy contempt. In the same way he brought dignity to the new government of the Constitution when he was placed at its head. The confederation had excited the just contempt of the world, and Washington as President, by the force of his own character and reputation, gave the United States at once the respect not only of the American people, but of those of Europe as well. Men felt instinctively that no government over which he presided could ever fall into feebleness or disrepute.

In addition to the effect on the popular mind of his character and services was that of his personal presence. If contemporary testimony can be believed, few men have ever lived who had the power to impress those who looked upon them so profoundly as Washington. He was richly endowed by nature in all physical attributes. Well over six feet high,* large, powerfully built, and of uncommon muscular strength, he had the force that always comes from great physical power. He had a fine head, a strong face, with blue eyes set wide apart in deep orbits, and beneath, a square jaw and firm-set mouth which told of a relentless will. Houdon the sculptor, no bad judge, said he had no conception of the majesty and grandeur of Washington's form and features until he studied him as a subject for a statue. Pages might be filled with extracts from the descriptions of Washington given by French officers, by all sorts of strangers, and by his own countrymen, but they all repeat the same story. Every one

---

*Lear in his memoranda published recently in full in *McClure's Magazine* for February, 1898, states that Washington measured after death six feet three and one half inches in height, a foot and nine inches across the shoulders, two feet across the elbows; evidently a spare man with muscular arms, which we know to have been also of unusual length.

who met him told of the commanding presence, and noble person, the ineffable dignity, and the calm, simple, and stately manners. No man ever left Washington's presence without a feeling of reverence and respect amounting almost to awe.

I will quote only a single one of the numerous descriptions of Washington, and I select it because, although it is the least favorable of the many I have seen, and is written in homely phrase, it displays the most evident and entire sincerity. The extract is from a letter written by David Ackerson of Alexandria, Va., in 1811, in answer to an inquiry by his son. Mr. Ackerson commanded a company in the Revolutionary war.

"Washington was not," he wrote, "what ladies would call a pretty man, but in military costume a heroic figure, such as would impress the memory ever afterward."

The writer had a good view of Washington three days before the crossing of the Delaware.

> Washington had a large thick nose, and it was very red that day, giving me the impression that he was not so moderate in the use of liquors as he was supposed to be. I found afterward that this was a peculiarity. His nose was apt to turn scarlet in a cold wind. He was standing near a small campfire, evidently lost in thought and making no effort to keep warm. He seemed six feet and a half in height, was as erect as an Indian, and did not for a moment relax from a military attitude. Washington's exact height was six feet two inches in his boots. He was then a little lame from striking his knee against a tree. His eye was so gray that it looked almost white, and he had a troubled look on his colorless face. He had a piece of woolen tied around his throat and was quite hoarse. Perhaps the throat trouble from which he finally died had its origin about then. Washington's boots were enormous. They were number 13. His ordinary walking-shoes were number 11. His hands were large in proportion, and he could not buy a glove to fit him and had to have his

gloves made to order. His mouth was his strong feature, the lips being always tightly compressed. That day they were compressed so tightly as to be painful to look at. At that time he weighed two hundred pounds, and there was no surplus flesh about him. He was tremendously muscled, and the fame of his great strength was everywhere. His large tent when wrapped up with the poles was so heavy that it required two men to place it in the camp-wagon. Washington would lift it with one hand and throw it in the wagon as easily as if it were a pair of saddle-bags. He could hold a musket with one hand and shoot with precision as easily as other men did with a horse-pistol. His lungs were his weak point, and his voice was never strong. He was at that time in the prime of life. His hair was a chestnut brown, his cheeks were prominent, and his head was not large in contrast to every other part of his body, which seemed large and bony at all points. His fin-ger-joints and wrists were so large as to be genuine curiosi-ties. As to his habits at that period I found out much that might be interesting. He was an enormous eater, but was content with bread and meat, if he had plenty of it. But hunger seemed to put him in a rage. It was his custom to take a drink of rum or whiskey on awakening in the morn-ing. Of course all this was changed when he grew old. I saw him at Alexandria a year before he died. His hair was very gray, and his form was slightly bent. His chest was very thin. He had false teeth, which did not fit and pushed his under lip outward."*

This description is certainly not a flattering one, and all other accounts as well as the best portraits prove that Washington was a much handsomer man than this letter would indicate. Yet the writer, despite his

---

*This letter, recently printed, is in the collection of Dr. Toner, at Washington. It contains some obvious errors, as in regard to the color of the eyes, but it is nevertheless very interesting and valuable.

freedom from all illusions and his readiness to state frankly all defects, was profoundly impressed by Washington's appearance as he watched him meditating by the camp-fire at the crisis of the country's fate, and herein lies the principal interest of his description.

This personal impressiveness, however, affected every one upon all occasions.

Mr. Rush, for instance, saw Washington go on one occasion to open Congress. He drove to the hall in a handsome carriage of his own, with his servants dressed in white liveries. When he had alighted he stopped on the step, and pausing faced round to wait for his secretary. The vast crowd looked at him in dead silence, and then, when he turned away, broke into wild cheering. At his second inauguration he was dressed in deep mourning for the death of his nephew. He took the oath of office in the Senate Chamber, and Major Forman, who was present, wrote in his diary: "Every eye was on him. When he said, 'I, George Washington,' my blood seemed to run cold and every one seemed to start." At the inauguration of Adams, another eye-witness wrote that Washington, dressed in black velvet, with a military hat and black cockade, was the central figure in the scene, and when he left the chamber the crowds followed him, cheering and shouting to the door of his own house.

There must have been something very impressive about a man who, with no pretensions to the art of the orator and with no touch of the charlatan, could so move and affect vast bodies of men by his presence alone. But the people, with the keen eye of affection, looked beyond the mere outward nobility of form. They saw the soldier who had given them victory, the great statesman who had led them out of confusion and faction to order and good government. Party newspapers might rave, but the instinct of the people was never at fault. They loved, trusted and well-nigh worshiped Washington living, and they have honored and reverenced him with an unchanging fidelity since his death, nearly a century ago.

But little more remains to be said. Washington had his faults, for he was human; but they are not easy to point out, so perfect was his mastery of himself. He was intensely reserved and very silent, and these are the qualities which gave him the reputation in history of being distant and unsympathetic. In truth, he had not only warm affections and a generous heart, but there was a strong vein of sentiment in his composition. At the same time he was in no wise romantic, and the ruling element in his make-up was prose, good solid prose, and not poetry. He did not have the poetical and imaginative quality so strongly developed in Lincoln. Yet he was not devoid of imagination, although it was here that he was lacking, if anywhere. He saw facts, knew them, mastered and used them, and never gave much play to fancy; but as his business in life was with men and facts, this deficiency, if it was one, was of little moment. He was also a man of the strongest passions in every way, but he dominated them; they never ruled him. Vigorous animal passions were inevitable, of course, in a man of such a physical make-up as his. How far he gave way to them in his youth no one knows, but the scandals which many persons now desire to have printed, ostensibly for the sake of truth, are, so far as I have been able to learn, with one or two dubious exceptions, of entirely modern parentage. I have run many of them to earth; nearly all are destitute of contemporary authority, and they may be relegated to the dust-heaps.* If he gave way to these propensities in his youth, the only conclusion that I have been able to come to is that he mastered them when he reached man's estate.

He had, too, a fierce temper, and although he gradually subdued it, he would sometimes lose control of himself and burst out into a tempest of rage. When he did so he would use strong and even violent language, as he did at Kip's Landing and at Monmouth. Well-intentioned persons in their desire to make him a faultless being have argued at great length that Washington never swore, and but for their argument the matter would never have attracted much attention. He was anything but a profane man, but the evidence is beyond question that if deeply angered he

---

*The charge in the pamphlet purporting to give an account of the trial of the New York conspirators in 1776 is of such doubtful origin and character that it hardly merits consideration, and the only other allusion is in the well-known intercepted letter of Harrison, which is of doubtful authenticity in certain passages, open to suspicion from having been intercepted and published by the enemy and quite likely to have been at best merely a coarse jest of a character very common at that period and entirely in keeping with the notorious habits of life and speech peculiar to the writer. (See *Life of John Adams*, iii. 35.)

would use a hearty English oath; and not seldom the action accompanied the word, as when he rode among the fleeing soldiers at Kip's Landing, striking them with his sword, and almost beside himself at their cowardice. Judge Marshall used to tell also of an occasion when Washington sent out an officer to cross a river and bring back some information about the enemy, on which the action of the morrow would depend. The officer was gone some time, came back, and found the general impatiently pacing his tent. On being asked what he had learned, he replied that the night was dark and stormy, the river full of ice, and that he had not been able to cross. Washington glared at him a moment, seized a large leaden inkstand from the table, hurled it at the offender's head; and said with a fierce oath, "Be off, and send me a *man!*" The officer went, crossed the river, and brought back the information.

But although he would now and then give way to these tremendous bursts of anger, Washington was never unjust. As he said to one officer, "I never judge the propriety of actions by after events;" and in that sound philosophy is found the secret not only of much of his own success, but of the devotion of his officers and men. He might be angry with them, but he was never unfair. In truth, he was too generous to be unjust or even over-severe to any one, and there is not a line in all his writings which even suggests that he ever envied any man. So long as the work in hand was done, he cared not who had the glory, and he was perfectly magnanimous and perfectly at ease about his own reputation. He never showed the slightest anxiety to write his own memoirs, and he was not in the least alarmed when it was proposed to publish the memoirs of other people, like General Charles Lee, which would probably reflect upon him.

He had the same confidence in the judgment of posterity that he had in the future beyond the grave. He regarded death with entire calmness and even indifference not only when it came to him, but when in previous years it had threatened him. He loved life and tasted of it deeply, but the courage which never forsook him made him ready to face the inevitable at any moment with an unruffled spirit. In this he was helped by his religious faith, which was as simple as it was profound. He had been brought up in the Protestant Episcopal Church, and to that church he always adhered; for its splendid liturgy and stately forms appealed to him and satisfied him. He loved it too as the church of his home and his childhood. Yet he was as far as possible from being sectarian, and there is not a word of his which shows anything but the most entire liberality and toleration. He made no parade of his religion, for in this as in other things he was perfectly simple and sincere. He was tortured by no doubts or questionings, but believed always in an overruling Providence and in a merciful God, to whom he knelt and prayed in the day of darkness or in the hour of triumph with a supreme and childlike confidence.

As I bring these volumes to a close I am conscious that they speak, so far as they speak at all, in a tone of almost unbroken praise of the great man they attempt to portray. If this be so, it is because I could come to no other conclusions. For many years I have studied minutely the career of Washington, and with every step the greatness of the man has grown upon me, for analysis has failed to discover the act of his life which, under the conditions of the time, I could unhesitatingly pronounce to have been an error. Such has been my experience, and although my deductions may be wrong, they at least have been carefully and slowly made. I see in Washington a great soldier who fought a trying war to a successful end impossible without him; a great statesman who did more than all other men to lay the foundations of a republic which has endured in prosperity for more than a century. I find in him a marvelous judgment which was never at fault, a penetrating vision which beheld the future of America when it was dim to other eyes, a great intellectual force, a will of iron, an unyielding grasp of facts, and an unequaled strength of patriotic purpose. I see in him too a pure and high-minded gentleman of dauntless courage and stainless honor, simple and stately of manner, kind and generous of heart. Such he was in truth. The historian and the biographer may fail to do him justice, but the instinct of mankind will not fail. The real hero needs not books to give him worshipers. George Washington will always hold the love and reverence of men because they see embodied in him the noblest possibilities of humanity.

Index

Ackerson, David, describes Washington's personal appearance, 485–86.

Adams, Abigail, on Washington's appearance in 1775, 93.

Adams, John, moves appointment of Washington as commander-in-chief, 91; on political necessity for his appointment, 91; and objections to it, 91; statement as to Washington's difficulties, 110; over-sanguine as to American prospects, 115; finds fault with Washington, 143–44; one of few national statesmen, 168; on Washington's opinion of titles, 266; advocates ceremony, 267; returns to United States, 321; attacked by Jefferson as a monarchist, 378; praised by Democrats as superior to Washington, 394; his administration upheld by Washington, 399; advised by Washington, 400; his inauguration, 412; sends special mission to France, 417; urges Washington to take command of provisional army, 417; wishes to make Knox senior to Hamilton, 418; censured by Washington, gives way, 420; his nomination of Murray disapproved by Washington, 423; letter of Washington to, on immigration, 445.

Adams, J. Q., on weights and measures, 285.

Adams, Samuel, not sympathized with by Washington in working for independence, 89; his inability to sympathize with Washington, 137; an enemy of Constitution, 278; a genuine American, 434.

Alcudia, Duke de, interviews with Pinckney, 340.

Alexander, Philip, hunts with Washington, 78.

Alien and Sedition Laws, approved by Washington and Federalists, 425.

Ames, Fisher, speech on behalf of administration in Jay treaty affair, 369.

André, Major, meets Arnold, 187; announces capture to Arnold, 188; confesses, 189; condemned and executed, 190; justice of the sentence, 190–91; Washington's opinion of, 191, 466.

532